MADNESS AND
SOCIAL REPRESENTATIONS

Medicine and Society
Andrew Scull, Editor

This series examines the development of medical knowledge and psychiatric practice from historical and sociological perspectives. The books contribute to a scholarly and critical reflection on the nature and role of medicine and psychiatry in modern societies.

MADNESS AND SOCIAL REPRESENTATIONS:
LIVING WITH THE MAD IN ONE FRENCH COMMUNITY

Denise Jodelet

Translated by
Tim Pownall

Edited by
Gerard Duveen

University of California Press
Berkeley and Los Angeles

University of California Press
Berkeley and Los Angeles,
California English language edition first published 1991 by
Harvester Wheatsheaf

Folies et Représentations Sociales copyright © 1989 Presses
Universitaires de France; this translation copyright © 1991
Harvester Wheatsheaf

Printed and bound in Great Britain by BPCC Wheatons Ltd,
Exeter

A CIP catalogue record for this book is available from the Library
of Congress

LC 91–050629
ISBN 0–520–07490–3 cloth
        0–520–07491–2 paper

Contents

Introduction

A transformation in psychiatric policy swings open the doors of the asylum, and the social situation which emerges overturns mental attitudes whose roots are to be found in the distant past. The insane, relegated for so long to the fringes of the community, reappear at its very heart. And what has become of the prejudices which justified their confinement? To borrow an image used by Lévi-Strauss, have we changed, without any intermediate stage, from the state of an "anthropoemetic" society which spews out the insane, exiling them beyond its frontiers, to that of an "anthropophagic society" which absorbs them? But will this not produce new phenomena displacing the rigour of society's relationship to insanity from the institutional level to another level, that born of direct contact and the representations it engenders? Will the decrees of the politicians overcome the symbolic barriers as easily as they circumvented the material ones? Or might it be the case, as so often happens, that the liberal measures of the law, however beneficent in their aim, cannot be applied with impunity, because social sensibilities obey a different logic, one which threatens to paint the experience of otherness with the colours of unreason?

These questions lie at the heart of the story which this book seeks to reveal. It is a story which goes back to the very beginning of the century and unfolds in central France around an open psychiatric institution which places the mentally ill in the care of the family. Such an institution is known as a Family Colony. This story documents what happens, mentally, psychologically and socially, when the mentally ill take their place within the social fabric.

What do we see? On the one hand there are the locals, people from a range of occupations, good, law-abiding citizens. They call themselves *civilians*. On the other hand there are the *bredins*, the loonies, the traditional name for the insane in the dialect of this region of France. It is in vain that they live on a free and equal footing in the rural community under the supervision of the Family Colony. They are the *non-civilians*. Marked by their membership of a psychiatric community, they are different. And a difference (whether it is national or ethnic in origin, based on colour or race or simply on language and way of life) has always invariably made those who manifest it seem alien to those who find in their territorial or cultural roots a natural reason for remaining with their own kind. It is true that a fundamental kinship exists between all situations in which different groups confront each other.

This kinship prompts us to ask whether common processes might lie behind these distancings which are always ready to appear, however remote the danger of contact; to ask whether these processes depend on political, economic and social factors as well as on the representations of the nature and constitution of otherness. This is the basis for the research which led to the reconstruction of the story of the life and the representations of a group of people confronted with insanity.

Three Questions in One

Three preoccupations combine to form the fabric of this study: How do representations function in a confrontation of this type? How are the mentally ill received in the community? How does the relationship to otherness develop? These preoccupations, heterogeneous at first sight, converge to form a single question: how far do social representations of insanity take account of the relationship with the mentally ill who are the embodiment of otherness? A study of these representations in a context of a close relationship with the mentally ill might be expected to yield a clarification of the still ill-defined status accorded to the mentally ill by society, such as uncovering something about what we make of the other.

No attempt has yet been made to approach these three types of phenomena head-on, not even in social psychology. However, such an attempt is necessary. To understand why, let us take these phenomena in reverse order.

First, otherness, which interrogates our times. The otherness outside us: of regions, of peoples whose discovery extends our knowledge of man and questions our image of ourselves. The otherness inside: of groups, of people whose otherness is defined, in a deceitful or violent implementation, by the lines of social division.

It is the relationship with the internal otherness that concerns us here, the relationship between group and group, between body and body. This relationship is often considered simply as a relationship of differences which can be explained in two ways. The first is to derive the relationship to the other, a group or member of a group, from a process of differentiation which finds its justification in a natural and social tendency to distinguish the self from everything else. From this point on, the other is only an empty form which is used to affirm one's identity. The second explanation has recourse to psychological traits such as the authoritarian character, or to social attitudes such as tolerance and intolerance, to account for the avatars of these relationships. These manifestations of autocentrism strip the other of all depth of being and life and, more importantly, prevent the understanding of the way people act. Equally, there appear to be social processes at work which, in defining as other that which is not me or mine, conceive of this other in a concrete negativity. This raises two questions: why is it that despite all resemblances of type and actual assimilation, the other is posited as such and remains so for us? What are the consequences of the other appearing to us in this way? To answer these questions it is necessary to examine the way in which this negativity is constructed. And this construction, an image whose contents are intimately fused with social practices, an image which in the world of social interaction furthers the process of differentiation and the work of alienation, comes from the field of study of social representations, which are constitutive of our relationship with the social world.

But let us continue. If the other is not reduced to a reliable void which allows people's identity to be posited, then otherness itself cannot be studied "in general terms". The construction of this negativity is always specified, even if we suspect that the processes of "defining as other" have a general validity and are supported by invariant psychological and social forces. Identifiable in our behaviour towards any and all others, this defining as other will be all the more instructive as a subject of study if it keeps us within our own society and refers to a case where the effects of cultural, racial or social difference cease to be of importance. Seen from this angle, the insane are a privileged case. However, that is not the only motive for choosing them as an object of research.

We still lack a unified viewpoint in our approach to the destiny of the mentally ill within society. Much has been written on the mentally ill without a lot being known about the fate reserved for these people by the public. Although descriptions abound, they are only poorly understood and the psychology of social representations has its own contribution to make to this topic.

Researchers have been interested in the perception of, and attitudes towards, the mentally ill for more than twenty years[1] and yet the results of their studies are neither conclusive nor coherent. Analysis of the psychiatric institution has become increasingly refined and effective following the lead set by Foucault (1971) and Goffman (1961). Not so with the analysis of the

---

[1] The literature in this field is too abundant for us to burden this introduction with references which have elsewhere been the subject of exhaustive reviews (Dufrancatel, 1968; Le Cerf and Sébille, 1975; Rabkin, 1979; Dulac, 1986). Our bibliography contains only a number of authors who are representative of the most specific trends in research during the past twenty years.

public response. The state of affairs has scarcely changed from that which Dufrancatel outlined in 1968: assessment of naïve conception by psychiatric knowledge, a knowledge which searches in this way for its own justification; an obsession with methodology which fails to question the presuppositions of the researcher; a vacuum in regard to the examination of social representations of mental illness. However, it is possible to make out a few shifts of emphasis, notably the decline of the interactionist view which finds in deviance the definition of the pathological and makes the mentally ill the object of a labelling process. Increasing attention is paid to a symptom-based interpretation of the behaviour of the mentally ill and to cases of purposeful coexistence with them.

This perspective, which is less symbolist and more "objectivist", may seem like the counterpart to the one which emphasized the institutional constraints moulding the development of the psychiatric patient. On the contrary, the two are moving in different directions. Whereas the contestation of a psychiatric power and the consequent functioning of psychiatric institutions and their staff have been called into question, this new perspective has moved from a sceptical distrust of the public to an ostrich-like serenity.[2]

In fact, most research into attitudes towards the mentally ill has gathered increasing amounts of evidence of public prejudice, its ability to reject and its resistance to information campaigns. Today, these results are open to criticism from a number of angles. On the one hand, the validity of attempts to analyse and modify attitudes has been questioned. Not only are they said to be unreliable and ineffective; they are also claimed to lead to results opposite to those expected because they accentuate the awareness of extreme cases which themselves arouse reactions of fear and refusal. Other critics emphasize the prejudicial role of medical officialization which is seen as provoking rejections which would otherwise not exist. The psychiatrization of answers is thought to elicit negative responses which contradict the spontaneous practices of the everyday world. The response is to advocate the policy of the *fait accompli*: to place the mentally ill in the social world and then wait and see; t'iis approach will work out better than the alarmism of the 1960s would have led one to believe.

The transformations made in psychiatric practice, with the opening of hospitals and the development of a community therapy sector, are responsible for a change of perspective which, however, fails to focus on the real problem of the relationship with the mentally ill. That is the problem of the representation of their illness and their condition, out of which their otherness and their social status are constructed.

---

[2] A special edition of *Psychologie Médicale* (15), which appeared in 1983 and presented the deliberations of an international symposium on attitudes to mental illness, is illustrative of the current ambiguity in the analysis of social reactions to mental illness.

If we look at it in more detail, this change of perspective goes beyond merely recording the consequences of a new policy which returns the mentally ill to the fabric of society. It corresponds to a change of paradigm in the approach to intergroup relations. Attention is shifted away from attitudes and towards behaviour, partly as a result of the failure of researchers to demonstrate the effects of the former on the latter. To illustrate this change of paradigm, let us cite two famous experiments conducted within this sphere, that of Griffin (1961) and that of Lapière (1937). By blackening his skin, the first demonstrated the systematic, conventional character of the "colour line" and racist attitudes in the South of the United States. For many years, his experience fuelled the pessimism concerning racial prejudice. Nowadays, we prefer to share the belief of the second, that behaviour is more positive than attitude. Lapière, together with a Chinese couple, succeeded in gaining admittance to 250 hotels and restaurants, 92% of whose proprietors had, in a questionnaire completed earlier, answered that they would refuse a Chinese entrance to their establishment.

This is what should be done, one might think, in the case of the mentally ill. Mental health programmes must *de facto* lead to changes within the population (Katsching and Berner, 1983), as is proved by results obtained in Canadian cities, made famous by research carried out by Cumming in 1959, on account of their negativity towards insanity and their resistance to change (Wattie, 1983). And yet many questions remain unanswered. The truth of this can be judged from, amongst other examples, the experimental closing of psychiatric hospitals in Italy following the 1978 reform which, inspired by Basaglia's ideas, was swept forwards by a wave of popular consent. It took only two years for fear of the insane and their "demonic character" to grow; for the families to develop a feeling of "victimization" and demand protection. And despite the increase in available information and a greater sensitivity of opinion, we see today an acknowledged fall in the all-round care accorded to the mentally ill (Bertolini *et al.*, 1983). The results of research conducted in North America confirm this tendency (Dulac, 1986). We observe that, if in the last twenty years the quality of people's knowledge of mental illness and the accuracy of their appreciation of symptoms have improved, then the image of the mentally ill is simultaneously becoming increasingly associated with the idea of danger. Equally, at the same time as the expression of social distancing is diminishing, we are witnessing a growing tendency to avoid contact with the mentally ill. Attempts to reintegrate "deinstitutionalized" patients into society reveal that communities develop a high degree of resistance as soon as the numbers of such patients grow. Rapid saturation of the social environment leads to their concentration in reserved or increasingly isolated areas.

To account for these contradictions, we have to progress further in the analysis of the public response to contact with the mentally ill. As we shall see, to have recourse to attitudes such as tolerance or intolerance is to fail to perceive the heart of the problem, whilst to confine oneself to the formal acceptance of the presence of the insane on the social scene is a way of evading the question. Those authors who advocate the *fait accompli* of this copresence are not unaware of this fact. Indeed, it seems as if they are formulating a self-fulfilling prophecy, expecting that what is denied does not exist or, going further, that the prejudices, left-overs of outdated beliefs, will die out by themselves. We shall have the opportunity to demonstrate that this is not the case. On the contrary, the evolution of the psychiatric system and psychiatric therapeutics could well provoke social responses and reactivate visions of insanity which place the fear of otherness and the defence of integrity at centre stage. Whence the importance of exploring a facet of the relationship with insanity which has as yet remained largely free of study, namely its ideal and symbolic dimensions.

The path leading to these dimensions is the study of the social represen-tations which bear on insanity and the insane. This study will be crucial to our progress in so far as we see in it the key to an understanding not just of the methods of treatment, the way the mentally ill are treated and located in society, but also of the way in which otherness is constructed. This is a perspective which differs from the dominant trends in the study of the relationship between society and insanity.

In fact, until now social representations of mental illness have attracted little study. They are rarely approached head-on and their manifestations are seldom investigated in their entirety. Certainly, we do encounter them in historical and ethnological works on the popular practices and knowledge which bear on insanity (Charuty, 1985), in the examination of the institutions and agents who are entrusted with their care (Morvan, 1988) or with reference to the areas of behaviour which are affected (Giami *et al.*, 1983). But it is important that social representations should be accorded the central position which they claim in the effort to understand society's approach to the mentally ill. We also know that the various masks and forms of insanity have peopled society's imagination as far back in history as we care to delve (Bastide, 1965), and this fact is related to the treatments society has reserved for the insane (Foucault, 1967). Similarly, recent research has shown the coherence of systems of representation of mental illness across different cultures or sub-cultures along with their articulation in the practices developed in the course of everyday life or within a professional framework (Bellelli, 1987).

This state of affairs is based partly on the fact that the attention of researchers has been primarily fixed on the role of the practices and ideologies of psychiatry in the control of mental deviance. Such a perspective subordinates representations to definitions and to the social rejection of illicit behaviour engendered by social and cultural antagonisms. The consequence is a reduction of scientific interest in the response of a public dispossessed of its traditional methods of exerting control, swept from the scene by the intervention of a medical authority into whose hands it commits itself. In future, changes to the institutions and the therapies they apply will reinvest this response with its social significance by giving it control of the position of the ill outside the official domains to which it was once banished. What is more, although attempts have been made to show how the criteria for the exclusion of the insane have been determined in relation to the struggles and schisms within the social body, little has been made of the conflicts which can generate the presence of people considered to be deviant because of their psychiatric categorization. These conflicts are decisive for the fate of the mentally ill and lead us to an understanding of the "profound level" of society's "intimate life" and "dramas", assuring us "access to its most fundamental and real relationships and to the practices which reveal the dynamic of the social system" (Balandier, 1971, pp.6–7).

This situation can also be explained by the fact that social representations have not always been considered to be a legitimate object of scientific investigation. There are two reasons for this. On the one hand, they were thought to reveal secondary phenomena, effects or reflections of social, economic, ideological and other processes considered decisive in themselves. On the other hand, it was feared that no analytical tools were available which could enable us to pass beyond the level of a mere description of expressive images of cultural attitudes. This was to ignore the contributions made by the study of social representations which was introduced to the field of social psychology by Moscovici (1961) and which finds an echo in other psychological and social disciplines. Evidence of this is provided by, amongst other things, a collective work (Jodelet, 1989) which gives a perspective of the scope of the ideas which originated with Durkheim and the body of research which has built up over a period of twenty years. Nowadays the importance and feasibility of the study of the production and the efficacy of representations within a social whole have ceased to be a subject for doubt. All that is required is a careful definition of the conditions for its empirical implementation.

This is the direction we have taken. We are following the path traced by Moscovici in his research into the representation of psychoanalysis in which social representations are conceived of as "theories" which are created and operative at a social level. This research focused on the involvement of social representations in the construction of everyday reality, in the behaviour and communications which evolve from it and in the way of life and means of expression of the groups within which these representations are forged. Our path gives us a sight of one aspect, to use an analogy with an architectural project, which is predominantly that of a psychosociology of knowledge. This is what is engaged in the perspective developed by Moscovici. We shall concentrate specifically on an examination of a naïve theory of insanity and the insane and on the analysis of the latter's formation and appearance in a defined social context. There are two reasons for choosing this perspective.

First, the existential significance of mental illness leads to suppositions about its nature, its causes and its consequences both for individuals and their surroundings. Yet there exists no real "hard core" of knowledge about this affliction and the scientific and medical world has been unable to agree on any homogeneous position. Thoughts, judgements, opinions on the subject frequently lead the thinker back to an autonomous social construction in which expert, legitimate knowledge plays only a minor role, despite the flow of knowledge resulting from the commitment of the insane to the medical and institutional authorities from the nineteenth century onwards. What is more, the vague and unresolved map of the psychiatric world offers the public little reassurance, a state which will favour the proliferation and survival of the vagaries of everyday common sense. From this point of view, mental illness is an ideal vehicle for the study of social thinking and its functioning.

Second, these elaborations on mental illness, if they are to be spontaneous and removed from the sphere of expert knowledge, cannot be formed arbitrarily in a social void. Considered in relation to an object of crucial relevance to the field of social interactions, they have a social basis, are of practical significance and exhibit the properties of a true understanding which has something to say about the state of the world around us and guides our actions within it. However, we still need to treat such elaborations as social insights and remain aware of their relevance to individual and group behaviour. This requirement is reaffirmed by the criticism directed at research into attitudes towards mental illness. The validity of past research has often been contested because it has reestablished the categories of the psychiatric approach and imposed them on the public, whose own categories it has disregarded. Researchers today, however, have recognized that evaluative attitudes are grounded in shared representations and beliefs, and are seeking the causes of collective practices in the cognitive dimensions of the social response, linked as it is to historical and socio-ecological factors.

We, too, shall progress on two fronts, on the one hand seeking to pinpoint the conceptions which shape the relationship with the mentally ill, while on the other trying to define how the context in which this relationship is anchored furthers the development of such conceptions. In a word, we shall approach representations as the product, expression and instrument of a group in its relationship with otherness. This closes the circle linking our three questions. Representations of insanity will help us to understand how the otherness of the mentally ill is conceived, whilst the examination of a concrete situation of contact with the mentally ill will reveal the manner in which these representations are formed and function.

Representation, Knowledge and Social Practice

To apply the standpoint of a psychosociology of knowledge in the approach to the relationship between a community and those members which it considers alien is not to adopt a resolutely "rational" and intellectualist point of view to the detriment of other dimensions, notably the institutional, symbolic, axiological and affective. On the contrary, it is an attempt to embrace in their totality the processes which bind the life of groups to a social ideation, by applying the properties of the idea of representations, a concept which has become crucial in the explanation of psychological and social functioning, of individual and collective action. Such an approach cannot fail to establish connections between trends of research which have developed the notion in a similar manner but which have never effectively converged in the comprehension of a concrete social milieu. In fact the importance of representations has been well-known in all the domains of the human sciences for more than a decade. But from psychology to the social sciences, the concept has become bound up with so wide a range of meanings that it is possible to speak either of its explosion or its dilution. Drawing from the phenomena discovered within intrapsychic processes or within the mental constructs of society, in cognition or ideology, in private behaviour or public action, it has given birth to a wide range of conceptions and has become part of the approach to a variety of problems. However, a common ground can still be discerned among these tendencies: the recognition of the pertinence and efficacy of representations in the process of explaining behaviour. And as I have attempted to demonstrate elsewhere (Jodelet, 1985), it is possible to find kinships and correlations in these various fields which clear the path towards a unified approach whose development will no doubt lead back to social psychology, a discipline which mediates between the psychological and the social, the individual and the collective. In particular, social psychology faces a double challenge: to think of the social in terms of the cognitive and the properties of cognition as something social, and to think the affective part of social thought.

An analysis of the results of research in the different disciplines reveals that although, here and there, certain properties of representation have become firmly established, they are always incomplete. In spite of agreeing on the fact that representation is a form of knowledge, we still have trouble accounting for its full conceptual implications, that is to say the extent to which it is implicit, as a psychological and cognitive phenomenon, in the dynamics and energies of social interaction. Let me present some rapid sketches of the current state of the study of representations.

If cognitive psychology has shed light on the structural properties of representations, then the dominance of models based on the processing of information and the computational study of artificial intelligence has produced or strengthened a conception of the mental process severed both from social bonds and from psychical and corporeal bases. Based on the representation of knowledge in a computer, human knowledge is conceived as a process of modelling certain aspects, traits, relationships of the represented world. This knowledge is analysed as a *structure* – by distinguishing between its contents and forms (declarative knowledge) and its operations (procedural knowledge) – whose retention emphasizes the importance of *memory*. However important it might be, this formalization, subordinating as it does psychological analysis to the constraints of information technology, has failed to take account of a number of aspects of representation.

First, its symbolic aspect. Knowledge is studied without any evaluation of its correspondence to reality (Mandler, 1983) and without drawing any implications from the fact that the representation "takes the place of" and signifies an aspect of the world, to itself or to others. By neglecting the referential and communicative functions of representation, we arrive at a hypothetical formalization in which the intra-mental is closed on itself. Now, as is evident from an examination of the best-known formulations of this perspective (for example, Minsky, 1977; Schank and Abelson, 1977), the omission of the symbolic aspect from the theoretical model has led to the necessity of reintroducing it to take account of cognitive functioning in real situations. The postulated structures (*frames, scripts* etc.) can only be applied with the help of the language, experience and knowledge shared within a particular culture. This is confirmed by other authors dealing with knowledge of the world and the conceptualizations introduced by language (for example, Johnson-Laird and Wason, 1977; Miller, 1978). This suffices to underline the necessity of including the social dimension and the aspect of communication in any model of knowledge. If we also view matters from the standpoint of works which analyse the conditions of comprehension and linguistic exchange (for example, Clark and Haviland, 1974; Flahaut, 1978; Grice, 1975; Searle, 1983) we encounter the postulation of a collective medium (cultural background, tacit knowledge, conventions, etc.) which is social in its representation. The time has come to treat it as such, and in this way to correct the inadequacies emphasized by Cicourel (1973):

> The problem of signification, as it is tackled in modern philosophy, in linguistics, in psychology, and in anthropology, is that the fact that knowledge is socially distributed is not made evident.

What is more, this kind of cognitive isolationism, which focused on the *what is known* and *how it is known*, says nothing about the *who knows it* and the *perspective from which they know it*. Consequently the expressive function of the representation and its relationship to affective and emotional life is eliminated, an error whose gravity is repeatedly underlined in the relevant scientific literature. Also little interest is shown in action or in the body which supports it. And yet the motor, postural and imitative basis of representations has been brought to the fore in connection with cognitive functioning and its development (Bruner, 1966; Jodelet, 1979; Piaget, 1972, 1962; Wallon, 1942). These omissions prevent any recognition of the role of the social bond in the formation of knowledge, of the affective investment in cognitive organization or of the drives underlying the emergence of the semiotic environment (Green, 1984). Difficulties result when it comes to dealing with the relationship between representation and practice and with the articulation of thought at the level of desire and negative affects. This is the task in which psychosociology is currently engaged within a clinical environment inspired by psychoanalysis. The work performed by Kaès (1976, 1980) is an example. Nor should it be forgotten that Durkheim had already insisted on the importance of the physical foundations of individual and collective representations, their bond with the emotions, with the pheno- mena of social memory – for which neither cognitive psychology nor the neurosciences can account (Changeux, 1987) – and with social customs and ritualizations.

Finally, the cognitivist perspective has brought about a dissociation of cognitive representation and social representation by means of a double opposition. First, between processes which refer solely to intra-individual mechanisms and contents which are deemed to form the distinctive mark of the social, with the affirmation of scientific precedence for the study of the processes, given the cultural and historical variability of the contents (Codol, 1984; Denis, 1976 and others). Second, the cognitive is opposed to the ideological, whose social representation is seen to take on the nature of the empirical. Researchers have even gone so far as to affirm the secondary character of the cognitive component in the latter, and indeed of the danger of autonomy and reduction involved in its recognition (Robert and Faugeron, 1978; Ramognigno, 1984). Corresponding to different visions of the place of the individual and the social in the production of representations, this dissociation fails to grasp the specificity of representational phenomena in the sphere of ideology (Jodelet, 1985) and can account for neither the characteristics of social cognition nor the cognitive conditions of ideological functioning.

This last remark applies in part to the treatment of representations in the social sciences. Recent trends in anthropology, history and sociology (see in particular Augé, 1979; Bourdieu, 1982; Duby, 1978; Faye, 1973; Godelier, 1984; Héritier, 1979; Michelat and Simon, 1977) accord representations the status of an originating factor in the constitution of social orders and relationships, the shaping of collective behaviour and the transformation of the social world. But at the same time we observe, with a few exceptions (Sperber, 1985; Douglas, 1986), a tendency to play down the truly cognitive aspects of representation whilst emphasizing its semantic, symbolic and ideological aspects or, alternatively, the performative properties of the speech which carries it.

Due emphasis should be placed on the decisive contribution brought by these currents of research when they demonstrate the intimate interaction of mental productions and the material and functional dimensions of group life. This contribution consists primarily of: the transcendence both of a hierarchical stratification of the levels of the social structure and of a linear determinism of the nature of thought in accordance with its infrastructural conditions; and the enlightenment of the place of representations in social practices which, within each social grouping, precisely characterize the specific forms of implementation or transformation of a process of structural organization. It is a contribution which has renewed the approach to the social production of knowledge and its relationship to social practices. However, even if in all cases we approach representations as "knowledge", "theories", "versions", "visions" of reality, which enable individuals and groups to interpret and master that reality, to justify or to invalidate its orderings and the position we occupy within them; even if we see in them phenomena which exert a genuine influence on the institution and evolution of societies, it still remains true that, as the representations do not form the central object of these theorizations, their status as "cognitive forms" is not elucidated. This knowledge is seen as a content which is operative in relation to processes which are exterior to it: discursive logic which assures its "acceptability" in social exchange (Faye); the "ideo-logical" process which simultaneously defines both the intellectual and the social order (Augé); the "performative magic" of the utterances which legitimize the cohesion and the dynamic of groups (Bourdieu), etc. No questions are asked about the cognitive properties of these contents which, generated within society, favour their adoption into a community and their operation in the social totality.

Nevertheless, in order to see how representations function within this totality we are forced to return to these cognitive properties and consider them in the light of the notion of *structure*. Here I refer to the "formal structures" in social narratives (Faye); the "organizational schemata" at the heart of material and discursive practices (Godelier); the "constitutive schemes", some of them "universal", which articulate the practical, symbolic and ideological registers (Augé, Héritier). Duby, in a discussion of the feudal imagination, has detailed this role of representation as "heart", "latent structure", "simple image" of the social organization, ensuring the transition from speculative systems to ideologies. Here, as in the importance accorded to language and the circulation of speech, we see how the social sciences and cognitive psychology can join forces under the banner of social psychology.

In effect social psychology, together with developments in the study of social representations, provides the means for theorizing representations without contradiction – not just as content but also as structure and cognitive form, expressive of the subjects who constructed them – in terms of their relationship to symbolic and ideological processes, and to social dynamics and energetics. This is the potential which we shall attempt to realize by putting the concept to work within a concrete social totality in which a relationship with otherness has been formed. We shall see how, to an extent determined by their position and their personal investments and passions, the members of that society link the different registers of collective life within a socially marked construct which enables them to manage their contact with otherness. It is an enterprise which seeks to benefit from the implications of research into social representations and to surmount certain difficulties which continue to be a stumbling block for such research. We shall identify the main thrusts of this research without entering into a detailed discussion of the work which is currently the object of numerous discussions (the most recent include: Doise and Palmonari, 1986; Farr, 1984, 1987; Farr and Moscovici, 1984; Herzlich, 1972; Jodelet, 1984, 1989; Moscovici, 1976, 1981, 1982, 1984).

In Moscovici's seminal model we find elements which, widely corroborated in the field of study which has grown up around social representations, furnish us with irrefutable premises. In particular, the role of these phenomena in the institution of a consensual reality and their socio-cognitive function in the integration of the novel and in the shaping of communication and behaviour. There is also the fact that representations can be studied in two ways. Globally: when we concentrate on the positions held by social subjects (individuals or groups) towards objects whose value is socially asserted or contested, representations are treated as *structured fields*, that is to say as contents whose dimensions (information, values, beliefs, opinions, images etc.) are delimited by an organizing principle (attitude, norms, cultural schemata, cognitive structure etc.). Specifically: when we concentrate on them as modes of knowledge, representations are treated as *structuring nuclei*, that is to say, knowledge structures orchestrating the totality of significations relative to the known object. The first perspective finds an echo in numerous enquiries conducted within real environments. The second has shown itself to be a paradigm of considerable value when generalized or applied to the study of social thought in the laboratory or in the field. This approach has made it possible to discern the constituent processes of representation and to identify its specific forms and effects in terms of cognitive organization.

The constitutive processes of objectification and anchoring are related to the formation and functioning of social representations and contribute to an explanation of the conditions for their emergence and circulation, namely social interaction and communication. As our primary aim is to emphasize that these processes provide the means of conceptualizing the intervention of the social in cognitive elaboration, we shall restrict ourselves to mentioning in more detail their "moments" in the presentations cited above. Objectification explains representations as a *selective construction*, a *structuring schematization*, a *naturalization*, that is to say as a cognitive whole which retains, from the information provided by the external world, a limited number of elements linked by relationships which form them into a structure responsible for organizing the field of representation and which is accorded the status of objective reality. The process of anchoring which comprehends a *grounding in the system of thought, an allocation of meaning, an instrumental-*

ization of knowledge, explains how new information is first transformed and integrated into the ensemble of socially established knowledge and into the network of significations available to society for the interpretation of the real, and then reincorporated in the form of categories which serve to guide both understanding and action. There are two points to emphasize here. This analysis permits us to describe the structural nature of representations, not as a hypothetical organization obeying an empirical, mechanistic model of information processing as cognitive psychology would suggest, but as the result of interaction between experiential data and the social frameworks within which they are apprehended and memorized. At the same time, this analysis allows us to recreate the genesis of representations and to find in their origins and functions a law of organization. This represents an advance on the approach of the social sciences which, in their observations, identify structures but are unable to account for the specific structures except to appeal to mental universals replicated at differing symbolic levels, or through recourse to linguistic models.

The analyses performed by social psychology have advanced the discipline in two directions: by examining the social mechanisms which determine how the terms of the structure are selected and by deepening the structural properties of social representations. In the first case, in an attempt to account for the accentuation or suppression of certain characteristics or dimensions of the represented objects, a number of authors have studied the effects of values particular to a social group or culture, namely the effects of normative constraints linked to the position occupied by the social actors within an institutional system, or of collective models which allow individuals to give a meaning to their social experiences (see in particular Chombart de Lauwe, 1984; Gilly, 1980; Herzlich, 1973; Kaès, 1968; Jodelet, 1984; Moscovici, 1961; Robert, Lambert and Faugeron, 1976). In the second case, laboratory research has brought to light certain aspects of the composition of this structure, while distinguishing between central and peripheral elements of social representations in order to study their relationship with behaviour and its transformation (see in particular Abric, 1988; Flament, 1984, 1987).

However, despite the extraordinary progress achieved by researchers in this field, we should note that we do not yet possess a unified perspective allowing us to theorize about the representational phenomena at work in the life of groups. There are two types of limitation to be noted. The study of representational production suffers a restriction in its field of exploration to the extent that research has sought a direct link between the social position of individuals and their cognitive constructions in relation to a specific sector of activity. At the same time, this study also suffers from the difficulty of establishing a link between representation and practice in so far as it has almost exclusively concentrated on the expressive value of representation with regard to the lived experience of the subjects, with no evaluation of the significance of the cognitive construction as a definition of the object through which these subjects are situated (Jodelet, 1985, 1987). The structural study of representations, despite its greater degree of generality and its demonstration of the effect of certain structural elements in the shaping of action, suffers from its failure to cast light on the question of the genesis of representations.

At the intersection of the diverse points of view examined all too briefly in this short survey, it is possible to discern some more exhaustive avenues of investigation. It is these we shall follow, fixing our attention on a number of central problems. That of comprehending the interrelationship of the cognitive and expressive aspects of a representation shared by a group with reference to an object such as mental illness which involves the emotions and identity of each of its members; that of examining the way in which social conditions, language and communication are involved in the formation, manipulation or preservation of a system of representations, in particular in the selection and organization of the elements which give it cohesion; that of delimiting the conditions under which this structure is operative in the establishment of a consensual vision and the orientation of individual and collective behaviour, in particular the cognitive conditions necessary if we are truly to account for the social efficacy of representations and their articulation at the symbolic, axiological and ideological levels. To this end we shall treat representations as a form of social thought whose genesis, properties and functions have to be viewed in relation to the processes which affect social life and communication, the mechanisms which tend towards the definition of the identity and specificity of social subjects, individuals or groups, as well as the energies which underlie the relationships formed by these with one another. If we are to implement such a perspective which unites the psychological and social approaches we must concentrate on real social contexts and adopt a multidisciplinary standpoint.

One Field, One Perspective, One Method

This has led us to search for a field of study which will allow us to identify the conditions under which representations emerge and function, and their place and role in the dynamic of interactions with the mentally ill. Responding to requirements concerning the validity of an analysis of social relationships to insanity as much as of an analysis of representations, we have chosen to work within a context in which a situation of daily contact with the mentally ill is effectively realized. From the choice of real situations, we have selected a geographically and institutionally circumscribed social framework in which both representation and practice are based on an entire past and present life of proximity to the mentally ill: the Family Colony of Ainay-le-Château. Within this institution, more than a thousand psychiatric hospital patients are placed in nearly five hundred local homes distributed over thirteen *communes.*[3] With the exception of Dun-sur-Auron, this Family Colony is the only one of its kind in France and is reminiscent of that in Gheel, in Belgium, whose long history served as an example.

In both locations an entire social system has established itself and functions around the presence of the mentally ill with the benefits they bring and the problems they cause. It is this fact which invests such a field of study with all its validity. The diffusion of the mentally ill throughout the social space, their participation in local life, the variety of their contacts with the population enable us to observe, as if through a magnifying glass, the phenomena which emerge in a diffuse and fragmentary way within the framework of our everyday lives. What is more, a long-established institution reveals forms of coexistence with insanity which have already stabilized and allows us to examine how and why they were formed. In this way we have at our disposal a rare chance of comparing our approach with that of other social sciences.

As we shall see, this approach was inspired by certain of their methods. Their viewpoint, and the anthropological viewpoint in particular, has clarified many aspects of the ideal and practical realities which we have discovered, illustrating what Sapir said about the "subtle interactions" between "systems of ideas which have their roots in global culture and those which the individual creates for himself as a result of his special spheres of participation": "The more we examine these interactions, the more difficult it becomes to distinguish between society as a cultural and psychological entity and the individual member of society whose culture he must espouse. If we are to be realistic we should never formulate any propositions of social psychology whose premises are based in the traditional opposition between individuals and society. It is almost always more correct to form an image of the exact nature and the implications of a constellation of ideas which forms the counterbalance to anthropology's 'cultural model', to establish its relationship to other constellations, to see how it is modified by the process of contact and, finally and most importantly, to locate the precise position of this constellation" (1967). And it seems to us that this centrifugal movement of opening to the social sciences should be accompanied by a centripetal movement back towards social psychology. Sapir again: "By choosing to examine the practical problems of behaviour and not the ready-made problems posed by classical areas of specialization, we arrive in the field of social psychology which is no more social than individual. It is, or should be, the seminal science which gives rise to both the impersonal and abstract problems formulated by anthropology and the indiscreet probing into the heart of human behaviour which constitutes the work of the psychiatrist" (*ibid.*).

---

[3]   French urban or rural administrative district. Roughly equivalent to the area administered by a British district council [Translator's Note].

This heart of human behaviour, when addressed to the mentally ill, is not always easy to grasp. And most importantly, we have found that what we discover is not always easy to formulate. Equally, it seems to us that those who were confronted by a similar situation at Gheel encountered the same difficulty. The results available from this great research project, conceived and orchestrated by Léo Srole from 1960 onwards,[4] suggest that we might feel a certain embarrassment at uncovering realities which are at odds with what might have been expected from an experiment in the family care of the mentally ill based on a religious tradition going back to the Middle Ages. Similarly, a large number of silences hover above the reassuringly bright descriptions of the public life of the insane in the city (Roosens, 1977). We shall conduct our examination resolutely, even if it means demonstrating how a civil society can turn into a totalitarian one.

The concern of our investigation, which extended over a period of four years, into a context of proximity with the mentally ill was to identify at all levels of social life the forms which the relationship with insanity assumes, the conditions for its acceptance and the representations associated with it. Our path has thus taken us around a long spiral, encompassing the history of the institution and leading from the phenomena observable on the public stage to the processes determining the integration of the patients into the social fabric and to the interactions which have established themselves in the private sphere. In every case we have attempted to give voice to representations and practices, seeking to lay bare the psychological and social forces which underlie both the one and the other.

This project has necessitated the implementation of a complex methodology, related to the methodology of the community monograph and armed with procedures drawn from ethnography, history, social psychology and sociology. The theoretical reasons, detailed elsewhere (Jodelet, 1985), for choosing this option were of two orders. Certain inadequacies generally observed in field studies of social representations had to be overcome, as these affect the reliability of the collected material and thus the conclusions which are based on it. We need only think of certain criticisms levelled, in particular, at enquiries conducted by questionnaire or interview: notably the imposition on the population of the researcher's appreciation of the problem, his preconceptions and categories; the hypothesis of the transparency of speech; the enclosure of speech cut off from its productive context and its relationship to practice; the prevalence of accommodating or socially desirable replies or, again, rationalizations of the effectively adopted positions; the intuitive character of interpretations; hermeneutic interpretation of meaning without a mastery of the mechanisms which allow significations to emerge. To avoid these pitfalls it was necessary to return

---

[4] "The Gheel Family Care Research Project" (Srole, 1962) which has been supported by a number of foundations, both American and Belgian.

representations to the context in which they emerge and function. On the other hand, we wanted to have access to all the phenomena involved in the processes of representations (communications, structural and institutional basis of social relations, cultural models of behaviour, material and symbolic practices, ideological systems . . .). Seen from this point of view, the monographic method of study which has proved to be so fruitful in social psychology (Arensberg, 1954; Redfield, 1955; Becker *et al.*, 1961; Goffman, 1961 etc.), because it addresses a community in its totality and defines a field of analysis which is investigated in all its dimensions, seemed to us to be a profitable approach despite having fallen into disuse. In order to avoid an accumulation of observations which might threaten to overburden the monograph with the unique and the particular, we have complemented it with approaches designed to identify the mechanisms affecting the psychological and social life which has crystallized around a psychiatric institution and its inhabitants. This was the basis for the development of the phases and operations of the research project which we shall briefly present here.

First, observation through engagement in community life was maintained for the full duration of the investigation, with the aim of discovering the forms of the contact established with the mentally ill in different places and on different occasions: on the public stage (in the streets, at local ceremonies and celebrations); in socially frequented places (shops, cafés, church . . .); in private places where people meet the patients and put them to work. Such immersion in the environment has made possible an exhaustive survey of the collective and individual behaviour shown towards the mentally ill and of the stability or variation of such behaviour in accordance with the varying conditions of contact.

Second, two avenues were followed in the reconstruction of the history of the institution and the consequences of its development within the environment in which the placements were carried out. The first consisted of an analysis of the literature relating to the Family Colony from its creation, in particular in a meticulous examination of the annual reports given by its doctor-directors to its supervisory body, the French *Assistance Publique*. The second was the commitment to gathering the testimonies of witnesses occupying key positions both inside and outside the boundaries of the placement project (a specialist in regional folklore and history, leading local figures, councillors, officials of local associations). This has made it possible to identify the factors which have contributed to local acceptance of the system, those which have led to its rejection or condemnation, the psychological labours which the placement community has applied to itself in order to surmount the fears and conflicts thrown up by contact with insanity, the tensions which have characterized contact with the hospital and the images associated with dealings with the mentally ill.

Third, the organization and functioning of the system of family placement of patients and the conceptions of it formed by different actors were studied by questioning a representative sample of the medical and para-medical hospital staff. Of particular value was the contribution of the "visiting nurses" who are responsible for liaising between hospital, patients and the "foster parents" who are in charge of their accommodation and supervision. As bearers of the group memory, witnesses of real-life experiences of cohabitation with the patients, vectors for the transmission of the rules and customs which shape life in the placement homes, these nurses enabled us to discover their forms and principles, along with the signification of certain deviations from explicit norms and of certain dysfunctionings.

Four, the two preceding phases of study have served to construct an instrument for the survey and description of the totality both of the placement families (493) and of the patients (1,195). This questionnaire, administered with the aid of the visiting nurses, has provided information on:

> The placements: position, distance from the headquarters of the Family Colony, type of accommodation, level of comfort, length of time functioning as a placement, scope of accommodation, rotation of the accommodated patients, living conditions available to the lodgers (work, extent of association with family life, shared meals etc.).
> The foster parents: age, origin, profession, childhood experience of contact with the mentally ill, family composition, number, sex, age of children etc.
> The lodgers: age, psychiatric category, length of time in the Colony and in the placement, sociability rating, professional activity etc. The results of this enquiry, consisting in part of the quantitative data referred to in the text, have made it possible to identify the factors and tendencies which shape the functioning of placements and the relationship between the foster parents and the lodgers, and to identify objective indicators of the relationship with the mentally ill. It was this information which served as a basis for the selection of the sample for the in-depth interviews which were conducted during the final phase of the enquiry.

Fifth, in effect, by reversing the usual sequence of studies of representations which progress from the qualitative to the quantitative, we expected to master in their entirety the elements intervening in, or revealing how, the community positions itself with regard to the Colony and its inhabitants, in order to explore the representations involved in its mode of conduct.

In order to assure a systematic study of social representations and to verify certain hypotheses formulated on the basis of our investigations, we interviewed a sample number of the foster parents, selected in accordance with the criteria of representativeness and significance. The representative status of the sample was assured by a sampling rate higher than 10% (65 placements were visited out of 493). Within this sample, groups of foster parents were contrasted according to the indicators which emerged from the statistical enquiry so as to control the differences in representation likely to correspond to differences in the situation and the functioning of placements and in the relations established with the patients.

Both for reasons of locality and to ensure the validity of the information collected, the conduct of the interviews was inspired by the methods used in the ethnographic study of cultural behaviour (Maget, 1962). This consisted in going from the particular to the general, via descriptions of patients and stories of everyday life, in order to obtain reflections on mental illness. In this respect the "placement log", a register of all the lodgers who have stayed in the placement together with their dates of arrival and departure, proved to be a useful instrument. Referring to the individuals mentioned in the log, we asked for a description of behaviour and symptoms, for explanations of the illness and its causes and for judgements of the patient's practical and relational capabilities etc. Moreover, this helped to reveal the traces left in the memory by the various patients. In this way we could determine that the rare remembered cases corresponded to prototypical portraits. The large number of the forgotten illustrated how frequently it proved impossible to discern the characteristic pathological signs or how often patients were relegated to the ranks of the anonymous. The interviews also included questions on the everyday conduct of life in the placement and on the causes underlying certain habits and practices revealed by the statistical enquiry or by earlier observations (in particular everything having to do with measures used to isolate the patients and to separate their personal belongings and items which they had touched). The explanation of these practices has enabled us to bring hidden representations to light, thus revealing the system of relations with the mentally ill in its entirety.

This means of progress has answered the need to place our approach to representations in context in order to reveal the conditions under which they form, their manner of functioning and their involvement in the development of the institution, as well as in the practices and behaviour applied to mental illness. It has also sanctioned an explanation of the significations attached to mental illness. This explanation is closely bound up with the local system of behaviour and knowledge, avoids unfounded or fallacious speech and, as Wittgenstein (1961) predicted, returns

> words and phrases to themselves, that is to say to the elementary situation in which they are used.

But, above all, this combination of the ethnographical approach and an in-depth sociopsychological investigation has shown itself to be heuristic in nature, leading us to make unexpected discoveries. Since from the very beginning of the enquiry our approach drew attention to surprising behaviour – most noticeably in connection with the administration of medicines, patients' contact with the water reserved by the population for personal use and the treatment of items and belongings touched by the patients – it has been a determining factor in the discovery of secretly held ideas. These notions, at odds with the reassurances concerning the non-contagious nature of mental illness propagated by official statements to which our interviewees overtly adhered, reveal a belief in the transmission of insanity by the bodily fluids and anything which has been in contact with them. By concentrating for a part of the interview on habits associated with life with the patients, we were able to obtain information which would otherwise have remained hidden in spontaneous discussion. We thus succeeded in opening the door on a background of tacit representations which are decisive in regulating contact with the insane.

This enquiry, which was conducted at the beginning of the 1970s in what was apparently a highly specific community, has revealed fundamental aspects of our relationship to otherness. Our discoveries concerning the belief in contamination through the bodily fluids finds an echo today in the fears generated by AIDS and certain discriminatory modes of behaviour which have grown from them. This is reminiscent of the symbolic processes through which things are placed in the category of "other", processes which are based on the defence of an identity and which appeal to knowledge rooted in the social memory. It is this we shall try to account for whilst traversing the spiral at the heart of the history and life of this community, whose fate it was to live with the insane. Our journey will take us from an examination of the material and psychological bases of the social institution created around the family placement of the mentally ill (first part), to the forms assumed by their introduction to a social context within a community which invents ways of adapting an exogenous population without truly assimilating it (second part), to conclude at their representational base and the way in which it is linked to the material, symbolic, axiological and ideological registers which character-ize the social dynamic and to the affective dimensions of group life (third part).

In reconstructing the events and facts in this life history of a collective at grips with a danger from within, we have followed a progression from the most external to the most intimate, one which enabled us to explore, not without difficulty or resistance, the heart of a secret masked by the veil of habit. In so far as it is possible, we have left it to the actors to describe their own story. Not all the actors; only a few of the mentally ill were interviewed. This was the price we had to pay for entering an environment swift to erect barriers in the face of the alien and in the face of those who approach the *bredins* or give them credit. However, it has been enough to hear the long train of speech describing life with them to understand their fate and the reasons for it. The people whose conversations we quote are not identified, not even fictitiously. The experience shared by the population and the common vision they themselves have made of it are so homogeneous that we often thought we were listening to a single voice. This has enabled us, moreover, to respect a minimum of anonymity.

In fact, the institution we describe is unique in France. It is easily identifiable. It would thus have been pointless to disguise its name or location. This honesty will, we hope, compensate for the risk of indiscretion. All the more so, since these risks have been erased by the time it has taken to make public a study some of whose results we have long hesitated to recount. Many of those whom we met will certainly have died by today. Witnesses of the founding of the Colony, they helped us to a better understanding of the innermost core of a situation which, in the present, has revealed itself in abrupt and obscure terms. We honour their memory as we also thank those who might recognize themselves in this story even if, for some of them, it has now taken on the colours of the past.

From what is said today, it seems that recent years have seen a change in the institution. Yet the photographs recently displayed in the press and on television testify to the fact that the realities we describe here remain. It is for this reason that we have not sought to modernize the description of the world which we encountered nearly twenty years ago and whose characteristics throw the phenomena which have been revealed into full relief. Perhaps this will provide a spur for new investigations in this field with the aim of observing what might have changed.

PART ONE

LIFE OF THE MAD, LIVING WITH THE MAD

Chapter One

Framework and History of a Family Colony

> The Family Colony . . . is what is outside the
> central headquarters, in the town, in its suburbs,
> in the country surrounding it. In a word, in the
> placements, in the families of the foster parents.
> Director of the Colony of Ainay-le-Château,
> (1919)

Overture: The Scene and Some of the Personae

Nothing of note seems to await motorists travelling on the "green route" towards Moulins who, looking down on one side towards the final plains of the Cher, have passed the sign bidding them welcome to the Bourbonnais.

If they are in a hurry they will hardly notice any difference between the village they are now crossing, following the S-bend of the road, and the many others they have already passed through on the trunk road, with their lines of shops and houses, their pulled blinds and closed doors. Turning the bend, they will scarcely glimpse the dense obscurity of the village centre which here coils its white stone houses and its moss-covered tiles tightly around the church, and there unfolds them in a criss-cross of new alleyways. It is unlikely that they will notice the grace of the village; their attention has not been awakened: guidebooks and specialist works make little mention of this ancient stronghold, one of the powerful Bourbon Châtellenies of the 16th-century. They make no attempt to urge tourists to stop and feel the weight of the old town perched on a hillside where the river flows more slowly as it passes through a lake, to feel the power of the ramparts with the heavy vestiges of wild, luxuriant creepers, to discover amidst the age-old chestnut trees the austere mass of the 12th-century church echoed, on the other side of the hill, by the bare simplicity of a rustic chapel.

This reticence concerning Ainay-le-Château is due, no doubt, to the fact that, lying at the northern extremity of the Bourbonnais, it remains largely peripheral, isolated from the rest of the region, now a *département*,[1] by the

---

[1] French administrative district approximately corresponding to a British county.

curtain of forest which extends over some 10,435 hectares. This is the forest of the Tronçais, visible for miles around like a dark dam. But is this natural frontier really enough to explain such reticence in admitting as an integral part of the cultural heritage a town which testifies to the past as much as many other locations, less interesting but more often cited? The texts do not fail to underline the history, folklore and tourist interest of that route into the Allier. Yet almost no mention is made of Ainay-le-Château. Everything around and about is referred to. A brief example: a special 1959 edition of the magazine *Richesses de France* devoted to the Allier informs us that the detour to Hérisson is worthwhile, as are the churches of Urçay, Couleuvre, Lurcy-Lévis and the Tronçais with its oak trees and its ponds. Not a word of our town located at the crossroads which links these places from which it is a mere ten kilometres away.

What can be the reason for this silence?

Not that the remnants of this ancient stronghold are so extensive as to warrant a prolonged visit. Or that the hotel capacity would make this possible in any case. The elementary level of comfort and facilities of the few rooms which are available is far more likely to dissuade the visitor from staying. Nor is the *cuisine* any more encouraging. And this offers further cause for surprise. Any of the surrounding towns of equal size boast a pleasant *auberge* or *relais* inviting us to stop. Why this dearth?

After all, the town seems very much alive. In a region where many towns are suffering depopulation and dying out, it is even said that this is the last centre of activity. Things have not slowed down here as in the main towns of neighbouring districts. A number of cafés are wide open and doing non-stop business. The window displays of the food shops are brightly illuminated and, in some cases, full of choice products. If, as elsewhere, the craft shops have disappeared, then the banks on the other hand have multiplied along with luxury shops entirely devoted to television and audio equipment, to household gadgets, to the pleasures of reading. To judge by the buildings bordering the roads which lead out of the village the already considerable population seems to be growing. Along the ups and downs of the main road, private houses, as gleaming and new as they are neutral in inspiration, vie, not without ostentation, in their style and affectation. Some of the village's inhabitants find that the spectacle of this growth undermines the charm and disfigures the nobility of the old town.

But this growth contains no disturbing element for a "stranger" who has overcome his surprise at discovering a development of this dynamism and so evidently geared towards consumption in a reputedly poor agricultural region. A minor note of urban development is not displeasing when, for the rest, there is the softness of the wooded countryside to enjoy, with its fields bounded by living hedges, punctuated by heavily leaved trees and traditional rural habitations, disturbed only by the slow movement of the Charolais cattle. Especially when a splendid natural site is so close at hand: this oak forest which has been a source of wood since the days of Colbert, with its vast, deep lakes, its legendary fountains and its game – stag, deer, wild boar – flushed from its lair by the amateur practitioners of the "photo-safari" or, in accordance with a cruel and aristocratic ritual, by the hunts which are organized three times a week during the season.

What then is the reason preventing a village a mere four hours away from Paris from either wanting to detain, knowing how to detain or succeeding in detaining the everyday walker or holiday-maker? To those who regret this fact, and there are many of them in the area, the voice of resignation, evoking the failed attempts to provide a welcome likely to tempt an outside public, answers, "the country wants it this way."

Let us return to our motorists. If they have been watching the panorama unfolding from the top of the hillside leading from the Cher, they will catch a brief glimpse of a large building which looks down on the harmonious interplay of the little chapel, the church and the roofs in the background. Losing sight of this building as they enter the village, they will not rediscover it when they leave to the south or the east. Postcards bearing a view of the town also omit this large modern construction, not that it is a complete blemish on the village with its brick cladding reminiscent of the ochre of the roofs. But perhaps the design of the wings which flank the belltower hides something strange. Perhaps it is necessary to block out from the representation of the town the building which the locals speak of from the very outset as the "industry of the region".

To get a closer view of this building, you would have to stop and travel to the west, along a road which dwindles to a track. There, you would meet one of those men whom you had no doubt glimpsed on the main road or in the central square. One of those anachronistic figures pushing or pulling a box mounted on two wheels, like those towed behind a motor scooter. The apparent laziness of these men, the nonchalance of their gait can be disconcerting. At times incongruous, they lie at the side of the road or on top of a pile of stones left by the roadmender, even if it is drizzling. One wears a grey suit, decent but no longer fresh, another wears clothes worn out by work in the fields, another appears in more refined attire and yet another in cape and clogs. The cleanliness of their appearance, like the accuracy of their shave, varies. Their gait is often curious, almost mechanical, because their boots are too hard to allow them to bend the feet which, instead, slide along the ground in small jerks with the foot remaining close to the ground. Some of them are suffering from a visible infirmity, others just from the weight of their age or their weariness. Some carry a shopping basket in the hand, others, arms dangling, wander absent-mindedly, in a daze, or absorbed by the sound of a transistor radio carried like a furtive child in their arms.

The coming and going of these men becomes increasingly persistent the closer you get to the school, the church, the town hall, the monument to the dead, the cemetery or, on the edge of the town, the building you have been looking for. And then it appears, glimpsed behind a succession of carefully cultivated flower beds and small buildings around which an animated world swarms. More of these men seated on benches, gathered around the entrance to a spacious and noisy hall, male and female silhouettes clad in white blouses, carts. A low wall topped by railings delimits this area of gardens and buildings to which access can be gained freely via wide open gates. This is the "Family Colony", a psychiatric establishment whose infirmary, seen from afar, rises above the medical buildings, the service and administration blocks, the workrooms and meeting rooms. This is a psychiatric establishment of a rather special kind: here people are cared for and administered but they are not shut in. All these men are its inhabitants and they live distributed throughout the town and its environs, accommodated in the homes of the town's population which is reimbursed for accepting them. All these men passing freely through the streets and avenues are the *bredins*, the loonies. This is how the insane are known in the local dialect. Might this be the solution to the mystery enshrouding this paradoxical and secret region?

All this introduction has been intended to evoke the atmosphere and the feeling of having to unmask something hidden which seized me at the very beginning and did not leave me at any stage during the entire duration of this study into the relationship with insanity in a context of free contact between the patients and the others.

The hidden secret of a region open to the mentally ill and rejected by its environment. A region which in some way resembles one of those "wilderness areas" at the fringes of normality and social control, in which Mary Douglas (1973) sees the emergence of new cults/religions. In it I sought for representations of insanity, supplied spontaneously and far from the learned discourse which, according to Foucault (1974), "rejects from its domains a whole teratology of knowledge . . . immediate experience, the subjects of the imagination which ceaselessly bear and renew beliefs without memory". And, in this "area of wilderness" (*ibid.*), what I was to find during the course of a long and difficult process of revelation was redolent of these "untamed images" over which thought stumbles in emotion and displeasure (Freud, 1954). Follow me if you will . . .

The blurring of the buildings of the hospital into the countryside of the little town we have just entered nicely reflects the position of the Family Colony in the community in which it is embedded. It is as much, if not more, the business of the region and its inhabitants as it is of the psychiatric establishment. This is explained by the functioning of the hospital and the role given to the surrounding environment.

The Functioning and Objectives of the Family Colony

A Family Colony is a psychiatric hospital based on the idea of "foster family" placement. The patients who depend on it administratively and medically benefit from a free, family-based way of life. Their accommodation, food and day-to-day supervision are provided by families living in the vicinity of the hospital building although, properly speaking, these families do not form part of the hospital's nursing staff. Thus in the 1970s, in the case which has inspired our study, some thousand patients entrusted to approximately 500 families were dispersed within a radius of 20 km from the medical and administrative headquarters located in the town of Ainay-le-Château.

The functioning of the hospital has been adapted to this innovatory situation. Medical supervision is the responsibility of a body of doctors who receive patients for consultation at the hospital and periodically visit the homes in which they live. A team of visiting nurses ensures a regular link between the services of the Colony and the patients housed outside it.

The Family Colony for men at Ainay-le-Château is, together with the women's Colony in Dun-sur-Auron to which it was originally annexed, the only experiment in family help for adults carried out in France. Falling under the jurisdiction of the law of 30 June 1838 governing public asylums of which they are a branch, the two Colonies have their headquarters in the *départements* of Cher and Allier. However, from their foundation (Dun-sur-Auron in 1892 and Ainay-le-Château in 1900) until the decentralization of the administration of psychiatric care, they fell under the authority of the *Seine*. Their doctors and nurses fell under the administration of the psychiatric hospitals of the *Seine* and, with only a few exceptions, their patients were transferred from establishments in the *département* in which they were cared for. This status had considerable consequences for the way the mentally ill were perceived and accepted. Indeed, the specific manner of the Colony's functioning was bound to accentuate the dynamic between three often antagonistic forces (the population, the patients, the hospital officials), shaping the system we are going to study in a way which reveals much about our social relationship with insanity.

In comparison with a traditional psychiatric hospital, mixed family placement of the mentally ill reveals a number of innovations which might have encouraged the founders of Ainay-le-Château and a number of its officials to attribute to it objectives in terms of which the responses of the surrounding environment stand out and make sense. Amongst these innovations we find: a break with the asylum-based life – in Ainay the patients circulate freely outside the boundaries of the establishment; a way of life close to the one the patients led prior to their confinement, in which they can mix with the population and even participate in its activities; more intimate surroundings because they are entrusted to families.

In this way the Family Colony constituted the first formal attempt to realize the practice of the *open door* and of *no restraint* which was demanded at an early stage by the reformist movement in psychiatry (Castel, 1976, pp. 271–273). Despite the inescapable fact that the Family Colony has always had the function of reducing the population inhabiting the asylums, it has acquired for some a revolutionary character. And, at the very minimum, it has followed a specific vocation which distinguishes it from other psychiatric establishments which have generally been accorded (Biadi, Faraut and Paoli, 1979) three principal functions, namely repression, assistance and therapy, sometimes supplemented by the fourth function of social rehabilitation. Opening the doors of the hospital minimized the repressive aspect while enhancing the role of assistance. From the therapeutic point of view, the Colony was intended, in the eyes of its initiators, to realize an innovatory form of "moral treatment" in which the aid of family placement was expected to augment the benefits of isolation in the fresh air of the country and the tranquillity of rural life, far removed from the noise and bustle of the city. This was later extended by the possibility of patients engaging in local life and activities along with the readjustments this implied.

That these explicit aims have been pursued over the years with greater or lesser degrees of conviction and of success by the officials of the Colony is testified to by the reports submitted to the supervisory body. These objectives have established the principles of in-family care with regard to which the way of life reserved for the patients by the population which accommodates them has to be defined. For, in opening its doors to the outside world, the establishment has made itself dependent on its environment, both ecologically and functionally, for the accommodation of its patients. It has consequently had to revise its aims in accordance with the reactions and expectations of the environment of which this study is, in part, the description.

Let us start by describing two aspects which characterize the Family Colony within its full context: its spatial distribution and its history. The first is important in that it represents one of the fundamental differences between an "asylum" and a "Colony" and because, as part of the everyday framework of the patients' lives, it is the stage on which the nature of the relationships established between the patients and the population which houses them are shaped. The importance of the historical aspect comes from the fact that it alone allows us to understand the construction and dynamics of this mutual adaptation of the milieu, the hospital and its patients.

The Framework of Family Placement

Just as the spatial distribution of an asylum was considered by Esquirol to be "the most powerful therapeutic agent against mental illness", so too was the ecological distribution as such of the patients in itself thought to be a factor in their treatment, primarily because of the family life it made possible. Within the Colony, patients become *lodgers* once they are taken into the care of individuals known as *foster parents*. The hospital is simply the headquarters of the Colony whose functioning is decentralized to the homes, or *placements*, in which the lodgers are accommodated. But the ideas or the practices of the foster parents will on occasions lead the officials of the establishment to hold the ecological distribution to be a factor in the improvement in the state of a patient. And for some this may indeed be the case.

Spread over thirteen *communes*, the placements are very different in appearance. From the detached house, often with two stories and a garden, or the low-level block of flats found in the hamlets or the towns (60% of placements), right up to the "estate", a large agriculture holding of 60 hectares or more farmed by the owner, a tenant or an employee, the estate manager, with buildings organized around a central courtyard (8% of placements), and, between these extremes, the smallholdings whose few hectares are farmed by the owner or rented out and in which the living accommodation and farm buildings are assembled under the same roof (31%).

It follows that even if generally speaking the size and level of comfort of the living accommodation are superior to that usually found in the region, the accommodation provided for the lodgers varies considerably from one placement to the next. In one placement the recent construction of the building has made it possible to install running water, even central heating – one placement in ten possesses central heating, more than seven in ten are heated by wood; the specially purchased bedding and furniture lie on a tiled or lino-covered floor, the walls are papered. In another placement, in contrast, where an old local workshop has been used, the brick floor scarcely hides the hard-packed earth and the cracked, whitewashed walls show traces of moisture deposited by the persistent humidity of this region of impermeable soil.

The position of the room reserved for the lodgers affects the way in which their coexistence with the family develops. Accommodation in an outhouse located in the courtyard, in the extension to a house or in a lodging constructed in the garden leads to a relative separation between lodgers and foster parents. Contact is closer when the room is located within the family's living accommodation, even in cases where a separate entry has been provided to make crossing the kitchen or the hall unnecessary.

The closeness of this cohabitation is not solely a question of the resources of the accommodation. It also depends on the conceptions of life with the lodgers. There was even a time in the early days of the Colony when the doctrine of the institution advocated total integration of the lodger into the family, for the good of the patient and in the name of the therapeutic virtues of family life. What is more, this demand was made under favourable circumstances as the first placements, made predominantly amongst poor families, were opened in small homes with the result that the place reserved for the lodger necessarily impinged on the common space.

But within a short time the foster parents showed a tendency to isolate themselves from the lodgers, leading to a number of incidents which could be attributed to a lack of supervision. The result was that the officials of the

Colony were obliged to rule that at least one window, the "spy-hole", should be installed between the foster parents' room and that of the lodgers to ensure that communication with the latter should always be possible. Even today, it is still possible in some placements to find a glass door joining the family room to the lodgers' room, covered on the family's side by a net curtain which can be lifted to observe what is happening on the other side. This sometimes makes possible a beneficial, well considered intervention, as the following account testifies:

> Ours once had a little fight. Once my husband had to go in. They were arguing, him and that Alsatian. The other one wouldn't lend you a thing. What was his, was his. The Alsatian was quite different. He was good. He would give you anything . . . And after all, he had more tobacco to start with and then he had taken some of the other one's. Well, that caused a bit of an argument and the other one, a nasty piece of work, he called him a squarehead. Well, that set him off! He caught hold of him but the other one was bigger and more solid. I was with my husband and we heard them shouting from in here. We've got a window in our room which lets us watch them and see what's happening in their room. So my husband pulled back the curtain and said 'Wait a while. We'll let them have a bit of a fight. Seeing how he's been called a squarehead we'll let him get his own back a little' [*laughter*]. Well, they went on arguing for a while and then the fighting got a bit too fierce so my husband opened the door and went in. That cooled them off.

A number of people tell you that the existence of this fragile door is the reason for their lack of fear:

> I've got three of them behind that door. Look, right near by. And my neighbour's aren't far away. I say to myself: I'm all alone surrounded by seven but I'm not afraid of them. My neighbour, on the other hand, she's frightened of having them in her courtyard. That's why she has her room so far away.

It is this menace and latent uneasiness that the partition pens back. From there it is but a short step to segregation and a number of people feel this:

> I find it absolutely absurd, very bad indeed, to serve them as if they were in the lock-up. I'll tell you what we call 'the lock-up'; some just have a window, just a hatch and pass everything through that. I think that's really bad.

The privilege of a true life in the community has long since ceased to be defended. Today it is found in only a few rare placements. In the majority of cases, whilst the lodgers' accommodation cannot be completely independent, the presence of a private door prevents direct access to the main living accommodation via the communication door which retains a purely symbolic function.

The ability to effect this kind of separation was doubtlessly an encouragement for the opening of placements, more so in recent years. Many still refuse to accept lodgers precisely because they cannot satisfy this condition which has become necessary and even imperative in the conceptions of lodging the mentally ill within this milieu. A farmer with empty rooms within his own home explained that despite the real advantages to be gained from accommodating a lodging worker, he was not intending to accept one because of the location of the rooms:

> I am in rather a delicate position. My house is not suited to it. Lodging them isn't easy when they are together with you. You need to be independent. Very often, it's the problem of accommodation which stops people. You need a private entrance so that the lodgers don't have to cross your area. It's right that they should have their own rooms. And the others, too, should have their own rooms.

From the very outset, purely spatial and material considerations regulate the movement of lodgers within a shared living space. This is a minimum delimitation of the private territories, passage between which will, as we shall see, be regulated by a precise and nuanced code. The extent to which the lodger is integrated into – or excluded from – family life regulates the movement of these territorial boundaries. Integration defines the permissible level of penetration into the foster parents' domain and the latter employ both concrete and symbolic measures to control the lodgers' access to their private territory which lies on the other side of a threshold which they themselves have fixed. Environmental psychology has long since demonstrated the importance of the defence of privacy. We shall have a chance to return to this point when analysing the significance of these spatial dispositions which, on the one hand, are related to the exercise of a power whose many forms have been described by Foucault (1971, 1977) and which, on the other, correspond to a "process of social semiosis", to the creation of "situation-signs" (Schaff, 1968).

It is possible to account for these spatial arrangements as forming part of the methods generally adopted with regard to a guest, tenant or lodger of any kind who is a stranger to the family. Certainly, the inconvenience of contact with strangers has a role to play and is admitted. Nevertheless, the significance accorded to the layout of the accommodation, which we have viewed in the light of the original objective of family placement, reveals the effect of more profound psychosocial mechanisms, with the elements of control and fear also having a role to play. In dealings with the mentally ill, lack of privacy is, to a greater or lesser degree, a source of anxiety. The relationship between the insane and the others is like the relationship between animals of the same species for which the sharing of a common territory represents a danger which results in the stronger driving the other to the furthest limits of the territory (Lorenz, 1966). Within the placements, partitions, protected access, reserved zones all appear as a primary mode of defence. This delimitation and defence of territory is a safeguard against threat which makes peaceful coexistence possible. In it we can see elements of fear and of veiled aggression:

> Nearly everyone in the Colony of Ainay-le-Château has the insane staying with them, they nearly all have children: *All in the same house; we can't help being near them, we don't bite one another.*

Thus a first paradox of family placement emerges. The routines of life put into practice by the foster parents run counter to the requirement to integrate the patients into the family. This discrepancy was to grow more noticeable as the practice of placement became more widespread in the population. It demonstrates one of the ways in which the environment in which the Colony was situated first adapted to the demands of the institution which it subsequently pushed towards the satisfaction of its own needs.

The History and Motives of Family Placement

This process of reciprocal adjustment has a long history. Long, because its beginnings go back to 1900. Long, too, because this work of transforming a community by an institution and of the human environment inflecting the aims of the institution has not been without confrontation and anguish. (Even if today the face shown by the protagonists in this adventure conceals these upheavals behind the smooth and silent solidity of tradition.)

Everything started in 1900, or even a few years earlier. A reformist wind blew through the asylums towards the end of the 19th century. A number of cases in which the mentally ill were spontaneously accepted in rural communities throughout Europe suggested a possible answer to the question of confinement. In this connection, Gheel in Belgium proved to be exemplary. A tradition of lodging the mentally ill had been established there in the Middle Ages around a church housing a saint's relics said to be beneficial in the treatment of madness. Arriving initially as pilgrims, the ill were increasingly entrusted to the care of the community which, generation after generation, acquired the custom of lodging them in their homes. This age-old custom had just been successfully rationalized and placed under the control of the medical administration. It was to serve as a model for the Family Colony.

In France, the establishment of a Family Colony was decided on at a national level and it was the poorer municipalities which took an interest in the project. Dun-sur-Auron was chosen because of its remoteness from railways and the main arteries of communication. The experiment commenced with a colony of women, some members of which soon spread to Ainay-le-Château where attempts were made to find places for men. The Colony of Ainay-le-Château was created in 1900. Initially mixed, it was soon to be devoted to the acceptance of an exclusively male population.

Some researchers (Vié, 1940) were able to propose the hypothesis that the region was sensitive and open towards the problems of mental illness because of the proximity of a place of pilgrimage, the "Déberdinoire" or "Debredinoire" (from *berdin, bredin*: madman in the local dialect) of Saint-Menoux, where the relics of a saint were said to cure the illnesses and fevers of the brain. However, we were unable to find the slightest trace of this tradition in the population, and a specialist in the folklore of the Bourbonnais whom we consulted on this matter could offer no support for an interpretation which embellishes a reality whose sources were of a different nature in a population totally unprepared for the task which awaited it

The reports prepared by the successive directors of the establishment in the years following its creation provide an idea of the reactions and motivations of the population. There was an initial fear that the patients would be wicked or a nuisance:

> They were thought to be unmanageable, violent, even dangerous. So much so, that at the time a certain amount of courage was needed and the rumour was that to be a foster parent great physical strength was needed. (Report 1900)

But the doctors, anxious to "keep to a minimum level of social danger", selected for entry to the Colony those whose illness "remained in the intellectual domain without being transformed into action". So successful were they that the anxieties soon calmed, giving way to an astonished curiosity amongst a "gentle, polite, welcoming" population which treated the patients "with much consideration":

> At present the Colony is no longer discussed, although initially everyone regarded the patients with a certain amount of distrust and was astonished to find them to be quite different from those erroneous images each one evokes in his mind when thinking of psychiatric patients. And so we heard people say: 'For madmen they are very quiet'; 'You would think they were quite middle class'; 'If you didn't know, you would never guess'; 'They are real gentlemen'; 'But what illness are they suffering from?' (Report 1901)

The dangerous nature attributed to the behaviour of the mentally ill, and too often used as a reason for confinement, soon ceased to be a major cause of apprehension amongst the population. Over the years, various factors have helped to confirm this undeniable state of affairs, in particular the choice of the patients admitted to the Colony and the system of supervision set up by the establishment. This fact reveals that the argument of danger is frequently no more than the mask of social prejudice. There are other cases, however, in which it is the rationalization of more deep-seated fears whose existence will be demonstrated in the last part of this study

Prejudices towards mental illness were not to show themselves in their true colours until steps were taken to extend the boundary of the placements. Some regions rejected the idea but never sought to justify their opposition by invoking the danger posed by the patients. The reasons advanced by both those agreeable and recalcitrant towards the housing of lodgers reveal the role of economics as a central determining factor and also as a mask. The bitterness of some conflicts shows how vital the stakes were, both materially and psychologically.

In the case of the foster parents, the benefits gained from the lodgers in the form of extra money or the provision of services were sufficient to overcome any reticence. In the direct vicinity of the Colony, the obvious importance for the local economy enabled the scheme to gain many converts. In contrast, those who did not benefit directly found the presence of the mentally ill difficult to accept. In some cases these were "people of private means whose peace of mind is disturbed by the possibility of contact with the patients", or those who found that "too dense a population of patients will end up completely changing the face of the town or village." (Report 1903) However, when speaking with the authorities, opponents of the project defended their position by falling back on the economic argument, thus attacking their opponents' strong point and concealing the weakness of their psychological resistance. From 1905 onwards, a number of councils complained about the competition lodgers recently settled in their *communes* represented to local workers.

At a time when the lodgers had not yet emerged as a "consumer group", the opposition between acceptance and rejection found expression as the opposition between gain and nuisance. The gain consisted of money and work for individuals, the nuisance was professional and moral for the community. The patients were stigmatized for the threat they posed to the social equilibrium, on the one hand because of the unemployment they created by offering themselves on the labour market as a competitive workforce, and on the other because of the laziness they induced amongst the men by providing a new source of family finance.

The problem of work seemed to be all the more difficult to resolve as employment opportunities for the inhabitants of the area were limited at the very time when the officials of the Colony were recommending professional activity as beneficial for the mental equilibrium of the patients and their integration into the family. The problem, however, was one of appearance only because, even though the work performed by the lodgers could be bought cheaply, it did not equal that of local workers or day labourers in either productivity or quality. Moreover, the labour market was soon to feel the benefits of a boom caused by the Colony, whose establishment put an end to the problem of depopulation which had first made itself felt at the end of the 19th century:

> An industry has been created in the region: that of home patient minder, of foster parent, of nurse, and this industry is arresting the rural exodus. (Report 1906)

This state of affairs lies at the root of the prejudice concerning the attack on the morale of the working population. It was alleged that the presence of the lodgers was responsible for weakening the will to work of the men with whom they were housed. To overcome this prejudice it was necessary to entrust formally the financial and administrative responsibility for the patients to the women. Even today, it is still the women who have to apply for the opening of a placement, the number of patients authorized to live with a family being proportional to the number of adult women it contains.

However, we should emphasize that the reports of the directors make no further mention of any opposition after the 1914–1918 war, which played a key role in consolidating the practice of lodging the mentally ill. With the men leaving for the front, increasing use was made of the lodgers' labour. The last vestiges of resistance were overcome and the attitude of the foster parents also changed:

> The new foster parents ask for, and some specify that they 'want' only patients as workers. Whilst previously this demand was merely a set clause, there is now a note of decision and determination underlying this condition, especially in the case of rural smallholders. (Report 1921)

Since that time, the financial incentive has never ceased to play a crucial role in the anchoring and extension of the system of placements which, gradually accepted and adopted by all, made its consequences felt in every sector of social life. When, shortly after the Second World War, the number of patients doubled thanks to the happy conjunction of the introduction of chemotherapies and a new establishment policy, the economic aspect affected the way of life and the identity of the entire community.

In the early days of the Colony, the practice of placement had spread predominantly within the most disadvantaged sectors of the community. The small amount of numerical data contained in the administrative reports shows that the first foster parents were recruited from the professional groups which were most deprived or under threat of extinction. In particular, a number of crafts, which had been under threat from industrial development and rural depopulation since the beginning of the century, were able to continue to exist thanks to the placements. Similarly, widows and labourers found in the placements a means of surviving or leading a decent existence. Later, as certain occupations died out, it was the farmers who turned to the Colony. The supply of money and labour which the lodgers represented seemed like a means to continue living and working on a property too small to be profitable. This was also doubtlessly a way of acquiring and maintaining a property. Thus right up to the beginning of the Second World War, foster parents were recruited from the ranks of the smallholders and owners of farms of fewer than 20 hectares. The accommodation of patients was only later to become of interest to the farmers of larger estates, whose numbers remained low. The involvement of the latter in the practice of family placement was to take place during the expansion of the 1950s and testified to new modes of interest. From this moment onwards, the development of the Colony ceased to be dependent solely on the crises experienced by certain occupational branches. Its rapid growth corresponded to a widespread demand for placements at all levels of the population, including the middle classes and the wealthy.

From then onwards, family placement ceased to possess the same universal economic value. For some it remains a vital resource, even a last resort against poverty and unemployment, or the only assurance of having a "bit of money coming in" in the future. Of the foster parents, 41% of the heads of the household were without work at the time of the enquiry. In the case of pensioners, placement abolishes the need to continue working without having to break into the family inheritance and brings the assistance of the lodger in day-to-day affairs. Married women see in it an "occupation" which prevents them having to search for work outside the house which is both difficult to find and which prevents them from devoting themselves to their children. In cases where a second salary is not needed by a family, they like to have a surplus of money at their disposal which can be used to improve their standard of living or the quality of their household appliances. This income, which the women receive directly, also provides them with a measure of independence from their spouses. For the large landowners, the lodgers represent a supply of cheap labour, while the well-off expect them to provide an extra income and a human resource "to do the shopping or a hundred-and-one other things". The difference in the profit expected from the placements is reflected in their capacity: in the case of farmers, who are looking for an extra worker rather than money, the number of lodgers is low (one or two) as it is with the poor who have neither the space nor the means to maintain a large placement. In contrast, the middle classes, who live in the towns and are building up their savings, and single people or pensioners, who live just from the income from the patients, are able to accommodate larger numbers (three to four lodgers or more).

Whether the patients are accepted "because of the money", whether they are "thought of as working automatons" or whether they are housed "because of all the little jobs they do" we always find that "you can't live off the placement but it helps," "it's a little bit extra". Everyone finds their own way to explain how the ten to twelve francs received per day (at the time of the enquiry) are eaten away by the necessities of housing, heating, lighting, laundering, feeding and supervising a mental patient and on top of all this, if the foster parent thinks of it, even giving him a little attention.

Everywhere you can hear the calculation of profits murmured like a litany: "If you grow your own vegetables, if you keep your own poultry, if you don't have to buy everything, then it's profitable." It is the litany of the small speculator, the impoverished litany of survival addressed to the desirability of material comfort.

> There's nowhere else where the people do as well as these people here. I tell you: a worker who's got two or three lodgers and a good garden . . . it's less so in the town. I can't understand the ones who have to buy everything. But a worker who's already got a little bit of money coming in, or a farmer with an income, his food, a little milk, some rabbits, that's good.

Significance and Repercussions of an Economic Choice

The sometimes obsessively meticulous enumeration of profits is the foster parents' major topic of conversation. During the enquiry it proved possible to obtain from some interviewees accounts of the financial advantages of the placement system which lasted for half an hour or more. We noticed a general tendency on the part of the people we spoke with to return periodically to this topic of conversation when starting to explain or evaluate their life of contact with the patients. It was as if, to make it acceptable or plausible, it was necessary to underline emphatically the profit gained and to stress its compensatory function. In this way, as it became more widespread, the system of family placement characterized the community, becoming bound up in its prosperity and its image, its life and its identity.

First of all the question of prosperity. It seemed like deliverance for a region threatened with suffocation: "Ainay would be a bankrupt region, a deserted region, if it had not had that."

The image of "it's the industry of the region", employed at a very early stage by the advocates of the Colony, has become the expression of an economic reality in the eyes of the population:

> Ainay is focused on that. It's quite simple. This is a region which still has big houses. That's why the Colony was put here – because they need houses for accommodation. So if anybody buys a flat around here then it's in order to fit it out for lodgers. Houses which aren't equipped to have lodgers here are absolutely worthless. And if they do have any value at all it's because there's money in the region. Prices here are much higher here than

anywhere else in the *département*. Houses sell for fantastic amounts. That's because there's money here. Placement is the reason why Ainay is still alive. It's not even an area of full-scale cultivation or full-scale stock breeding. The soil isn't good. There's no industry for the simple reason that Ainay's situated off the beaten track and is difficult to get to. The region would be dead without that. There were no resources. Tourism is seasonal and there's no tourist accommodation. The cafés are quite well appointed but this isn't a town tourists stop at. There's no beach or anything. Once Ainay lived from the wood industry with its woodcutters, its charcoal burners, its oak hewers, its coopers, its clog makers; and then there was steel and all that brought with it; and to top all that, agriculture here has been practised none too carefully. It used to be a region of charcoal burners and now it's been converted to a region of placements.

Industry, the only form of production known as a remedy for the death of the country areas, is related to the system of placement because the majority participate in it, and it maintains and breathes life into the consumer sector. The effects of the Colony appear to the local inhabitants as indisputable benefits of which they can be proud: the same is true of the commercial upturn which is explained directly by the presence of the lodgers. Placement is equivalent to increased consumption: more mouths to feed and more money as well – "you have to spend more" – and, as we have seen, increased investment in the home: television, refrigerator, washing machine etc. In fact the shop windows, not least the displays in the food shops, testify to a refinement, a variety and a luxury which contrasts with the simplicity of the shops in similar towns.

The lodgers themselves now constitute a real consumer group as their numbers have grown and their habits have altered. Thanks to their work, their savings, funds sent by their families, they possess a certain amount of personal money and they have become more ready to consume than in the past. The most obvious mark of their freedom seems to them to be the freedom to purchase.

The influence of the Colony extends beyond the limits of the commercial sphere to transform the basis of the community's economic life. In a region characterized by population loss, the area within the placement boundary is distinguished by a growth in population which has been sustained over a period of fifteen years. We have seen how the institution has contributed to the preservation or reestablishment of occupations in danger of extinction; furthermore, its existence also provides openings when these occupations are abandoned – offering prospects in the commercial sphere which even attract the inhabitants of other districts, or of a career in the hospital: "That brings activity to the surrounding parishes, that brings work, an atmosphere."

At the time of the enquiry, the hospital itself employed 96 people of whom 80 came from Ainay and had been recruited from the craft industry and more poorly represented occupations. The consequences of the placement system for agriculture, too, are more far-reaching than immediately appears. Not only does it provide a replacement for a declining workforce, it also shores up outmoded structures. Just as it has enabled a number of farmers to acquire their properties, for many others it has provided a means of remaining on land which they would otherwise have had to abandon. As we have already said, it enables a living to be made from smallholdings which are barely profitable, as well as making it possible to extend the area of such smallholdings and the benefits obtained from them.

Taken together, these elements incline one to the view that this commitment to the practice of lodging and employing the mentally ill is an original form of development within a traditional framework. This, in conjunction with the "pioneer" role played by the foster parents who agitated for the introduction of placements in new areas and the extent of the resistance to their initiatives, tempts one to compare the choice facing the inhabitants to what Merton described as "anomic innovation". The preservation of traditional modes of existence and social advancement are the stakes in an economic choice, admittedly made under the constraints of the crisis in the agricultural world, but made in order not to suffer from it as so many others have. It is in relation to the social environment that the anomic nature of the choice appears. The arguments of those who criticize this choice involve the local system of values: the code of practical morality, values related to work, taboos concerning mental illness. As a response to the failure of the global system, the choice is not to everybody's liking: seen from the point of view of the politics of the "red country",[2] it is a decision of expedience, its retrograde character exacerbated by the exploitation of man by man.

The use made of the revenue provided by the system of placements confirms the external nature of the economic choice with reference to the current modes of production and distribution of goods. As a supplement to traditional means of subsistence, it injected resources into the economic cycle in the unaccustomed form of regularly renewable assets:

> It would be a catastrophe if the Colony were to disappear, because people have got into the habit of living well. 300 francs a month multiplied by 1,200 lodgers makes 360,000 francs entering the town each month, plus the salaries of the employees, plus the medicines . . .

The placement system thus constitutes a "revenue sector" in the functioning of the economy. The available funds are treated as a "surplus" exceeding "the level socially recognized as necessary for the subsistence of the members" of that society (Godelier, 1966).

---

[2] This part of the Allier, known as the "red country", which had long since supported the currents of left-wing politics, was a communist constituency during the post-war period. The district capital, to which the headquarters of the Colony was attached, had a communist town council, radically opposed to the placement of patients within its precincts.

Everything happens as if the resources provided by the placements devolve to activities which are not themselves directly productive and should therefore show up as a surplus, even amongst the poor:

> The lodgers play a very important role in regions which used to be poor. Saint-Bonnet was a region where the people were poor because the soil isn't rich. There are parts where everyone has lodgers: that has let them improve their homes, to do a bit of painting. It's a lot better now. There's been some building. I'm absolutely certain that if there weren't any lodgers in the region, well, it wouldn't just have remained poor, it would be a lot poorer still.

In most cases, income received for placements is used for increased, if not ostentatious, immediate consumption or for the pursuit of non-material goods such as prestige, pleasure or culture:

> It allows us to keep the land we inherited. It allows us our pleasures, clothes, a car, television. It keeps the money moving, doesn't it?

In a manner reminiscent of that of the "windfall economy" (Poirier, 1968), the Colony short-circuits the local economic cycle and modifies the hierarchy of social needs by enhancing the value of external signs of wealth and improving the standard of living. Evidence for this can be found in the care showered on the comfort of the home, the car, the pursuit of leisure or the importance accorded to educational advancement. The satisfaction taken by the inhabitants in the contact with cultured lodgers assumes a similar level of importance:

> Some of the people who stayed in the Colony were most distinguished; and if the population is in some ways sympathetic to the lodgers, it's because it benefits from the presence of some of them. There was a violinist who was quite extraordinary. He used to teach pupils and certainly spread the taste for music here in the days before the radio could be received everywhere. And there was another one who used to give lessons to the children of the region. He was in touch with the population and they benefited from it.

This enhancement of social status from which eminent persons are most likely to benefit has its counterpart, amongst the less cultured elements of the population, in the delegation of subservient everyday chores to the lodgers.

The inhabitants are well aware of the benefits they draw from the presence of the Colony: "Without the Colony this would be a dead region." And it is not possible to escape from death without finding some glory in the fact:

> If it wasn't for that Ainay would be a drab place, let's be truthful about it. Because after all it's only the country and this makes it into a town. If the

lodgers weren't here, the shops wouldn't be as attractive. Because of that it's more important than Cérilly, which is a *canton*. Although it's smaller, there's more going on than in Saint-Amand.

And they show their pride, to the displeasure of the population of the surrounding areas:

> When I go to Cérilly they tell me they can recognize people from Ainay because they look so proud. The representative of the Board of Trade told me: 'I can recognize an Ainay shopkeeper immediately by his air of superiority.'

Criticized for their choice by the surrounding population, the members of the community are forced to stress the compensations they receive for "putting up" with their status as deviants. But can they avoid feeling a sense of unease because of it? Apparently not, as their evaluation of social life testifies to an anomic state of mind, characterized by pessimism and dissatisfaction. Their pride seems to them to put a strain on social relationships: "It's impossible to have a social life here"; the appetite for gain: "no one gives anything to anybody", the taste for social ascendancy and prestige seem to them to entail rivalries, jealousies, disagreement:

> They don't form a group, they detest and envy one another; they can't do anything together. There's no longer any social life.

> Life has been thrown off balance, there's no give and take any more, no more social life.

This social unease then crystallizes around the institution of the Colony and its staff. Young people of the region who have joined it are rejected because, so it is said, they form "a privileged aristocracy", "a caste, like the upper middle class, and stick together like a family", "they set themselves up and then turn against society, they won't have anything to do with the people of the region". The doctors of the Colony who complain of "not being accepted in the town" are reproached for their isolation:

> If there aren't a lot of people who sympathize with the Colony, it's because of the medical set: they're a closed set and they don't want contact.

> There's nothing between them and us. They aren't interested. They stay here briefly for a year or two and have their contacts back in Paris.

The reproaches become more bitter the more the Colony is expected to compensate socially for the withdrawal of individuals entrusted with functions or services of public interest:

> Before, there used to be two doctors. One had been here since 1913. Now there's only one. He's been here for five or six years and he followed two who had been here for four or five years apiece. It's the same thing with the vet. In a small place you have to be there body and soul if you're going to stay; and what's more, the people here are unfaithful.

> The Colony chases people away. When the old priest died, the diocese had trouble finding a replacement. It had seventeen refusals before finding a priest who volunteered. It's the same thing with the teachers. Just think of all the teachers who didn't want to come. Once they arrive, they stay.

But the hostility shown towards the personnel of the Colony, whilst expressing the rejection of those who come into contact with the mentally ill, is also the result of the conflicts, overt or latent, which have grown out of the opposition between the demands of the institution and the demands of the population over the question of the care of the lodgers.

The Law of the Milieu

Within the milieu which lives in contact with the mentally ill, specific attitudes and behaviour towards the patients were quick to make their appearance. Four years were enough for signs of discrimination to emerge, an affable reserve making way for denigration:

> The patient is primarily regarded as a source of profit. We can be sure that in time the *bredin*, to use a word from the dialect of the Bourbonnais, will be considered more charitably and more fraternally by certain inhabitants, whether foster parents or not . . . We still sometimes have to complain about the behaviour of the children towards the patients whom they torment. (Report 1904)

As the fears dissolve and the interests of the population are asserted, the patients' numbers grow to more prominent proportions and disparagement of the patients becomes more obvious:

> Whilst it is bad for the inhabitants, the patients themselves suffer even more from their high numbers. Now that their great numbers have made them unwelcome, our patients are no longer respected as they should be. An atmosphere of contempt towards the *bredins* is emerging. (Report 1911)

For their part, the foster parents form their own rules of conduct which are not always compatible with the demands of the Colony. In the town of Ainay, despite wanting a monopoly of placements and rebelling against the introduction of patients into other parishes when their demands were not met, the foster parents showed a tendency to eject the lodgers from their houses outside mealtimes and the hours of rest. The inadequacy of supervision and care, indeed the repugnance at allowing the patients anything more than their material upkeep, the economies made in providing them with food and heating are all further obstacles encountered by the directors in their attempt to institute a better mode of accommodation.

In this field, also, the 1914–1918 war was to bring about a decisive change in the way of life originally desired for the patients. An implication of the notion of in-family assistance was that the patients should take their meals with the fostering family, and this was indeed the case during the early years of the Colony. But the period of impoverishment caused by the war favoured meals taken in separation and offered the families an excellent pretext for escaping from an unpleasant requirement.

> The price of foodstuffs has risen and the price of wine in particular. Many foster parents have complained that, not drinking wine themselves, they find it unreasonable to give it to the lodgers who eat with them at the same table. For this reason, I have permitted a slight relaxation of the regulations as, in principle, the lodgers should be treated in the same way as the foster parents' own families. It has happened that in certain placements where we have authorized separate meal arrangements for the patients, the lodgers continue to receive wine while the foster parents drink none. I have noticed no significant difference between these menus and those served prior to the war. The best way of judging nourishment is the health of the lodgers and their expression of satisfaction or discontent. (Report 1915)

From then on, meals were no longer taken in common and this relaxation became the rule which the environment imposed on the establishment. Today, as we shall see, the custom of eating with the lodgers is considered to be a deviation from a norm which only a few families permit themselves at the risk of appearing deviant.

Little by little, the region asserted its law, one which was to its greater profit no doubt, but also one which allowed it to come to better terms with insanity. Even at this stage the influence of the environment affected the decisions of the institution. The officials were forced to compromise with the population to gain acceptance of the Colony. Whilst they resorted to a mixture of authority and persuasion to secure the observance of certain imperatives, they also accepted the most basic demands of the population. Successive officials enjoyed varying degrees of success, with their stays in the institution being all the shorter, the more intransigent they showed themselves to be on the question of the well-being of the patients. Those who, amidst the interplay of the environment's expectations and the Colony's demands, helped fashion the institution we find today, enjoyed long periods of control. For these individuals, the realities of the region were often more decisive than the principles of the hospital, the point of view of the inhabitants often a more important factor than that of the patients.

As long as the medical authorities were able to shape local reactions these remained, be it through conflict or negotiation, an object of attention. But from 1920 onwards nothing more was said about the milieu's response, as if, finally captured and fixed in an immutable mould, it was henceforth known and dominated, an essential, intangible cog in an organization whose agents and beneficiaries would in future be the preferred objects of consideration in the study of the Colony's functioning.

Over the years, however, one concern has remained constant amongst the directors. They have always been anxious to avoid harming the region by introducing to it overly disruptive patients. At odds with the doctrines of their time, which advocated the confinement of the mentally ill, they were still unable to abandon the scruples which accompanied these doctrines. The choices which they asked to be made before cases were submitted to them from Paris, and which they were later able to make themselves in the asylums of the *Seine*, were just as much responses to this criterion as to the desire to find a better way of caring, or a more suitable way of life for certain types of patient, or even the simple desire to free patients from confinement. Ideas concerning the types of illness which were admissible for placement within the Colony have varied in accordance with the psychiatric beliefs held either individually by the doctors themselves or in common with the general notions of their time. These ideas have been further influenced by the question of the number of patients necessary for the efficient functioning of the hospital. Further considerations exercising a varying degree of influence have been the revenue made available to the population and the benefits expected from it. This last factor has sometimes brought about the termination of experiments or the withdrawal of certain categories of patient. Moreover, the system of control set up by the establishment, the gradual increase in coordination between the hospital personnel and the foster parents, has made it possible to minimize the number of "incidents", which have always been remarkably few.

This policy has proved to be effective in every respect: there is no doubt that the population currently feels itself to be most secure. At the same time it cannot be denied that as a consequence the advantages of this form of hospitalization have been refused to certain patients who might have benefited from it without harming anybody had the scruples and fears been less intense or found less support in psychiatric ideologies. Nor can there be any doubt that the policy has indirectly encouraged or contributed to the entrenchment of defensive or preventive behaviour which has proved or may still prove to be prejudicial to the improvement and curing of certain cases. But at least it has helped in the creation of a more open attitude towards mental illness and, in doing so, has improved the quality of the human environment within which the Colony is located.

But, most importantly, the effect of this policy has been to restrict the range of psychiatric categories admitted to the Colony in a way which has proved to be relatively stable over the years, favouring cases of retardation and chronic illness. Moderate mental retardation (imbecility) represents 24.5% of cases, debility and chronic schizophrenia each account for 22.5% of cases, with chronic deliria amounting to only 10% and alcoholic psychoses to only 8%. The preference for certain categories shown in this distribution reflects the obsessions, needs and history of the Colony. The category containing the older lodgers and stabilized illnesses – and, conversely, the relatively small number of cases bordering on the criminally insane or manifesting character disorders – testify to the fear of social and sexual danger; the retarded and sufferers from certain chronic afflictions are the categories which respond to the need to provide a trouble-free rural workforce. The few places left for cases of neurosis, depression or certain forms of alcoholism reflect the difficulty in obtaining foster parents prepared to go beyond the provision of material needs and be of assistance in the psychological support of such patients. Finally, the minimal proportion of places reserved for epileptics results from the care needed in the handling of a population very sensitive to the spectacle of fits, which even today remain a source of fear.

The stability of this representation of pathological types gave the region a specific experience of mental illness which was bound to exercise a degree of influence over its representations of insanity. The introduction of chemotherapies served in some way to modify this state of affairs. That this was to a lesser extent than some doctors would have wished reflects the resistance shown by the local population to any change in its way of life or its relationship with the lodgers. Above all, it reflects the latency of certain beliefs, reawakened by the use of medicines, which overturned the cognitive balance established by the community during the period over which the image of the mentally ill population was formed. But that is another story and one to which we shall return after a detailed examination of the relationships maintained with the patients. These relationships, whose framework we have just described, cannot fail to be structured by those elements which the Colony's history has enabled us to identify: the unease felt in the presence of the mentally ill and the economic benefits of their accommodation. Both factors have contributed to the creation of an institutional system which has moulded the destinies of the Colony's lodgers.

Chapter Two

Custom and the Defence of Identity

Last year some people we met on holiday came to
visit. They stayed for two or three days. We
hadn't said anything. Imagine if we had told
them that I work in a psychiatric hospital! They
said: 'Who are these people?' And we told them:
'They're the patients.' 'What do you mean, the
patients?' 'They're the psychiatric patients.' 'It
isn't possible,' they said, 'it's unbelievable!' 'It's
strange here. Everyone gets used to it. It's a
question of custom.'

A nurse

What then was the image presented by the Colony some seventy years after
its creation? Seventy years: enough time for successive generations to live in
close contact with the mentally ill; for the patients to grow old and die here;
for the children to be born under their gaze and sometimes even by their
work; to grow up in the midst of them and, having reached adulthood, to
settle down and house them. How do we live with the insane today?

Learning-to-Live-With and Custom

Time. That is precisely the argument used by the population to explain the
custom of living with the mentally ill which they think of as original and
unique. It has allowed this "custom" to prosper, this *leitmotif* which everyone
puts forward as if it were an explanation. "The custom of the region" is a
point over which every interrogation stumbles. Sometimes it takes the form
of a rebuttal: "You don't understand. It's the custom and that's all there is to
it." We frequently met with this response at the start of our enquiry when we
began interviewing the population. In the mouths of members of the
psychiatric establishment, local people for the most part, this argument took
on a variety of meanings. It took the form of an irrevocable scepticism, often

tinged with irony, at the naïvety of an investigation into what is accepted as a social rule. It is encountered once more in the "that's all there is to it" of the refusals to explain, the attempt to protect what is hidden. And buried under the rule of silence lies the denial of any hidden problems. This question of denial is one which has frequently been raised by researchers interested in the attitudes held towards the mentally ill (Cumming and Cumming, 1959). Should we share Dufrancatel's view (1968) that this is a negation of insanity in a public environment, a negation which is equal to acceptance, toleration? The question deserves our attention and we shall return to it once we have elucidated the meanings ascribed to the idea of custom.

This idea is summoned up as the outward appearance of a collective fact which is no longer questioned:

> People from other regions, outsiders, ask us how we get on: It's the custom. We're used to it. We don't notice it any more.

In fact, this notion covers a range of intimately connected processes, each implying an effect of familiarization due to prolonged exposure to the patients. First of all, it is applied to the very acceptance of the system of placements which is based on observation, example, imitation and soon spreads through the community with the force of a tradition:

> Everyone's got them. Everyone takes lodgers. It's the life of the region and it's been like that for as long as you can remember.

> In 1909 my husband's mother was one of the first to have them. Since then, every generation has taken them. It was the daughter's turn next, my husband's aunt. And now it's me. Our family has always had them. My son's the latest one.

> To me it feels like a tradition. Everyone, nearly everybody has got patients and so we take them as well. That's all there is to it.

Being rooted in the customs of the region in this way confers an appearance of normality on the accommodation of the mentally ill:

> There's not much to say about it. They are the lodgers. Everyone thinks that's normal. No one finds it strange.

At the same time, the very fact of referring this practice to a long process of habituation shows how deeply the community feels that this practice deviates from common reactions to insanity:

> If you want to understand something of the relationship with the patients you have to bear in mind that it has become established over a very long

period of time. It's a custom passed on from generation to generation which
you wouldn't find anywhere with an open asylum. In those places things are
still brutal. It's shocking. What you have to bear in mind is the way the
patients have been introduced. At the moment there's a detached attitude
after three good generations.

It's because the people here have got used to it. If we had never seen them
before . . . I'm sure if it was a question of a new settlement, of taking an
asylum and setting it up in a region where they haven't got a clue, where
they have never seen them, it would probably be received badly. It would
certainly be received badly. People would find it hard to get used to.

The work of time operates through a whole psychological transformation of
the community, at the end of which incongruity has been erased, unease has
been effaced or masked, and that which was rejected as external has become a
component of the community. A transformation assisted by familiarization.
At present, everyone from within the Colony's boundaries, even the oldest,
say they "have always been used to" the patients. If they were not "brought up
with them", that is to say, did not come from a family of foster parents, then
at least from school age onwards, they have rubbed shoulders with the lodgers
on the way to school. The patients who have been seen "as long as you can
remember", "since you first opened your eyes, as familiar as television",
become everyday actors on the social scene, as familiar as the rest of the
environment. They neither shock nor surprise. They are even defended:

It's all the same to me. I've always been used to them. I've always seen
them. When I was little they were already there and I liked them well
enough. But as for the people who don't come from here! I know a lad who
goes hunting in Ainay and he's shocked by it. He finds them standing,
watching, at the street corners and it makes him laugh. But it shocks him all
the same. For people who don't come from here . . .

Thus custom transforms experience. It is a process which makes everything,
even the strange, seem familiar and self-evident. The power of familiarity and
acceptance accorded to the simple fact of seeing, however, only makes sense
if it is acknowledged that this experience is socially coded. We learn to see,
or not to see, "not to notice", and those who "have always lived together with
those people, always been in contact with those people" have, from the very
beginning, received from their environment the rules for learning-to-live-
with: "People are used to them, they have got used to seeing them around."
At the end of one interview the daughter of the house, a student, joined in
the conversation. As I was trying to get her impressions from her, the father
butted in and said on her behalf what she was supposed to think:

Since you were very little you've always seen them. You don't notice them.
You find it perfectly natural. That's all there is to it . . .

At this initial level, the learning-to-live-with-the-patients, which implies a wide range of regulated behaviour to be examined later, limits itself to controlling individual reactions which might be provoked by the behaviour, remarks, gait, physiognomy etc. of the mentally ill. By eliminating any aberrant events from the realm of consciousness, or by investing them with the character of an insignificant fantasy – "you think to yourself that it's the patients and don't take any notice" – the process aims to make the patients as invisible as possible, to merge them into the surroundings and accord them as neutral an image as possible. Even before any direct relationship is entertained, a social model makes it possible to "apprehend" the mentally ill by shaping the cognitive and emotional process triggered by the simple fact of their presence.

In order to transform this presence into an "everyday affair", the model regulates the manner of "viewing" it, of defining it, by assigning a negligible value to any appearance of abnormality: "Life is quite easy for us. We don't notice any more, we just don't notice."

The model also orients the responses to its appearance through a way of assuming responsibility, controlling the intimate repercussions which it generates and classifying them under the category of "shock". One interviewee was surprised at the fear shown by a number of drivers who were passing through the village at the sight of an exhibitionist who, at one time, had the habit of waiting for nighttime to fall before opening his cape and showing himself naked in the headlamps of passing cars. Her astonishment reached its peak when friends who were out with her one evening were seized with panic and escaped by car, leaving her standing there right in front of the lodger. She, however, calmly returned home as if nothing had happened, but added, "when things like that happen you're not frightened at the time. It's only afterwards . . . " When dealing with the alien, the custom established by tradition and familiarity finds support in habit which provides a social means of processing it.

This method of approaching an alien neighbour, which consists of not noticing or sensing in him any elements of incongruity, has a certain affinity with the basic psychological mechanism of denial. For this reason it is not without ambiguity. In its most radical form it can lead purely and simply to making the troublesome element invisible: "it's quite simple. I just don't see them", or in a refutation of their human quality. But by placing the other in the category of the normal, it implies an attitude of acceptance of daily contact. And in this way the evident ability to live in close contact with the "insane" spreads through the population.

This ability, however, does not ignore the difficulty or the specificity inherent in it. However small the temptation to forget the self-application necessary to "put up with that", the reactions of visitors to the village are enough to recall it. The villagers are happy enough to have a laugh at the expense of the driver who, asking for directions, is shown on his way, frequently down the wrong road, by one of the lodgers, or at the woman who turns "pale, shrieking with fright" because a lodger is circling her car. In this connection, commercial travels provide a particularly varied sample of pitiable and laughable events. As for those Parisians who rented a house in the town and had "even paid a deposit. When they saw these people in the streets they took fright and the next day they were gone, we don't know who was more ill, them or the people who frightened them." But whatever it might say, the slightly disdainful population measures how much it differs from others in and through its process of habituation.

> I've never known anything different. They are part of the region. People visiting from elsewhere are shocked. It's a question of habit. We don't feel afraid. We don't feel anything special.

From here it is only a short step to feeling oneself to be different:

> You see, *living here has marked me* . . . *Marked? No, better not say that, shouldn't say that.* But in the end you realize how different you seem to those who don't know. Nothing seems very different to us. There was one bloke who came from fifty kilometres away and had never seen a patient. Never seen a patient and then he comes and settles down here. But we've always been used to them. There were patients when I went to school.

Before proceeding with our exploration of the consequences for the population of this process of habituation, let us stop to examine what its different modalities, located at the meeting point of the social and the individual, imply from the point of view of contact with otherness.

Custom and the Normalization of Aberrance

Behind the idea of habit, we find the phenomenon commonly cited by anthropologists when their informers, unable to supply the unconscious or implicit reason for certain collective practices, invoke tradition or custom (Lévi-Strauss, 1976). We also encounter the process identified by sociologists as the preliminary to institutionalization: habituation which, by subsuming the variety of situations under a single predefinition, eases the adaptive effort, reduces tensions, facilitates action and takes root, disguised as routine, in the obvious facts of communal knowledge (Berger and Luckmann, 1966).

But in the community we are studying, the appeal to the customs of tradition also has the function of a mask donned in response to the attempt to penetrate and research the milieu. It is possible to see in this the mark of a process generated by collective psychology and it is important to analyse its dynamics. This process is the counterpart to the work performed by individuals on themselves to control their reactions to the presence and sight of the mentally ill.

This psychological aspect might incline one to see in what the respondents call custom the generalization of a purely individual mechanism. All the more so as many works in the literature of psychosociology attempt to account for the phenomenon we are interested in through the application of a behaviourist or psychoanalytical approach, by addressing its twin aspect of familiarization and defensive neutralization of the signs of aberrance and the reactions they provoke. We shall not adopt this viewpoint here for the following reasons. First of all these works, which all attempt to explain attitudes as a response mechanism to an object stimulus, human or otherwise, social or otherwise, fail to grasp the social dimension of response and behaviour (Moscovici, 1970). Then there is the fact that it makes it impossible to explain the collective character of a response, other than by the identity of individual reactions in the face of the same situation – which amounts to discounting the social – or by a "diffusionist" hypothesis of collective sharing which postulates communication without integrating it as an element in the explanation. This seems to us, at least, to presuppose the idea, which is gaining acceptance, that attitudes, beliefs, representations are social because they are commonly shared. Yet no interest is shown either in what might be socially "moulded" in individual responses, or in the way such an element might become operative, or even in the effects of communication and what is carried by it.

What is true of habituation is also valid for familiarization. The behaviourist model accounts for the formation of a favourable attitude or acceptance by the simple fact of repeated contact, "by mere exposure". This effect of contact has been studied across a range of fields, including the relationships between social groups, without ever truly accounting for the mental process which underlies it (Fodor, 1981, pp.6, 28). This process has to be reconstructed by focusing on the actions employed by subjects to integrate the new into their own frame of reference, to situate it in their own field of information and evaluation. This frame and this field are socially structured in that they spring from a background of symbolic interactionism and ethnomethodology (Schutz, 1962; Garfinkel, 1967; Cicourel, 1973) which have established the role of everyday life, of social organization and corresponding practices in the shaping of attitudes. Moscovici (1976, 1981) has contributed to an explanation of this mental process by showing how, in the cognitive universe, social representations help in the "familiarization of the unfamiliar", by re-forming, even by transforming, all new information on the basis of socially constructed models which enable individuals to situate themselves and act in their environment, harmonizing their position with that of their social circle. This approach can be applied and extended here.

In effect, what our interviewees described as custom concerns the social method of integrating this strange and alien object, which is the mentally ill patient, into their cognitive universe, and to an even greater degree, into their practical and emotional universes. They are not content to react in a private way to a shared experience, that of the presence of an aberrance in the social landscape. They respond to it, and learn to respond to it, in standardized fashion. In their speech, custom presents itself as one of the *natural facts of life* which are equally *moral facts of life*, to use Garfinkel's apt formulation (1964, p. 225). It is the custom of the community which erases the strange, which makes the spectacle of confusion and fear in the face of the insane visible and pitiful, which exhorts all its members to a self-control and a common response. And from this fact two questions arise. On the one hand, by bringing us into the presence of the group production and control of social affects, it raises a problem which, as Garfinkel rightly pointed out (*ibid.*, p. 233), remains for social sciences *terra incognita*: that of the effect of the background of common understanding on the genesis and evolution of social affects. This concern will occupy a central position in our investigation. At the same time, the why of this social control still requires explanation. What processes are at work behind this codification of the way the patients are perceived on the public scene and the reactions they provoke? Might this be a question of defending a collective equilibrium?

For discomfort, fear and unease are not absent. They must simply not show themselves. Whatever it does, the population never completely erases the silent and close menace of insanity from its consciousness:

> I get the impression some people are going to raise objections because they're afraid. Because you do see it, you know! I always wait for my little girl when she leaves school, in a square with a bus stop. I wait there along with lots of other mothers, in the car. Some of them come up to talk to you, to joke with you because you're a woman. All the same, I don't think some of them are very good for the community. Some of them you don't notice, but there are others . . . There's one of them, on the road up towards Saint-Mamet, one of them who I don't like one little bit. If I went out by bike I know I would meet him. Perhaps he's quite harmless. I don't know. It's just the way he looks. He makes an impression on me. He walks a bit like a dancer, and he's got a black face, and his eyes . . . he stares at you. It's really dreadful and it scares me. There's something about him which frightens me. His face is . . . I don't know how to describe it but it worries me. His eyes stare at you. He stares at you when he looks at you. That's all. I can't describe the effect it has on me. It upsets me.

In the face of this multiform, incessant presence of insanity a subtle knowledge evolves, one which makes it possible to stifle the onset of this obscure apprehension, transformed into the terse *leitmotif* "he frightens you", and which sometimes overwhelms its victim with a specific illness: the "attack of fright". Seen from this viewpoint, the smoothing away of emotional reactions seems to result from a collective technique for maintaining a calm, harmonious social façade. This leads us to suppose that individuals draw on the know-how of the group for the forms of control because they have to elaborate for themselves an experience congruent with that of their social surroundings and express themselves in conformity with it.

That is why the view of a universal elaboration of a defensive position, leading its holder "not to notice" or even "not to see" the mentally ill, makes it difficult to interpret this kind of denial in terms of defence mechanisms which are purely intrapersonal and subjective. Some psychosociologists have recourse to a psychoanalytical schema to show that when people are placed in similar social conditions, the unconscious dynamic to overcome conflicts associated with these conditions operates in accordance with similar defence mechanisms (Dollard and Miller, 1950). Applied to the phenomenon we are describing, this conception would amount to saying that this copresence with the patients activates the same type of intrapsychic adjustment at an unconscious level. But in that case, how are we to explain how the mechanism which dictates the response of denial reaches the conscious level, and how it is communicable and transmissible as a mode of behaviour? If, as we have seen, a socially-shared and collectively-cited custom conceals an unconscious component, then this is of another order from that used in the psychoanalytical interpretation of the resolution of a state of conflict. Rather, the unconscious character of the custom is concerned with the reasons and significations which lead to its collective adoption.

The cognitive and psychological control of the avatars of confrontation with the mentally ill is learned as a socially transmitted technique. It results from a collective regulation of the process of coexistence with difference. By unifying this group response, regulation blurs differences and makes coexistence possible. This fact legitimizes the idea that such regulation responds to a feeling, a state, which affects the community and has the aim of reducing a conflict felt at the group level.

In fact, the process of denying deviant behavioural characteristics is frequently employed when the identity, the respectability, the normal face of a group is put at risk by the actions of one of its members. This is particularly true of responses to mental illness. Scheff (1967) has seen a phenomenon of bipolarization between labelling and denial in the way society perceives mental illness; Cumming and Cumming (1959) have registered many forms, both primary and secondary, of the refusal to admit the problem posed by mental illness when a community finds itself directly involved with it. The phenomenon is aggravated in the case of restricted groups such as the family. Star (1955), Yarrow *et al.* (1955), Freeman and Simmons (1963) have underlined the disinclination shown by families to define the disturbed behaviour of one of their members in terms made available by psychiatry, and a tendency to consider the symptoms of mental pathology as normal. Numerous researchers have shown that this tendency to normalize mental illness in order not to identify members of the community as ill and declare them as such to the others, even at the risk of preventing their treatment and rehabilitation, persists in different countries and across different cultures (Lyketsos, 1983). The denial process seems to us to be based on a social defence mechanism protecting against a narcissistic wound, the threat posed by stigma to the identity of a group and its members. This defence requires the symbolic effacement of the disruptive element and its distinguishing characteristics and can extend to the negation and isolation of the ill person.

In this connection, we can apply the notion of "stigma symbols" to the community we are studying and the consequences of the presence of the mentally ill within it. Goffman (1963) contrasts these symbols with "prestige symbols", saying about them:

> [they] are especially effective in drawing attention to a debasing identity discrepancy, breaking up what would otherwise be a coherent overall picture, with a consequent reduction in our valuation of the individual.

The phenomenon of habituation used by the population to accommodate itself to the presence of the Colony's patients serves to reduce their negative symbolic value. The significations of this phenomenon clearly remain unconscious and its functioning resembles that of a tacit idea (Polanyi, 1966). At the level of daily contact on the public stage, habituation is responsible for a filtering off of aberrance, a perceptual repression, a "subception" of disquieting characteristics and consequences. It performs an adaptation which maintains the group equilibrium through the application of a social know-how which internalization in psychological functioning has made tacit.

In questioning this "explanation by custom", our intention was not solely the methodological aim of penetrating behind the surface response, apparently vague or superficial, given by a group unaware of its interpersonal mechanisms; neither was it the psychological aim of elucidating the individual implications of the invoked process. Its distribution and its profound impact on the attitude of the people we interviewed obliged us from the start to consider custom as the first, generic expression of the acceptance of the mentally ill. Its investigation seemed to us to be a prerequisite for the understanding of the processes at work when a community integrates a population which is not only exogenous to it, but is also characterized as different. These processes have been little studied, irrespective of the difference concerned: illness, sex, ethnic origin, nationality etc.

If custom is indeed as we have just defined it, it should be possible to recognize its effect which, throughout the community, serves to guide contact with the patients, and in the expressions of the anxieties and threats it helps to surmount and mask.

This point of reference should be visible first of all at the level of contact in the public arena, since something of the group identity clearly has a role to play in social interaction. Especially when, wherever it might be, the doors of the asylum are opened and the conflicts generated by the presence of the insane enter the community. Mostly, however, this involves only a few individuals in brief and episodic encounters. The Colony is a different case, however. The number, ubiquity and implantation of the mentally ill impose a human mass whose encroachment the public can elude as little as the repercussions of its image.

This situation results, of course, from a concentration of patients which at times reaches a critical threshold in the eyes of the officials. However, the dispersal of some thousand patients throughout thirteen *communes* creates widely differing conditions of contact. The proportion of patients within the population varies greatly from one *commune* to another, from one corner of the region to the other, varying between 5% and 32% of the local population and, in some cases, even exceeding the number of foster parents in the population. And if, in some villages, the volume of patients is highly impressive, it remains minimal in some of the hamlets and in some places falls to so low a level that the individual patients are practically lost at the bottom of a farm, itself isolated at the end of a road or in the clearing of a forest. What is claimed to be tolerance is, in the rural environment, sometimes only this oblivion in a vast agricultural expanse.

Figures and Images of Public Contact with the Insane

The relative density of the lodgers has an effect on the way their contact with the population is organized. This is especially visible when, as we were able to observe in many different places, contact occurs on public occasions such as ceremonies or festivals involving large numbers of people.

Three fairs proved to be particularly illustrative in this respect. Two of them, announced by posters displayed in the region, drew a public coming from the entire district and even further afield. One was organized on an Easter Monday and was centred around a *roulade*, a traditional festivity during the course of which hard-boiled eggs are given away and eaten together with a *brioche* and a glass of wine. We were at the very edge of the Colony's territory where placements were seldom opened. In the *commune* itself, only one farm accommodated a lodger and he attended the fair as the sole representative of the institution. We were able to recognize him because we had already seen him, but only a practised eye could have told from his clothes or his bearing that this man, who remained at his foster parent's side rather too timidly for his age, formed part of the Colony. No one in the public noticed anything about him and when he had grown a little bolder, the man disappeared into the crowd behind the procession of majorettes. There was no distance between him and the others, none of whom suppressed those looks or gestures which betray the effort to act as if nothing had been noticed. After the parade, he joined the others who were returning to the rest of the fair in small groups. Perhaps it was then that he noticed the off-handedness of these young people who, laughing in complicity, were teasing a poor wretch, the village idiot, who had just emerged from a ruined building. Moving as if in a ritual, the youths approach the idiot, address him using a familiar but inoffensive nickname, tickle him with a wooden stick until he trembles and shakes the *baguette* he is holding in his hand. Then a warning voice is heard: "Watch out, he might get angry and turn nasty. He might give you a good bashing." And they retire. Soon, however, they continue the teasing as long as the object of their fun does not become over-excited, in the same way that one might play with a dog, making sure that "he does not get too angry". After a short time, they withdraw, tired, taking their playmate along with them. No one takes offence. Watching this unconcerned, natural sparring, we are far from the embarrassed reserve felt by those who, surrounded by numerous lodgers, discover among them a native of the same region, someone who is "one of them".

In this locality at the edge of the zone of placements, too distant to be visited by lodgers deprived of a means of transport, the only one who had access took his place on an equal footing with the visitors who harboured no prejudiced attitude or watchful air. It was necessary for "madness" to make its appearance dressed in the buffoonery of folklore to trigger a customary style of behaviour aimed at revealing the wickedness expected behind the inoffensive mask. An impression of symbiosis and openness emanated from these Easter festivities.

This impression was to be absent from the second festivity, of more recent tradition, in which the lodgers shared, *en masse*, the fun of the fair with the local population. This took place at the very heart of the Colony's territory, a mid-summer celebration for the "old soldiers" of France. The fairground was situated at the edge of a pond, complete with stands and, between them, a raised stage for the show, opposite which was a platform with a number of folding chairs for more comfortable viewing. A number of lodgers, regular visitors to the fair, had arrived early to take possession of the chairs for the duration of the afternoon. There they sat, their gaze looking down on the bustling public. Whenever there were musical interludes or displays of folklore, the crowd would gather around the stage while a group of women, children and older people seated on the ground accumulated around the square of chairs occupied by the lodgers. Some of them took care to maintain a distance between themselves and the lodgers. No one, however, challenged their position. By arriving early, the lodgers had earned their privilege and, knowing with whom they were dealing, the locals considered it better "not to pay attention". In this way the patients were able to enjoy a temporary superiority in the tranquil isolation of inattention.

The crowd around the stalls was more varied. Small groups gathered briefly at a stand or were detained by a chance encounter and then melted again into the mass of people. People came and went ceaselessly. Although many had come from far away, no one stayed for long. In fact the rhythm of these brief visits proved to be a greater contribution to the general animation than the liveliness of the visitors themselves, amongst whose numbers a few dozen lodgers could be counted. Whether solitary or in groups, a discreet void formed around these lodgers who were left unanswered whenever they tried to engage in conversation. Everywhere parents were taking care of their children, holding them by the hand or watching over them from a distance, discreetly making sure they kept away from strangers. This unstated vigilance was the cause of a climate of tension and reserve which makes itself felt at any gathering where the lodgers are present in large numbers. This crowd, composed both of locals and visitors from all over the region, manifested an ambiguous mixture of reserve and acceptance in the presence of the lodgers. The locals were quite indifferent, acting as if they could not see them, moving amongst them, whereas the visitors remained alert, maintaining a void of silence and distance between themselves and the lodgers. Although, because of the location of the fair, they had expected to encounter lodgers, they had still come, thinking that their numbers would be small compared with the rest of the crowd and that constant alertness would protect them from the necessity of contact. And yet in some places they have had to stop holding fairs because the lodgers are so numerous they have dissuaded the public from coming.

At the village of Ainay, however, it is only those who are used to the patients who attend public occasions and the patients, for this reason, do not risk isolation. Indeed, the fair partly belongs to them:

> Whenever there's a festival, they are at it. They're present at the parades. They're there and they're part of it. There are a lot more patients at the processions than there are locals.

Just as on one 14th of July, while the crowd waits for the 10 o'clock torchlight procession, the lodgers flood into the road. As soon as the band strikes up from the war memorial, silhouettes emerge from the houses and line the 200 metres the procession must pass on its way to the market square. Not everyone comes down to the road.

Some people arrive singly. Parents come with their children. There are also a large number of those single middle-aged women dressed in grey or black, with carefully permed hair which is protected by a scarf, with something neat about them, something correct and slightly stern in which you can see the modest income and the ever watchful superiority of the widowed foster parent.

You can feel their vigilant gaze surveying the scene and, most of all, its actors. If a lodger goes a little too far, speaks too loudly or addresses a passer-by in words thought to be a little too forward, one of them is quickly at his side, ready with the word and the gesture which bring him back to the established order of the ceremony. Like a child. What is more, the festival of the 14th of July belongs, in some ways, to the insane and the children of Ainay. The band is followed by a group of torch-bearers: they are lodgers trying to march in step, almost stiff with the effort of trying to stop the enormous torches, which they carry in outstretched arms, from wavering. The torches, unprotected by any shade, are more reminiscent of funeral candles than a joyous gathering and their unstable lights augment the fantastic appearance of those people who, for the brief and unique instant of 200 metres, are invested with a solemn social duty. The children, sensitive to the unaccustomed solemnity of the procession, surround and follow it, tempering their exuberance until they reach the square where the firework display will take place.

Here the procession dissolves. The public, swollen by spectators who approach from every road, divides into groups. A great mass of lodgers gathers at a slight distance from the square. They speak, some move around a little, but the vast majority remain completely immobile during the entire duration of the firework display. The locals circulate, stop to chat, allowing the few patients who are avid for company to mix with them. The children are separated from their parents and play beneath the trees or in groups, free of any constraint towards the lodgers. As a nurse from the Colony has pointed out, the behaviour of the parents is different:

> Two years ago I went to a fair at Dun-sur-Auron. The locals didn't go near the patients. One of them approached my daughter. I let her. Maybe it comes with the job. I'm sure if the patient had been dealing with a foster parent the same thing would have happened.

In between the salvos of fireworks, the orchestra carries on making its own contribution. The children take advantage of it to dance farandoles with their ribbons streaming amongst the spectators, breaking up or encircling their groups. It is of no consequence to them that these groups are composed of patients; and you can see the children's little silhouettes losing themselves in the imposing mass of lodgers, which stands slightly apart from the rest, as if they wanted to reduce this spontaneous separation. Close to us, one lodger, already advanced in years, breaks into tears and, passing from one person to the next, tells through his sobs that he was born on the 14th of July and that none of his family is there for his birthday. Everyone listens to him and, before returning to their own conversations, finds a phrase with which to express their condolence. When he turns to us with his tale of woe, a couple approaches and removes him discreetly from the strangers that we are: "We know, we know, you're very unhappy," says the woman and the lodger continues: "the 14th of July. It's the day I was born. My poor mother will be in tears because her son isn't with her. She will think of him and be so unhappy." The man takes him by the arm: "Oh believe me. She'll remember your birthday. She won't have forgotten that!" The joke is harsh, but spoken without laughter, with just a glimpse of irony for the benefit of the spectators. The old couple leads the man off towards the dance. This, and the protective attention which accompanies the words, quietens him.

There are other public occasions when the population of Ainay is less prompt to lower its defences. At the dance the lodger is allowed to watch but not to take part. When films are shown at the local hall, the darkness proves to be a cause for reticence and the patients are consigned to a corner whose seating is separated from that of the public. On other occasions the patients are helped to affirm their right to a share of the collective well-being and to show themselves as equals. In church, where once they were grouped together in a special area close to the side door, they are now perfectly free to sit wherever they please. Although the priest, once attacked as a "revolutionary" for opposing these segregatory measures, has been unable to gain them access to seats traditionally reserved for certain families, some of them are, at least, allowed to approach the altar. And if most of the lodgers are to be found at the sides rather than occupying the more central seats, then at the moment of communion they come together without distinction with the other believers. That should be enough for those who want to point out that all God's children are equal – and what does it matter that the main door of the church should be barred to them!

But whatever their density, the lodgers appear in everyday life as if embedded in the natural and social landscapes. The freedom they enjoy leads them to disperse amongst the villages or to ramble through the countryside. Nearly half of them prefer to live away from their place of residence or are more or less forced to do so on account of their foster parents, especially in the towns. In this way, even in places where they appear in no significant numbers, they remain a diffuse, insinuating presence, signs of which can be found everywhere: in the tireless walker who has marched many kilometres into the heart of the country; in the shuffling silhouette pushing its trolley along the road or letting a pair of boots dangle from the end of its arms; in the perpetual dreamer lost in reverie on an embankment or sitting on a bench; at the approach to the village, in the line of pedestrians whose limp, often uncoordinated, steps carry them towards the Colony's annex; or in these curious runners of errands carrying a basket full of shopping, jugs of milk or large loaves of bread for the family.

And back in the village everything speaks of their presence: the strange, stooped man washing the shop floor who wrings out his floor cloth with the skill of a servant; in the resigned patience of these shoppers waiting their turn to be served at the ironmonger's, the greengrocer's, the chemist's, a turn which will only come when the locals have been dealt with. In other places the unending ballet around the lavatories danced to the constant rumbling sound of the flush contrasts with the discretion of furtive visits to the café and with the placidness of these groups of men who rest together, talking or silent, in the shade of the bus stations or in the sunlit squares. Sometimes, indeed, this presence is the only one to be encountered in the little towns buried in the heart of the countryside, all but deserted when the last of the residents abandon the streets for the fields or the kitchen, leaving the lodgers to look after the children. And in this unpeopled silence, in the shelter of a closed chapel, you can hear a faltering voice searching for a tone of authority: "Don't do that or you'll make your mummy cry; don't do that or you won't have any lemonade." The three-year-old girl continues to play.

This continual presence takes on an appearance of destiny:

> We were made to live with these people. If the younger generation carries on living here, they'll live with them as well.

This ubiquitous presence is on view everywhere and multiplies in the imagination:

> You can say that there are nearly as many patients as there are residents living here. 1,800 residents in the *commune* and 1,200 patients. We're always in contact with the patients.

We were told this by a woman living in the village of Ainay which, in fact, possesses only 130 placements with a total of 330 lodgers. That this presence has been adopted and familiarized is suggested by the expression "they're part of the region", which refers less to the volume of patients than to their ubiquity, their penetration into the spaces of everyday life, and also their activities, their participation in the rhythms of life. And, in this respect, perhaps the presence has made its impression:

> But for us, you know, living here is quite straightforward. We don't take any notice any more. We don't take any notice. For us the patients, they are, they are . . . If there *weren't any more patients, I think that would throw us off balance. We've got used to them.*

But this "used to them" is a hollow habit, threatening a transformation of the self. What power do they have then, what threat do they pose, those people whose presence can change you if you accept it?

> It's true. *When you get used to it, it's as if you were infected, as if you can't do without it.*

Habit, therefore, is the mark of a kind of intoxication. But the nature of this mark, this stigma – that you are never told.

The Anticolonist Struggle

To get an idea of this stigma it is necessary to search the Colony's recent history, to the 1950s when there was a rapid expansion of the number of lodgers, which rose from 500 to 1,000, and an enlargement of the placement zone. These developments provoked new conflicts and public debate. The opposition was no longer between "consenters" and "opponents" as it had been in the early days of the institution, but between "colonists" and "anticolonists", a choice of terms which itself denounced the Colony's power to conquer and to harm the invaded populations. These conflicts were to escalate to a previously unknown degree, reaching onto the political stage on which entire town councils had their destinies at stake. The arguments appeared to be a defence of the social body rather than conflicts of opinion or interest. And even if this episode in the life of the Colony has been strongly underlined during the course of the enquiry, it has still proved difficult to obtain from the informants any clarification of its underlying motives. Resistance was blamed on "personal interests", "people not as intelligent as they might be", "pig-headed", "as thick as they come". Only through indirect questioning could conversations with individuals directly implicated in this public affair (wives of prominent figures, officials of foster parents' associations etc.) uncover the psychological reasons underlying opposition to the spread of the practice of lodging. What was at issue in these collective debates was the simple fact of the physical, visible presence of the mentally ill in the *communes* and the anxiety it provoked.

Within this opposition to the Colony the protection of a kind of social façade was to find an ally in fear. The sight of the mentally ill is disquieting and, because it can be seen by others, it also becomes embarrassing:

> Believe me, there are plenty of people in the region who don't like it. They're afraid, some of them, afraid that we'll have patients really mentally ill. And then they think it's not a very pretty sight to see them wandering around in the streets, people like that.

> These people are, after all, not like the rest of us and there are people who don't like that and that causes a certain coolness between some members of the population. There are a number of people, of a certain social position, who find it embarrassing, and a few families have created some disagreement in the *commune* by saying that it's not the right thing for a town, because they are worried about the appearance of their town.

The stigma of physical and mental distress is sometimes reminiscent of the visions of Hieronymus Bosch and the local inhabitants cannot approach it with equanimity:

> There's one aspect of it which is a bit like the *Courdes Miracles* of Paris and it's an unpleasant sight. For me that's important. The others are more interested in the end of the month.

A way of basking in the sun without undue modesty takes on, for some, the colours of provocation:

> I've heard that some people have complained because, after all, it is sometimes rather embarrassing. The ones who are in the town and don't have anything to do, they're always in the square, lying, sprawling. Well, of course it's annoying to the population!

> Some people were furious with the Colony. They said they were all good-for-nothings, people who were fed and didn't do a thing for it. Some people think of them as parasites.

These arguments derive additional force from the expectation that people from outside the region will feel that its inhabitants are tainted by this presence: "People are afraid of the region's reputation."

The freedom enjoyed by the lodgers is a source of threat to the image of the group. They fear that an observer, ignorant of the fact that these people belong to an institution, will mistake the appearance of full civic status and put them in the same category as the rest of the population:

> People opposed it because they didn't want others to see the patients wandering around the town. They said that the example of one or two might lead them to . . . But anyway, a lot of people pass through here and there are never any problems with the patients. Of course they are ill. We know that. But all in all the ones we've got here aren't unpleasant!

The arguments and quarrels which characterize each region newly opened for the integration of the mentally ill clearly demonstrate the collective significance of the conflict experienced by the inhabitants. The initial numbers of patients do not have to be high for the locals to voice their reactions and, in fact, the existence of a single placement is sufficient to set the defence mechanism in motion. When it is a question of a single individual, the practice of placement seems to be a deviant action and the foster parent is quickly the object of attacks from the surrounding group which wants to prevent the spread of the practice:

> In the region they thought it was funny that we wanted to have a lodger in the house. They were astonished that we were taking a patient.

> My grandparents had one. But at that time there were a lot less than there are now. There were only two in the region. And, good grief, people were dreadful about it . . . they were up in arms against my grandfather and then they had the lodger taken away again.

When, despite everything, the practice begins to become more widespread, it appears for some time as a choice whose consequences are injurious to the group. Evidence of tangible benefits for the local economy have to come to light before opposition dies down and many of those who argued against the system become its advocates.

> They all screamed when I had one and then afterwards they all went running after them. It's always the same. It's those who open the way for the others who are criticized. Everyone knows that. A lot of placements have been opened since then. Now you see lodgers all over the *commune*, nobody would insult them.

> There are people who used to criticize and then got lodgers themselves and changed their minds: I don't know how these things happen.

But the economic incentive itself remains a blot on the group image in the eyes of an environment whose system of values has been shocked. Leaving aside the question of the reduction of the labour market, today the stigma is focused on turning altruism into a profit-making occupation, living and benefiting from the misfortunes of others. Something of the dignity of the social body is lost in turning insanity into a business:

> Some people think we have lodgers because we get money for it, because we're paid at the end of each month.

> They criticize, they say we take the patients because it's profitable. Some of them think the lodgers are here to be exploited.

The reproach of "profiting from the patients with added interest" is exacerbated by the disapproval of a way of life which does not conform to received models. It is striking that all the external evaluations of the benefits to be gained from placement emphasize the trouble the inhabitants save themselves by entrusting everyday tasks to the lodgers. These assessments give a financial value, the value of a bonus, to the walking the foster parents save themselves, the work they escape by not having to cut their own wood or do their own shopping, the extra work available to the farmer. The money they gain without doing anything is counted. Everything offends against the principle of effort, of hard work.

The apparent indifference to the taboos relating to insanity is also perceived as a break of faith with the social code, and observers call into question the responsibility of the State which, in setting up the Colony, has imprisoned the population within a degrading set of circumstances.

The "shame of showing this human face" – the face of poverty profiting from the face of insanity – which the public authorities were unable to avoid, is augmented by the "degrading of the foster parents" through a natural tendency to allow oneself to deteriorate through contact with the insane – "the children are stupid and the adults have lost their moral and religious qualities." For the first and only time, an allusion to sexual relations with the lodgers is expressed openly with reference to the danger of the region being ruined if the State does not do its duty and protect it. As we shall see, this side of things is rarely mentioned within the region where the people are directly involved in the Colony, but this state of "being at fault" implied by others is a severe wound to the identity of the group and reinforces the impression of "contamination".

The Other is the Same

This impression is always present within the community when proximity to insanity mobilizes its reactions to the risk to its integrity. And as we have seen, the disquieting menace of insanity is always at large, even where a whole system of protective knowledge has been formed. This lies at the root of a new paradox which is without doubt the most delicate of all. At the same time as it makes it possible to approach what others reject, this knowledge will make insanity more immediate on two counts. Experiential knowledge blurs the differences between the insane and the self, whilst defensive knowledge, however effective, must be ceaselessly deployed, and will always be a reminder of the imminence of danger.

In fact, what insanity teaches this population, more thoroughly even than an observation of the workings of the illness, is that it spares nobody, that its surreptitious or explosive imprint makes no great distinctions, as the procession of its victims shows. This experience provides the local population with the argument of indulgence in the face of the frantic resistance of prejudice:

> The people who are against it are wrong. They don't understand in the slightest. Because those people there, they're people like us, aren't they?

> They were stubborn. We told them, 'we don't know what's going to happen to us, you don't know what's going to happen to you, the same is true of your children.'

The closeness of the contact with insanity changes the general appreciation of the illness:

> When we arrived twenty-two years ago we were like anybody else who doesn't come from Ainay-le-Château. There were the insane and the sane. We never asked ourselves if there was a line between the two which was sometimes difficult to draw! . . . How much can you be thought of as insane? I don't know, the barrier between . . . It's like 'size', how tall do you have to

be before you're of medium height, before you're tall? What criteria do you use to say a man is bad, or a little less bad? You can't define it!

Even if real-life contact with the lodgers has not, as we shall see, fully expunged the traditional images of insanity then it has, at least at an overt level, deflated the caricatures of moral degeneracy and evil which were associated with them:

> Having the Family Colony here in the region has done something big because, you know, people who get illnesses like depression go for treatment as if they had a more common ailment like bronchitis. People here don't hesitate to see a psychiatrist. Yet in other places, not far away, just twenty kilometres from here, people think of it as a shameful illness.

> In Ainay we have a better understanding than in other rural villages where the mentally ill are considered bad people. Here they don't try to make it anybody's fault, they don't accuse you of being bad, they just realize that you are ill . . . For people outside, the mental patient is a dangerous man and they don't realize that there are a lot of others who are mentally ill as well. Here the mentally ill are people who are suffering from something. People often say 'it could happen to us one day'. That's something which people in other places don't expect.

The affability of this new popular wisdom reinforces custom in its role of reconciling those who "are part of the region" and those who "have made a life with them" and gives the patients the status of elements in the social whole. The breadth of participation publicly permitted them confers on the patients considerable scope for penetrating into the social fabric and the mental panorama of its members. At the symbolic and material levels the patients impose themselves as irreducible, even obsessive, facts:

> In earlier times the lodgers were treated as an unimportant factor, 'he's an idiot, he's insane.' You had no respect for a lodger because he was an idiot. Today, behaviour has changed. They are part of everyday life, part of us. It's rare for a family not to have discussed the patients. Women say to each other, 'mine did this, he did that.' Not a day goes by without you commenting about the patients. That's perfectly normal. If the patients were all taken away overnight we would find it strange here. We're so used to them, integrated with them. They are integrated because we talk about them all day long . . .

The lowering of the frontiers of normality, the penetration of the patients into the activities, preoccupations and conversations of everyday life gives their group an invasive power of another order than that observed at the simple level of physical space. By making the lodgers an integrated part of the "we", the identity of its members is even modified. Proof of this is provided by comments made about the idea of their absence which, from the "it's a way of life, it's true we would miss them" to the "it's as if you can't do without it" and even the "if there weren't any more patients, I think that would throw us off balance", suffice to show the extent to which coexistence with the patients is felt to be a true impregnation by their presence. Although it is only articulated in connection with attitudes and living habits, this transformation is equally felt at the level of psychological integrity. But on this point the older the practice of placement was, the more discreet and indirect our interviewees were.

Certainly, the rapid, almost involuntary, allusions that occur in conversation reveal a certain unease, whether it is the woman who greets you saying, "here's me all muddled up as well", because she hasn't put the saucepan in its proper place, or someone evoking the image of the town, "when I go to Creilly, they say 'you come from the idiots' village'", or the person who echoes public opinion:

> Some people say that the mental patients have had a bad influence on the region, that, for example, it's because of them that the children are like they are, that they pull faces, that they are badly behaved, that they don't answer you.

But there are more deeply hidden signs which reveal this unease. Thus in the town of Ainay, four fifths of the mothers we interviewed had consulted a psychiatrist about one of their children or asked me if I found them too nervous, if they ought to see a specialist. This is without doubt the effect of a better appreciation of mental illness, partly due to a more practised eye, partly to a less derogatory conception of it.

However, the type of motive cited for the consultation, the irritability of the child or "freezing" in exams, indicates that the question is prompted by a more deep-seated anxiety, the fear of reduced protection against mental illness. Similarly, although they claim to be "used to abnormal behaviour", it is not without a certain shame that they turn to a psychiatrist. The women who took me into their confidence would, under no circumstances, have gone to the doctors of the Colony and took care to conceal their actions by turning to a doctor from outside the region in Bourges or Montluçon. And one of them concluded:

> Earlier we wouldn't have accepted anyone with a depression. 'What's wrong with them?' I would say. When you get older you realize it's not always something serious that sets off a depression. I understand better now. My daughter suffers from anxiety so I was told to go for a consultation. They said, 'there's nothing to it. This neurology can belong to lots of things.' Before they would have said, 'they're nutters, they're idiots.' Now they accept it. But like my friend says, the doctors should put 'neurologist' on their nameplates, not 'neuro-psychiatrist'. The 'psychiatrist' is too much.

This proximity to insanity is a cause of closer relations and a convincing intimacy. The wisdom drawn from everyday confrontation leads to both increased openness towards the insane and towards a greater sensitivity to their presence. As a consequence, it is a small step from this feeling of penetration to that of one's own fragility and of contagious impregnation. Acquired through contact with the patients, the knowledge which makes them seem less different and renders participation in their suffering more immediate has, as its consequence, a paradoxical duality. Whilst this knowledge manages to overcome its initial anxieties, all the more so since they are articulated in the language of prejudice, the increased contact it allows reinforces these anxieties by modifying their mode of expression. Denied in speech, these anxieties are subsequently manifested in "concrete action" such as the preventive or curative behaviour we have already investigated or the practices relating to contact with the patients which we shall examine later.

But the community which finds a common method of overcoming in secret this intimate conflict is unprepared to see it revived and brought to light by an outside observer who is quick to denounce the misdeeds of a shameful illness. The eyes of another, when you are yourself aware of the proximity of illness, imprison you in it and you start to fear being thought of as mad, if not actually becoming it:

> There are people hostile to it in the population. But often the hostility doesn't come from them, it comes from the others. It's stirred up by the others. We call them 'the lodgers', but seeing them, living together with them, you realize that they aren't at all extraordinary, that they are ill, people like everybody else. But you often hear people talking when you leave the *commune*. Straightaway it's, 'V . . . , it's a village of idiots.' No, it's stirred up by the others. Once you've seen them, you realize that they are people who often aren't that ill at all.

The young woman who told us this had only just opened her placement. Herself the daughter of a family of foster parents, she worked in a carpentry shop in the Tronçay forest. When her children were born it had seemed quite natural to her that she should take lodgers and thus continue to make her contribution to the family budget while staying with her children. She described the reactions of her companions at work:

> A lot of my workmates came from other regions. Although they weren't from V . . . they used to talk about it. They just couldn't get used to the idea that I live in V . . . and that I have two lodgers. Some of them even joke about it amongst themselves. They wouldn't dare to in front of me, or at least not too much. That's a laugh, isn't it? They would never have thought I could have taken patients. They say we'll go mad, too. That say it's going to rub off on us. They weren't able to understand and they were frightened,

very frightened, just like I was. But they expected the patients to be evil. And they said we would grow like them. Because we look after them, we'll listen to them and start believing them. It's the others who put these ideas into our heads.

In this way we observe the emergence of new, indirect signs of anxiety in the face of insanity, signs associated with the similarity noted today between the lodgers and the local inhabitants. There, too, the effect of a combination of the awareness of the non-distinct and the anguish of the indistinct can be found in the search for effective methods of observing the patients in the social environment.

The 1957 reform of the clothes worn by members of the Colony, the aim of which was to reduce the feeling of difference and confinement by substituting a varied, modern style of dress for the earlier tragically bright uniform, met with an ambiguous reaction in the region. Although pleased to be spared the sight of bizarre and sometimes ragged clothes, the inhabitants were unable to avoid a feeling of unease, all the more so because changes in behaviour induced by the effects of chemotherapy made the signs of mental illness more difficult to identify. The population, which, in a sense, was comforted by being less marked in the eyes of outside observers, was confronted by greater difficulties in distinguishing the patients within its own boundaries. The consequence was a constant, sometimes obsessive, concern to identify them:

> Nowadays they are very well dressed. But they still wear a kind of uniform and you can still identify them in spite of everything. If one walks down the road, 'Look, there's a new one!' It's their behaviour. If they have the same habits as the civilians and they bear themselves well, then you hesitate. If they look a bit strange on the road, if you see they're a bit disoriented or they have nervous tics, then there's no doubt. If they are alone and wearing civilian clothes you hesitate because there isn't anything to tell you that they are lodgers.

A conversation between two farmers touches on the criteria for recognition:

> Me, I say that you can recognize them. You can't miss them. There's the way they walk and all that, even if they're dressed normally. A lot of them are great smokers. Heaven knows what they wouldn't do for a packet of tobacco!

> All the same, some of them look quite normal. Look at the one who stayed with . . . always in his working clothes. He didn't look as if there was anything wrong with him.

> That's true. But there's something else which tells you if it's one of them or not. That's when the time for their tobacco comes round. They only get their tobacco after they've shown their pair of boots. Because they have to keep their boots in good condition and because in order to keep their boots

in good condition they have to grease them, they have to look after them, take care of them. That's why you see them out walking in their shoes or slippers. That lets you recognize them as well.

Underlying and closely associated with this desire to identify the patients is a fear of identification and identity:

> You know. There are some of them who are just as well as the civilians and some civilians who are as ill as they are. As we say around here, there are some people from both groups who aren't all there [*laughter*]. Of course, they do have their clothes. It seems to me it's the way they dress that distinguishes them from the others. Because there are some, you know, if they're well, some who have their own clothes. Some of them are so well that you just can't tell. You have to find them a bit outside Ainay, on foot [*laughter*]. Then you can say, 'if he's on foot . . ', because there aren't many people who go anywhere on foot these days. I tell you. It can be difficult to tell them apart . . .

The reassurance conferred by the ability to identify the mentally ill from material indications becomes all the more imperative as the population, itself unsure of its ability to distinguish, fears that others may be taken in by some affinity or other and judge the local inhabitants to be just as affected as the patients it has taken in. This mistake was made by an official originating from another region:

> I have been here for twenty years. I was surprised at the establishment of placements. I couldn't understand how people with children could accept lodgers. But there are people here who are no different from the lodgers, who are every bit as mad as the people from the Colony at Ainay.

And the less it feels able to guard against the risks posed by the patients, no longer distinguishable by their appearance, the more the group is motivated to search for new modes of protection, taking its model from the period of history when the yellow star condemned to the opprobrium and vindictiveness of society those in whom others denounced as a threatening defect:

> There's one astonishing thing here. *In the past you could tell them apart. They wore a uniform. Now they wear civilian clothes. They dress better than we do.* They go into the cafés; if they are somewhere where the people don't know them they can drink whatever they like . . . It's like the children in care, just the same. *You need something to distinguish them, something that would give you a badge.*

Thus the logic of the process of acceptance, by making the foreign "implant" an undifferentiated, integrated element of the social context, ends up transforming it into an internal danger and erecting new and more subtle barriers against it. This contradiction, acted out in an environment saturated with the mentally ill and sensed by those who seek a final resistance to their presence, is one of the motors of the dynamic of the relationship between the inhabitants and the patients. Although it does not always cross the threshold to full consciousness, this contradiction, together with the expected benefits which justify the acceptance of the lodgers, lies at the base of the social system which the group response instigates around their presence.

Conclusion

From Contact to Impregnation

The veil enshrouding the secret of the Family Colony has started to lift. It has allowed us to glimpse the slow, sometimes insidious, work which the accommodating community has applied to itself and to the psychiatric establishment, revealing the twin motors of the social institution as we observe it today: unease in the presence of the mentally ill and economic interest in their acceptance. Both call into question the identity and the image of the group, compromising the objectives of the hospital, transforming the partners in this interaction between society and insanity. An exemplary case of coexistence with a form of otherness, represented in large numbers within the population, this dynamic questions the way we conceive of the relationship with difference when difference becomes the defining characteristic of a group.

One of the conceptions of this relationship bases the possibility of coexistence on tolerance. Of particular value for the relationship between society and the mentally ill, it assumes, in its naïve and sometimes even knowledgeable representation, the privileged form of an opposition between two terms deriving from heterogeneous but closely associated universes, danger and tolerance:

> Simultaneously festival, mystery and menace, insanity has always troubled society. This unease and this uncertainty have justified the continual oscillation of the collective attitude between *tolerance and approbation, liberalism and confinement.* Within this framework, the psychiatrist has often appeared as the opponent of these attitudes: austere in denying the festival, rigidly scientific in denying the mystery, *philanthropic in denying the danger.* (Pélicier, 1964, p. 86)

The opposition between danger and tolerance has been of primary importance in the evaluation of the characteristics of the psychiatric institutions and continues to be so. Originally the danger which the patients were thought to pose to the population was considered to be the prime obstacle. This idea frequently conceals prejudices and fears of a different nature, and we have seen how persistent it has been. It is thus the tolerance of the community which is emphasized as the key factor:

> The fact that such a concentration of mental patients should be tolerated, even if the assistance given by the population is not prompted by purely philanthropic considerations, is a valuable experience when one considers the difficulties encountered by all psychiatrists when their patients reenter the community and consequently society's frequent reluctance to accept just one patient whose condition has been improved or cured. (Bonvalet *et al.*, 1966, p. 229)

In the same way, danger is the overwhelming argument used to oppose the opening of psychiatric hospitals, as shown by press articles, opinion polls and spontaneous testimonies. But here too, as Foucault (1971) pointed out, confinement has other causes than protection against the aggressive potential of the insane. Rather, it seems like a case of "primitive social behaviour in the face of mental illness" (Daumézon and Bonnafé, 1946).

Confronted with this perception of danger, doctors, legislators and others seeking to identify the conditions which favour the acceptance of patients in society, have always, like a leitmotif, called upon the tolerance of the public. They have seen that the fate of the patients beyond the walls of the asylum rests on this tolerance. An illustrative example of this tendency can be taken from the pages of a report commissioned by the Quatrièmes Journées de la Santé mentale (1959, p. 39):

> The full significance of mental illness can only be viewed within the surrounding context. The importance of the problem posed by mental illness is a function of the tolerance shown towards it by society . . . In a highly tolerant environment, confinement, a devaluing measure, is never necessary for the treatment of patients and this tolerance facilitates their social reintegration.

According to the authors of the report, the social environment affects the moral and mental state of the patients who no longer present "these *pathological reactions* which are thought dangerous and which are *often triggered in less tolerant environments*". Moreover, the patients are able to regain their "*human dignity*".

To some degree the idea of tolerance is linked to an unquestioned common ground, a pyschosociological assumption, as an instrument of analysis of a specific social relationship, the relationship to difference. But does it offer a pertinent viewpoint? What does tolerance denote at the level of behaviour and social symbolism? Do its connotations fully embrace everything that is at work in the relationship between a social group and those who bear the mark of mental illness? At this level, the least that can be said is that the texts themselves present the idea of tolerance as belonging to both the medical and ethical fields. And often, the organic image and the moral vision are mixed; their significance hovers between that of a biological phenomenon and that of a moral virtue.

On the one hand, all that happens suggests that the social group is assimilated in an organism capable of receiving within itself a foreign body, an implant, whose presence it can support without showing symptoms of pathological reaction or rejection, in conformity with the medical definition of tolerance. This organic vision of the social reaction to the introduction of the mentally ill contributes to the emergence of a representation of society as a living tissue able to absorb an external human mass which is different in nature. On the other hand, to use the term tolerance to describe an attitude of mind is to remain bound to a normative viewpoint. At this level, the domains of usage of the term are not without importance, and the same is true of the history of its use. However old the idea, the word tolerance made its first appearance with reference to the 16th-century wars of religion and implies the freedom accorded to others to think, or indeed to express, beliefs which we do not share, and thus the coexistence of world views which have ceased to engage in violent confrontation. This definition has been extended by a legal dimension referring both to the unprotesting acceptance of attacks on one's own rights when in a position to suppress such attacks, and to the latitude of interpretation established by law or custom and extended from the monetary to the moral sphere by France's so-called "houses of tolerance" or brothels.

But let us leave the images of the insane and insanity which are articulated by these notional formulations: the image of the foreign implant in an organic whole which absorbs it without reacting; the image of a heresy towards which a policy of inaction results in scepticism rather than acceptance; the image of injured rights. This summary of current representations contains nothing very positive or beneficent. But at present the thrust of our enquiry is aimed elsewhere.

We are concerned with the model of social relations, of an orientation towards others which implies the social attitude designated as tolerance. As a type of social intentionality, a value-bearing vector which is inscribed at the level of the individual or the group, in both effective and symbolic behaviour, tolerance emerges as an issue in the moral more than in the psychological field. The analysis conducted by Jankélévitch (1970, pp. 32–39) gives us a glimpse of its implications. This relationship with otherness or with difference reveals two faces. The first, the relationship of love – but this is neither requested nor obtained in connection with the mentally ill – has the positive force of an effort of understanding, of respect, and, if empathy proves impossible, of sympathy. The second, that of "peaceful coexistence" – and this is what society is expected to show the mentally ill – is no more than the empty form of abstention. It accepts others as they are and not for what they are. It limits itself to saying what is not permitted, the use of physical or symbolic violence to interfere with another's existence. And in so doing it "admits the *de facto* physical existence of the stranger. Nothing more." It supposes a non-communicating juxtaposition within a common social space and, psychologically, almost a social void. It is "a virtue on which to found a disunited world, a world in which humans ignore each other".

The ethical model is similar to the medical model. Neither provide the means to describe how, and with what consequences, heterogeneous human elements are able to exist together in a real social entity. To borrow the medical metaphor as an articulation of social tolerance leaves unanswered the question of whether a socially structured and psychologically integrated group can limit itself to receiving an external element without adopting any other form of accommodation (of which habituation is an example) or assimilation, to use Piaget's terms. In the same way, recourse to the model of peaceful coexistence says nothing about the way in which dissimilar elements live together as "stuck pigs", whether as "embattled brothers" or as "condemned men".

In short, to explain the relationship between the mental patient and society in terms of tolerance alone is to preclude an understanding of the pyschosocial dynamic through which strangers, or those who bear the brand of otherness, are received and maintained in a space where nothing necessarily demands their presence. Not that the forms of a silent copresence, deaf or blind to others, cannot be observed. But if people coexist separated by a screen, if, in the absence of frontiers, they erect barriers between one another, then we still need to know how and at what price to themselves and their partners. The social environment is a melting pot, not an inert shell. Contacts are formed there, positively or negatively, in accordance with the modalities which are generated by the interplay of the peculiarities, needs, expectations and feelings – experienced or projected – of groups, and which also influence the groups themselves. It is here that we must seek the causes and forms which determine how the mentally ill find their place outside the asylum, the Jews outside the ghetto, the Africans, Portuguese or other foreigners outside the factory.

The notion of tolerance does not seem to us to form part of a precise psychosociological analysis. At best it is of some use to us in characterizing the apparent result of the complex relationships formed within the system of the Colony. An obvious result if you observe public behaviour or refer to the discussions of habituation. But the repercussions revealed to us by a glimpse of the various phases of the introduction of the mentally ill are sufficient to show that the phenomena accompanying the establishment of a divergent group within a community motivate something other and more complex than a simple attitude of tolerance.

Already the study of the mechanisms which, known by the locals as custom, make it possible for the inhabitants to adapt to the influx of lodgers into their daily lives, has shown us how an attempt at accommodation regulated by the social framework has affected the psychological functioning of the population. At a later stage, the analysis of the processes which lead to the appropriation of the social space by the patients, processes which we have already seen at work in the control of personal territories or in certain social conflicts and behaviour, will reveal the importance of protecting both the social body and the group image and identity.

At the same time, the economic element, a motor of the Colony's system, far from explaining the processes regulating the relationship between the patients and the others, appears, because of its role of justification and compensation, to be one of the forces of the psychosocial dynamic which leads to the production of an institutionalized system of relationships. The question now is to find a framework within which to analyse these processes.

The models which suggest themselves to us for the examination of this relationship are derived either from social psychology with its research into prejudices and intergroup relationships, or from sociology with its work in the field of race relations. Let us briefly examine what they have to offer us in the treatment of the interaction of two groups, distinct from one another despite being embedded in a common social whole which is itself delimited or defined by this interaction.

In the field of social psychology, a large volume of literature has associated the cause of attitudes expressed towards an out-group with intrapersonal mechanisms and structures (Allport, 1954; Adorno *et al.*, 1950; Rokeach, 1960; Eysenck and Wilson, 1978 etc.). Two further major currents of thought, elsewhere intimately linked, have sought a more precise definition of the social variables of position and behaviour manifested "within" and "between" groups and enable us to go beyond the purely individual level in explaining the relations between members of different groups. The first of these currents is characterized by the work of M. Sherif (1966). The second is associated with the perspective provided by H. Tajfel (1972) on social categorization.

The significance of Sherif's work lies in its deduction of the characteristics proper to one group from the relationship it maintains with another. These characteristics relate to the structure and functioning of the group as well as to the choice of its value system, the orientation of its goals and the social definition of its members (distribution of roles, authorities, determining and anchoring of attitudes etc.). But although this model bases an understanding of these characteristics on a knowledge of the mutual position held by the groups, it is nevertheless limited in its ability to explain interactions between groups. In effect, it defines for itself a preestablished set of relationships as an irreducible precondition. According to this, interdependent group actions can take the form of partnership in competition, conflict or cooperation, or in a context regulated by a higher interest. It is within these imposed frameworks that the analysis of mutual perceptions and evaluations is conducted. As it envisages only a small number of abstract types of situation, this perspective offers no way of understanding the complex relational situations and states which are encountered in concrete social contexts, either as a function of the global system in which the groups are situated or as a function of the social affects which are mobilized.

Tajfel's theory of social categorization attempts to take account of individual perceptions, the formation of stereotypes and prejudices, social comparison and discrimination, and the relationships between groups. In this theory, cognitive need for the organization, interpretation and mastery of the physical and social environment results in a classification of its elements. The pertinence of the categories to a subject depends on the subject's membership of a social group, and there is a tendency to differentiate systematically between individuals sharing membership of the same social group and those not sharing it. The theory holds that this differentiation is based on the accentuation of similarities between members of the same group and of the differences between members of different groups. Its corollary in the fields of evaluation and behaviour is a discrimination which is expressed as in-group favouritism. This discrimination is then manifested automatically as soon as individuals are classified into groups even when this classification is an arbitrary process.

Tajfel's theory has an individualist connotation. The cognitive perspective which lies at the root of the theory cannot fail to accentuate the intrapersonal character of the categorization, with the result that it concludes in the vision of a cognitive, adaptive process which organizes the environment for the survival of the organism, and in this way questions our conception of human nature and confers the status of normality and necessity on social discrimination.

A number of authors have tried to extend Tajfel's work to complete the cognitive model of categorization with elements of a motivational nature, with precisely the aim of accounting for its social character. But, with the exception of the work of Rabbie and Horwitz (1969) which related social categorization and the in-group bias to the fate and intentions shared by members of that group, this attempt seems to us to return to the individualist approach. To give one example, this is the case with the theory of group identity (Turner, 1984) which uses the group members' need for positive self-evaluation to account for the discriminatory character of group conduct which is produced by social categorization. As group membership is used as a means of definition and evaluation, there is a tendency to evaluate one's own group positively in order to evaluate oneself favourably. We are faced with the same schema that we rejected in connection with habituation and denial, namely that similar collective attitudes and behaviour within a given social situation are mediated by intrapersonal processes even if the motivation for these is social in origin.

This is clearly not what we encountered in the relationship between the population and the patients in Ainay-le-Château. It seems to us that what is at work in this situation is the defence of a group identity through the bias of socially regulated individual behaviour. And we shall have a chance to test this hypothesis in the context of the regulation of interpersonal relationships with the patients. Whilst the difference between the groups is established from the start, we have encountered demands for discrimination arising from the experience of proximity and the risk of identification. This risk implies observation by another, judgement by a party external to the two groups involved in the contact. Is this third element not a determining factor in the processes delimiting the relationships which form between the patients and the population which receives them? We think it is. This third element, to which Moscovici refers when proposing a "ternary" structure conception (1984, p. 10) of social relationships, is not present in the category-based approach to intergroup relationships. What is more, because this approach is primarily experimental, doubts have been cast on the limits imposed on the experiment by the context (Saint-Claire and Turner, 1982). In that study, however, the effect of observation and judgement by a third social entity was not the subject of investigation. Perhaps the time had come to consider this aspect, as in this way it is possible to escape from a certain cognitive formalism and grasp the social, motivational dynamic which lies at the root of differentiation and its expression in terms of categories. In effect, we are of the opinion that categorization is just one of the possible modes of operation of social division; that, far from producing discrimination, it is secondary to the need for division which is based on social affects and the representations provoked by situations of contact with difference.

In any case, the two models we have just examined seem to us to be inadequate to define the different effects of contact or the initial production of forms of interaction as a function of the global system within which the groups are situated. In this respect, sociological studies into race relations may offer some assistance, however wary one is of admitting an equivalence in the attitudes shown towards strangers and minorities in general and those shown in connection with the mentally ill. In a study of this field, Banton (1959) analyses all the forms of contact between groups or societies belonging to different races, taking as his basis various ethnological and sociological studies conducted in multiracial countries (Latin America, United States etc.), in countries characterized by ethnic, tribal or social pluralism (Africa, the East) or placed under the domination of a foreign power (whether colonial in nature, or whether the settlement is of an industrial or commercial type) or in countries with high levels of immigration such as Great Britain. All these studies show how, depending on the type of relationship defined by the objective social situations, a single difference, the racial difference, is accorded clearly delimited social roles, is attributed variable social functions, is the object of diverse social relationships and provides the scene for internal modifications in the groups concerned. This makes it possible to characterize various forms of social relationship:

peripheral or institutionalized contacts, domination, integration, cultural adaptation, paternalism, pluralism, symbiosis etc. (ibid., pp.84, 113).

However, these tools are difficult to transpose to the context of the placements, first because of the range of the phenomena studied, and second because the procedure is the reason why they are of interest, namely the description of the effect of contact between groups on the cultures and the economic, political and social systems associated with them. It is true that the hospital institution imposes on the population an internal contact with elements which are external to it and it is equally true that it appears to be an organ of authority which dictates its will to the community and changes it. But the context within which it is operating is radically different to that in which two societies confront each other in search of economic advantage or conquest. On the one hand, the institution, the community and their members form part of a larger common framework which is determined by the global social and cultural system. On the other hand, neither the culture nor the political system of the population is under attack. For the patients form a group without their own structure or culture and even if, coming from the outside, they seem to overrun the region, their lack of social and psychological defences soon gives them the status of a group dominated and ruled over by the local population.

Nevertheless, the repercussions of the system of the Family Colony are related to those observed in many cases of interracial or intergroup relations, as can be deduced from the language of the region itself when it evokes the "encroachment" of the patients, their "transplanting" or their "integration". Whilst it seemed sensible, for the reasons we have described, not to adopt terms used in parallel fields, it will prove necessary when analysing the circumstances of Ainay-le-Château either to adapt them or to redefine them for our own ends. To do this it is necessary to bring to light the particular nature of the relationships which unite the patients and the environment into which they are introduced, and thus to identify the consequences which result for both groups and to find a definition of these in conceptual terms.

So far we have limited ourselves to examining the external forms of the contact between the lodgers and the population on the public stage, devoting ourselves to a description of the repercussions, in a sense the psychological cost, of what has the appearance of integration. Already at this stage we are able to transpose an idea such as "acculturation" which is applied to the changes in way of life and culture undergone by a group which is forced to adapt by contact with another. Turning to the psychosociological domain, it seems to us that the term "impregnation" might prove able to describe the modifications experienced by the population in its attempt to live in contact with the mentally ill. The idea of impregnation allows us not just to designate the type of transformation which takes place in the customs and mental habits of those who live in close proximity with mental patients but also to define the mode of action attributed to the latter. They bring no coercive culture to the everyday life of local representation. They act, because of their illness and the economic consequences of their presence, through a diffuse influence on the identity and integrity of the group which receives them. Although it is produced by different means, the result resembles that of acculturation. Moreover, the metaphorical value of the term "impregnation" also suggests the almost phantasmagorical emotional dimension which characterizes the experienced relationship as the immersion of the other in the social body and which lies at the base of all social symbolism which organizes the construction of both otherness and the relationship with insanity.

We must now proceed with our exploration of the relationships maintained with the patients, penetrating in the next part of our study to the deeper level of the practical organization of life with them in order to observe how they are integrated as partners in the life of the social fabric, how their "entering into society" as a distinct community operates.

PART TWO

THE BARRIERS TO INTEGRATION

Chapter Three

From Difference to Separation

> You have to maintain a certain distance. You
> have to familiarize yourself with them a little, but
> you mustn't get too close . . . You take them for
> what they are. That's all there is to it. You do
> what you have to for them, but you have to keep
> your distance from them all the same.
>
> You wouldn't want one like we've got coming
> into the house, even though he isn't bad.
>
> Mealtimes are special. It's the people who keep
> them busy with work who give them a family life.
> We serve them in their room. Those who work
> get their reward. But to have them at table. No.

Demarcation

The story was already some years old when I heard it. A man who had just
arrived from somewhere or other became a regular visitor to one of the village
cafés. Every day after dinner he would sit at the bar to drink his coffee, alone,
always silent, with a strange look to him. His beard was of a rather old-
fashioned cut. His clothes spoke of a neglect which accorded badly with his
well-tailored city dress. Every day the waitress served him a cup of brown
liquid, taken from one of the percolators, always the same one, reserving the
coffee from the other percolator for local customers. It was customary at this
bar to serve two sorts of coffee, both costing the same, one for the inhabitants
of the village and the other, of lesser quality, for the lodgers. The waitress
had summed up her client at first sight. He could drink from the lodger's pot.
He sipped his coffee without saying a word. This went on for a number of
weeks, up to the day when he revealed his identity. He was a house doctor
working in the hospital. Had his timidity led him, day after day, to drink the
insipid brew offered him without complaining? Had he been putting on a
show to get to know the way his charges were treated? Nobody could say.

This story is grist to the anticolonist mill, always ready to denounce the vices of the system. It is also illustrative. Any male, a stranger to the region, who passes some time there without looking like a tourist, or a commercial traveller, or a lorry driver, is treated like a "non-civilian", a lodger.

We have already seen how the obsession of identifying the insane is intensified by the lack of clear signs distinguishing them. The ever-alert attention of the population then resorts to a sense of intuition which it believes to be infallible:

> I can always tell when there's a new arrival, however well he's dressed. I couldn't tell you why but I sense it. In other places, too, I can tell if somebody's off the rails.

> Maybe we've got some kind of mental twist which makes us see madmen everywhere. It's possible. Maybe it's a characteristic of these parts. Perhaps I don't see you in the same way I see a Paris lady who has come to visit her brother.

Thus anxiety finds a sure way to calm itself in the act of discrimination.

But is the motive of suspicion sufficient to explain the discriminatory treatment received by the patients and the mentally ill in the placements? A glimpse of this treatment is provided by the story of the house doctor and perhaps by something which happened to me at the very beginning of this enquiry. At the end of my second week's work at the Colony, at a time when I was still unknown in the village, I found I was early for the bus which was to take me to the railway station. I decided to wait underneath the chestnut trees in the church square, seated on one of the benches which look out over the valley. The sun was setting. Nothing could be heard in this corner of the village except the echo of the river below. Suddenly there was a dull sound at the back of the bench. This was followed by a second and then a third. My belongings were jolted and stones as big as pigeon's eggs landed at my feet. As I turned around the children ran away. Children who, without even laughing, were bombarding a stranger, a stranger who kept company with lodgers. People in the village thought I was a social worker at the institution. One lodger had shown me around the village and some of them had accompanied me from the Colony to the hotel in the evening. My incongruous presence in this poetic, deserted place resembled that of the social workers, and like them I had earned this mark of distinction. I got off with a fright and a warning.

Examples of discriminatory treatment abound. For instance, the level of priority accorded to the lodgers in the shops where they are always served after the locals even if they arrived first. Their presence in the cafés also obeys a set of rules. There are three cafés bordering the main road. Each has its own appearance and its own clientele. The largest, a *brasserie*, is frequented by workers and, during the school holidays, by the local youth. The coming and going of the customers follows an inflexible rhythm. A few lodgers venture into the café during the empty hours of the afternoon but make way, before six o'clock has struck, for the workers stopping for a drink on their way home. In the summer, the lodgers retire in the face of large numbers of young people. The inside room of another café opens onto the road through a wide door. At all hours of the day this room gives shelter to farmers, salesmen, managers and foremen who meet to discuss business or just to have a quick chat. Only one or two of the working lodgers, acquaintances of the landlord, drop in briefly to quench their thirst at the bar. The others feel out of place. They prefer to go to the hotel-restaurant, a small establishment consisting of two buildings. The first, situated at the end of a courtyard, is the restaurant with its small, attractive American bar. This is separated by the hotel entrance and two doors from the front room whose view over the road is entirely shut out by a thick curtain. Each section of this establishment is reserved. The restaurant belongs to the hotel guests, the upholstered bar to the good-time seekers and certain "ladies", and the front room with its long tables and its white rough-hewn benches along the bare walls is reserved for the lodgers. Nobody else frequents this room, hidden from view, where sad silhouettes silently consume their half bottles of wine. However, it is enough for it to adjoin the little bar to deprive the latter of its local custom.

These spontaneous demarcations are the most obvious signs of an order which specifies the place of the lodgers in the community. They are accompanied by other discriminatory measures, more formal or more subtle, which extend to all the patients irrespective of their individual characteristics or qualities. The patients are aware of this, suffer from it and say so:

> The population of patients here contains many types, from oligophrenics to alcoholics. The schizophrenics, when they aren't in the middle of an attack, are normal people. But they are thought of in the same way as all the others. There's no difference in the way they are treated. When I arrived here, I went to church to attend a service. The priest rushed up to me, saying, 'Join your companions at the back of the church on the benches without backs.' It's the less intelligent people who make distinctions. Later he accepted me because I gave readings for him. But there's no total integration.

This process involves the social constraints which mould the "career" of lodgers in the Colony and the social controls which govern the relationships maintained with them. A number of procedures combine to reveal the heterogeneity of the patients and the partition within the community which orients the relationships regulated independently of the individual characteristics of the actors.

Civilians and Non-Civilians

The first tool which makes it possible to establish a formal, stable dichotomy is the designation of the Colony's members. This bases their separation on their legal status which establishes the opposition between "civilians" and "non-civilians".

Because he came from a psychiatric hospital, the patient is immediately considered to have a *deprived status*. He is not what the others are, a fully acknowledged citizen. He does not enjoy all their rights. The idea of "non-civilian", despite finding general and systematic use, is not clearly conceived in the minds of the population. As an immediate fact of social apprehension, it posits difference without explaining it. It is sufficient that the category should operate to permit a self-orientation in the social universe, where it regulates everyday behaviour, for its employment to be accepted without any further analysis: "There's no point in drawing a grid. It'll just rack your brain."

The use of the privative category acts as a cognitive operator of discrimination like a social categorization or the "structural opposition" (Evans-Pritchard, 1940) which derives membership of a sub-group from the non-membership of the groups opposed to it. The "civilian–non-civilian" bipolarity arises from the principle of a formal division which defines identity by according the designation of membership or non-membership. However, the overtones of the term "non-civilian" have implications for the status accorded to the patient which derive from both judicial and group prohibitions.

The fact of belonging to a psychiatric establishment is a determining factor in that it implies the status of a prisoner and the suppression of certain rights. In fact, it is the status of confinement and not the status of patient that lies at the root of a number of devaluing or negative attributions. There is no doubt that the state of hospitalization with its attendant misfortunes, the loss of autonomy, commitment to residential care, an alienating hospital regime, evokes all the other situations of constraint and withdrawal from the world of freedom. The uniform which the patients wore for so long has left its mark on the imagination:

> When I arrived here on my return from captivity, after five years in a prisoner of war camp, I wasn't shocked to see these poor wretches. After all, I had been a poor wretch as well. In those days it was very different from what it is today. They just had one set of winter clothes. But at that time it was still a concentration camp. Nowadays they are freer.

> It's a bit like it is in the army. I was in the sanatorium during the war and I surprised myself by saying 'when I'm demobilized'. I've felt what it's like. I don't know why they call them non-civilians. It's like in the army. It's as if they had been called up! But I understand it. I've asked myself the question

'when am I going to be demobilized?' I was properly immobilized, that's for certain. They remind me a little bit of that. They are immobilized as well, because . . . they haven't even got the right to vote, nothing . . . I don't know why. I don't even know if they ever had it.

But that is not the most important thing. For the population, entrance to the psychiatric institutions leaves a doubly negative mark. These establishments are thought of primarily as places of repression, of a penal nature and with a policing function. The nurses are viewed as representatives of the rule of order, the hospital ward merges into a prison. As for the lodgers, they are readily attributed the dark misdeeds which result from a mental illness, as we shall see later. The potential for delinquency attributed to the patients is aggravated by the idea that the asylum causes the deterioration of the individual by relieving him of any sense of responsibility or action:

> The hospital deprives them of any idea of readaptation. The inactive individual soon falls into laziness. He has no need to earn money, no responsibilities. They automatically grow to like their inactivity. They can no longer readapt.

Confinement only deepens the inactivity of the patients, transforms their legal status into an irremediable condition: "They are no longer human. They are stripped of all their civil rights and so they are no longer human beings."

This is the reason why the desire shown by some of the lodgers to lead a way of life similar to that of the population, taking part in all its activities, including its leisure time, seems to be an inconceivable pretension:

> Big D . . . said to me, 'When is he going to come back?' [*referring to the son of the interviewee, who was performing his military service*]. I told him, 'He's just got five days left to go.' – 'Ah, so he's free then. If I could, I would take his place.' We started to chat and he said to me, 'I don't understand why, at twenty-two, I can't go to the dance. I've got the right to go with girls.' I've noticed that these boys are perfectly well aware that they aren't all that distinguished, aren't anything special. And generally speaking they think they are less clever than the others.

The ever-watchful care to take even the slightest opportunity to show the lodgers that they are not civilians prevents any attempt on their part to immerse themselves in the life of the group as equals:

> In effect, they are still locked up: they aren't allowed to have a drink, to go out, to go dancing, to see people. They are still locked up, however much you say that they are allowed to go out for a walk. That's all they have . . . The great pity of it is that the supervisors tell them that they are free. Freedom for some of them is to go to the café, to have company, to live like

other people. But they aren't supposed to. All they're allowed to do is eat and drink, obey the rules of the Colony, and go for a walk in the streets. And that's all. Those are all the rights they have . . .

This separation lies at the root of all the relationships with the patients and the status assigned them in the community of which, however, they remain an integral part. The privations which distinguish the patients help the community in which they are received to express its expectation to the Colony and to see these fulfilled. It is in this way that the conditions which determine the destiny of the third group in this triangle are established.

Commodity and Use-Value

Since being transferred from Paris, this third group have been neither simply patients receiving a new method of treatment, nor simply detainees to whom the doors have been opened. They are also a cog in the exchange mechanism operating between the hospital and the population. Their placement, the pivot of the mechanism which transforms services into prosperity, invests them with the quality of a product, a commodity for transaction. This impersonal status of commodity infuses both representation and practice. A whole field of terminology has been reserved for their movement between and their installation in the placements. A transfer is known as a "load" or "delivery" of patients in the same terms that are used for livestock. In the placements, they speak of receiving "stock". When a lodger is removed the placement is out of stock. The installation of new lodgers is known as restocking. An old foster parent told us of her problems: "At the start I was completely satisfied", but now, without knowing why, though she thinks it is because she once refused a lodger who frightened her, or because of her age, "I'm badly stocked . . . You can't have your cake and eat it too." The lodger takes on the nature of a "commodity" which is distributed and retained depending on his prestige, one of those "goods" which, as Lévi-Strauss (1969) emphasized, "are not only economic commodities but also vehicles and instruments of realities of another order such as power, authority, sympathy, status . . . ", the truth of which we were able to demonstrate.

The lodger thus becomes an object of direct transaction because of the value he embodies *per se*. Formerly it was the task of the visiting nurses to find a placement for each new arrival and it is said that they used to walk from placement to placement offering the patient:

'Do you want him?' They would show us the patient: 'Oh no. We don't want one like that', we would reply. But when acceptable lodgers were brought around people would compete for them.

A barter system grew up around the lodgers:

> There was a tradition of giving presents, a kind of bartering. If the foster parent could satisfy the nurse with her chickens, her Barbary ducks, or with herself, she was well served. And if she didn't, she still got her patient, but not such a good one.

This qualitative "added value" depends on the social utility of the lodger. The exchange value of the lodger is solely dependent on his social utility. Whether this is measured as services performed, as productive work or as positive character traits, it is always with reference to the foster parents' own criteria. Even the personal qualities shown by the lodger (politeness, cleanliness, sociability etc.) are evaluated with respect to the expectations of the foster parents which, without being a subject of consensus, are always linked to the functioning of their placement and their professional role.

At this stage, the scale on which this qualitative added value is gauged already asserts elements of the role which will be assigned to the lodgers. It is no longer a question of being stocked, but of being well or badly stocked. When a new lodger is introduced, the old question is always repeated: "will he be a good lunatic?", even if today it is formulated in other terms: "that one can't be placed" or "that one can be"; "we're well served with that one" or "we're not with that one", and in a discreet return to the idea of service: "that one's serviceable" or "that one isn't". The loony becomes a thing, a *that*, and any positive appraisal concerns the services he is able to receive and render. The only other appraisal is by some external characteristic, for example his age group (the young one or the old one), his origin (the Russian, the Arab or the Alsatian), his previous profession (the parachutist or the engineer), or, if he is truly accepted, by his family or Christian name, generally preceded in French by a 'le', or by the place he occupies in the family, "Grandfather loony". The use of privative forms of language generally lead to the rejection of the lodger. They represent the verdict of the foster parent on the patient's adaptation to his role, his suitability to what might be called the "explicit standard for the good lodger" formed by the community.

Nowadays, the administrative regime forbids negotiating the installation of a patient on his arrival, with the result that the process of adjustment is performed by trial and error. If things are not working out well within a placement, the lodger is moved on to another one and so on until a foster parent is found who can keep him for longer, sometimes for a very extended period. Occasionally too many failed attempts mean that the lodger is classified as "unsuitable" and is sent back to Paris. One example cited was that of a boy who was returned to the asylum after passing through 17 placements in three months. A full-scale circulation of patients takes place within the placement boundaries. The lodgers may remain for a long time within the Colony, but how many can remain for long within the same placement?

A study of the internal turnover at each placement registered in the placement log kept by the foster parents has made it possible to estimate the length of stay of the lodgers. With the exception of a few cases, this data demonstrates their instability and, indirectly, the lodgers' status as object. The average length of stay amounts to between one and three years. Sixty-one per cent of placements have housed lodgers who stayed for fewer than one month and all of them have known lodgers to stay for less than a year.

This circulation of lodgers causes a problem. Although part of the basic structure from which the placement system gains its flexibility, as it allows for the best possible adaptation of the lodger to his surroundings, its intensity provides evidence of certain functional defects. The frequency of short stays and the reasons for change of residence reveal the complexity of the mechanisms of adaptation (43% of departures are due to the incompatibility of foster parents and lodgers, 25% to practical difficulties generally resulting from the distance between the placement and the Colony). "We bet on how long stays will last", people say to the Colony, which seems to have difficulty in controlling the factors at work in the settling of the patients. There is an emphasis on the variability of conditions which admit no systematic viewpoint because they involve both psychological and material considerations.

When talking about the foster parents the psychological elements mentioned are "temperament" (familiarity or reserve, distrust or openness), "character" (calm or excitable, affable or impulsive) or the family status (with the presence or absence of a husband implying a greater or lesser degree of authority and protection: "a difficult patient won't be placed with a woman on her own if he needs authority"), and age (on which different habits of contact depend). Important, too, are the conception of the role of the lodger (worker or guest), the lifestyle offered to him (greater or lesser integration in the family) etc. As far as the patients are concerned, character is also mentioned, as are their capabilities and their expectations of life in a placement (desire for activity, taste for solitude or social contact, desire for comfort etc.), their social origin (which may lie at the roots of any incompatibility), and of course their illness (primarily because of the level of activity and sociability it entails). As far as the placement itself is concerned, its ecological position, and the comfort and food which are provided are cited as considerations, as is the small community established by the lodgers who are housed there.

To believe the officials, adaptation within a placement supposes an adjustment between these diverse elements, susceptible to multiple combinations, which depends on chance and psychological imponderables. This point, on which institution and milieu, patients and population all have something to say, reveals a certain disorder which disrupts the functioning of the establishment, reducing the ascendancy and the control of its agents. Behind the flux of concrete cases, everything happens as if the incompatibility of foster parents and patients, which causes nearly half of the changes of placement, were not simply a question of temperament; as if the goodwill of the foster parents and, beyond that, their expectations, to which the lodgers conform with a greater or lesser degree of ease, dictated conditions which the institution itself finds difficult to accept as rules. Does this change-over of lodgers not represent a means of pressurizing the institution and obtaining one's demands by blocking or furthering its functioning until the desired lodger is obtained?

Good and Bad Lodgers

Assuming that the circulation of patients depends on the pressures exerted by the environment in which they are accommodated rather than any regulation within the hospital leads us to search for the source of these pressures in the conditions involved in the "job" of foster parent. Evidence for this assumption is provided by the personnel entrusted with the supervision of placements, the visiting nurses whose "social importance", as Dr Vié pointed out in his study of family placement (1940, pp. 1–29), "appears to us to be so great that, as we understand it, they constitute one of the principal motors of these institutions [. . .]. The visitors are, so to speak, the prime movers (of the life of the Colony), they monitor the placements, they supervise the patients, preside over the relationships between them and the rest of the population. They assume a triple function, medical, moral and social."

A touchstone of the system, they occupy a pivotal position in the organization of the hospital. To a greater extent than the doctors, it is up to them to know the relations between foster parents and patients. And their task is a difficult one, not only because they have to exercise a control and supervision which is ill received by the local inhabitants to whom they are bound by ties of family, neighbourhood or friendship, but also because they "play a buffer role between doctors and foster parents in the case of both good and bad lodgers". Bound to apply the regulations of the hospital, they also have to represent and gain acceptance for the viewpoints of the population, to testify to the validity of its behaviour towards the patients and, if necessary, to arbitrate on or bring to an end any disputes which arise in the placements. It is at their level that the conflict between the demands of the establishment and the constraints of the environment is manifested, that the criteria of social evaluation are expressed, despite the defensive haziness in which they are masked. In some respects, they are the vehicle for the "norm of the good lodger" against which the patients are measured from the very beginning.

In fact, a patient arriving at the Colony has to comply with certain formalities, one of which immediately makes it possible to judge the kind of lodger he will be. This is the moment when the inventory of his belongings is drawn up, when he is taken to the linen room to receive his clothes.

Undressing in front of the nurse and trying on his clothes constitutes a "test" in which his reactions are judged:

> It lets you see how he behaves, how he reacts. If he makes a sharp retort, if he acts grudgingly, throws open the cover of his suitcase, you can tell straightaway that he isn't calm, that he won't make a good lodger.

This search for an attitude of submission and docility raises the question of the kind of network of restraint in which the patient will find himself enmeshed. The first restraint is the discipline of the placement itself. This is because it is expected that if a service is due to the lodger then, because it is poorly remunerated and not paid for directly by the recipient, it must entail the minimum possible cost and exertion and incur the minimum possible responsibility.

This accounts for the necessity of observing mealtimes. These are generally precisely specified so that they do not encroach on the life of the family. The lodger is also expected to return home by a specified time, as all absences have to be reported to the foster parent to avoid the risk of an escape which might be blamed on inadequate supervision. Cleanliness and order are also demanded of the patient's personal belongings and his room. Alongside the preparation of meals, cleaning is the main and most visible task in the placement. But whilst the first seems self-evident, clearing up after the lodgers always takes the guise of a disagreeable servitude whose unpleasantness is to be reduced wherever possible. The care of some patients who suffer from urinary or faecal incontinence, from motor impairments which prevent them from eating normally, or who simply abandon themselves to dirtiness because of either renunciation or morose enjoyment, can seem repulsive. However, this is not the case with all the lodgers, whilst the concern with cleanliness is general. Distaste – which is a point we shall return to later – leads to the desire "to avoid work" and also to a calculation:

> Dirtiness demeans the foster parent. If you have two or three dirty patients then your placement can't be as tidy as one with two or three clean patients. The difference in bonus counts. The bonus is higher in a clean placement.

The result of this is strict supervision, sometimes accompanied by the demand that the lodger should absent himself from the placement for the whole day. This kills two birds with one stone – the placement remains clean and all contact with the lodger is avoided.

Almost as important as cleanliness is the patient's readiness to take his medicine. This new responsibility, difficult to instil in the foster parents, is all the more onerous because many patients refuse to submit to medical treatment and because it is the subject of strict control. Failure to observe the prescribed regime can be punished by the closure of the placement.

Discipline, cleanliness and acceptance of treatment represent a minimum level of cooperation in her tasks which the foster parent demands from the lodger. Other expectations relate to the functioning of the placement. Sometimes the good lodger is the one who "stays in the placement and doesn't go up to the hospital". In fact, it can happen that a lodger needs to spend time at the infirmary because of a psychopathic episode, an alcoholic bout or some complicating illnesses. Payments to the foster parent are then suspended for the entire duration of the hospital stay. In the same way, when a number of patients are accommodated in the same placement, it is necessary to ensure their tranquillity and sociability, so that no quarrels spring up between them and degenerate to a level where the patients have to be withdrawn.

A further factor in the definition of a good lodger is his reaction to measures taken to assure the profitability of his accommodation by cutting down on the related costs such as heating, upkeep of furniture and clothing and, most important of all, food. Although the Colony constantly monitors the nourishment of the patients and the restrictions imposed on the patients are spoken of in the past tense, it seems that today there are still two weights, two measures, as in the story of the café. This fact cannot be disguised by claiming that in the past "it was quite different. There were practically two sorts of cooking. At the butcher's you could get meatballs and blood sausage for lodgers, made with leftovers, which you only ever bought for them." You can still hear the grocer, whom a shopper has asked for peas, reply, "what sort of peas do you want, the small ones or the big ones for the lodgers?" Meals taken separately also serve to hide these differences in menu, making it possible to withhold the family's steak from the rooms occupied by the patients. From this point of view, the good lodger is one who accepts without balking or complaining, one who "doesn't complain about everything, the food, the room, any excuse!", one who doesn't make a fuss.

Here we can discern some of the attributes of the role given to the lodgers who benefit from a contract to which their only contribution can be refusal. The lodger has to be a quiet, submissive guest, neither burdensome nor demanding, causing the foster parents the least trouble and bringing the greatest profit to the placement. Entitlement to the little he is allowed is paid for with a mute subservience or with his person. Because the most important factor in the evaluation of a lodger is the work he can provide: "he ought to do a few jobs", "his day's work" – that is what is expected of him. "We let him have a little bit for it" or "we overlook his faults, we spoil him." To obtain recognition he must offer a payment in kind, his social utility.

Working Lodgers

In a population which historically, as we have seen, has linked the acceptance of lodgers to their value as workers, this criterion always remains preeminent and is always sought after. But even though the demand for workers is general, it is, in fact, rarely fulfilled.

In fact, the number of lodgers working at the placement is not as high as the assertions of our informants would suggest, and that the same is true of their level of occupation. Fifty-seven per cent of lodgers engage in no work, 16% work only occasionally, 18% work relatively frequently and 9% are fully employed. The locals have to count on the willingness and ability shown by the lodgers and, here, neither they nor the Colony can wield any real power. The same is true of work outside the placement where, again, the number of working lodgers is considerably overestimated: 78% of patients do no work of this kind, approximately 8% are employed by private individuals and 15% work for the Colony.

It is clear that this expectation results from real needs within all sectors of the population. It is equally certain that it corresponds to a taste for easy living and that it encourages this tendency. But as a fundamental and unanimously acknowledged dimension of the social definition of the lodger, does it not also express a process of differentiation in which everyone has their place? On the one hand, the civilians, a free and superior caste, enjoying the right to demand services of the other, the non-civilians, an inferior caste which is deprived of its rights and destined to perform servile tasks. This appears to be the representation of the relationship between the two groups which conforms to the colonial type of relationship, spontaneously evoked by the population,[1] in which the dominant group assures its power and its prestige by using the dominated group for the most ignoble, subordinate tasks which, if necessary, it can create or delegate at will. The most striking cases in Ainay are not the men who weed, hoe, gather the hay or collect the wood. They are the men standing at their sinks, "the washers-up", the men who scrub the floor or buy the milk (17% of active lodgers are employed solely to do the shopping or help in the house).

This relationship is illustrated by the remuneration given to the working lodgers, a practice which has become established by custom. The administration has drawn up no regulations to cover this point, itself paying the daily wage fixed as remuneration for work by patients within a psychiatric hospital. Known as the "allowance", its value at the time of this enquiry was that of five 30 centime postage stamps per day. What is a rule for the hospital is only an indication for the population, but no one can object to it taking this sum as a guideline. In fact, the wages paid to the lodgers are determined by a tacit arrangement. The foster parents base their estimate on what they would have

---

[1] The comparison is with the only case known to the interviewees, North Africa. The lodger is a bit like the Arab and admiration is shown for the ability of certain farmers to "make the Arabs sweat". "The country people have a strange authority, like in Algeria, we ask the lodgers to come and do the gardening for 6 francs a day. They don't come. They aren't interested. But the farmer comes and finds ten of them. He gives them 200 francs for some dreadful job and they work for him. It's awful. They have that power. They say that the colonists had the same power."

to pay a "civilian" worker, the revenue brought in by the lodger and the threshold defined by the allowance. In some cases the professional status of the patient allows him to negotiate his own wage. When the employment is episodic or incidental, the idea of wages is replaced by that of a "reward" which is left to the judgement of the foster parents. Which amounts to saying that the amounts paid are totally arbitrary. Arbitrary but not unstructured, for an examination of these "rewards" reveals two things.

First of all, rates vary on a scale delimited by generally applied boundary values which correspond to definite activities.[2] It seems as if the community – over which the officials of the Colony have no power except that of defending the patients in legal disputes – has drawn up its own regulations which it applies rigorously: the social institution defines the functions and rewards of the patients, the scope of their duties and their rights. Next, the financial recompense given to the lodgers – if they exist at all, as 38% of the workers receive no money – is very small. Admittedly, the lodgers are treated more generously than at the hospital (45% of those who are paid receive more than the allowance) but the upper limit is still low, with wages of over 60 francs (10%) being the exception. Most significant, however, is the fact that 40% of wages are lower than or equal to 20 francs. This amounts to a complete exploitation of the lodgers of which they themselves are aware:

> The region is short of workers. The employment office is the Family Colony. If the Colony didn't exist they would have to find workers and to get them to come they would have to pay them legal rates. And on top of that there would be the welfare contributions and a union to deal with. My companions in poverty from the Colony – poverty, I exaggerate, we are fed, housed, our washing is done, but there are deductions – here we are all the servants of the population.

What are the reasons for this, whether clear or obscure? On the part of the patients: the obvious absence of legal or psychological protection; sometimes reduced means, despite the desire to be integrated into the active community; easy monetary satisfaction after having known harder times in the asylum. On the part of the local inhabitants: the abuse of their weakness and their aspirations to a social status other than that of psychiatric patients, their lack of social defences; not to forget the negative evaluation of the mentally ill as depleted individuals, non-civilians, diminished, destitute

---

[2] When the lodger works in the placement he receives no payment in 20% of cases. In 18% of cases he is paid in kind (tobacco, sweets, wine), in 18% a payment which varies in accordance with the work performed and in 43% a fixed wage. External work is always paid, with the nature of the remuneration depending on the nature of the employment: 26% of instances of occasional work are paid for in money as against 81% of cases of frequent or continuous employment. The demand for workers is higher in country areas and cash payments are higher there, at least in instances of regular employment

human beings, an evaluation which results in the devaluation of their needs
and their human rights.

A testimony is provided by this lodger who had been confined for thirteen
years and a member of the Colony for two years:

> A human being who has spent X years in psychiatric hospitals is offered the
> chance to go the Family Colony. When they suggested I could come I knew
> what would happen (some had come back, some had written to me), and at
> first I refused. But then a nurse told me to come. He told me it was my only
> chance of getting out, but he thought the opposite. I think the social
> services should open an enquiry into the workers. Anyone who has done the
> work of an agricultural labourer, and often more, and who has been working
> for more than a year should be allowed to leave, to be reintegrated into
> social life with his rights and duties as regards work, family and citizenship.

The lodgers consequently share the fate of all peripheral or inferior groups.
They become a sort of sub-proletariat which, in the absence of any law,
remains unprotected from the excesses of exploitation by any moral
imperative. Is that all? And if that is all, what are we to say of the significance
their work has taken on since the founding of the Colony? And how can we
fail to see that its value as a compensation for the unpleasantness of contact
with mental illness implies that it is not treated as real work? How would the
process of differentiation work if full monetary recompense of the patients'
contributions meant that they were no longer relegated to the symbolic
fringes of the group?

A Status Unlike that of Others

In establishing the rules for the integration of the patients through the social
definition of the status of the lodgers, the group in which they are received
has simultaneously fixed the modes and limits of their recognition. For a
member of the Colony to be anything other than the anonymous object of
the negotiations between the hospital and the environment – goods to be
bartered for at the level of the placement, cause or manifestation of prosperity
at the level of the community – then he has to prove himself at the level of
social utility. The use to which he is put is like a fee he has to pay if he is to
accede to an individualized way of life. Employment is in some ways an
obligatory route for escaping a reified condition. The patient has to play his
part as an actor on the social scene, as servant, as valet or as farm hand, and
for a pitiful wage.

Once this assurance has been acquired, the patient becomes necessary to
the equilibrium of the environment for two reasons. By developing in the
population certain customs of service which it can ill do without,
participation has given the lodgers an indispensable function in the

maintenance of the standard and style of living of the population: "they have their place" and "we would miss them if they weren't here to do the shopping, fetch the bread and so on." But more than simply making things easier for the locals, the employment of the patients diminishes their aberrance, attenuates their status as assisted persons, one of whose most irritating and ignominious signs is laziness, a synonym for parasitism. When the expectation of employment is not satisfied by the patients, the locals become uneasy. This explains the feeling of worry and revolt which has accompanied the changing attitudes of the patients who today no longer wish to work, and the nostalgia for a time – not so long ago, as running water was only installed in 1952 – when the lodgers used to go to fetch the water and took the washing to the washroom:

> It wasn't the same as it is now. They were useful and that helped them and helped the region. There were five wells which they used to walk to in order to fetch water. You didn't see them wandering around with nothing to do.

At that time, "they were treated like people who might have been part of the family," whereas now "it's pitiful to see grown-up men like that, in good health, lying about on the grass."

> They aren't given enough to do. At the beginning, the Colony did a lot of little jobs. To say that they were well paid is going a bit too far. We gave them something to eat, a glass of wine, a nice afternoon snack. They were paid in one way or another. Later on they got the idea into their heads that all work should be paid for in cash. They all thought they worked like the civilians and that they should be paid like the civilians. It's a recurring theme in every conversation. They talk about it all the time. It's their great craze. I know one who works on a farm. He says, 'We do the same work as the farm hands, don't have any holiday and earn 5 francs per day.' I reply, 'You get your food, heating, clothes while those who earn more have to pay all that themselves as well as all the deductions.' I don't think 5 francs a day is unfair to them. When you consider that they are here to get better, that the people who employ them don't demand a great deal of productivity. Well, they shouldn't demand too much in the way of money. That would give them a much better image in the region.

At the symbolic level, work assures the longevity of the acceptance of a difference which low wages confirm and maintain.

The social character of the lodgers is highlighted by their large numbers. Their most distinctive characteristics are linked at various points within the life of the society, articulated with the explicit expectations of the population. Depending on the reception reserved for him, the lodger is a guest, a member of the family group or the professional group, an element within the community, a part of the country:

> They are absolutely a part of the region. They are absolutely integrated into its life. People live with the lodgers just like they live with their companions at work.

The result is a role and a position unique of their type, "exclusive to Ainay":

> The women speak of them as *their* lodgers. It's an indefinable nuance. I can't explain it to you. They speak of them as if they were responsible for them. That's all. They don't speak of them like their son who is at school, they speak of them as their lodgers. For them it's an absolutely novel idea, and one that is unique to Ainay, absolutely exclusive to Ainay.

Thus as soon as they take their place outside the walls of the Colony, its members receive a double definition from the environment in which they are settled. The attributes of this definition are related to those of "label" and "role" as identified by Nadel (1970). The label of the non-civilian identifies the "we" and the "non-we" in the social universe; the behaviour which it shapes performs a placing apart. The designation of "lodger" implies prescriptions which allot specific places and functions to the patients and creates an ideal for their participation and their image as social actors. The behaviour which corresponds to this image obeys expectations which are normatively regulated in accordance with the needs of the community. This social response introduces a dual trigger process in the otherness of the patients. It manipulates the distinction between the "we" and the "non-we" to produce a model of the "almost-we" which confers a proper physical weight to the other. It also transforms an order of separation into an order of arrangement in which the "almost-we" is bound to the "we" by socially coded relationships. But in effecting this integration, the community which receives the lodgers is not content to coexist with and tolerate the presence of a group which is heterogeneous to it. It characterizes its exteriority and its modes of insertion. What is more, it regulates its difference and legitimizes its presence by putting it to use. The functionalist interpretation of this kind of process sees a group absorbing a difference in order to benefit from the resources it offers, whilst assuring its own survival. What we have seen of the usefulness of the lodgers suggests that this interpretation is inadequate. Indeed, it seems that utility is sought for and excessively attributed to the lodgers in order to make it possible to absorb their difference. If this is the case, then we should expect that the role whose ideal image is provided by the norm of the good lodger does not exhaust the full range of social relationships established with the patients. And this is further suggested by the organization of everyday life as it is described by the foster parents and the observations of this enquiry.

The Arguable and the Unarguable

Seen from the viewpoint of the foster parents, contact with the lodgers appears oriented along three dimensions: institutional (the normative expectations concerning the "good lodger"), functional or practical (the demands relating to the utility drawn from the lodger which depends on the type of placement), and interpersonal (the proprieties which relate to contact with someone external to the family core, a person who is, moreover, a mental patient). That these dimensions are perceived as deriving from different universes can be seen in the distinction between the "arguable" and the "not arguable" or "unarguable" in the way in which the locals live with and evaluate the patients.

The "unarguable" resides in the "objective" sphere of the constraints which are defined by the usefulness and functioning of the placement. The appraisal of the lodger and the regulation of his life then depend on a material base – situation, extent of profitability of the placement etc. – and not on the temperament of the foster parent or the patient:

> A good lodger, that depends on what you've got him for, whether he's there to work or just a lodger for a month. There's no question about that. There are some lodgers who the foster parents take just to get their money for the month and who don't work at all. Then it makes a big difference whether they are pleasant or not. But at the moment, if it's the other way, if the lodger does a bit of work, well, there are some lodgers who are worth a lot more than others. That's how they distinguish between good and bad lodgers. It's not a question of them being pleasant or not. That's how they tell the difference. It's unarguable.

This material judgement imposes criteria for assessment on the foster parent:

> The people who haven't got anything to do prefer an old one. It depends on the type of placement.

> In the country people are tolerant of them as long as they do a bit of work. It's not the same in town. They aren't accepted so willingly.

At the same time this judgement differentiates between the lodgers in accordance with the extent to which they are able to fulfil the exigencies of their role:

> Work is something else. You'll get some lodgers to work for you. You'll ask them to do something which is worth a bit to you, and then there are others . . . That's unarguable! . . .

Although evaluation varies depending on the nature of the placement, the criteria on which it is based remain stable, depending, beyond the goodwill of the foster parent and the lodger, on the context in which they fulfil their functions. That is why the assertions which are "not arguable", whilst pertaining to a discrete reality, are the object of a consensual acknowledgement and thus acquire the status of an experienced truth which cannot be questioned. Each lives the truth of his own condition.

The "arguable", on the other hand, emerges from the sphere of the subjective. Where it touches on opinions and behaviour relating to the lodgers it is an effect of the personal fancies and psychological attitudes which are directly implicated by mental illness. Just as in questions of taste, what is simultaneously admitted to be an irreducible private belief and a subject for conversation and controversy is related to the feelings each individual can experience in the face of a patient. On the one hand, the "arguable" has as its object the reactions of a receptive subject and not those of an agent embedded within a network of determinations. On the other hand, it deals with a specific property, insanity, and not with the attribution of a role or the ability to accomplish it:

> It doesn't make any difference to us if he's a mental patient or not. If you had asked me that twenty-five years ago I would have given you a different answer. It's only after a lapse of time, how can I say it . . . It's only by living together like that, how shall I put it, by seeing one another all the time . . . Time has changed us. Of course, if you talked to someone who had just been given a lodger today, maybe he wouldn't talk like I do. There are some people who can't adapt. *That's unarguable.*

This reaction may be one of habituation or of an affective, emotional nature deriving simply from contact with a patient:

> People who have never had a lodger probably wouldn't talk the way we do. They aren't used to it, of course, and then there are some who don't want anything to do with them. Those who don't have the right temperament to keep lodgers, what do you expect of them?

It may also be associated with the types of investment and interpersonal obligations demanded by the illness or with a subset of these. Thus some people might prefer to deal with an adult patient rather than with a child sent by the social security services because the responsibilities are fewer and because the probability of attachment is less. In other cases, the opposite applies because the foster parent does not accept the impossibility, posited *a priori*, of growing attached to a mentally ill man. In the same way differing reactions are shown to certain manifestations of melancholy because they demand an attention or psychological support which requires the acceptance or refusal of an interpersonal relationship with the patients. Finally, this private relativity of attitude leads to an admission of the multiplicity of ways of living with the patients.

> Personally, I talk to them. But whatever I tell you, someone else will tell
> you the opposite. Other people won't talk to them like I do.

> It all depends on their contact with the foster parents. The differences
> between the foster parents are 100% important. It's difficult. You can go
> into another house and find that the foster parent never talks to the lodgers,
> that there's no contact. They get their food and drink and go away again . . .
> In houses like that the foster parents won't tell you what I tell you.

If this type of behaviour is open to debate, it is because it derives from the
repercussions subjective evaluation has on the object and thus allocates the
latter to no consensually acknowledged practical or functional criterion. The
debate is fuelled by the unstable material of impressions based on personal
criteria, variable but still admissible as a subject for discussion. All in all, the
arguable is the domain of opinion.

The two types of assertion between which the foster parents distinguish
spring from the sphere of social judgements which consist in the evaluation of
others and, indirectly, of oneself, in accordance with internal or external
scales of value. That which is "talked about" is etched on a field of
communication which requires a community of experience or circumstance:

> People who don't have lodgers don't talk about it because they aren't able to
> judge, or because they don't want to get mixed up in it.

The social communication which grows up around the lodgers with its
necessary shared basis of "having them" refers to a socially moulded reality.
Although at this point we cannot avoid evoking Festinger's (1954) model of
"social comparison", we must, however, insist on an additional nuance,
namely that "arguable" and "unarguable" designate two kinds of "social
reality". In the first case, communication elicits a reality made of a collective
experience which swarms with viewpoints coexisting in mutual acceptance.
In the second case, it records a reality whose different facets are defined by
the constraints of the situation and are consensually acknowledged.

This linguistic subtlety therefore gives voice to a conception which assigns
the social relationship with the patient and the personal relationship with the
patient to different registers. These registers are irreconcilable and can
intervene in the organization of life in the placement because this implicitly
places them in opposition as the social and the private, the determinant and
the contingent.

Nevertheless, those aspects related to non-utilitarian contact with the
patient as a person do not appear to derive solely from the unforeseeable and
the individual. When seeking to paint an exact picture of the relationships
which develop within the placements, our informers always referred to the
initial model of the Colony, that of family life into which the patient is
integrated as a member of an extended kinship network. This model has

remained applicable. It makes it possible to condemn placements in which purely utilitarian considerations prevail:

> People think of it differently nowadays. It's not a family any more, more like a hotel-restaurant – not even a family bed and breakfast.

> They aren't foster parents any longer, they've become employers.

This model also makes it possible to define the status of the patient within the foster parent's home. Here, the model retains its validity thanks to a slippage of meaning which equates "family" with "familiar" in the sense of "accepted", which designates the simple fact of contact when the patient ceases to be treated as a "stranger", is "more highly regarded" and benefits from "better", "freer" behaviour. This slippage distorts the normative character of the family model and introduces gaps into the continuum of relationships which extends from integration to rejection, gaps which cannot be explained by the instrumental aims of the foster parents. It implies the search for a rule to regulate the crux of the problem posed by the relationship with the patients: distance or proximity at the interpersonal level.

In the House, Not of the House

From the start the patients' membership of the home circle is articulated in the speech of the foster parents by the categories of "more-or-less" and "as if":

> We do what we can to give them a family life. If you can really call it family life, that is . . .

> They have their room, they are . . . we are . . . it's a family, so to speak.

The management of nuances testifies to a continuing effort to master the implications of an illusory familiarity which is accorded to the patients: "They even think of us a little bit as family," and ". . . if they end up with the right people they can believe that they are at home." The signs of this pretence situate the welcome reserved for the patient on a scale progressing from simple presence, "in the house but not of the house", to the fictive bond "as if they were part of the family". This is clearly far removed from the original inspiration of the Colony, whose founders saw shared habitation and companionship as the bases of community existence. By a slow process of distortion, acquired at an early age, distance has been reintroduced into the aspects of life which most clearly signify close contact. It has been reintroduced by the symbolic distancing which derives from the terminology of approximation and by the separation which results from its practical application. The result is the development of an order which social thought neither appreciates nor masters for what it is: a form of social control whose rules of action cannot be deduced from explicit norms but which nevertheless exist at a stable supra-individual level.

A number of indications revealed by the statistical enquiry provide us with information regarding this implicit regulation of the customs of contact with the patients. Beyond the rigid control of their circulation within the living space of the foster parents which we have already identified, two sectors of the organization of everyday life retain a crucial importance today, namely meals and extra-professional activities. The way in which the patients are admitted to the family dinner table, or included in the family's leisure time and festivities, remains in the minds of our interviewees, as it was in the past, a mark of their deprived status.

In the same way, entrance to the house signifies entrance to the home:

> My mother had one. It was as if he was part of the family. He saw me come into the world. He had his chair in the kitchen, as if he was one of the family.

Similarly, a place at table, whether for the daily meal or for a special occasion, or just a chair in front of the television, represents an opening of the family circle:

> They live with us, eat with us. We think of them as family. Fourteen of us sit down to eat. My patients are like the rest of us.

> When he talks about eating with the family, it's important for him. Every year it's the same. We have a family reunion, brothers, sisters, children. For him a family reunion is important.

> Every evening the serial came on and we let them come and watch the television. We did what we could to treat them as family.

But these instances of close contact are very much the exception. The lodger is not treated as a companion and, in the vast majority of cases, does not eat at the foster parents' table. Everyday sharing of meals occurs only in a few placements (12%) and only a small number make it an occasional practice (6%). In contrast, a strict separation of meals is the rule in 82% of placements.

We find a similar reluctance to concede the right to share evenings together, evenings in front of the television, Sunday outings or festivities. A mere 9% of lodgers are permitted to participate in such activities. The close correlation of these statistical data concerning meals and family contact points to the workings of a social process of distancing.

Modulations of Life in the Placement

Badly perceived in its potency and in its social character, surely the roots of separation lie in a "lived order" (Lévi-Strauss, 1976) whose duality regulates situations of contact, exercising a rigour proportional to the closeness and age of these contacts, reproducing at the interpersonal level the phenomenon of hardening which is observed at the collective level. At least this is what is suggested by the analysis of the variations in the practices of the foster parents both from a quantitative and a qualitative point of view. In fact, the evidence we have gathered of interpersonal contact permits us to adduce certain arguments whose principal thrusts weaken the naïve hypothesis which sees the relationship between foster parents and lodgers as exclusively dependent on the interaction of material determination and chance.

Thus separation remains a majority practice[3] irrespective of the character-istics of the placement (type, situation and distance from the Colony, capacity), the foster parents and their families or the family to which the lodgers belong (length of stay, age, psychiatric category).

Two factors seem to contribute to a relaxation of this distancing. First, the objectives of the placement and the status the lodger derives from it along with the way in which he adjusts to it, Second, the cultural distance, the breaking away from dominant values and group pressure.

As far as the functional constraints of the placement are concerned, there is no doubt that expectations concerning the activity of the patient exert an influence. Lodgers who are frequently or fully occupied are more often admitted to the intimacy or the table of the foster parents than those who work only rarely or are totally unoccupied.[4] The value of their work, estimated on the basis of their remuneration, also has an effect on meals and relations, although with a different significance. The more highly he is paid, the more likely he is to be accepted at table, but he is also more likely to be considered a worker; whilst the increasing intimacy of relations, clearer when there is little or no payment in kind, seems to take on a compensatory value. This is confirmed by the way customs change with the type of placement. There are significantly more meals taken in common and closer relations between foster parents and lodgers in agricultural holdings than in other lodgings. At the same time, the separation increases as the number of lodgers in the placement increases. The type of profitability expected from the placement therefore has a direct effect on the relationship with the patients.

---

[3] As far as the separation of meals is concerned, the figure scarcely falls below 70% (compared to a mean of 88%, including exceptions to separation), and scarcely below 80% in the case of absence of relations between foster parents and lodgers (compared to a mean of 91%).

[4] x^2 significant at $P < 0.001$.

The role of functional factors is balanced by the adherence to the dominant norms of the environment. Certain differences observed in the way of life of the various *communes* which depend on the concentration of placements, their longevity or their distance from the centre of the Colony, can be explained by social pressure and the hold of tradition. The scope for acceptance increases as the density of patients falls. The *communes* which were slower to adopt the practice of placement show a much clearer tendency to forge close relations with the lodgers than *communes* in which placements belong to an older tradition[5] and in which the number of lodgers is higher. At the same time, the simple fact that placements are situated further than 8 km from the headquarters of the Colony and thus from the historic core of the institution is enough to relax the lifestyle led by the lodgers.[6]

This tendency for a norm which has developed over an extended period to crystallize and harden is confirmed by the differences observed in the customs established by foster parents who are themselves members of a family of foster parents. Those who take their place in a family tradition of fostering reinforce the tendency to separation in the case of both meals and relations.[7] Not having grown up with lodgers makes foster parents more receptive to those who do little or no work.[8] The subordination of close relations to interest is similarly reinforced by the effects of tradition, as is the underestimation of the monetary value of the work of the patient.[9]

All these observations suffice to confirm the presence of the dualist principle in the relationship between the foster parents and the lodgers. And it is reasonable to ask whether the minority adherence to the initial model of the Colony does not appear deviant in comparison to the established practice of its rejection. This is what is suggested by the way the organization of life with the patients is described. You "open up" your placement or you "keep a certain distance". In the first case you always remember that different habits are practised elsewhere and willingly concede your marginal status:

> Let me explain to you how our placement works. We all eat at the same table. All my lodgers have always eaten at the same table as us. But let me tell you, it isn't the same in all the placements . . . They are no different to mine but they are treated like children. You won't find all this in some placements . . . You know, I don't know if you'll find many placements in the *commune* where they eat together. It's a habit of mine. We don't have to. In other places the placement is a 'room of their own'. A room of their own means they eat on their own. But mine have never eaten on their own. You don't always have to keep them in a cage like some of them are.

---

5 x^2 significant at $P < 0.001$.
6 x^2 significant at $P < 0.10$.
7 x^2 significant at $P < 0.05$.
8 x^2 significant at $P < 0.02$.
9 x^2 significant at $P < 0.10$.

This contrasts with the second case where foster parents often find it difficult to conceive of others leading a way of life different from their own:

> They live there in their room, they eat in their room, there aren't many who let the lodgers eat with them, nobody. Nobody does.

Separation, a long-standing habit, an unquestioned custom, is justified by the "principle" of a protective legality or a judgement made about the lodgers. Close relations, on the other hand, question the justification of received customs and the values attributed to others and oneself.

In fact, in the speech of the foster parents, the maintenance of distance is decreed in the form of a "that isn't done". The interdiction may be implied by the incapacity of the patients. This incapacity may be of a legal nature or refer to their status:

> They aren't in an asylum but they are supervised all the same . . . If they were allowed to do anything! You still have to stop them coming into the house.

> These are people you can't give to somebody else. They're ill, after all. They can't live with us or eat with us or anything.

The interdiction is also justified by the breadth of action allowed by the Colony, which is interpreted as a negative prescription:

> Down the road [at another placement] they let them do whatever they want. They all eat together, they let them do this, that and the other. But me, I don't want any of that. Besides, the nurses have told us that we don't have to. So what should we do? We don't have to!

In the final analysis it is based on a "protectionist" perspective:

> From the start they have had their room and I've had my house. I let some of them come here if they have to, either to bring something or to fetch something. Otherwise I never, never let them come here. Not even to watch the telly. Otherwise I wouldn't feel at home.

Distancing is articulated as the rigidity of a regulation:

> I'm not a supporter of patients eating with you. Not at all. It's a principle I don't like in the slightest.

On the other hand, non-distancing behaviours are rarely expressed in the imperative mode, even when they are articulated as an accusative alternative:

> People shouldn't mistreat the lodgers. I can tell you that the big one, he
> used to be in another area, I've often heard him say 'I never watched the
> telly at my old place'. You get the impression that everybody doesn't treat
> them in the same way . . . Personally I would rather give my lodgers back
> than lay down the law about this, that and all sorts of ridiculous things. It's
> not worth being here . . .

Rather, such behaviour comes from an attitude of appreciation, responding
with "it's right to" or "I can't do otherwise" to the concern to manage for the
best a concrete relationship with the patient. Justification of this concern
takes many forms, by taking account of the lodger's individual merits, as in
the case of the working lodger, "it's the people who take the trouble to get
them to work who give them a family life", or of his human qualities, "not to
treat them simply as patients", or by attempting to satisfy some deep-seated
need to give the lodger something:

> They know very well if you like them. When you tell them off they are
> unhappy. When you let them watch the telly they are happy.

> Perhaps there are others who don't think the same way but I think the
> patients are here to be helped, not to be exploited . . . The patients are
> people like anybody else and there's no reason not to take an interest in
> them . . . Maybe you won't find this in all the placements.

In other cases, the "best" is related to the foster parents themselves, either
because proximity improves the organization of their lives:

> We eat with them principally because it makes a bit less work for me. I feel
> all right about it and they get hot food to eat. Otherwise, if I were to take
> their meals to them in the room at the side, well, it gets quite cold in the
> winter.

or because it testifies to a need for communication or the impossibility of
living at a distance at the affective level:

> They keep me company. I've been completely alone on the estate. I
> couldn't have remained alone if I hadn't had them.

> I immediately made them a part of the family. They are already deprived,
> There's no reason. I couldn't . . .

> Yes, I like living as I do, understanding them and not treating them just like
> animals, keeping them at a distance like they do in some placements. I like
> family life since they've put them here, going from door to door, sometimes
> exchanging a few words. I'm so alone that the oldest of them, we talk and
> that helps pass the time, even though they aren't too charming.

Thus being a minority practice, close relations, even though they are value-oriented practices to the foster parent, are experienced as purely private attitudes which have a psychological sound. Being a marginal practice, even if they find something reassuring in the family model, such relationships cannot acquire the force of a norm in the face of the widely diffused norm of separation to which they stand opposed, in the same way that anxiety opposes good conscience or flexibility of adaptation opposes the rigidity of prohibition.

An understanding of the way these processes of distancing come to function as rules should help us to understand the normative character of the lived order which they realize.

The Transmission of Recipes and the Rules of Tradition

Nothing in the organization of life in the placement is left to chance and very little to personal improvisation. When questioned about their own behaviour, all the foster parents have recourse to the same language, and the customs they describe are obviously related, deriving from received modes of action which they follow as if they were the articles of a professional code and a veritable guide to life.

An immediate cause of this state of affairs is the fact that opening a placement implies the contraction of a certain number of responsibilities about which information is desirable. Furthermore, it is to introduce into your home an alien element against which you want to be as well armed as possible. This is the reason for the preparatory concern with finding out what to expect and what you have to do to make sure that everything runs smoothly, both at the professional level and that of adapting to life with your future guests. Whilst it is the task of the Colony's staff to provide information on the management of the placement, the responsibilities involved in the job and even some practical advice, foster parents still far prefer to seek information from their peers: "I've seen some people, seen the way they handled it, taken their advice."

Of all the foster parents we interviewed, not a single one had embarked on the enterprise without equipping themselves, either directly or indirectly, with a considerable amount of information. From the oldest to the youngest, whether they had been born in the region or had just moved in, whether they had themselves grown up in a family of foster parents or worked in one, all of them took advantage of the good offices of more experienced foster parents. In the same way, the keeper of the oldest placement in the Colony was to tell us, "There were some people I knew very well. I asked them and they gave me advice."

Like the woman who had just finished preparing her accommodation but had not yet received her first lodger:

> There were a lot of people who had lodgers. They told me, 'You ought to take some'. Everyone has them and says that they are pleased with them . . . I've been thinking of doing it for a long time but I didn't have anywhere for them to live . . .Then I got my husband's workshop . . . I took some advice . . . I went to see Mme L's . . . and Mme B's and Mme C's. I talked to them, asked them 'how do you do it, how do you manage things? . . .'

From one end of the scale, a woman with fifty-six years of experience in accommodating lodgers, to the other, with no personal experience whatsoever, the language used was exactly the same.

By means of this initial advice in which the tricks of the trade are passed on – tried and trusted techniques and habits concerning the drawing up of menus and the management of time, the upkeep of the house and the maintenance of discipline – an entire convention of behaviour is transmitted: "We all go about it in the same way." And this exchange of information continues well beyond the opening of the placement, as:

> We're always talking about it. Nowadays we don't get quite so much of a chance to talk about it because our pay arrives by post. Earlier, though, payday, the 30th, was when the big conversation happened . . . Someone would be having problems, someone else . . . We would give them a bit of advice, how to go about it, how we did it ourselves.

Through such exchanges the recipes are codified as a repertoire of obligatory behaviour, social customs, conventions and treatments strictly reserved for the patients, and become, under the influence of peer group pressure, the "law of the placement" with which even the most independent finally comply, as a case told us by an interviewee illustrates:

> She was a strange foster parent. She wasn't from the region. At first she was hesitant. When she arrived here she went six months without a patient. Then after she had become integrated into the region she had four of them. At first she didn't see things the same way as the people of the region. She didn't treat the patients as different. She served them rolled ham. After three years and after meeting more experienced foster parents, she changed. She started saying 'that one' instead of 'Monsieur Untel'. It was a strange case. When she arrived she never tried to find out why her lodgers had changed placement and gone to other foster parents. After three years, she always tried to get information from more experienced foster parents, to find out what had happened earlier.

This process of the consolidation of customs, of the passage from recipe to rule is accentuated by its transmission from one generation to the next. Simple usage becomes a guide to acknowledged action:

> You have to be used to it. That wasn't a problem for me. At first I worked in a house where there were some of them. I got used to them. I've been living

with lodgers for nearly twelve years. When I got married we took some almost immediately. Because I already knew how to behave with them, how to feed them, how to treat them. When I worked in other households of course I had to deal with the lodgers, how to change their linen and all that. That's not a problem when you're used to it. But there are some of them . . . I can imagine myself in the place of a young woman who takes lodgers without being used to them! She must wonder how she's ever going to get by.

This phenomenon becomes even more significant when transmission is from parents to children. For the latter, the opening of a placement seems less like a choice imposed by an economic necessity than the perpetuation of a family system, the acceptance of a common destiny:

> We've all been foster parents in my family, it's like a tradition. It's more that than anything else. It's still handed down from father to son.

Which, in consequence, supposes obedience to the models imposed by the elders by virtue of the principle of authority which is reinforced by the skills acquired in the course of a long-practised career:

> I had advice near at hand because my mother-in-law lived next door. My mother-in-law gave me advice. She told me 'do it like this, do it like that'. It's so familiar that it's quite normal.

The path is open to the formation of traditions which cannot be broken:

> My parents had them. I saw how my mother went about it and I followed her example.

> Me, I work on the same principle that my mother used with hers.

The daughters and granddaughters of foster parents are more prone to the employment of a normative language than the others, speaking of "rules" and "principles", articulating their customs in the categorical mode – "Personally, as a foster parent, I think you should . . . " – sometimes manifesting a rigid authoritarianism which explains the extremity of their behaviour.

This can be seen in the case of one of these "heiresses" who received us in a recently built house. It is neat and tidy and she is very proud of it, as she is of the special accommodation built on the first floor for the lodging of patients, independent of the rest of the house, with bathroom and central heating. She explains how the meals are organized:

> As far as that's concerned, I've got my rules: It's 7.30, midday and 7 o'clock. They work at the Colony. But it's still necessary to have them here on time,

and no nonsense. I take everything to them. My husband made me a two-tiered tray so that I can take everything up at the same time. I've told them to bring the crockery back down. They put it in the little recess over there.

In the model kitchen, fully equipped with the latest gadgets, under the white tile draining board, near the door, the recess opens onto the enamel-painted, two-tiered tray. But it reveals no crockery. Instead we see the heavy pottery which in earlier times was reserved for the lodgers: *large, rugged, earthenware bowls and wooden spoons, such as were used in 1900, like mother used.* This gulf between the modern and the archaic shocks the observer. Why should those who act in this way perceive it as a duty: special treatment for the lodgers, separate earthenware for mealtimes and accommodation with every comfort on a different floor?

Communication is thus the channel for the diffusion and anchoring of models of behaviour towards the patients which, under the guise of organization, introduce a particular personal regime which becomes all the more constraining as the group of foster parents is strengthened in its power by its size, and in its certainty by its tradition. The processes at work in the transmission of recipes and their transformation into a normative system underline the autonomy of social control and the extent of its involvement in social constraint as far as the management of the day-to-day relationship with the patients is concerned.

At the same time as it embodies the concrete and symbolic barriers of differentiation implied by the label of "non-civilian", the rule of distancing guarantees that the patient will remain an external element despite the obligatory intimacy of forced coexistence, and sets limits to the integration sanctioned by fulfilment of the role of good lodger.

Chapter Four

Similarities and Differences in Everyday Life

We study them all the same . . . we try to change
their ways . . . We try to get them to do things
our way.

They aren't all the same. You have to find out
how to manage them to get them to do what you
want, to try to adapt them to our ways. As long as
you don't have any who are too obstinate!

We bring them up like ill people. You don't have
to live with them as if they were animals.

If action inspired by tradition and social pressure accounts for the
transformation of recipes into rules allowing for the management of everyday
life with the lodgers, it is still insufficient to explain the intensity and
generality of the quest for information carried out by the foster parents. What
are they looking for and to what do these techniques apply? For those who are
both responsible for the lodgers and also the guarantors of the equilibrium
and safeguarding of the home is it not, in the last resort, a question of
mastering the contact with insanity in the face of which they feel exposed
and threatened?

The first concern of the foster parent is "to make herself a life with" the
patients. This is a delicate task, demanding the reconciliation of the
aspirations of the lodgers and the requirements of the placement at a
minimum of cost to the foster parent and her family, and the habituation to
the customs of the household of a stranger who has his own habits and brings
with him his pathological peculiarities. All this demands subtle skills which
are difficult to acquire: "You have to go without to get used to the lodgers,
make sacrifices to put up with them."

And the control of others is no less difficult than mastery of oneself:

It's difficult to know how to handle them, whether they want to adapt to our
way of life, be polite and all that. That means there has to be understanding

on both sides. I manage all the same. You learn. But you have to put a lot of yourself into understanding them.

The Three "Hows"

This is why, despite appearances, advice acquired from the surroundings goes beyond the limited boundaries of material organization to bear on the general regulation of life with the lodgers. And it is a guide to action that is sought for in the triple question, "*how to treat them*", "*how to adapt them*", "*how to manage them*". These three hows address different informational domains which, however, still imply one another. To know how to treat a lodger requires a knowledge of his status; to know how to adapt him requires a knowledge of the corresponding rules of education; to know how to manage him, a knowledge of the techniques used to gain admission of both the first and the second.

In asking herself how to "treat" the lodger, the foster parent is showing that she feels exposed on two fronts. At the start, she does not know how to define the social individual with which she is confronted. She has no way of gaining an immediate understanding of the peculiarities – habits, psychological traits, mentality etc. – of the real individuals with whom she is dealing. The specificity of the individual is not exhausted by the attributes of his instrumental role, and his assimilation into the professional and family group is never total. The lodger is never truly treated as "a" (worker, child, friend etc.) but rather "like a" (worker, child, friend etc.). It is thus necessary to invent, discover or borrow ways of life adapted to a universe of the "as if", to treat the lodgers "as if" they were "children", "part of the family", "employees", "workmates" or "not at all like animals", even if no one goes so far as to say that they are "like part of the furniture". It is necessary to find a behavioural register which prevents the lodger identifying fully with one of the categories which he is continually approaching and yet from which he is being continually distinguished. It is a strict control exercised through permission and interdiction which makes clear the lodger's situation in the indefinite nature of the "as if". It is education which imposes this situation in the form of the principles or customs of the house. It is the knowledge of how to manage the lodgers which gains acceptance of this situation either by persuasion or manipulation.

Knowing "how to treat" the lodger is also used with a second significance: acquiring knowledge about his way of life, his mode of action and his social attitudes, his resources and his needs, his ability to adapt and so on in order to find a way of guiding his actions. This demands that two conditions are met. On the one hand, it is necessary to apply pertinent criteria for judgement in order to identify and evaluate those particular characteristics of the partner which have a direct bearing on the chances of mutual adaptation.

As far as functional criteria are concerned, beyond the practical constraints which the foster parent imposes, she refers to the consensually acknowledged dimensions of the role of the lodger. As for relational and personal criteria, the foster parent confirms her direct experience by borrowing the more generally acknowledged categories recognized by amateur psychology. On the other hand, a certain amount of time is necessary for the deployment and application of this knowledge. Only observation of the lodger can help the foster parent to apply these categories and apprehend the uniqueness of the individual confronting her, or to select from her repertoire of responses and procedures those which will best serve her aim of adaptation. Again the model of collective experience will guide this slow process of living together, the first stage of which will prove to be crucial.

Observation: A Time for Understanding and Learning how to Manage

Everyone, both interviewees and foster parents, is unanimous in emphasizing the importance of the phase of entrance and settling into the placement. The future relationship between foster parents and lodgers is almost completely determined during this period, in which each gauges the other and attempts to impose his or her own definition of the situation. The reception reserved by the foster parent, the conditions of life which she is anxious to establish at the very outset, suffices to make the situation clear to the lodger. Sometimes a single remark is enough to extinguish any chance of adaptation, as in the following change of placement narrated by a nurse:

> When we took him there the foster parent asked straight out right in front of the patient, 'Who is he? What's he done?'. You know, that's very painful for a patient. He made a sign to me and said, 'I don't want to stay in this house.' I took the patient with me and we went elsewhere. After that, everything went well. We never heard speak of him again. In that house he had been greeted with distrust . . . The foster parents can ask us for information, but not in front of the patients . . .

The foster parents have to weigh up the risks of this first meeting. It is often the cause of premature departures and escapes: "You have to encourage them to stay where they are. If you don't, some of them will leave." Each new arrival is something of a lottery: "You don't know who you're going to get", "how well you're going to be served". Always the old question, "will he be a good loony?"

The chances of adaptation have to be calculated rapidly: "It's up to you to see if you can keep them. You don't have to keep them." And whilst maintaining an attitude which will be of benefit in the future, it is necessary to establish the customs of the household immediately. It is up to the lodger to accept them or not: "You say what you want to say and that's that. If they go, it's because they want to go." The significance of this confrontation is such that during the first week(s) of the stay, it plays a major role in many departures from the placements, either because of refusal on the part of the lodger or rejection on the part of the foster parent. It is also during this period that the highest number of escapes take place.

For it is during this period that a fundamental characteristic of social behaviour is judged, the capacity for submission. This "docility", which is first evaluated when the lodger's clothes are handed out, is manifested in a number of ways at the placement: passivity articulated as "tranquillity", "not unpleasant"; acceptance of basic prescriptions; conformity to the model set by other lodgers. The opposite is found in indications of reserve, an insolent attitude which may give rise to a suspicion of obstinacy, opposition and demands which are then called "wickedness" or "annoyance". Acquainting the lodger with the restrictions in force in the placement makes it possible for him to react and show his potential for obedience:

> From the very first day they are brought to me they are treated the same as the others and that's all there is to it. I can tell then if he's going to behave like the others or if I'm not going to be able to adapt him. If he doesn't do things my way, I can see straight away if he's bad or not.

The most significant of the first impressions is related to constraint:

> The one who only stayed with me for a day, we had him taken away because he wasn't able to adapt. In the evening he started sweet-talking the others. He wanted to be in command, to stir up trouble everywhere. You can see immediately if they have a gentle character or if they are less easy to manage, if they are communicative or if they are withdrawn.

In this game it is cards on the table, take it or leave it. The partner is evaluated. You see him come without knowing him at all. More detailed observation is necessary to reveal his true nature, to discover what in the long run will turn out to be intolerable or amendable. Finally, it is necessary to distinguish between the effects of illness and the effects of character and to adapt one's behaviour accordingly. This is called "studying" and is generally thought to require a period of at least three weeks to a month, sometimes more, before the new arrival grows used to the way of life, becomes manageable. What is required is a discreet, vigilant attitude. A prudent reserve can limit both risks and damage:

> We give them confidence straight away. I speak to them gently, give them a bath. Then little by little we see if there is something not quite right . . . we get there bit by bit.

There's no point getting suspicious during the first few days. At the start, you don't know them. It takes them several months to adapt. You know a little bit before, but not much. We leave them free as well, we watch them. By the time five or six months have gone by, you know their character. In a new placement everything is fine. They always show their best side. It's after six months that you see what they are really like.

The foster parent's lack of knowledge makes her a prey to systematic doubt:

The beginning, that's important, because you never know. You don't know what he's like. You want to know about a lodger, you wonder.

This ever-present doubt is sometimes augmented by a negative first impression based on more or less explicit signs – the silence which makes the lodger appear withdrawn and sullen, the abruptness of his gestures or, less precisely, his bearing, his untidy clothing which raises fears of violence etc.:

There was one of them who immediately made a bad impression on me. He was a bad-looking lodger. He looked as if he wanted a fight. It's difficult to explain, but you can tell immediately from the way they behave whether they're going to be difficult or if everything is going to run smoothly.

When such suspicions grow stronger, the foster parent considers rejecting the placement without even trying to "adapt" the lodger. The sole point of observation is then to reveal the motive for this rejection:

There was one of them who used to sleep on the grass, a gloomy man. In the second week he wanted to start a knife fight. I didn't keep him.

There was an evil-looking one. I saw him in the fields taking off his belt. I said to myself, 'no need to keep him'.

We had a Spaniard. My husband said to me, 'We won't keep him. I don't like the look of him. We won't keep him.' So I said to him, 'Let's wait for a bit, see what he's like.' He was very young, twenty years old. In the end we didn't keep him. Not because he wanted to harm anybody, us or the children, but because he treated the animals badly. And it was never him. He was a liar, such a liar.

In fact, an operative criminal capacity seems to find rapid expression in concrete acts and constitutes, together with a refusal to obey, one of the causes cited for the immediate rejection of placements. In many other cases, however, criminality is simply imputed and serves as an explanation for the lodger's unruliness. A lodger you have no hold over is presumed to be "bad". It would be more accurate to describe this initial aspect of observation as a period of uncertainty during which "the lodger will show himself in his true light" than as a period of study. The foster parent "monitors", "examines", "watches" what the lodger is "capable of doing", and she does this while keeping her distance, without entering into any closer relations with him. He is not yet asked to perform any services or do any work and he is given only what he is due. The absence of spontaneously manifested negative behaviour is enough to reassure the foster parent. The time needed to form an opinion of the lodger is such that foster parents continue to demand the withdrawal of certain patients even after stays of relatively long duration. In contrast the number of lodgers who ask to change placement after the first month has passed is low and continues to fall as time passes.

Properly speaking, the period of study commences when observation merges into an interpretation of the way the lodger "reacts" to his social environment. It takes the form of a search for an evaluation in "psychological" terms, an effort to "understand" the patient. To gain this understanding, watching alone is now insufficient. A remark or a question slipped in casually whilst serving dinner or in between the household chores can provoke a revealing response. The reaction to the request for help or a reminder of a rule of the house may confirm the foster parent's judgement. It is even possible to find ways for the lodger to express himself without granting him too great a scope for action.

This approach is necessitated by the quest for mutual adaptation. First of all it makes it possible to evaluate the lodger by providing information on his "good" and "bad" qualities, by revealing the areas of behaviour which are susceptible to influence and those which are impervious to change. To do this, the foster parent applies a selection of behavioural classifications. These may refer to disposition such as goodwill, order or cleanliness, to aspects of temperament such as reserve or timidity, or to modes of response such as fear or opposition. In every case, however, such classifications are based on the visible behaviour of the lodger and not on his hidden needs or intentions, on his acts not on his words. "Understanding" consists of specifying what behaviour is by referring it to a class which defines either its origin or its determination. Four categories are used. Behaviour may result from "nature" or "character" (it is "in the nature" of the person), from "education", from "mentality" or from the "illness". This classification does not serve to establish a mutually exclusive typology of behaviours. A single behaviour may belong to one or other of these classes. Thus a lodger may "shout" (lose control, get angry, throw insults) "by nature" or because of "the illness". He may be dirty "by nature" or because of "the illness". If a lodger is clean it is because it is "in his nature" or because he has been "educated" like that. The refusal to work may result from "education", "mentality" or "illness" and so on. It is the task of interpretation to perform this breakdown of behaviour. In doing this, it is following purely practical aims and is subordinate to practice. Its objective is to discover whether behaviour changes as a result of the attempt to channel qualities in a useful direction and to improve negative characteristics and, more generally, to discover, at the very least, if and how adaptation is possible. The evaluation and assessment of behavioural characteristics can lead to a great variety of attitudes and to surprising situations such as that of "putting up with" a grave fault in the name of habit or because, in other respects, the lodger "isn't unpleasant". However, extreme situations remain where, in the face of an immutable negative trait which makes communal life impossible, the foster parent gives up the attempt to get the better of it or "put up with it" and rejects the lodger.

Techniques of Control and Laisser-Faire *Attitudes*

As a guide to action towards the other (what has to be adapted) and towards oneself (what you have to adapt to), the study of the lodger serves to define "the way to manage him", that is to say, the way to influence him and gain a hold over him, the approaches to which he is receptive, the attitudes or demands which may offend him, shock him or wound him. You have to be able to impose your will on the "obstinate" ones, not to get angry with the "timid" ones for fear of distressing them, to choose your words carefully with the "touchy" ones to avoid antagonizing them. Equally, it is important to discover the clearest, quickest routes to getting what you want.

During the observation stage, the foster parents select their modes of adaptive action from an already codified repertoire of behaviour. What they call "knowing how to manage the lodger" is no more than the application to a specific case of one of these methods of influence which form part of amateur psychology.

In the same way that the "psychology" which underlies observation is a phenomenal psychology which only takes account of the face value of behaviour, the psychology which guides interaction is "behavioural", aiming to produce changes solely at the level of the partner's manifest conduct. Here, too, knowledge has a technical character and a practical intention. It aims to obtain certain results at the level of conduct and maintain control of the situation.

The psychological recipes used by the foster parents are thus means of exerting pressure, modes of manipulation, veritable methods of control. Limited in number, and generally applicable to all interactions which aim to exert a direct influence on the partner's response, these recipes differ from *laisser-faire* attitudes (withdrawal or modification of one's own responses) which are adopted when the attempt to influence another person is abandoned. These methods of control are always presented as a bipolar schema which covers the full range of action towards another: *you control them by fear or by kindness*. Finding "the right way to manage the lodger" consists of discovering which of these two options is appropriate for his case and, when this has been determined, the way it can be applied most effectively. Fear appeals to the power of the foster parent, kindness to the satisfaction of the lodger. They can both be applied in the manner of a "punishment" or a "reward" as a direct response to a specific piece of conduct. They can be used in the form of a "carrot and stick" condition associated with the projected future appearance of certain modes of behaviour, or they can be the object of blackmail by intimidation or seduction. Equally, fear and kindness may simply be functions of the mode of address and characterize the type of expression thought fitting for the lodger, to "let him know what's what" or "to speak to him gently, without shouting". The choice of the method to be applied is always attributed to the nature of the lodger, his character, illness or sensitivity to others.

The mode of address depends on the character of the lodger, "easy" or "difficult", "timid" or "bold" and "insolent":

> There are some of them you have to frighten if you want to be able to control them.

> You have to find out whether to manage them gently or roughly. There are some you mustn't be rough with and some who have to be afraid of you.

> You have to react to their character, understand it, not antagonize it. There's one of them who flies off the handle if I antagonize him. He gets into a rage, shouts, stamps. A single comment can offend him terribly. You have to understand if someone is sensitive. If you're not gentle with him, you can hurt him.

Sometimes the risk of annoying the lodger, of turning him violent, dictates an attitude of kindness which is often close to the attitude of *laisser-faire*:

> I never say anything to them. We don't have the right to tell them off or anything. Perhaps that's an error. Maybe it would be better if they were afraid of us because those people, you know, you can hardly talk to them. It's better like that really, because when they get angry what can you say to them, what can you do? You can't do anything. You just have to let it blow over and take it calmly.

The instilling of fear remains a privileged method in so far as it necessitates the acceptance of the law of the placement by the lodger who may already be "afraid of the supervisors or of the Colony", that is to say he may be afraid of being sent back or of being punished with a period in the ward. It is then sufficient for the foster parents to evoke this threat whenever the lodger does not comply with their demands:

> I had one who was dirty. He used to go in his pants. Well, I told him what to do, I told him off, but it had no effect. The nurse told me to make him wash his pants. After that I told him. 'We can't keep you. If you're always

going to go in your pants the Colony will have to take care of you.' After that, he came round.

This real power exercised by the foster parents can also be used to manipulate a lodger who is not afraid of the Colony but who likes the placement and does not want to change:

If he had to change he wouldn't like it. Anyway, I always tell him if something isn't right. He's very frightened of me. I just have to say, 'I'm going to telephone and ask them to take you back.' That's enough. It's all over. 'Don't you like it? Are you moaning?' I reach for the telephone and it's over. I don't hear another thing.

If the lodger is sufficiently dependent, "a good talking to", an intimidating anger, is preferred to the arousal of fear:

Some of them need to be rebuked by the people they live with. You have to make them understand why they are being told off without saying it in a way which will shock them.

I don't think mine would get used to living anywhere else. I don't want to annoy him, of course, but you have to be in control. He has to feel that you have authority over him. You have to take him in hand when it's necessary, but without overdoing it.

The process of adaptation often takes the form of a true apprenticeship with each act receiving a positive or negative sanction. Here the power of the foster parents is based on their control of the rewards and punishments:

The young one. A year ago, when they brought him, he was quite diabolical. Now, he's no worse than the others. You have to know how to manage him, whether to reward him with tobacco if he hasn't got any, with sweets, with some other kindness. And sometimes you punish him . . . What I do to the children to punish them, I do to him. If he does something very bad I punish him when I give them their dessert. One day he killed one of my goats and to punish him I didn't give him any dessert when all the rest had theirs. That's the worst punishment you can give them without actually doing them any harm . . . It depends on how you manage them, whether you can lead them by their good points, if you know how to . . . It's the same as with a child. Some children you can get somewhere with by giving them a sweet and there are others where a good clout won't help you. I've got a son so I know. You could half kill him and he still wouldn't give in. It's the same with that one there. You could half kill him. It's all the same to him. So I control them with the dessert. I just have to make an ice cream and they're punished enough.

The little rewards which are given or refused in response to praiseworthy behaviour or a reprehensible act (or associated with the possible occurrence of one or the other) come from the everyday pleasures of the lodgers (treats, a cup of coffee, tasting the cooking, watching television, a Sunday walk etc.). They are manipulated as a sign that the foster parents are treating the lodger "as if he was part of family life". When the threat of the Colony or rejection meets with resistance, the power of domination, anger, scolding, punishment are enlisted as educational methods and are based on the techniques used with children. The lodgers are treated "like the children are" or "as if they were children".

Control by fear thus covers a range of techniques based on fear, intimidation, repression by threat of privation or punishment – frequent allusions are made to the cruelty inflicted in other placements:

> I've got one who was in a placement where he used to be beaten. They stupefied him more than anything else. I've improved him by treating him gently.

Control by kindness implies, beyond the recourse to rewards and "reasoning", explanations made without reprimands:

> When they do something stupid, something idiotic, you have to get them to admit it. But you don't have to pursue it all the time. If he breaks a tool I say, 'C. take care not to break things.' He says, 'It broke.' 'But you can tell me – it was the other day – you can tell me.'

Used as an incentive, kindness is also more specifically reserved for the acquisition or reinforcement of positive habits. It thus implies a consideration of the lodgers' expectations, an orientation towards the individual, whether this is presented as a sign of the recognition of a quality, as an indication of interest or trust or as an appeal to a sense of responsibility:

> I have a way of handling the good lads. I do what I want with them. I give them duties. I realized that that was important. When I send them off to work they're responsible for themselves. None of them are placed above the others. They are all equal and that works. They all have their work to do. They're under no compulsion and they're proud. That's how I go about it . . . I've always done it this way and I've seen that it's right. It's the same everywhere, you have to know how to manage them. There are little things which give them pleasure. If I make pancakes, they get pancakes and they're happy. If it's their birthday we celebrate it. We make a cake, they come to the house, have a drink . . .

This effort to assure oneself of the goodwill of the lodger can lead to the adoption of a certain form of seduction which is frequently used in social relations and is known in plain terms as "flattery".[1] This consists of addressing a sensitive point, according a moral satisfaction, flattering pride:

> We have one. When he was with his parents he did nothing at all, but we manage to get him to do something. You have to tell him that he's done very well, that he's an excellent worker, that he's better than the boss . . .

The attention shown is always subordinate to the performance of a service (professional work, household task etc.):

> But the lodgers aren't all the same. I've got two in their own room. One of them used to like to be left on his own. He didn't like me entering his room. It was sacred to him. And the other one likes me going to see what he's got, to pay him compliments: 'Well done, Adrien. You've done very well.' Some of them like you to say something to them. But the others, you have to moan at them to take their bedding off, to tidy their rooms. They're incapable of getting by on their own. It was Adrien's character. He used to say, 'I've done it. Do you want to come and see how I've tidied it?' You felt he needed encouragement. On the other hand, he didn't like being sent out to do things.

In short, the whole art of controlling the lodgers can be reduced to mastery, in accordance with the different partners, circumstances and events, of the variations of fear and kindness which are summarized in the table on page 125.

This summary of practical pedagogy in which priority is accorded to repressive techniques and to incentives based on the satisfaction of elementary needs – bodily needs and the desire for company – covers all the resources used by the foster parents to "adapt" the lodgers "to their own way of life". If these are inadequate, there is only recourse to a position of withdrawn *laisser-faire* or the rejection of the lodger. The course chosen will depend on whether the behaviour in question is considered to be of minor, secondary or crucial importance. Evaluation of behaviour is always relative:

> The fourth is a fine type. His great pleasure is to be in bed. At the start we told the supervisor about it. It was annoying to see him in bed all the time and he gets through a lot of bedding! He's always tired. It's too hot, it's too

---

[1] A fundamental category of affective relationships, flattery appears as a mark of indulgence, of submission to another person which makes it possible to manipulate his weaknesses in order to obtain his affection or his goods. It is opposed to the refusal to make concessions, "to give way". Illustrative of this is the description a grandfather furnished of his grandchildren, classing some as "people who never agree with you" and the rest as "flatterers who are cunning with it". This trait, identified in amateur psychology, coincides with the psychosociological analysis of "ingratiation" (Jones, 1964). In this examination of control methods it is impossible to ignore their resemblance to the models of social psychology.

cold. 'Yes, yes', we say to him when he tells us. The nurse said, 'You should try to get him to go out if you can.' We've shouted at him, we've flattered him, but nothing changes. We tried being kind . . . it made no difference. Now we leave him alone, we don't bother about it. We let him lie there. What can we do? He always says, 'Yes', never 'No', and he doesn't move. We don't disturb him and that's all there is to it.

Whilst reliant on a spontaneous psychology, this method of managing the lodger is clearly characterized by its objective, and the full significance of the prevalence of control by fear can only be appreciated by identifying the education it supports and the order it establishes.

Table 1 Repertoire of Control Techniques

a) *Methods used to control the lodgers*

By fear (Repressive techniques)	By kindness (Incentive techniques)
Appeal to fear of the (F*)[1] institution	(F*) Comments and explanations made without anger – Precautionary
Appeal to the fear of (F*) rejection	(F*) Rewards (oral, social)
Intimidation (roughness, (F*) anger, reprimands, affirmation of authority)	(R) Proof of esteem and recognition
Penalization by privation or the (F) refusal of a need	(R) Appeal to responsibility, to goodwill, marks of trust
Punishment (including (F) corporal)	(F) Flattery

b) *Modes of employment*

- Mode of address (roughness–delicacy)
- Direct response to actual behaviour (reinforcement–suppression)
- Response conditional upon the appearance of behaviour (negotiation or blackmail)
- Response to a need (denial/satisfaction) promoted by the behaviour
  If it is impossible to influence the other = rejection or *laisser-faire*

---

[1]F*: very frequently used; F: frequently used; R: rarely used

The Education of a Lodger

The objective of the community of foster parents is stated in perfectly clear terms: "to get the lodger to fit in". This means imposing a unilaterally defined set of rules on another person by changing his way of life and by overcoming opposition or the tendency towards opposition – hence the importance of docility, on the one hand, and domination on the other: "You have to find a way of training them. You have to train them."

But if "adapting him to your way of life" is called "educating" the other, then the phrase "giving a lodger's education" implies that this apprenticeship is based on a specific position and a specific status, the imposition of which may run counter to certain expectations or aspirations – hence the significance of repressive techniques. Not only does the lodger have to abandon his supports, he is also forced to adopt the limitative regulations of the "as if", to live in an uncomfortable balance between the rights obtained through the correct fulfilment of his role and the barriers erected because of his position of approximation.

This is the source of the rigour and vigilance of the foster parents for whom reiterating the principle of authority and maintaining distance also becomes an educative function, if not more important than the teaching of customs. Seen in this light, the foster parents are the representatives of an order which they have to express and affirm in their own terms.

This is why every interaction with an adaptive aim is stamped with a double character, both instrumental and normative. It is a duality which can be observed from the moment of initial contact on the lodger's arrival at the placement where, as well as "showing the lodger the ropes" and introducing him to the practical details of the house and its management, the foster parent stipulates unbreakable rules whose acceptance is an absolute precondition for communal life.

Showing the lodger the ropes includes providing information which is not classed purely as imperative. Some of this information relates to non-regulatory elements of the placement (layout of rooms, washing days etc.), whilst some concerns personal discipline and tasks. These demands vary in accordance with the inclinations of the foster parent, and thus allow a relatively flexible and differentiated application. This is the best example of the domain of mutual adaptation, which we analysed above. By way of contrast, those elements which are related to the definition of the services due to the lodgers (for example, time and nature of meals, method of serving, tray taken to room or served directly in the kitchen) and their rights is given a more strictly obligatory character:

> We have to teach them to live with us. They should be comfortable but *they should be able to get by in the life they have to live*. They do their washing-up. They get by with one or two things they need to be able to do. If you've got

the flu they have to get by, so you have to teach them to do a few things. If I need it, one of them must be able to come and help his colleagues. *You have to put up with them asking you when they need something but you shouldn't overdo helping them.*

This type of constraint determines the position of the lodger and sets the unpassable frontiers in his relationship with the foster family. Whilst the foster parents describe their own habits and preferences in an informative mode and with a certain amount of latitude: "A lodger might say to you: 'We get used to it somehow or other, everyone has their own ways'", they use the categorical mode to deal with questions of right and position, accepting no deviation and no delay in the execution of the commands which seem to come from a transcendent order rather than from their goodwill or beneficence. This is because the delimitation of living spaces and the organization of daily contact establishes a differential way of life for the lodgers which obeys the rule of separation. And separation is neither justified nor negotiated; it is the unconditional ante paid to enter the game:

They are people you can't put together with others. They're ill after all. They can't live with us or eat with us or anything like that. From the very start, they had their room and I had my house. When it's necessary they come here, either to bring something or to ask for something. Apart from that, they never come, not even to watch television. Otherwise, I wouldn't be in my own home.

I get them used to it. They have their room. They walk through the courtyard. You have to get them used to it. If they want something they come to the door to ask for it, 'Please Madame.' *They are used to it, they're not ashamed.* When the last one arrived, he came into the house straightaway. I said to him, *'You're not allowed to do that.* If you want something, ask for it.' Now that's all over. If he needs something, he asks me for it. He never dreams of coming into the house.

Nor is there any hesitation to use material means to instigate this separation, in particular when it is a question of forbidding the lodgers to cross the threshold to the house. In many placements a small, 50 cm high barrier is used. Formerly this served to prevent the poultry from the courtyard finding its way through an open kitchen door. There is no more poultry, but the barrier has stayed in place to signal the presence of an uncrossable boundary to the lodgers.

Authority, however, remains the most important attribute of the role of foster parent:

You have to stay a bit aloof, keep a certain authority. It depends on the way they react. You have to be able to put them in their place. When you have to tell them off you should treat them like you treat some children. As long as they are calm, they realize they have a different life from the life of confinement. It's not the same life.

Authority has an instrumental value and a normative basis. In saying "You have to make them respect you," "You have to maintain a certain authority," the foster parent is expressing her need to affirm her power in a relationship of strength:

> You shouldn't be scared of making them frightened of you. If you are, you won't be able to get them to do what you want. I know I've gained a lot of confidence in that respect . . . When you live with them, you grow in confidence. You tell yourself that you have to show them that you are stronger than they are and that they have to obey you.

This need is felt all the more deeply because, as a woman, the foster parent has to oppose a masculine resistance. In this connection, the presence of a husband seems to be of a certain amount of help:

> It's a support, even though all the ones I've had so far have been scared enough of me. All the same, though, I feel more secure because otherwise I would be on my own. I would possibly be less confident. I would make them less scared of me because I would be frightened of their reprisals.

But recourse to a husband – where he exists; many foster parents are alone in their homes – is mostly only a moral support because, already occupied by his work, the latter is, by definition, in no position to busy himself directly with the patients. The order of the placement is primarily a women's order.

Because they feel themselves alone in the face of the lodgers, the foster parents feel the need to establish their authority and note, not without a certain pride, that "they are obeyed more readily than their husbands". In fact, the husbands seem to allow themselves a greater familiarity with the lodgers which their wives interpret as a lack of authority.[2] Authority does not have the simple function of assuring power. It is also indissolubly bound to the idea of distance. This is one aspect of its normative value:

> You have to keep a certain authority over them. You really shouldn't . . . I've got one now. He comes from a good family and all that but you have to treat him just like the others, because if you do him a little favour then you'll never get to the end of it. He had only just arrived and there he was at the door, waiting, yawning . . . I'm telling you this to show you that you have to keep a certain authority over them, a certain distance.

---

[2] We shall see later (in the Epilogue) that the closer relations between the men and the lodgers, frequently the result of a shared workplace, has consequences which are linked to the representation of mental illness.

Entrusted with the maintenance of an order which applies to the home as a whole, the foster parent, in demanding respect, also defends the hierarchical position with which she is invested and thus also the rule which she embodies. Authority both serves and expresses a real and symbolic relationship which must be imposed from the very start and maintained by constant control:

> All the same, there are times when they are quite easy to deal with. One of mine, before he came to me his longest placement had been a month and I've had him for two years. Even the doctor can't understand it. She said to me, 'How have you managed it?', and I replied, 'Madame, I've done my best, I've done all I could to get him used to it.' He's a strange case. How shall I put it? He's strong willed. And when he arrived here . . . I'm not saying this to boast . . . he was very cheeky . . . and he's stayed like that towards my husband. I don't know why. Perhaps because he's so seldom here. Or perhaps that gives them . . . while me, straight away . . . Earlier we could never get him to say Thank You or Hello or anything. At the start, I remember, I was picking beans . . . and he said to me, 'Do this for me . . . ', 'Well,' I said to him, 'where were you brought up?' Then he said to the other lodger who was at his side, 'She has to do it. The other nurse, she did everything like she should!' – So I told him, 'Things don't work like that here, take it or leave it.' And in the end he got used to it. We had a few rows but in the end I was able to manage him . . . You have to make them a little bit frightened of you . . . You have to try to educate them. At the beginning he was very coarse, and now when I go upstairs in the morning he always says hello. And I don't give him anything unless he says please when he asks me. And he could easily come into the kitchen without knocking or anything. I told him, 'M, I should like you to knock before you come in.' He came when I was washing the kids, so I said to him, 'No M, when I'm looking after the children you mustn't come into the kitchen. You have your own room. Stay there. You've got everything you need. If you want something from me, tell me and I'll see what I can do about it.'

This speech provides the proof of the close relationship, and even the equivalence, between fear, authority and distance, and establishes their normative character. The vehicle of a power which is realized through fear and respect, authority is thus both the expression and attribute of a legitimacy which inspires fear in order to establish distance as a value over and above any functional barriers. Is it possible to decipher something of the sacred implicit in this language? The idea of the sacred is always present in the minds of the foster parents. As we have just seen, one of them said of her lodger, "He didn't like me entering his room. It was sacred to him." This point, which still has to be investigated,[3] does not fully explain the question

---

[3] The protection of private and personal space which forms the subject of a large body of literature in the field of environmental psychology (see Lévy-Leboyer, 1982) is generally

posed by the correspondence between the lodger's nature and the exercise of educative functions as they are conceived by the community of foster parents.

Education here supposes the acquisition of new codes of conduct and the adaptation to a specific structure and way of life. What then is the reason that those who dispense it do so in the form of so violent a domination and what implications does this have for its recipients? The emphasis given to the domination of behaviour on the one hand, and to docility or the willingness to obey on the other, demonstrates that the crucial point in the relationship between foster parent and lodger lies in submission. This necessity for submission may derive from the excessive constraints of the law imposed by the milieu. That these constraints run contrary to the aspirations of the recipient of the education is indicated by the opposition he expresses through escaping or demanding a change of placement, and the resistance he shows in what is called his "stubbornness", his "wickedness", his anger or his perpetual discontent. It is clear that opposition of this magnitude can only be overcome by the application of effective methods. The same strong approach is necessary to restrain demands which are judged excessive.

> You have to watch out that you don't let them do whatever they want. Because if you give them everything you lose control of them. There needs to be an element of fear. They need to be a little bit frightened of us.

But one facet of the recourse to fear and domination remains unexplained, namely its widespread application. Everywhere you can hear it advocated, irrespective of whether the willingness to submit was established on first contact, whether obedience was assured slowly or quickly, whether the foster parents are lax about the establishment of rules or disposed towards closer contact and integration into the family. It is as if the relationship thus established were constantly endangered by a risk or a threat which each lodger carries within himself.

Boldness

This danger is clearly indicated by the idea of *boldness*. Boldness, either potential or real, is attributed to every lodger, and, because it appears as the inevitable corollary of adaptation, every foster parent seeks to eradicate or minimize it through education and repressive vigilance:

---

explained by the defence of identity, the protection of property and the protection o᷍ ᷍ᴛhe group. Following the work carried out by ethologists, Lorenz (1966) in particular, reference is also made to territorial behaviour in animals. Less attention has been paid to the potential contributions of anthropology to the understanding of the "making sacred" of social spaces, notably that separation and spatial distance create a hierarchical order (Dumont, 1981) which can be clearly observed in the case we are studying.

Adapting the lodgers is to try to understand them and that can easily make them bold. If he's not such a bold lad and has too much contact then he learns it. If he's too bold by nature . . .

Some of them turn out well and don't get mixed up in things too quickly. Others start to grow bold.

At the same time it is the reverse of fear, an enemy of authority and distance and the object of control, boldness retains an ambiguous significance. To discover the meaning of this term, common in the local speech, we shall follow the example of ethno-methodology and seek the circumstantial contexts in which it occurs and the situations in which its significations are rooted.

As difficult to define as it is common in use, boldness constitutes a general category for the comprehension of social and interpersonal relationships:

It's the same with everybody. There are some people you like better than others among the civilians as well. It's the same with the lodgers. There are some you shouldn't allow to get too bold, as we say in the area . . . When they grow bold, you know. It's difficult to explain . . . After I've told them to come into the house once or twice they might start coming in without me asking them. You always have to keep a certain distance from these people.

When it is manifested as a behavioural characteristic (insolence, recrimination, rebellion etc.), boldness can be explained either by character, as a natural disposition opposed to timidity and fear, or by mentality, as a disregard for social conventions:

Nowadays the lodgers don't have the same mentality at all. They don't behave like they used to. They are bolder. Before, they paid attention when you said something to them, and they didn't answer back. But nowadays you really have to lay down the law before you can get them to listen to reason.

By contrast, boldness cannot be explained by the patient's illness, except indirectly in that it prevents an understanding of the situation to which the lodger is exposed. But rather than being an inherent characteristic of the individual, it is a dimension of any social relationship and is implied in a relationship where there is insufficient domination of the partner or inadequate defence of the hierarchy established between the two partners. Boldness marks the failure of the interaction between two individuals of unequal rank (superior–inferior, man–woman, civilian–lodger). Seen in this light, it is not inevitable and can be corrected through constant supervision of attitudes and actions. When a consensus on the relative positions of the partners exists, the spontaneous observance of certain codes of conduct is sufficient, for example in the demonstration of reserve and non-familiarity in the relationship between the sexes. If no such consensus exists, one of the partners must act against boldness and defend his standing, by force if necessary. In the relationship with the lodger, a relationship in which everything is imbued with the ambiguities of the "as if", in which everything is destabilized by the lodger's willingness to be or illusion of being "one of the household", the prevention of boldness is an absolute imperative which operates through the foster parent's attitude of authoritarian domination.

Like its antitheses – fear, authority, distance – boldness concerns the instrumental and normative aspects of the relationship between the foster parent and the lodger. To confer boldness upon the lodger or to allow him to develop it is to run the risk of the lodger permitting himself liberties which are incompatible with his status. These may be liberties of speech – "answering back", familiarity, the expression of disrespect or insults etc. – or liberties of behaviour – familiarity towards the foster parent, playing with the children etc. – which claim unacceptable rights such as the demand for excessive attention or unauthorized entry into the house. In short, the risk is that the lodger will cease to respect the constraints and obligations imposed upon him as rules by the foster parent. In the application of a logic of "all or nothing", the foster parent views boldness as a loss of authority, a reversal of the relationship which she entertains with the lodger, her capitulation and his victory:

> I know foster parents who let them speak to them familiarly. They call them 'tu'. They let them grow bold. It's not like that with us and the children are the same. I want the children to respect them and, equally, I want them to respect the children, because if you don't have that, they grow too bold. It's always the same. If you have lodgers you don't want to make life too awful for them, but at the same time you have to maintain a certain authority. If you don't, if you allow them too much freedom, you never hear the end of it.

Authority also seeks to prevent the assumption of boldness by forbidding both the self and the other to use any gestures or words which might suggest a reciprocity of roles, a freedom of exchange:

> Personally, I look after them myself. It isn't the same everywhere. Out in the farms it's a different life. To start with, it's different if there's a couple, if there's a husband around. Then you can chat with them, let them do a few things. As for me, I don't let them do anything because I don't think I would have enough authority over them afterwards. If you're a woman on your own you shouldn't let them become too bold. You have to keep them in their place and be quite firm with them. Of course, you mustn't be too strict or too bad-tempered but all the same . . . you shouldn't joke with them for example. They are quick to interpret your words, to interpret them not in the way you meant them . . . You have to be reserved with them to stop them growing too bold.

This specifies for us the significance of boldness at the normative and symbolic levels and its relationship to the rule of distance. Certainly, the control of oneself and others which prevents the growth of boldness guarantees the observance of the proprieties and conventions and avoids the unpleasantnesses and incidents which may arise from thoughtlessness:

> Even if they didn't have bad manners they would grow too bold, they would start getting familiar, it would get on your nerves. I don't insult them but I make sure they respect me. I don't let them get too bold. I don't put up with them insulting me or swearing.

Certainly, the authoritarian repression of boldness makes the job of foster parent easier to perform and prevents the lodger from "gaining the upper hand":

> You shouldn't be too good to them. You should keep your distance, because if you don't they'll grow too bold, they'll gain the upper hand, they'll answer back. You can't manage them any more.

At the same time, repression is the guarantor of the foster parents' power, in particular the power to "do what you want with them".

Crucial values are at stake in the struggle against boldness. It is a question of keeping each individual in a position which is based solely on the unilateral, social definition of status and role, of maintaining a regime imposed by the community of foster parents. At stake also is the protection of an order, contradictory because what is licit with regard to the institution – the desire of the lodger to adhere strictly to the principles of family life and to live in the placement freely and on a basis of equality – is not permissible to the foster parents. All the fragility of an impossible situation in which integration is achieved through separation is revealed in the compulsive concern "not to let them grow too bold", that is to say, the concern to act in unison to fix and delimit the rights of the lodgers. Thus boldness, always potentially present as a claim to an equality of rights, finds its purest expression in the negation of distance, the entry into the placement:

> If there's too much contact with the lodgers then even a lad who isn't so brave will grow bold. If he's too bold by nature then he'll be troublesome.

> You mustn't let them grow too bold. If they are bold then they're more likely to bother you when somebody arrives at the door. They take advantage of it to ask me for this or that. It's boldness. I'm not worried about the big one when someone comes. He's an educated lad. Deep down it's really to educate them, to get them used to it.

All the symbolic or actual signs of distance are used to curb its growth:

It's like this. I wouldn't like to have them eating with us. It seems to me that it's good for them to be together and for us to be together . . . There's no question of that. I think it makes them slightly scared of us, we have a certain amount of authority over them. But if they were here, then they would get bolder.

The rule of distance becomes a prohibition, boldness a transgression. The social order and the moral order meet in this freedom which, unchecked by distance, respect or authority, degenerates into lawlessness as a result of the two dangers associated with it, theft and sexual freedom.

My mother had one. He was like a child to her. But she had to send him back, he started to . . . It's always the same. If you have them for too long they start to get bold. He stole the neighbours' washing. She said, 'I can't keep him.' He had never done that before. It was no good telling him off. There was nothing to be done.

Some people pretend to take them seriously without really taking them seriously. That's not a particularly good state of affairs. I've got one, for example. His parents come to see him and take him with them to the hotel. They keep him there with them. And when that happens he wants to leave, he wants to go back with them. They said, 'But you aren't able to work you know, you can't take your place.' And he said, 'I'm going to get a mistress and tell her to work.' His mother said, 'That's all you have to do!' People like that don't realize the state their child is in. Because it doesn't end with saying that to him. Afterwards, he'll get the idea into his head, he'll get bolder, he'll start chasing the girls. Well, when that happens you don't know what . . . And although there's not much to him he could frighten someone. That's not the way to treat them.

It is revealing that the corollaries to the interpersonal manifestations of boldness at the moral level should be seen as the unjustified appropriation of belongings and the release of urges. This imputation can be interpreted as a rationalization of the distress which denotes the defensive conflict engendered by coexistence with the lodgers when privacy is shared, the home invaded and the barriers of propriety broken down.

In fact, the language of the local population confers a psychological importance and a social significance on the idea of boldness which could not be predicted from its more general usage, creating a specific type of social conduct from a quality which is normally perceived only in limited aspects of behaviour.

By elaborating this notion, the group transforms it into a category of thought which is, in its own way, as original as that of the lodger. But what is created in this manner is not simply a conceptual instrument which makes it possible to distinguish a potentiality or a state specifically associated with the status of the lodger. The very way in which the group relates boldness to authority, fear and distance reveals the expression of an experience of the reality of the relationship with the lodger which we must try to comprehend.

What lies behind this dramatic, everyday conflict in which both the order and that which it represses define one another in a reciprocal tautology? What significations does boldness possess that it should attain a special status as an object for concern at the level of interpersonal relationships where it provides its full, if not new, content for the rule of distance? In a way, the fact that the foster parents fight this assumption of an opposed "position", which demands an equality and a freedom denied to the lodgers, shows that the rule of distance consists of more than just the erection of barriers intended to establish and maintain a formal differentiation or to manage coexistence with difference. It also serves as a protection against a threat, the menace which arises precisely from the suppression of this distinction.

Conclusion

Beyond Principles:
Fear and the Social Threat

The preservation of exteriority within coexistence – this appears to be the paradox of coexistence which a dualist order surmounts by managing its relationships with the members of the Colony. However, this division is affirmed in a different manner in the collective and the interpersonal spheres: in the contact between group and group, it works through the withdrawal of the inhabitants and through geographical isolation; in participation in social life, it functions through cognitive differentiation and the barrier of a reserved status; in the family unit and face-to-face contact it functions through the barrier of distance.

The processes involved in effecting this distancing also differ from one level to the next. The anonymous, little-codified phenomena at work in the public arena are distinguished both from the uniform, rigid modes of categorization and labelling and from the statutory constraints which are rigorously defined and imposed by the functioning of the social group. Distance itself is maintained by a direct hold on the person of the patient. In order to assure permanent control over the lodger's access to the private goods of the foster parent, an access which the principle of placement has made legitimate, distance requires special procedures which the foster parents apply like transmitted rules of life and which are respected as norms.

These principles and methods, which, from observation to education, have the function of implementing a dualist order, also have a defensive function. The durability and force of distance, the authority and fear which serve it, and the boldness they oppose, all reveal the association of the order with something menacing. Might the normative character of these usages be related to the way the order is grounded in the function of protection? Beyond the appeal to the phenomena of diffusion, of social conformity and the generalization of social control, we would need to explain these phenomena in terms of the risk they counter in lending their practical modes to a formal order. This is what is suggested by the following remark by Lévi-Strauss: "By establishing a general rule of obedience, whatever this rule may be, the group asserts its jural authority over what it legitimately considers an essential valuable" (1969).

This idea, formed in connection with the prohibition of incest and related to the enjoyment of privileges, possesses a general relevance, even when its prescriptions are negative, in so far as it reveals "the beginnings of an organization" and most importantly "the spontaneous resolution of psychosocial tensions which constitute the immediate facts of collective life". In emphasizing the importance of the psychosocial as a motor for the transition to the cultural or the social, the author opened up new perspectives for research. This is why it has seemed legitimate to us to extrapolate his reflections, especially the following passage:

> If it is objected that such reasoning is too abstract and artificial to have occurred at a very primitive human level, it is sufficient to note that the result, which is all that counts, does not suppose any formal reasoning but simply the spontaneous resolution of those psychosocial pressures which are the immediate facts of collective life. In non-crystallized forms of social life, such as communities arising spontaneously out of accidental circumstances (bombardments, earthquakes, concentration camps, children's gangs and so on), which still await psychological investigation – and are so rich in both elemental and universal processes – it is soon learnt that the perception of another's envy, the fear of violent dispossession, the distress resulting from collective hostility, and so on, can wholly inhibit the enjoyment of a privilege. The renunciation of a privilege need not be explained by the intervention of authority, nor as being calculated, but may be merely the resolution of an emotional conflict, the pattern of which has already been observed in the animal kingdom. (1969)

Despite all the reservations made necessary by the difference in the objects of study, this interpretative scheme seems to agree with the phenomena described, and the line of investigation it inspires should prove fruitful for the approach to the relationship between the foster parents and the lodgers. In effect, after forcing ourselves to follow the milieu's own analysis of this relationship, stated in its own terms, we have discovered the presence of a conflict closely associated with a feeling of menace lying below the surface of practical, normative statements. In instituting the rule of distance and in raising its prescriptions to the level of a practical moral code, is the group of foster parents not trying to overcome the contradiction of its life of openness towards those who are normally hidden behind the walls of the asylum? And whilst participating in their social integration, are its efforts to prevent their intrusion into the private domain not an attempt to avert contact with insanity?

The problem of the fear inspired by mental illness now becomes a foreground issue. We have frequently noted both the signs of this fear and the refusal to acknowledge its existence or to confront the awareness of it. In this connection, let us recall the role played by the affirmation of custom. The protection provided by the Colony, the reassurances given by experience and the refutation of certain prejudices serve to expel the anxiety aroused by contact with the mentally ill from the field of everyday concerns. But this anxiety, which is mastered at the rational level in social perception and organization, reemerges in the interpersonal relationship where it is expressed in the form of a system of control elaborated by the milieu. This system, the principle of which is guided by the relationship with insanity, then assumes the imperative character of a safety measure. But if, despite the denials, everything functions as if to parry a danger and dominate a fear, then it must be possible to bring to light the raw indices of the anxiety which inspires this defence of the rules and to understand what the group is protecting itself against with its dualist organization which serves to conceal both the defensive process and its object.

When speaking about their contact with the mentally ill in the private context of the placement, our interviewees showed themselves little inclined to give direct expression to the associated fears, a reticence we had already noted in the case of public contact. It is sufficient, however, to consider some of the modes and contradictions which modify the practice of lodging the patient to discover proof of this fear, and this is corroborated by the explanations offered by the foster parents.

An example is provided by the condition for the opening of a placement. Apart from those who perpetuate a family tradition, the majority of foster parents allow a considerable period to pass before taking up their "career". As proof of this we can cite the relatively advanced age of the foster parents at the opening of the placement and the delay in taking lodgers observed by those who come from the Colony:

> When I arrived I already knew the region vaguely. No one had ever spoken very well of it because . . . Some relatives of mine lived here and we used to visit them and I used to watch the lodgers. But originally I didn't think of coming to live in the region and I thought to myself, 'My God, one day if I had to come here and have them I don't know if I could get used to it.' At first I was frightened. When I arrived I said, 'I don't know if I'll be able to get used to these people, because you don't know who you're going to get.' That was it. When I arrived I said, 'When we've settled in here, later on, then I'll see whether . . . ' But you have to live in the region for a while before . . .

In general, material contingencies are blamed for delays in opening a placement. These may be a shortage of premises or too much work for the mother of the family etc. However, even if the required installations are present, a waiting period is still frequently observed. Furthermore, the argument of family responsibilities is fallacious as these depend on the number of children and do not decline with their age. In any case, it is sufficient to press the point, and the reason for the delay reveals itself as the anxiety of living in continual contact with the mentally ill. An old tenant farmer and his wife tell how they became foster parents in 1935.

(The man) We had relatives at Valigny. We visited them quite often and they had lodgers. That's where we saw them. And then luck played its part. We took a farm in Valigny in 1933, in the place where our relatives had the lodgers. Well, we said, 'We don't want them'. No, we were scared of them.

(The woman continues) We were young and we visited our cousins. The lodger was there too, eating at a little table in the kitchen. And I said, 'I wouldn't like to have a lodger because if I had one I wouldn't dare let him eat with me. I would be frightened of him.'

(The man again) I asked the owner of the farm, 'Madame, I'd like you to have a servant's room built for me.' She said, 'Yes, but I'll have a lodger's room built for you.' Well, I told her, 'That doesn't mean a lot to us.' 'If you ask me for a room it's as good as done,' she said. And that's not all. She had lodgers as well. – 'I'll ask for some for you. When you arrive, you'll find everything waiting for you.' Straightaway. Well, we weren't too happy with that.

(The woman) Straightaway. We weren't all that, not all that . . . What scared me most was being all alone when the men had gone to work in the fields. I was scared that he would come. I was scared. I was scared . . . I wasn't so sure about it. I said to myself, 'What if I was alone one day and he came . . . to attack me. You know, like that, to ask something of me. Well, I wasn't so sure, not so sure at all . . . In the end we got used to them and when we had got used to the way they were, when we saw that they weren't wicked, we got used to them very quickly.

This apprehension is overcome by the guarantees given by the psychiatric institution, the knowledge gained through habit and the precautions the foster parents arm themselves with when they receive the lodgers. This makes it easy for them to display a feeling of security, to deny any fear or any problem. And if an initial fear is admitted at a personal level, then its persistence in everyday life is never acknowledged.

Nevertheless, a more obscure, more profound unease remains, identifiable only in the actions it provokes. An example is provided by the relationship between the age of the children and the opening of the placement. From what is said, the presence of children appears to be no problem for the accommodation of lodgers. Why then is the installation of patients delayed until or even long after the children reach school age? In fact, it is a question of a measure of which the foster parents remain ignorant, both in its existence as a very general tendency and in its significance. However, some 76% of foster parents act in this way and, in doing so, reveal the implementation of a protective mechanism which veils the fear on which it is based. The work of the mother sometimes explains the postponement of the acceptance of lodgers. But the fact that families with children tend to have higher capacity placements does not accord with the hypothesis of the extra burden the lodgers cause the mother, unless the supervision of young children becomes an integral part of her work and that, exacerbated by the presence of the lodgers, she takes on responsibilities which are not compatible with the rest of her activities. What does this mean, if not that preserving the children from contact with the patients is an obsessive and imperative duty which alone can confer a feeling of security?

> My son has never been in contact with the patients. When he was with them, we were there as well . . . He was six or seven when we had them. And right at the start we explained to him that they were people . . . patients who he should keep clear of . . . I was lucky to have a sensible son. He paid attention to me and I've never had any problems with him and the patients. He listened to what I said. To start with the patients don't really live in the house. I make them stay in their room and my son doesn't go there. He never disturbs them. He's never had the bother of going to their room. I've never had any problems on that score . . . Because children, you really can't leave them with the patients.

This anxiety comes from the ignorance and incomprehension of the children together with their habitualization to the lodger's presence and even the attraction the lodgers have for them:

> The children are used to seeing the mental patients. It's like the children who are born nowadays. They've barely opened their eyes and they're watching television.

> And it's strange, isn't it? The children like them. They like to be with them, you can't stop them. They like to play with them . . .

It is also associated with the risks which might be posed by the behaviour of the child or the carelessness of the patient. For example:

> A lot of people have lodgers and young children as well. The children get used to being with them. They don't pay attention. There may be parents who say, 'Try to keep away from this one or that one . . . '. They're quite all right to start with . . . It all depends on the way their parents bring them up. The small children don't give me anything to complain about. But there are places where it's different, where they are frightened. If you leave the children with them they can turn nasty or suffer an attack of nerves if they are always in the presence of children who irritate them or interrogate them, who ask them embarrassing questions.

> You have to watch the children. You never know what some of them are going to do, take them walking with them and then lose them, get them to climb onto something and then let them fall, get them to do stupid things or give them something to eat which . . .

> Places where there are young children, I have to say, before they go to school, well I think that's shocking. What's that like for the children! They can't behave like they do with the lodgers around them. Me, I don't have any, but if I did have kids I wouldn't take any lodgers until the children had started going to school . . . because there are a lot of lodgers who get quite friendly with the children. Because they don't have anyone to . . . they need affection as well. I think that's how the bad habits develop. They get them from the lodgers.

Also of importance is the fear of the risks which are linked to a mental pathology whose potential manifestations are more worrying than the established forms which the region has become used to:

> My mother had lodgers before I had them. We used to be together with the lodgers. They were always around us. We used to tease them then much more than they do nowadays. That's changed a lot. The children don't notice them now. I've got a grandson who doesn't even know what a lodger is. When he was little he used to say: 'I want to be two things, a vet or a lodger. I want to be a lodger to do Mummy's shopping and to look after the little animals.' I know he meant it because he never said anything bad. Earlier there were a lot who were like children, they played with the kids . . . They were harmless. And we were more indulgent with them about a lot of things because they were, how shall I put it, because they were unfortunate. Nowadays we get the bad ones. It's not the same. You mustn't. I've told my children not to play with them.

In fact, before the age when the child can understand her commands, the mother only feels reassured if she can exercise complete control and operate an absolute separation:

> I'm not scared for the children. They're all on the look out. They're always careful.

> And the hardest thing is when a baby starts to walk. That's very difficult. That's the time when they have to get used to the lodgers. Later they won't realize that there's a danger. Because even if you've got a lodger who isn't dangerous and you can leave the children with him, you don't know if you're going to keep that lodger . . . You can't forecast anything. And then you can't tell what's going on in a patient's head, can you? You should try to get them to avoid the lodgers as much as possible because that can cause problems. Because a baby likes to be on someone's lap. You can't let the lodger keep the baby on his lap. It's not that I'm frightened of the lodgers or that they disgust me. But personally I think that it's better to bring up the children to get by on their own without being together with a patient . . . My daughter, who is eleven, she helps me, she takes the lodgers their food and all that. But she never clings to their side or sits next to them. She

> knows that I don't like it. With the children, there's no question. They
> know that they mustn't.

Even though the strictness of the mother's vigilance can be relaxed as the
child grows older and internalizes these prohibitions or even if older children
are present who can supervise the younger ones,[1] it is only going to school
that offers total safety:

> It interests them for a while when they understand [the children]. When
> they go to school, it's over. But up to school age . . .
>
> You shouldn't let the children have any contact with them. When they go
> to school there's nothing to stop you having lodgers.

This removal from contact with the lodgers makes protection certain and
makes it unnecessary to justify a separation whose necessity is not always clear
to the children:

> It's quite a problem with young children. Later on they understand better.
> It's different, you can reason with them. They can understand that these
> people are not like us. But they don't really understand that they have to be
> on the look out, that they mustn't get too close.

At school it is the peer group that takes over from the parents and transforms
obedience into absolute adherence:

> We're all used to seeing it but we don't take any notice. At school if there's
> a child who spends a lot of time with the lodgers we exclude him until he
> understands. And really the children shouldn't be together with the
> patients. They get used to it when they are very young.

The order which he previously obeyed is now internalized by the child as an
unchallengeable norm. The distance which was based on a fear whose causes
he never understood is transformed into a mode of discrimination. Waiting
until the child is older bypasses these stages of supervision and admonishment
in which fear appears in a raw state. This fear is that constant, explicit
reminders will become intolerable and that the spontaneous regulation of the
practices of the placement will be blurred as a result of their constant
acceptance. The relationship between the child and the lodger reveals the
dynamic by which the distance which originates in fear erases an awareness of
this fear when the distance is institutionalized as a norm. This, too, is clearly
expressed: "We're not afraid that they'll come. They won't enter the house."

---

[1] Lower ages are considerably less represented when brothers and sisters belong to the same age
group than when they belong to different age groups, irrespective of their sex.

At other times, when fear is thought to have been suppressed, it re-emerges and displays the contradiction in the way in which the relationship with the lodgers is conceived and lived. This contradiction lies at the heart of the conflict between the familial and instrumental models of behaviour. It may wear the mask of chance which is used to explain the durability or the failure of the relationship between the foster parent and the lodger, or it may appear in the disorder of the characteristics which make a good or bad lodger. By way of example, let us turn to an elementary means of evaluating the lodger, the opposition of cleanliness and dirtiness. The good lodger is always clean and the bad lodger is always dirty. In accordance with the ideal scale of attributes given by the explicit norm of the lodger, we should not expect to find any degree of compromise with dirtiness. It is a grave fault which causes the foster parent the most work, reduces the value of her household installations and damages her standing with the Colony.

A reason for rejection because of these practical considerations, irrespective of whether it provokes disgust, dirtiness is also a reason given for separation of foster parent and lodger, in particular in the case of meals. And yet, they "put up with it". There are numerous foster parents who, despite what they say, "have done everything" to keep a lodger who is well known for his dirtiness. What is at work here? Why this contradiction between actions and words, if not the fact that dirtiness, however unpleasant and troubling it might be, seems to be a lesser ill than other, more frightening characteristics? If we follow the paths taken by these women, we find that the initial period of observation leads to the diagnosis of dirtiness as attributable to nature, illness or education. This is followed by the attempt to correct it and the prognosis for the future, and finally the weighting which relativizes the theoretical importance of dirtiness. The seriousness of the case and its interpretation dictate the final attitude of the foster parent, but the correspondence between dirtiness and insanity results in distortions of judgement. If the foster parent fails to improve the lodger's behaviour she will be more intransigent the more adaptable the lodger initially appeared to be. Persistence in dirtiness is then attributed to a refusal, a resistance, and is then seen to reveal a potential for wickedness, that other face of insanity which may have consequences for other spheres of existence and which can lead to rejection. If there originally seemed to be no likelihood of eradicating the behaviour, the foster parent shows herself to be more indulgent towards cases caused by "illness" than cases caused by "nature" because her failure emphasizes the aberrant character of the behaviour in a different way. Dirtiness which is "part of him", in his character, forms part of the personality of the lodger and expresses a troubling disorder. Equally, as the product or deviation of a disturbed will, it sheds a negative light on all his acts. On the other hand, persistence in dirtiness caused "by illness" reinforces its pathological nature and does not impair the personality or responsibility of the lodger: "He isn't free." Moreover, dirtiness seems to syphon off the major part of the negativity of insanity and is a less disturbing manifestation of the illness than others. Ultimately, it is reassuring. One then begins to understand the foster parent who declared, "a bad lodger is a dirty lodger" and then told us of her oldest one, "He's been with me for twenty-seven years. He's not bad at all. I'm not frightened of him." Of course, "He's dirty. I could kill him sometimes. Every day he goes in his trousers." To have to wash a pair of trousers every day for twenty-seven years! But, "He's not wicked. That's what I'm most afraid of. I would hate to change. I would prefer to put up with it." Dirtiness which is due to illness is unthreatening. That alone makes it worth putting up with, whatever unpleasantness that entails, provided that it does not exceed a limit of revulsion which appears to be quite high:

> We're not too badly stocked. Y has got one, X . . . , who pees upstairs and always in the same place! . . . He does all kinds of things, all sorts of dirtiness . . . This morning I did the washing and it was all wet yet again. And he never puts his sheets out to dry. He puts the sheet away somewhere, you know . . . that smells dreadful. The doctor said, 'You can smell it . . . ' You're not used to it smelling like that when you visit someone, and urine has a strong smell. I don't know . . . We have trouble looking after him. We've tried everything, everything . . . I've got used to it. It went on for a week at the start. And then after that, every night or near enough. I've got used to it. He's not wicked. I mean to say, he's the sort of bloke who doesn't lose his temper if something doesn't suit him. He keeps it in. He doesn't say anything. He sulks a bit, but it's not that bad. No, I don't want to change.

Fear makes unpleasantness a choice of preference, causes the renunciation of comfort and the contravention of an order based on material determinism.

This is the explanation of the apparent disorder derived from a superficial analysis of the relationship between the foster parents and the lodgers. The reaction to contact with insanity influences the functioning of the placements and modifies the relationship with the lodgers, causing deviations from the way these are structured by the statutory and instrumental constraints. Equally, it does not operate solely at the level of simple personal and psychological contingency or at that of disorder. Of course, the level of anxiety induced by contact with insanity differs from one person to another, as does the importance attached to a particular quality, a particular failing or a particular compensatory characteristic. But the examples which have allowed us to illustrate its workings show, on the one hand, that it produces a system of social regulation which aims both to dominate the unease and the dangers, whether imaginary or real, as well as to diminish the intensity of the foster parents' awareness of them, and that, on the other hand, it plays a motivational or supporting role in the processes of separation and discrimination.

This discovery of an emotional source for the institutionalization of the relationship with the lodgers opens the gates to a flood of questions. To start with, the way in which behaviour is discussed in the examples we have just looked at underlines the importance of the role played by the conception of mental illness. It becomes necessary to explore the different contents of these representations if we are to explain the phenomena we have observed so far. In the second place, if social organization is held together by the distress occasioned by images of insanity and the contact with the mentally ill, we still have to explain how defence of the individual is transformed into defence of the group. One example of this is the transformation of the forbidding of children to enter into contact with the patients into the exclusion from the peer group of those who infringe the prohibition. Our aim now is to identify the representations of insanity and to link them to the dynamics and symbols of society.

PART THREE

THE PEOPLE OF THOSE HOMES

Chapter Five

Understanding without Knowledge

> The illness? I don't know. We don't know
> anything about that. They are ill. They've got
> this or they've got that. But we don't know about
> it. We open a placement and we take them in.
> We don't ask what they've got or what they've
> done. As long as they aren't unpleasant.
>
> There's a mystery surrounding all their lives.
>
> All the illnesses are pretty much the same.
>
> You need a while to get to know them. That only
> happens in the long run. You think of them like
> the others. Because it's only in the long term that
> you learn how to handle them.

One trait of striking consistency was marked in all our discussions concerning the lodgers, the difficulty of speaking of them as mental patients or, more precisely, that of approaching mental illness through them. The more said about their profitability and their role, the greater the reserve or awkwardness on this point. The embarrassment and reticence shown by our interviewees at directly confronting in conversation any aspect of the lodger's psychiatric state was shown in their statements, their hesitations, their refusals, their silences, their evasion or recasting of questions, physical signs of discomfort (blushing, sweating, trembling of the hands, laughter etc.). This mode of silence threw a new light on the assertions contained in their speech. Might it be that the strictly delineated social profile of the lodger conceals the significance of insanity in the shadows, far from the anxious gaze of the foster parents?

But the most pervasive form of evasion manifested itself at the register of consciousness itself. "Mental illness? I don't know about that." From the very start, all our interviewees forbade themselves any statement expressing knowledge of this subject. Ignorance was, at the level of representation, the counterpart to custom at the level of contact with insanity. It was as if by becoming the object of an explicit knowledge or formulation, the power of mental illness to generate anxiety would be released. Yet at the same time surely a population so closely involved in the functioning of the psychiatric hospital would have had the opportunity to acquire an outline knowledge of the subject thanks to the combination of personal experience and contact with the hospital staff. Surely the exchange of information between nurses would further the circulation of such knowledge. Our enquiry was to discover that many conceptions existed of what the mental patient is and does, the way in which he is attacked by the illness, of what mental illness is and where it comes from.

However, many detours were needed before we could get through to these conceptions which always referred to a dual object, forming an indissoluble bond between patient and illness. We passed through concrete descriptions of cases, comments on events, behaviour, expressions, real-life narratives etc. These conceptions always emerged indirectly, sometimes without the interviewees knowing it, and were almost invariably preceded by an absolute refusal to admit any psychiatric knowledge: "We can't imagine the kind of illness they've got."

The Absence of Psychiatric Knowledge

At an initial level, ignorance affirmed in this way can be explained by a delimiting of function. The foster parent is not a nurse and hospital regulations state that no medical details concerning the lodgers should be revealed at the time of placement. Obedience to this rule assures the security guaranteed by the hospital authorities:

> The illness? I couldn't tell you. You'll have to find out from up there. That's not my responsibility.

> We don't know, we can't know. We haven't seen their files. It's better that way and, anyway, we're not entitled. It's all well organized. They're well supervised. The administration looks after that.

> We're quite happy not to know too much. In any case, we know that when they are placed they're so full of drugs that they can't . . . when they're placed they look well cared for, well-groomed and everything.

A part of this discretion can be accounted for by a head-in-the-sand mentality: "I can't tell you much about the illness, perhaps it's better not to try to understand too much." The denial of knowledge is an effect of the fear of knowing too much, of stumbling on hidden defects in the lodger which may be waiting to emerge at any time under the dual face of criminality and the uncontrollable fit.

In fact what is understood as knowledge of the illness is not a medical approach to the case but rather knowledge of the past life or event which led to the patient's confinement and which can be discovered either by recourse to the "file" or by direct communication with the patient, both of which are difficult to countenance.

The "file", with the administrative and legal aura it evokes, is the repository of obscure and disquieting information. Even the use of the ambiguous term "homes" to denote the psychiatric hospitals reveals that they are more readily attributed a function of imprisonment and repression than one of assistance and care:

> Some people say they are sent up to the ward as a punishment . . . Mme X . . . got told off because she said they had taken one of her lodgers to the ward to punish him. They say it's to treat them, not to punish them . . . But really they take them to punish them . . . Once big C . . . insulted us, you should have heard the way he swore at us, and as for the gestures he made. We told the Colony and they kept him naked in the cell they use for people in straitjackets. He was like that for three days. When he came out, he didn't start again.

In the same way, the equating of "knowledge" with the "file" reveals a vision of mental illness as criminality:

> We don't want to know what the lodgers have got. You can be sure that among those people there are some who've done bad things. Maybe they've stolen. No murderers though. We don't want to know what's in the files.

Even the opening of the file appears to be related to a police procedure. The psychiatrist who performs this act exercises considerable skills. The interview with the patient becomes an interrogation, clinical analysis becomes an enquiry, diagnosis becomes a verdict:

> There are some strange cases, you know. There was a patient the doctor wanted to get to talk. I didn't know the case very well but he was dangerous and the doctor kept on trying to make him talk. The patient didn't want to say what had got him there, nothing about his life, absolutely nothing. In the end he talked. The doctor recorded it on a tape recorder. The doctor said: 'He told me a lot but he didn't tell me everything.' He left the next day because the doctor thought he was dangerous.

The investigation seems to have less recourse to medical science than to an interrogatory skill and a somewhat esoteric kind of insight which justifies the discretionary powers of the psychiatrist within the coercive organization of the hospital:

> I think it's the file that's important at the start. We had one who stayed for two months. It was all the same to us. He was very happy here. He was an

excellent worker, a big, strapping man. He certainly knew how to work. And they sent him back! They wanted to take him back to the Colony. He was desperate. 'No,' he said, 'I don't want to go back.' He left in the lorry with my husband. He'd liked living here and we'd tried to make him comfortable. But the doctor. I don't know what was wrong with him but the doctor sent him back to the asylum. He had asked for him and interrogated him and then he kept him. Well, he really raged. 'I want to go back to X . . . ,' he said, 'I was happy there. If you don't take me back, I'll escape.' So they brought him back and then there was another visit and the doctor sent him away. I asked the supervisor about it and he said: 'He's got a very bad file, you know.' We didn't notice anything. We really didn't think . . . We had had no trouble at all with him. So you see, they watch them carefully after all. They know things which we don't notice.

The proof of the fact that we don't know what they are or what they've done is the case of the boy who had killed a child. Perhaps it's just an idea of mine, but the psychiatrist didn't recognize it. If he had recognized it he would be in a home.

And every year some of them leave the Colony. The director lets them leave and become civilians. According to him it's possible to tell which ones can leave. There are some he's recognized. It's difficult to say.

For those who lack the specialist's mastery and means of control, such troubling discoveries remain inaccessible and undesirable. The fact that his past is enshrouded in mystery makes the relationship with the lodger tenable, removing the threats he is thought to pose from the foster parent's conscience.

A further danger of revelation comes from direct communication with the patient and with his relatives, whom the foster parents treat with considerable reserve and discretion:

I asked little Paul's mother about him. She didn't say anything. You know, you can't ask people too much. It's unpleasant. It's embarrassing.

Still, there's something wrong with them. Thank heavens everybody isn't like that. But as for what they've got, it's the doctor who can tell you that. Me, I don't take any notice. I don't ask. Oh no, and anyway, why humiliate them?

The presumed contents of the "file" reveal a criminal vision of the illness which metamorphoses into an image of ignominy because of the reticence to discuss it. The shame of the illness reappears, and with it comes the fear that on seeing his faults exposed the patient will react to his questioner with a fit of rage or annoyance:

We ask them as little as possible. Perhaps it wouldn't be a bad thing but they wouldn't like it. They might take offence at it. What would you do? They've been in the homes, they could . . .

This prudence is redoubled by the magic power of words. To talk about the illness is to summon up its symbolic presence and, through its recollection, to provoke its resurgence:

> I don't like to talk about the illness with them. Like M . . . who is, after all, . . . You couldn't say that he's a genius, but at least you can talk to him. But it's still better not to talk to him about it. If it were to happen to him again. You have to think how someone like that, who had learnt a profession, was in the army, was a normal person. I could imagine that to talk to him about it, that could . . . He would talk about it again, that might bother him. He would think about it again. On the other hand, he has talked about it lots of times since he's been here. But I never take the conversation any further when he's talking about that.

> I've never asked them why they were in the homes. Speaking about it might do some harm. It might make it worse. Because there are some who have done certain things. I'd rather not know . . . You don't know for sure but you have your ideas.

Fear impedes conversation just as it diverts attention and suspends discussion in order to prevent the emergence of this still undefined something which the patient carries in him and which seems to escape awareness.

The Patients Who Are Not Ill

In some ways the foster parents' profession of ignorance and refusal to provide information place insanity outside the domain of the medical. It is never analysed or described as a medical condition. For example, it is extremely rare to find medical terminology being used to designate its forms. Alongside notions such as "innocence", "alcoholism", "epilepsy" heard frequently in popular speech, we only encountered the word "depression" some ten times, "schizophrenia" just once (and that in the mouth of a relative of one of the nurses), as was also the case with "neurasthenia" and more popular expressions such as "persecution mania", "sexual disease", "syphilitic disease". This paucity of denomination can no doubt be explained by the silence of the hospital. It also points to a reluctance to turn to nosographic frameworks in the constant juxtaposition of multifarious minute descriptions of symptoms and the unified designation of their cause: the illness.

> Look, they aren't ill. You can't really say that they're ill. They're abnormal. That's what it is with the mental illness they've got. Me, I don't think of it

as an illness, like X . . . who died of illness, the sort of illness which everybody gets.

This is why the psychiatrists and, to a lesser extent, the relatives are reproached with not knowing the lodgers or how to treat them "as patients". The competence of the psychiatrist is contested if his approach to illness is anything other than medical or repressive. Those who simply listen to the patient, who pay attention to his desires, who are interested in the conditions surrounding his life, are reproached with forgetting, or never knowing, that they are dealing with a "patient", and exceeding their functions in impinging on the domain of the foster parents:

> They listen to the patients and then afterwards, when the women come round, they tell us off. They have no idea what the lodgers are like.

> You have to be strict with them, you know. And we have a better idea of what they're like than the . . . director. After all, we live with them every day, and you should hear the lies they tell. At the Colony they don't really know what it's like, they listen to them too much. The doctors listen to them a bit too much because they aren't always with them. And they tell them things which aren't at all true.

The same attitude is shown towards families who come to visit the lodgers:

> When the relatives arrive, it hits them. It does something to them. The foster parents understand the lodgers better because they live with them. But the relatives, they're there for three or four days. None of the relatives understand cases like that. O.K., their child is a patient. They see their child in the countryside, well looked after, enjoying the fresh air. They don't see what he would be like if he hadn't been treated, drugged. That wouldn't do. The parents don't know about the illness. They never see their child for what he is. He's a patient, he's not . . .

Juxtaposing the approaches of knowledge and inexperience, the claim to know more about how to understand the patients implies a conception of mental illness whose initial elements are indicated by the prognosis which determines both the actions of the foster parent and the criticism of intervention on the part of the relatives or the doctors. This pessimistic prognosis is partly based on assumptions associated with confinement, partly on the outcome of attempts at adaptation:

> They're there because they've got something.

> What's more, we don't know where they come from or what's happened, but . . . how I shall I put it, it's difficult to say, maybe some of them improve, but none of them are cured. I get the feeling that if they're at Ainay it's because they're there to stay.

> They don't improve mentally. In a certain sense they're incurable. On the other hand you can teach them to do the odd thing.

> If you tell them to do something they don't react like someone . . . normal. You get the feeling that there's something wrong.

What do these incessantly repeated words indicate if not the material, irremediable character of mental illness?

To say that the patients are incurable, that their ability to learn is limited, that "something" disturbs their functioning, is, at the very least, to suggest that they are attacked in their very being. And one might well dare suggest that this attack is itself material in nature:

> Some of them improve but it stays there. It's there. It's there. There's nothing to be done. It's there. It's there.

The distinctions employed to designate the illness and its subject confirm that it is seen as natural. Contrasted with the "normal illnesses", it is not "an illness like everybody gets". Instead, mental illness is situated and situates its subjects at the level of being. Itself different – "Mental illness, it doesn't trouble you, it's different" – it is not linked to its subject by a "to have" but by a "to be": "They haven't got any illness, they're ill." The quality it designates becomes a state: "They aren't ill, they're patients." The workings of insanity, neither transient nor external, are inscribed in the sufferer as a condition of his being:

> The one who died, he said that if you're ill through some illness, you can get better, but if you're ill in the brain, then it's impossible. You can't get better, never. He admitted it!

The reproaches levelled at the doctors and the families show, moreover, that mental illness produces a qualitative transformation which places the patient in a separate category:

> No, they're not like the rest of us. They've all got something, all of them, they're all abnormal somehow or other. All of them are abnormal. Some of them seem all right for a little while and then later you hear them say something which shows that they've got something. They're all lads who have been drugged, been treated, had lumbar punctures. They've had something. There are all types here.

This category comes from a different regime: "They're patients, they aren't able to live like we do."

Any intervention which seems to call this regime into question appears as an error of judgement, the error of seeing the patient as a normal man. This regime thus also delineates the image of a nature-of-the-normal-patient, or in other words an implicit theory of man and his madness. It is from this image, as it is revealed by the methods of behaviour and the differential treatments reserved for the patients, that we must proceed if we are to grasp how insanity is conceived and understood despite and beyond the initial negation of any specific knowledge.

What it Means to Understand

In effect, the greater the reserve shown by the foster parents when it comes to formulating a general knowledge of the mental patients, the more intent they are on emphasizing the necessity of understanding each of the lodgers they deal with at the practical level, and in insisting on their own competence in this regard. Far from being contradictory, these two attitudes are complementary. For the foster parents, knowledge only exists if it is particularized by its object, its purpose and its mode. They feel that experience has made them competent to pronounce on the apprehension of the individual characteristics, attitudes and behaviour through which each case reveals its "character" and "nature". This apprehension has two objectives: first, to evaluate the level of conformity and scope for adaptation made possible by the illness with regard to the practical and psychological expectations of the foster parent; second, to discover, in favourable cases, the means to achieve and preserve this adaptation. In its particularity, understanding – in the sense of knowing and influencing – involves a general knowledge, and the passage from the former to the latter confirms the analyses we have already made.

Each new arrival at a placement is greeted as the bearer of a full range of potentials and only closer examination is able to distinguish those which are present from those which are not. This is the significance of the observation phase:

> During the first few days we just don't know! You learn by having them. You keep them and you study them a little.

> You need time to get to know them. If you were asked the next day, 'Is it going well, is it going badly?' you wouldn't be able to give an answer.

The directing of this preliminary study at the pathological dimension of the person known as "the patient" and not yet as "the lodger" possesses a number of objectives. At the very least, it aims to discover whether the pathology is compatible with life in the placement. Seen from this viewpoint, two types of patient are quickly judged. A positive evaluation is accorded to retarded patients and a negative one to very "nervous" patients (besides indocility which is related to the lodger's readiness to submit to his role, the reasons for immediate rejection of a lodger are nervousness, restlessness, twitching and epilepsy because of their "frightening" nature). Things become more complex when it comes to interpreting ambiguous characteristics such as certain forms of silence or withdrawal, certain ways of looking. What are they? Expressions of discomfort or unease felt by the patient who suddenly finds himself in a new placement, signs of a timid or frightened nature or, on the contrary, indications of a potential for evil so often attributed to the withdrawn, silent, brooding man?

> He used to lie on the grass without saying anything. I sent him back. I don't like silent people. I get the feeling they might be dangerous.

What can be done? The patient has to be acclimatized and, at the same time, he has to be observed "to see if he is a difficult or an easy character, if he starts to talk or if he becomes more withdrawn". It is only through a sustained period of analysis that the true face of the patient can be discerned behind the layers of presumptions, as one foster parent was able to tell us:

> Jean, that was five years ago. At the start it was always the same. Jean frightened me. I told myself that he looked at us strangely. I didn't know whether he was a Russian or a Pole. He looked a bit like the Russians. But now he's a good lodger, patient and polite as well. At the start it was because we didn't know him. Someone said to me, 'he watches you all the time, he's always looking for you . . . '. But in fact he was quite a timid man . . . At the start he was a man who never said anything . . . well, he still is . . . if you said anything at all to him, well! . . . I didn't say anything to him . . . but he had been in a very disrupted family. He fell ill. I got the impression that he was suffering from a nervous depression . . . We didn't really know. We didn't know. We didn't know what was in his file . . . We were scared at first because he was a lodger and he had been ill and we didn't know him. We didn't know what he might do. At that time we didn't think he was dangerous or they wouldn't have placed him with us, but, all the same, if you're not used to them, when you haven't had them around you for a bit, you say to yourself: 'The way he looks at me . . . It's a bit . . . ' And in fact you're quite often mistaken.

Observation can remain a permanent state because even if the foster parents fail to discover anything worrying, they are still always on the alert for signs which need to be suppressed or reported to the Colony. This concern lies behind the vigilant attention paid to the patient's character in order to evaluate the significance of any change in his behaviour:

> We live with them. They're with us all the time. You see if they are dangerous or not. You have to keep on watching them. You watch them and after two or three weeks you know what they are, what they're capable of doing . . . You're always in contact with them. And if they turn ill we tell the Colony to come and get them.

Finally and most importantly, it is the information garnered from direct examination which, in every case, acts as the surest guide to the mutual adaptation on which the stability of the patient depends:

> They don't make you keep them. It's up to you to keep them if you can. I take them as they are. I don't try to change them. If I ask for a patient, I ask for one without an incurable illness, but I don't care about the rest. I'm the one who tries to change. I try to find out how to behave, and as long as he isn't bad I try to find a way to adapt to his illness.

It is only at the cost of an unceasing supervision of their own and their partner's reactions during the course of their communication with the lodger that the foster parents will be able to choose which of the repertoire of "techniques of control" will be most efficient in surmounting any particular difficulty and in "making-a-life-with" the lodger, a life which should last as long as possible because each change represents another leap into the unknown:

> Once you get to know the patients, you prefer to keep them. Because they get used to you. And you, you get used to them as well, you learn how to handle them. The little young one. A year ago, when they brought him, he was quite diabolical. Now, he's no worse than the others. Of course there are times . . . you know perfectly well that they are ill. But when you know how to handle them!

It is a life in which adaptation and habit are equated with malleability and flexibility because of the necessity of ascertaining the right mode of behaviour which may change from one day, from one moment, to the next, depending on the circumstances, on the objective, on the patient's response, on the "whim" of the moment. In this, however, a number of foster parents show a rare psychological finesse in their apprehension of the patient's reactions, together with a considerable amount of what they call the "patience to put up with it" which helps them suppress their own displays of ill-temper. Let us listen to their voice through the words of this woman who wanted to "educate" her patient and, when all is said and done, succeeded better than his parents or the authorities:

> That one is very undisciplined, very obstinate, and his father was coming for a visit. I said to him: 'Go and wash yourself, go and have a shave before kissing your parents.' I gave him some *eau de Cologne*. Well, he didn't wash. His father said: 'I understand. You haven't washed. Your foster mother told you to. You haven't changed.' Then his father got angry. His father has never been able to do anything with him. Then in the evening I told him: 'Go and wash. If you don't wash you won't go for dinner with your parents.' And when I said that – 'And then I'll give you some clean clothes to wear.' – when I said that he went and washed after all. You have to treat them like

children. You have to tell them: 'You have to do this if you want to get that.' I'm telling you this because we have to live with them, and really . . . That one is quite stubborn. On Monday morning, I had a pullover of my husband's which I had given to him. I had washed it and I put it in the cupboard in case I have someone one day. Because at the Colony they don't always take very good care of their clothes. He took the pullover and he unstitched it and I wasn't able to get him to give it back so I could mend it. The supervisor said: 'You won't get any tobacco' and he replied that he didn't care about the tobacco, that he had some anyway. You have to know how to handle them. I got it back from him by saying: 'I'm going to wash it. If you don't give it back you won't have any more pullovers, you won't have anything else at all.' He had grown attached to that pullover. Before, I had said to him: 'The doctor has come. She says that if you don't give it back she'll punish you, she won't give you any tobacco' – And he said that it was none of her business, that she wasn't from the Colony. Well, I got it back from him yesterday by saying that and I think he took it again this evening. He's thirty-five years old but he's like a child. You have to know how to handle them and that takes a bit of patience.

The example illustrates both the development of the process of "knowing how to handle" (selection, by trial and error, of the method of control) and the pragmatism of the foster parent's thought. The foster parent knew how to touch the lodger at a sensitive point, his attachment to her. But the fact is that despite her ability to manipulate him, she did not truly identify this, the implication being that she evaluates the technique by its effect and not by the significance it bears. Moreover, she also denies the emotions on which she plays. Should we not see in this interpretation, which we have so frequently encountered elsewhere, a sign that depth of feeling, the affect, is denied to the patient? This point is worthy of attention and we shall return to it later. It also tempts us to see in all these situations of interaction the influence of something like a spontaneous psychological theory which makes it possible to distinguish between those aspects of observed behaviour which derive from the illness and those which result from other factors and which influence the type of conduct applied.

The Pathological, the Psychological and the Natural

As we have seen, the lodger's behaviour is judged as a function of the origin attributed to it. From this point of view, the pathological is situated on the same level as character, mentality or education, namely the level of causality. When considered in connection with the entrenchment and persistence of behaviour, the illness, like character, is assigned to an order which is in some way "natural" and more constraining than the "cultural" order which comprises mentality and education, twin functions of the group to which the individual belongs. In the case of mentality, the environment provides the normative framework which delineates the state of mind with regard to the fundamental values of life (work, effort, cooperation, sense of responsibility etc.) and, in the case of education, it provides the code of proprieties which moulds social behaviour. The social origin of these determining factors confers on them a certain plasticity with the result that the foster parents consider themselves to be in a position to adapt the lodger. The limits of this adaptation, however, are variable since other factors can interfere with or reinforce the factors of social determination.

Thus it is thought that the influence of age on the rigidity of behaviour differs depending on whether the behaviour derives from education or mentality. The chances of instilling new modes of behaviour are at their greatest when the age is low and diminish as age advances or social experience increases:

> In principle, the ones you can adapt the best are the ones you get while they are still young. Some older people adapt as well but you always do better in adapting the young ones to what you want, whatever that might be. It's not the same with a fifty-year-old who had a job in civilian life. It makes a difference.

> There's not a lot you can teach them. They're grown men after all. They've got the best part of their life behind them. It's difficult to change the way they go about things.

In contrast, the mentality of the young offers fewer possibilities of control than that of older individuals because it refers to values which are divergent from those of the adults:

> There's a great difference between the lodgers of earlier times and the ones we've got now. Then, we used to get people like ourselves, workers. Today it's not the same type of person. You don't find many young ones who want to work.

> The young don't have the same mentality. You find that in the lodgers as well, and most of all in the men. They don't have the same mentality as the women. They don't do as much, don't make the same effort as the women. A woman makes more effort than a man. And the kids are no longer brought up like we were. Out in the country, we used to go to school by bike. Nowadays, they take the kids to school by car. It's the mentality of the parents that changes, there's no doubt about that. They get the car out to go anywhere at all. It isn't good for the kids. You give them one thing and the next day they want something else. They do what you say then you let them do whatever they want and the next day they don't pay any attention to you. I wouldn't put up with being spoken to the way some kids speak to their mothers. They want to be served hand and foot. It's the parents who serve

them, and the parents aren't any better. It's the same with the young lodgers. I can see trouble ahead.

Sometimes the difference in education and the generation gap combine to form a double, insurmountable barrier between the world of the farmer and the world of the middle classes:

> The director has gone a bit far in wanting good rooms. At our place the night cabinet used to double as a dressing table. Now they want a dressing table as well. I can imagine that there are people, ones you wouldn't know were lodgers, who you would give a placement like that to. But there are others they could place in the country areas, people who know a bit about country life, who aren't middle-class. But today they're all educated, they're used to modern life.

> First of all I had some good ones but I haven't been well stocked since then. It's the shopkeepers who get the best lodgers. I don't want a middle-class one. People today, they've lived in the towns and they've been to school. They aren't country people any more. They don't have the same ways. They want napkins when they sit down to eat.

It is for this reason that the effort made to modify modes of undesirable behaviour which are attributed to mentality or education is soon replaced by an attitude of withdrawal similar to that produced by behaviour attributed to character or to illness. But this attitude is similar in appearance only: the respect and tolerant abandon it implies are not found in withdrawal, which is often a synonym for evasion or fearful rejection inspired by behaviour which is psychological or pathological in origin. Its social base, its involvement as a model, value or code of conduct, and its relative precariousness assign cultural causality to an order radically different from that of determination by character or illness.

The latter are, in fact, conceived as explanatory principles, inherent to the individual, which are impervious to the influence of any outside intervention:

> I want a patient who isn't bad either because of his nerves *or* because of his character. If it's the fault of the character then there's nothing to do. A bad character, that means he'll be there saying ridiculous things to me. Like I've seen in some places, you know. All the insults they can throw at a foster parent, they say them, even if the foster parent doesn't say anything to them . . . or where there are children, it doesn't make sense at all.

Illness and character diminish the role of influences from previous environments or the immediate surroundings. When they assume an unacceptable form and when their inflexibility points to a psychological or pathological origin, the foster parent attempts to put an end to interaction with the lodger either provisionally or definitively.

However, within this natural order, character and illness are accorded a distinct causal status. Any psychological explanation based on character – which, moreover, is the be-all and end-all of the psychological explanation – refers to characteristics which exert an invariable, specific influence on behaviour towards others. The reason for this behaviour is found in a certain type of *social reactivity* with which the individual is constitutionally imbued: "They've all got their own character." Thus the individual reacts to the other or to the situation he creates through his demands or his constraints in accordance with a constant mode of contentment or vindictiveness, sensitivity or indifference, expansiveness or withdrawal, acceptance or obstinacy, kindness or unpleasantness etc. This reactivity may be expressed in a more or less civilized manner. It is incapable of modification: "if it's natural for him to answer back" or "if shouting is part of him" there is nothing to be done:

> If it's because of their character, there's nothing you can do.

> They keep their character. If deep down that's what they're like, there's no point thinking of changing it.

Determination by pathology is interpreted in a variety of ways. Even if it produces behavioural characteristics as inflexible and persistent as those generated by character, it is not defined, as character is, as a set of dispositions which control a limited and specific sector of behaviour. The aspect of the unknown within mental illness makes it impossible to comprehend, aside from its distorted effects, but at the same time it reveals itself in fields as varied as social conduct, moral behaviour and practical activity. Treated as a state, assimilated to a "nature", pathology is thus radically differentiated from cultural determinations, even in cases where it appears at a relatively advanced age. Yet it simultaneously retains an autonomous status within the natural register: "They've all got their own character. The illness is separate from it."

This becomes particularly clear in the way the association of pathology with the other factors which determine conduct is conceived. On the one hand, in cases where the illness is advanced by way of an explanation as an alternative to character, then the latter is excluded and there is no combination of or interference between the two factors: "Wickedness, that can come from nerves *or* from character." When imputed to illness, behaviour loses the distinctive characteristic with which it was invested when perceived as an effect of character, namely that it is a self-orientation towards others. For this reason, temper or "shouting" which arise because of illness are less serious because they are denuded of intentionality:

> The big one, it's his illness which makes him shout. But he's not bad because of that. Anyone who came in when he's shouting might say they

were frightened. If they came in when he was like that it might scare them if they didn't know him. Me, I don't pay any attention. We ignore him and it passes over. When he starts shouting it's because he's ill, he gets angry. I ignore him. I listen to it and let him get on with it.

What is more, the pathological has no influence on the psychological. The solid entrenchment of character protects it from the illness:

The illness doesn't attack their character, I don't believe it. That comes from the nature of the patient. There are some who are perfectly happy. Well, that's in their nature, isn't it? You can find some who are very ill but who are always in a good mood. On the other hand there are some there's no point arguing with because you won't get anywhere. It all depends on character.

At most, the consciousness of being ill may "sour" the character or make the individual more "sensitive". Acquisition of the status of lodger may also reveal new dimensions of character. Reference is then made to the "patient's character" of the lodger. This covers the psychological traits which are linked to the exercise of a role (docility, fear etc.). But illness in no way affects the structure and the components of character which lie at the root of the patient's behaviour within society.

The same is not true of education and mentality. Codes and social values circulate, whatever the psychological inclinations of individuals, and character is considered as an element which acts as a counterbalance to education and mentality in the evaluation of the lodger. It may also be the case that certain aspects of character take precedence over, or allow a compromise with, cultural characteristics. On the other hand, it can happen that character aggravates differences in mentality, bringing to light a social difference which is unacceptable to the foster parent. Such is the case with this lodger whose proud and in no way timid character exacerbates his refusal to submit to the rules of the placement:

My second one. You had to be firm with him. He treated us like imbeciles. He was better than us and we were simply there to serve him . . . He was impossible. He was an impossible being. They gave him to me as their last attempt in this region. It was the fault of his parents who had wanted to give him a more comfortable life at the beginning, wanted him to be truly happy. Well! He ate at a separate table. He became quite impossible. He would say: 'I want this in my room. I want that in my room.' One day he said to me: 'You have an evil character, you are a bad person. You have only one quality, you cook well.' I had to go to Paris to see a Dominican monk who knew this man. He said: 'In his life of mental illness he is just as he was in normal life.'

On the other hand, illness is seen as a reason for the failure of attempts to gain acceptance of certain principles and models of behaviour. Sometimes it is even attributed the power to counteract or radically impair what the individual has received from his original environment. Products of the environment, mentality and education may be distorted by pathology and this distortion serves as the, sometimes unique, indication of the illness, as this foster parent explains with reference to a Muslim lodger:

> He didn't want to eat pork. His religion forbade it. And then one day last harvest time, we were all out working in the fields. My mother had prepared pork in aspic for dinner. She hadn't thought about what the lodger was going to eat. She said: 'Listen, just don't say anything and if he makes a fuss I'll give him a bit more of something else.' Well, we gave him some and my mother watched him and so did my husband. When he had finished eating, and he had eaten well, my husband said to him: 'How was that, Mohammed?' and he replied: 'Very good, boss.' My husband said: 'But do you know what you've been eating?' and he said: 'No but, good God, it tasted splendid.' We laughed. We found it quite amusing, you know. My husband said: 'Well my friend, you've been eating hallouf.' He didn't answer. I thought, 'My God, he's going to be angry.' I was frightened, good heavens I was. And he said: 'It was very good, Madame.' Afterwards I gave it to him again and he didn't say anything. Well, I'm telling you this to show you that there must be something about him which isn't quite right.

In this way the frameworks and categories used in the study of the lodgers posit pathology as an autonomous explanatory principle. However, the illness, ill-defined as it is, appears only as an operative force capable of affecting the diverse determining factors and expressions of the individual. A study of these expressions as they are described by the foster parents should help us discover how the illness is manifested.

The Symptoms of Illness

The resolutely practical perspective with which the foster parents confront the patients shapes their descriptions in a way which makes them easy to evaluate and, rather than looking at the illness itself, they focus on the particular effects and signs in each description. Each patient possesses his own pathological traits, sometimes unmistakably evident, such as those who lie on the floor to sleep like an animal, sometimes far more difficult to observe as we have seen earlier. The foster parents list all the signs around which the illness appears to crystallize, however minor they may be:

> I've got one who goes to pick grass for the rabbits. It's an odd habit of his, an idiosyncrasy. It doesn't matter what the weather's like. If he says he's going to gather grass for the rabbits, there's no point me telling him otherwise. Sometimes I get angry and say: 'You'll get wet' or whatever, but it's part of him. And anyway, they're his rabbits so I let him get on with it.

I had one. I don't know what was wrong with him. I couldn't keep him, it was intolerable . . . He made a real scene, he tore the lamp down, it was his illness . . .

It's one of his obsessions. When he's decided to change something, it has to be changed. He can throw a fit and destroy what he wanted to change.

When he gets it, he starts by scratching himself, he does strange little things like that, he gets down on his knees. He's not a stupid man. He's a professor and everything. And after that he makes piles of coins, because he hasn't any money of his own and he has to touch them . . .

When he was bad tempered we avoided saying anything to him. When everything was going well, he was very bright. When things were going well, everything was fine. But then, afterwards, if something happened which he didn't like, I don't know what came over him, a fit or something, it was his illness. He would get into a murderous mood. He was impossible . . .

My neighbour's got one who can't walk straight, you know. He takes up the whole road the way he meanders. He twitches.

Illness is also approached in a roundabout fashion, with case descriptions noting the sector of activity which is most severely affected:

He lacks judgement, lucidity. You can make him believe whatever you want. There's something missing in his head. If you explain something to him, you do eventually get him to understand. But you have to explain it well. He understands, but only if you explain well. Yes, there's something missing up there [*she points to her head*]. He hasn't got much in there.

He used to see things when there was nothing there. Maybe he was a bit unwell, perhaps it was a nervous depression . . .

Him, when he was angry, when he was nervous, during his nervous fits, he could easily break things. But he would be sorry for it afterwards. That was nerves with him. We saw him doing it: sometimes he would get hold of a bit of wood, or anything else really, and twist it . . .

Finally, a description is matched to an attempted explanation which refers to the conditions and period during which the illness started:

Illness, that depends on how bad it is, whether it's from birth or whether it's an accident . . .

They're all slightly lunatic, it's the illness at work, of course. It all depends on how the illness started. With some it's alcohol, with others it comes from deficiencies which are completely . . . Nowadays it also depends on the type of alcoholism . . .

> But still, there are gaps in their memory . . . gaps in the memory, that can be due to family grief.

> The young ones have done something, but the others are ill. It's attacked them like it could attack us . . . We've plenty of time for it to come. Some people get it when they are even older than us.

> There are so many things that can happen, because of alcohol, by accident, or even because of misfortune, a death or something like that . . . It's an illness which you get when something or other goes wrong . . .

The concordances and interrelationships between these elements are not always stable and systematic. What the foster parents tell us remains highly contingent, dependent on the experience they have gained of the individual lodgers placed with them, of the ones who have "passed through" and have remained in their memory because of some special characteristic. The first impression such contributions provoke is one of confusion in which understanding, based on the contact with a small number of patients, seems to dissolve into a haze of detailed, individual descriptions in which there is nothing constant to take hold of. And yet this diverse collection of case descriptions appeals to modes of conduct strictly reserved for and properly adapted to the mental patient. And precisely because these modes are grounded in a practical base, such descriptions already imply recourse to uniform categories.

The Little Catalogue of Loonies

On the one hand, this practical base upon which the foster parents act and of which they speak includes both their direct, concrete experiences and second-hand experiences transmitted through communication and confrontation with their peers and their parents:

> People who have patients living with them feel the need to discuss things with other people who have patients. All the placements don't work in the same way and all the patients aren't the same. There are often reasons to discuss things . . .

And we have already seen the extent of this need for communication and exchange when a placement is first opened, the strength of the tradition which is transmitted from mother to daughter, from generation to generation . . .

On the other hand, the policy of recruitment adopted by the Colony and practised relatively strictly and consistently prioritizes certain types of illness and consequently swells the number of some types of patient compared to other types. The resulting interplay of these two factors has made comparisons common and has given rise to summary but relatively consensual taxonomical frameworks.

This is why the hotchpotch of descriptions nevertheless yields five types of patient arranged within a classificatory system which applies to all the lodgers. This typology has evolved through a process of accumulation and decantation. Today it catalogues a variety of types which were once grouped together under the vernacular category of the loonies which the acquisition of experience has made obsolescent. In it, we find perennial characters and the characters of memory side by side with more recent characters and the characters who point towards the trends of the future. But, although defined with variable clarity, employed more or less implicitly, identified more or less expressly, these categories tend to be generalized to include all those who, satisfying one criterion or other, can be assimilated to them. We shall designate them here by the terms which, without being employed systematically, provide a specific designation and retain the greater part of the imagery encountered by us: *the innocent, the nutter, the epileptic, the crackpot* and *the head case.*

The innocent, a designation for the retarded, is, in a sense, a fundamental category because it is used by all and effectively applies to a large proportion of the placed population within which it nevertheless serves to effect a basic division. Retardation is clearly distinguished from all other types of mental illness. Before the foster parents say anything about the patients they take care to make a qualitative distinction between the innocent and the others. Easy to understand and easily comprehended within a schema accepted by all, innocence has a reassuring quality. Whether it is a result "of birth" or arises because "the brain stops developing", it manifests itself as an insufficient mental development which returns man to the state of a child or even of an animal, marking him with three incontestable characteristics: he lacks awareness; he lacks responsibility; he is not dangerous. He is the village idiot stripped of the idiosyncrasies of the "nutter" and stripped, too, of the potential for harm feared for various reasons in the others. These traits are associated with characteristics, positive or negative, which form the basic schema of the illness of "omission" which, as we shall see, applies to many other manifestations than that of mental deficiency.

Whilst the innocent has not lost his place on the stage, *the nutter* and *the epileptic* have become rather less common. At first sight the "nutter" does not seem to be a generic name since, over a period of time, it (*maboul* in French) has replaced the term *bredin* in local speech whilst retaining the pejorative connotations of this word. It is still used discreetly, especially in the presence of a researcher, even though it is not the worst insult that can be thrown at someone held to be insane. However, in a number of older people, it has retained a purity of use which makes it possible to understand how it took hold and the types of behaviour to which it corresponds. In the original meaning which it retains in such cases, "nutter" refers to those "who are obviously patients" because they "gesticulate", "shake", "make gestures", "twitch", have strange or eccentric habits, who speak or sing to themselves or continually repeat the same scene. These were the first patients introduced by the Colony. They were to cause a shock in the population which was divided between feelings of amusement, astonishment, unease and fear and was constrained to use an outside word to designate the aberrations whose excesses no longer fitted the vernacular category of loony.

Fully characterized by visible manifestations of strangeness for which, unlike the innocent, no explanation suggests itself, the nutter seems to belong to ancient history because today, as a result of the available medications:

> . . . You don't see as many as when I was young. There was one who was always pretending to be a train. Well, he had a big pipe and he was always being a train. Nowadays, you don't see patients like that any more. In the same way there were some who were always pulling a little cart, who came out onto the road to pretend to be a bicycle or to wave a white handkerchief, or again, who went out walking with their chests covered in mandarin peel to look like medals.

However, the idea of the "nutter" is still called on to evoke the twitching, the slightly different gait or gesture, a motor disability or simply a hello or sign of familiarity addressed to an unknown passer-by. This reference to an obsolescent but highly structured image, which continues to emphasize the unconstrained use of gestural signs, points to patients who display signs of a lack of behavioural coordination or coherence attributed to a nervous dysfunction, from which they derive their "shocking", "upsetting" and worrying character as members of a relatively differentiated class.

The same holds true for the case of *the epileptic* who, in fact, should be treated as a subclass of the "nutter" were it not for his isolation and the repulsive force of his image. Just like the nutter, he appears, if we heed the words of the population, to belong to the early history of the Colony. Yet he remains present in the imagination as a category as clearly identified and distinguished as that of the innocent. A *bête noire* of the past, all that is remembered of the epileptic is the paroxysms of a fit which invests nervous disorder with the aura of fear whose memory the foster parents cannot, even now, avoid recalling.[1] Everyone cites the epileptic as *the* patient they don't want, even if they are pleased to emphasize that new treatments have eradicated such manifestations. Where then does this fear "of nerves", whose

---

[1] The fear caused by the sight of an epileptic fit has, from the early days of the Colony, caused problems for the recruitment of patients. The number of epileptics has always been relatively low. The distorted perception of the number of epileptics, both in earlier times and now, fully emphasizes the imaginary aura which still surrounds the epileptic.

action is apprehended in the fixed, continuous "unhinged" twitching which is exemplified in the epileptic, have its roots? This we shall see later.

The crackpot and *the head case* represent the most modern figures in the Colony. These categories are applied to cases which cause anxiety without being identifiable as insane through an obvious and familiar defect. More specifically, these classifications refer to lodgers of recent introduction who "are difficult to tell from the civilians" and who are classified in accordance with their social attitude. The category of "crackpot" or "mental case" is generally used only for those who, in their appearance of normality, do not show themselves to be obvious opponents of the order established by the Colony but whose ambiguity shows itself in their speech, in the gleam in the eye, in an error of reasoning. Little used, with a meagre content and poorly elaborated and, for the same reason, menacing, the terms evoke a certain localized unease in the minds of the foster parents: "You don't know what's going on in their heads." It also evokes the diffuse presence of mental illness but is all the more worrying because it is little known. It is through the use of this term that the population indicates the criminal tendencies of a warped and therefore malign intelligence, or the force of an evil or maleficent intention which shows through the "deceitful air" or the "dark nature" which make the patient an object of fear unless his wild speech shows that he is "in a world apart" and withdrawn from the others.

As far *the head case* is concerned, he is always young,[2] an embodiment of the deficiencies and dangers of the new generation. He is familiar with the prisons:

> The young ones have done some bad things and their families have passed them off as ill. If they can do that it doesn't reflect badly on the family. The papers are full of it. I know a lad who used to start fires. They claimed he was ill. We're afraid of people like that. Families have to get extra money for having them. But the others are ill. They've got something just like we could get something.

Their criminal capacity is proportional to the opposition they show towards any attempts at discipline:

> They're young people they nabbed in hold-ups and all that sort of thing that goes on around Paris. The families don't get them out and they end up in the homes. They have a different mentality. They have an effect on you. And they're bold.

Indistinguishable from a change of mentality, the illness is equated with a moral deviance which causes its rejection from the social world:

---

[2] The "youth" of this type of illness is subject to the same distortion that we have found in the case of the numbers of epileptics. The social construction of this type is charged with the anxieties of the group and produces an image of invasion of the human landscape.

> Patients today are not the same thing at all. They aren't men. They aren't good. After all, earlier, even though they were ill, some of them were distinguished men, good people. In those days there weren't any of these special institutions for different types of patient. At that time they were all sent here. There were the innocent ones who were good men. Now, the ones who come here are young boys, they're little head cases.
>
> The young ones are appalling. They can be wild. The two young ones who came here, they were real . . . real savages . . . They weren't civilized!

Here we see the aggressive potential of mental disorder, its moral face stalking the shadow lands of the social framework when it is not the pure image of the criminally insane which is engendered by the almost police-like image of the psychiatric homes, of psychiatric doctors and policemen-supervisors.

Even if the totality of descriptions can find a place within this taxonomy, it is still necessary that these categories are strictly, indeed conscientiously, manipulated and proceed either from a precise inventory of the corresponding characteristics or from a clear hypothesis of their mode of operation and their genesis. Seen in this light, it is really only the innocent who fulfils the requirements for membership of a class. Nevertheless, the other types also function as classes in an implicit manner. This results in a certain confusion in the words of the foster parents which continually vacillate between the effort to go beyond particular references to the concrete cases on which their speech is founded and the evocation of the cases which provide the inert mass of details. Related to the concept of "prototypes", these types develop and operate in a different way from that postulated by cognitive psychology. Here, as our earlier analyses confirm, we are dealing with a constituent mode of thought whose order of classification, which is most frequently a latent order, combines past memories, borrowings from the framework of collective experience – both of which are passed on through communication – and information drawn directly from personal real-life situations. The characteristics proper to these types are identified through the action of a social theory of insanity and the distress it occasions. This classification becomes less strict as the perception of the patients grows increasingly blurred with the advance of time, as the introduction of chemotherapy reduces distinctions in behaviour, or as the replacement of patients provokes the fear that:

> Things might become more difficult. We might even have to ask ourselves if we dare take them. As one man from Ainay said to me: 'We don't know if we're going to be able to take real maniacs.' You have to realize that these people are abnormal and you can see the signs of their insanity.

The patients become "atypical", each almost indistinguishable from the next. This results in their different characteristics combining to form an amalgam which then reinforces the tendency, already induced by a uniformity of know-how, to confuse these characteristics in a single perception. Each individual, able to manifest all the symptoms attributed to one and the same type, becomes the recipient of a composite description which makes use of images of type which were previously separate. And during this process of fusion, these images give rise to new criteria which serve to maintain a clear distinction of type even in the absence of any indicative sign.

Thus the meaning of the word "knowledge", as it is understood by our interviewees, gradually becomes clear. It is a knowledge which serves as a vehicle for local stereotypes, for the past and present figures of a collective imagery, whose various faces are differentiated to a greater or lesser degree. It is a knowledge which progresses from an everyday contact with and orientation towards the patients to take the form of wisdom based on experience, a mode of pragmatic reasoning. But it is also a knowledge weighed down with presuppositions concerning the illness. It is through these presuppositions as well as through the workings of a lay psychology that this knowledge gives rise to a "portrait of the madman".

Chapter Six

The Three Faces of a Single State

The patients are made of flesh and bones like us.

They aren't able to be like us. They aren't able to take responsibility for themselves.

Incapable of earning their living, starting a home, making a life for themselves.

They're tough cases. They're not at all weak, although they might look like it. They can easily do something stupid. There are a lot of them like that, who can get worked up.

If a radical difference exists between the mental patient and the normal individual, then the establishment of a specific way of treating and managing the lodgers also confirms a similarity: "They're people like everybody else. You have to treat them properly." The imposition of an order is an acknowledgement of their human quality: "We give them a lodger's education. After all, we don't want to live with them as if they were animals." However, considering the means preferred in the social treatment and control of the lodgers, then the fullness and dignity of the attributes of this quality appear to be under continual threat from the illness. We are in the presence of an order apart for men apart whose characteristics display an affinity with those of the animal world, the world of childhood and the world of exogenous "races" or "populations".

People of Flesh and Bones

These admissions of similarity are made against a community background which is never denied, that of the species. What the patient is least grudgingly accorded by his fellow human beings is a corporeal brotherhood.

Without humour and in a literal sense: "The patient is a person of flesh and bones like us. We have to treat him like us." In the use of the term "people", the passage from the singular ("a person like anybody else") to the plural corresponds to a shift of accent. Collective assimilation gives way to a qualification which is distinctive to the type of organization. Here, the metaphor of "flesh and blood" which unites human beings in their mortality is understood literally. It denotes, of course, the material nature of the body without soul or spirit. But more than this, it designates the organic element which, as the lowest common denominator shared by the patient and the others, becomes the dominant feature in the patient's make-up. Although it varies with the seriousness of the case, this domination always derives from a specific organization of the system which turns the patient into a distinct person or "microcosm".

The foster parents' analysis of the activity and the resources of the lodgers reveals a schema of biological functioning in which the organic is articulated by reference to two independent terms, the *brain* and the *nerves*. The dominance of the organic both accounts for and is explained by the often antagonistic juxtaposition of these terms. In its most radical form this dominance, which reduces the individual simply to the biological dimension, implies failings and is explained by a failing. The patient's life appears to be purely vegetative, regulated by primitive needs: "Eat well. Sleep well. That's all they ask." Inaction appears as the corollary and most striking indication of this state:

> They're always lying at the side of the road. They live a bit like animals. All they're interested in is eating. They lie there at the side of the road like pieces of wood.

It appears as a passivity which often manifests itself as complete prostration:

> I've got little J there. He's a wretched specimen. I'm not criticizing him or making fun of him or anything. But he's very ugly, all doubled up. It's the best thing for him to stay in his corner and sleep.

And in this passivity the patient is closer to the animal than the human:

> Some of the patients I'd far rather see dead than the way they are . . . They don't have a life. They're like animals. They just lie there like animals. They don't do anything, nothing at all. They drink, they sleep and they eat . . .

Reserved for cases which are considered the most serious, descriptions of this type form the corollary to behaviour obtained through imperative commands designed to produce blind obedience rather than cooperation: "You have to find a way to train them, don't you? You have to train them." The patients are trained as one might train an animal. Discipline is imposed by "fear" and "threats" rather than by positive encouragement. The fact is that this absence of life which organic existence represents is, more than simply the absence of work, the lack of a fundamental dimension, the hedonic dimension, the source of activity and social bonds:

> But that isn't the case with all of them. There are some lodgers who take some pleasure in life, who try to do things . . . They have a walk, do a bit of tinkering here or there to pass the time, to amuse themselves . . .

The achievement of pleasure signifies attainment of the "reflexive" mode. In it are manifested the beginnings of a "comprehension" or an "awareness", demonstrated by the ability to distance oneself from corporeal functioning, to guide one's actions towards the search for satisfaction which also lies at the base of social exchange. By contrast, the being which is not animated or guided by any self-awareness is abandoned to the urges of his organism and the constraints imposed on him by the environment. The self-regulation of the vegetative existence excludes any social relationship. There is only one possible hold over this impenetrable organism, the fear of the privation or suffering which can prejudice biological peace. This is the reason underlying the recourse to negative motivations and the arousal of fear.

At this zero degree of human existence, the lack of concerted activity and pleasure indicates the operation of the illness in the absence of any reflexive guidance:

> It's the illness in them. It's different. They don't think. I don't know if they realize they exist. I don't know if they realize that when it rains, it would be better to be under a tree. Even a dog realizes that. It's their brains, their spirits that are empty.

This automatism and this organic domination are measures of the failure of the brain. Here, cerebral activity finds its basic functional specification. Before being comprehended as the seat of thoughts which are referred in some way to productions belonging to mental life, the brain is understood as exercising control over organic and active life:

> It all comes from the brain. Their brains aren't in control of them any more. There's something stopping them . . . they are ill . . .

Lacking this guidance, the patient is prey to the spontaneous and often excessive needs of the species:

> They're not like normal people, not even without . . . there's a type . . . They've all got something. And then there's something else which I forgot to tell you. They eat a lot. I'd like to show you just what they can eat . . .

They're all the same. If you watch them you won't find a single one who eats in moderation . . . L, it doesn't matter to him . . . You can't imagine the amounts he eats . . . He's as thin as a rake. He'll tell you it's not true but you just have to see him at it . . . We don't mind it because he works. If he didn't eat, he'd waste away.

He is also unable to suppress his bodily functions:

That one was so dirty in that way. It used to cause difficulties. It wasn't his fault. He wasn't free. He couldn't control it. It was the illness that's part of him.

Equally, the attempt to surrender to a rudimentary activity also bears the mark of automatism and organic drives:

It ought to be possible to get them to work. They tell you yes. They start off doing something, a little bit of wood cutting or little jobs like that which you show them how to do to keep them occupied, to liven them up a bit. And what do you think? They cut a piece of wood or two and that's it. They leave everything and clear off . . . The brain isn't in control of the body. It's their brains which aren't in command.

But despite its self-sufficiency, self-regulation cannot be applied to all aspects of existence. And the failure of the brain, which abandons the body to its inertia and its demands, clears the way for the action of another force, that of the nerves. Independent of the brain, the nerves proceed to dominate the organism in its relationship with the environment. Where this is the case, any direct and immediate intervention in the activities of the patient risks triggering a nervous reaction. Although privation or punishment can be applied as an effective means of adaptation, reproaches, reprimands, admonishments are quite inappropriate in the case of a patient who is inaccessible to reason and remains "obstinate" in the kingdom of nerves which he inhabits:

If they do something stupid and I scold them, you can see them getting annoyed straight away . . . What's the point of annoying them? All you can do is leave them be. They get annoyed more easily, and violent more easily than others. We're always living on the edge of our nerves ourselves, and those people are mental patients to start off with. It's worse with them. When one of them does something stupid, I prefer not to give him any dessert when the others get theirs. That's the worst punishment you can give them without actually doing them any harm.

You have to leave them free, not force them to do anything, otherwise they turn obstinate. And if I make them stubborn, that's it. They get angry, they shout, run around . . .

This omnipotence of the nerves, which assures the dominance of an unfathomable fantasy, closely linked to the nature of the patient, emphasizes once again the animality of the patients which no social action can uproot:

> They're lunatics. The illness is at work in them, there's no doubt of that. We've got two and they're both very sensitive to the weather.

> It's mainly stormy weather and changes in the weather. It's things like that which affect them. Especially changes in weather. It makes them nervous. You can see how it affects them. A bit like animals, isn't it? Because the brain has no control. They don't know what's happening. There's nothing you can do.

And in this interplay of material forces, the nerves, which cause a transition from cosmic effects to the expression of drives, reveal their relationship to sexuality, especially in the women:

> The women react more to stormy weather and changes in the moon. One day at my parents'-in-law, my mother-in-law went indoors and the [female] lodger slapped her twice. My father-in-law went in and he got a couple of slaps as well. He managed to give her a slap. That calmed her down.

> The women are more nervous, even though they're drugged up. They're all quite sensitive. That's more true of the women than the men. One stormy afternoon there was one who got undressed in the middle of the town. She walked around in her knickers. Changes in the moon affect their nerves. If she got undressed, it's because of her nerves.

In this way the analysis of the dynamic underlying the behaviour of those patients who are judged to be most seriously affected reveals a double representation. The first is that of the functional nucleus of the human organism. This elementary structure includes the biological, cerebral and nervous levels which are themselves uniquely defined by a regulatory activity. Fundamental to the organism, it operates as a system of forces whose equilibrium is a basic necessity for the development and differentiation of higher functions. Central to this system, the brain plays a primal and primordial role of control over organic and active life and dominates the nerves. The second representation is of the effects produced by mental illness within this structure. The illness modifies the relative importance of the three constituents and the relationship between them. Organic domination becomes a symptom of the dysfunctioning of the brain and a shift of power to the nerves. "Lost", or in other words, deprived of cerebral control and abandoned to the domination of the nerves, the mental patient slumps into animality. And even if his activities tend to suggest a lesser disturbance they still follow a course which is delineated by this state.

Big Meals, Sweets and Tobacco

This is borne out by the closer relations which are formed with lodgers who are seen to possess more valuable qualities, the most important of which is, as we have seen, the hedonic dimension with its implicit capacity of "awareness". What happens when a foster parent notices that a lodger possesses this dimension? What is the order of the "pleasures" which he thinks the latter is able to attain? First of all, this recognition, acknowledged in terms of "consideration" or human respect, is expressed in the material conditions of the life of the lodger. This, at least, is the sense attributed to the change of attitude associated with the minor "revolution" which occurred when the administration introduced and supervised rules of cleanliness, comfort and nourishment in the placements. Testimonies suggest that prior to this, the "bestiality" identified in the state of the patient found a direct echo in the life he led:

> In some placements they were worse off than the dogs. They were thought of as animals. And they were fed just like the dogs. I've seen potatoes swimming in the stew together with lumps of wood. That disgusted me so much . . . Those people, they lived like animals. The beds which you saw sometimes! . . . Old bedsteads with canvas sacking stuffed with straw where the springs should have been . . . and dirty! They're human beings. You can't feed them on steak morning, noon and night . . . but at least you should feed them, treat them like people . . . like human beings.

Although the material management of the placement now provides a qualitative surplus over and above the satisfaction of the elementary needs of the organism, it continues to demonstrate the dominance of these needs, as did, at other times, the small attentions which provide everyday pleasures to the patients. It seems as if the only pleasure the illness can recognize is that of oral satisfaction:

> He likes sweets. I buy him a packet and he's happy.

> All the lodgers like cakes and sweets and desserts. It's because of the illness.

A cup of coffee, a pancake, sweets, "it's the best thing to make them happy", and the same is true of tobacco:

> Mine's a smoker, like a lot of them. It's his little pleasure. He can't do without it. Smoking is something they all do all the time. They need to smoke. If you want to give them a reward you just give them a cigarette. They don't want anything else. That's what they prefer.

By the same token, oral satisfaction becomes a privileged medium for the establishment of social exchange and communication. Whether she is trying to win his affection, put him at his ease or assure him of his integration into the family, the foster parent plays on the lodger's susceptibility in this respect:

> It encourages them, a cup of coffee, a piece of cake, they like that. It doesn't take much to win their confidence.

> One day at four o'clock he came to ask for something to eat, he said: 'It's like I was hungry, but I'm not hungry for bread, I'm hungry for cake.' You know, it's like with children. So I give him his bit of cake or whatever I've got. They don't go without. They eat like we do. It's the same food as well. It wouldn't feel right to eat . . . That matters. It's like with children. These lodgers, if they left us they'd be unhappy. It's not everywhere they get a family life.

But most significantly we see here the motivational basis on which the foster parent can base her attempts to adapt the lodger:

> It's always the same. There are little things which give them pleasure. If I make pancakes, they get pancakes and they're happy.

> The other one, the one who was changed because he used to argue with his foster parent, he does what I tell him. It's the way you handle them. You give him some cake and he eats it with the others or with us. They're not dogs, especially when they're not in too much of a daze.

The same is true if the foster parents want to gain the lodger's cooperation, motivate him to some effort:

> At harvest time, it's good that we've got them with us. It makes them more gentle if they're working hard and we bring a jug of wine and give them a glass. It's a marvel for them.

Within this vision of organic dominance, the importance accorded to the need for food and its satisfaction fulfils a dual semiotic function. On the one hand, it is the sign of the seriousness of the lodger's cerebral dysfunctioning. On the other hand, in those who are considered to be close to a state of normality, it is the sign of the persistence of a pathological state and an "egoistic" thought pattern which is indifferent to others, foreign to the social norm, cut off from the world:

> The one who left. When the illness attacked him he really was a little bit mad . . . Like at dinner time, for example. I used to take him a good dinner and I would say to him: 'Is that good?' In two minutes . . . he didn't like what I had given him. In two minutes, three changes of mind. He had

already brought down his tray . . . finished eating. The other one sleeps all day. He gets up for lunch. Then he goes straight back to bed for the whole afternoon. I take him his dinner at 7 o'clock and when he's finished it, he's back in bed immediately.

There are some of them who are really mentally ill. They don't know what's going on, and they go at their food like animals. We've got one, L. He was quite young when he lost his parents. He's always been a farmer. But you can feed him until it comes out of his ears. It doesn't have to be good as long as there's plenty of it.

You have to see what they carry around on them. There's not a single one who doesn't eat a lot. They're all like that . . . the ones who eat with us. There are times when it's annoying. Because even the one who's in quite a good state of mind, he only lives to eat and drink. And when you have people with you, really! When you have people to eat he doesn't wait until he's finished what he's got. He just helps himself to three more pieces of meat. When he's still got one left, he helps himself to more . . . At harvest time when we have people eating with us he helps himself to all the best pieces.

They aren't all that interested, not very interested in life, not normal life. They don't try to find out the whys and wherefores of things. They just live like they are, eat, sleep and that's all. They're not interested in anything. They never come if something's happening in the region, sporting events or anything like that . . . It all depends. Some of them go to the fairs but all the same . . . It's a difference which I think is mainly due to the effects of their illness.

Many others testify to the limits and deviations of cerebral functioning which corroborate the other indications observed in the spheres of everyday activity, work or social behaviour.

Drifting and Self-Direction

Equally revealing of the state of the patient is the sphere of practical activity, a sphere which is particularly rich in observations on account of the benefits and comfort that the foster parents derive from the practical abilities of the lodgers. There exists a whole range of behaviours whose gradations correspond to the levels of control and resources attributed to the brain or to the influence of the nerves.

The patient who remains at the threshold of animal-like lethargy only seems able to abandon himself to the pleasures of the moment, to the intoxication of freedom:

They think of it as an escape. They feel happy to be here, to wander, to drift.

This explosion of aimless, unchannelled physical energy gives way to those rovings to which the local inhabitants are so sensitive:

> They need to relax, to get out. It would be painful for them to stay seated all day. They have to walk. They have to wander. They mustn't stay shut in.

If these unsettling wanderings are often the clearest mark of insanity, it is because they express not only a rootlessness but also the impulsiveness and disorder of an unmastered nature. This is exacerbated by the instability of the nerves and the failure of cerebral control:

> You can't say they're stable enough to keep animals. You can't leave them alone or they'll drift off somewhere.

The way in which these wanderings serve to distinguish the lodger from the civilians shows that the foster parents doubt that this blind, inner compulsion for movement, sometimes akin to agitation, can ever be completely mastered in the person of the patient:

> I've got one. When it comes over him he'll leave the house ten times a day. Off he goes, whistling to himself. What can you do, it's the illness. And he travels. He goes to Paris all by himself. He can't stay in the same place.

> There are some who change placement non-stop. It's a craze of theirs. They change placements like they change their shirts. It's stronger than them. They have to change.

Providing that the regulatory function of the brain is not too disturbed, it is possible for these wanderings to be transformed into coherent activity. The walks whose function is to amuse, to "distract", are replaced by useful movement, such as the accomplishment of a task, which occupies the mind. Once this is acknowledged, the patient becomes capable of spatial orientation:

> When my aunt had her first lodgers, they brought her one who didn't want to stay. It was the innocent one who's died. She kept him right up to his death. They said to her: 'Come and pick him up in the car and drive him around a bit to confuse him.' Well, she took the horse and rode all over the place so he wouldn't get to know the roads. As soon as he saw her saddling the horse, he had his raincoat on his back and was standing ready at the door. And he got used to being there. Later on he ran errands for her. He invented his own names for everybody. His habits were his habits. *Although he was lost he had enough intelligence to find his way.*

In some ways, behaviour is a direct and literal expression of function. One does what one is. Aptitude, its extent and its limits, are all fully present in the performance of an activity.

The Three Faces of a Single State   181

It is because of this that the work performed by the lodgers acquires such significance. Quite independent of its profitability, such work always has a value because of its significations. As an indication of the state of the patient and, at the same time, a means of channelling his energies, work is reassuring. It is reassuring in the first place because it turns the lodger's thoughts away from morbid rumination:

> It distracts them. It keeps their ideas moving. It occupies their minds. They don't have to keep on thinking about . . . I don't know what they think about but at least they don't get bored any more.

> If a lodger works, his mind is occupied, he doesn't think about doing harm. He thinks about what he's doing. He doesn't shout. If he's inactive, who knows what's going on in there!

It reassures, too, by draining off nervous energy and diminishing the danger of violence:

> The big one is extremely nervous. If he would only start to work that would calm his nerves, that would do him some good.

But the greatest reassurance is that it proves that the functional equilibrium of the lodger is not too weakened: "there's nothing to be afraid of in a patient who works" because a cerebral element which is strong enough to direct action must also be strong enough to "govern" the nerves:

> The ones who work forget, they can forget more quickly. But the ones who think all day long, who sit there and don't do anything, they are incurable. What's more, the ones who don't work are the ones who are really ill. The workers manage to recover a bit. It all comes from the brain. It's not in charge. There's something which stops them working, I don't know what. The other one, he tries but he can't manage it. He hears noises and that worries him and then he's off and that's that.

Despite these guarantees, work still fails to provide any assurance of normality. Whatever the level of competence shown by the working lodger, the foster parents always find shortcomings in his execution of the task which testify to his fundamental inability to be like the others.

The difficulty of the tasks given to the lodgers accords with the levels of functional organization and intellectual or practical ability attributed to them, and in this way the field of work reveals the same differentiation as the field of food; in some placements the patients are given repetitive tasks which reduce them to the level of automata:

> There was one in the region who was given the job of killing crows all day long. He used to go up and down the field without stopping, from morning to night, to stop the crows eating the corn. Is that what you call work?

> There are different ways of treating the patients. There was one who had to
> clear the ice from the ponds with his hands. He nearly cut his fingers off.

As far as motor activity is concerned, the passage from wandering to walking
to "errands" corresponds to the movement from incoherence to direction
towards an enjoyable or useful goal. The degree of responsibility accorded to
the patient in the minimal form of work known as "shopping" varies with the
confidence the foster parent has in his intelligence and his honesty. The
shopping can be simple and unvarying from one day to the next – fetching
bread or milk whose quantities, which never vary, have been agreed by the
foster parent and the shopkeeper – or it can vary in nature and amount
depending on the needs of the moment, with the result that the lodger must
visit a number of shops to pick up orders placed in advance or, better still, has
to purchase the items himself in accordance with a shopping list, payment
being made either in cash or by means of a "running bill" which does not
involve the immediate transfer of money. The mode of shopping employed
depends on the lodger's ability to read, to count, to remember a number of
things at once, to express himself clearly etc. The same is true of productive
activity. Starting with a helping hand in the house or farm, this can extend as
far as sharing a real job or even to professional activity. And it is in this
sphere that the restrictive judgements of the lodgers' mental function are
most clearly expressed.

   Thus the patient may be deemed to possess sufficient "understanding" and
"calmness" to be given a definite activity (doing the housework, looking after
the courtyard or the livestock etc.) or the tasks he performs might be reduced
to the fragmented and mechanical which demand no initiative. There are a
number of reasons for this and they point to either mental deficiencies or
mental disturbance. At first, "it's because the brain's empty", which is to say
the brain does not know how to acquire and, most importantly, to apply
knowledge, because it has never learnt how:

> At first we said: If he had been well looked after he would have been able to
> learn. But afterwards you realize that it isn't so. They're incapable of getting
> by on their own. All they do is follow a routine.

The work they do is repetitive, imitatively reproducing a demonstrated
procedure:

> Making their coffee with milk in the morning, they're able to do that, or
> prepare a meal if I'm ill. That's to say, they're used to seeing me do it.
> They're with me all the time. Now that they're used to the house I say to
> them: 'Today we're going to make mashed potato, you're going to . . . '
> After that, they're able to do it.

Automatism appears to underlie all their behaviour: the automatism of repetition in habit, in apprenticeship, and the automatism in gesture, in thought, in execution:

> The one I've got to work, he always does more or less the same thing. Personally speaking, he takes a lot off my hands, I have to admit it, but he can't . . . You mustn't change his habits. In the winter we get up, I call him, we drink a cup of coffee together and after that it's off to the fields where he does his work. He cuts the beet, he pushes the wheelbarrow. Like that, everything's fine. But you mustn't change anything. I have to get up a little bit earlier than him in the mornings. If I try to speed up the work at all then it's all over.

> I sold the pigs this morning. Every morning when we get up, we feed the pigs and I've got him used to that. Of course, this morning we didn't, and he didn't know where he was. If I explain, it takes half an hour before he understands. He said to himself: the pigs aren't going to eat today.

This automatism is reinforced, or indeed instilled, by the foster parent to whom it is a source of security, and as such it reveals a number of things. Primarily, it reveals the weakness of the inner control which is seen at the root of fragmented effort, unstable attention and superficial awareness:

> The one who says he's bored, I told him: 'But R, you work but you're not consistent. You start something and then you don't finish it the next day.' He gets bored but he doesn't understand that he isn't capable of acting for himself, of living a worker's life. It's impossible. The work they do isn't the same at all. For example, if they're doing the washing-up, you have to stand behind them and make them wash things again. I don't think they're capable of making their own way in life.

This makes necessary the external imposition of the frameworks of habit and the exercise of a constant supervision aimed at compensating for the lodger's incapacity to evaluate the significance or the result of his work, an inability which makes any adjustment or correction impossible:

> If you give them something to do, you have to be there with them. You have to stay with them. The other one who's here with me, he does the washing-up. But I have to be there because otherwise there are pans which haven't been properly scoured or forks which haven't been properly washed. You can't trust them. It's not possible.

Furthermore, there are the limitations of memory which make it impossible to remember instructions concerning multiple tasks or tasks which are to be performed at different times:

The old one we've had for the last thirty years. He's a good lodger when it comes to performing little jobs. But we don't ask him to do much. He can't remember much. You have to be with him all the time. He never refuses to do anything but he doesn't remember much of what you tell him. You can't ask him to do three or four things at once. But the other one, J, is very good at remembering what has to be done. I never have to give him any instructions.

Properly speaking, it is an "empty" or a "shrunken" brain that is revealed by this failure of memory which is also observed in other fields in which mere mechanical apprenticeship offers no solution:

I don't know what to do to get them to be cleaner. Because if you tell them something then they've forgotten it two minutes later. Take that one there. Every two or three days I have to change his sheets. He simply goes to bed in his shoes and socks or in his wet trousers. And if I tell him today then he's forgotten by tomorrow! How can you expect them to be clean? They're ill, after all.

The difficulty experienced in "trusting the lodgers", "having confidence in the patients" is not simply a result of the weakness of their resources. It also occurs in the distortions which may derive from reflective thought. The risk of stupidities and accidents prevents the foster parents allowing the lodgers to exercise any real initiative and still less any autonomy. They continually expect to see execution of the task halted by some aberration of thought, the sudden eruption of a ludicrous idea, "you never know what's going through their heads", the incoherence of the lunatic mind, or the defects of reasoning which make it impossible for the lodgers to gauge the consequences of their acts, relate their action to its context or anticipate a risk:

There's one next door. He doesn't look stupid but heavens above. The foster parent hasn't been able to teach him how to drive a tractor. When he gets to the end he doesn't think of braking. He ends up in the hedge and that's that. There must be something wrong. His reflexes don't work maybe. I don't know what . . . Once they said that he does it on purpose but I don't believe it. Because after all you don't end up in a hedge like that for fun, do you? You've still got a reflex which tells you, I don't know what, it's instinctive. When you see the danger, you stop automatically. But on the other hand, if you're going to drive into the hedge, you know what to do about it. They don't have the reflexes to avoid danger like we do. You see animals doing exactly the same thing. They get themselves kicked a hundred times a day. But they haven't got the sense to think, I won't lie there because if I do I'm going to get kicked, someone will step on my head. They just keep on doing it. You really get the impression that they haven't got a clue about life. But you do manage to give them some idea, like teaching a baby who's just starting to walk.

These evaluations of the practical capabilities of the lodgers are based on a constant presupposition, namely their inability to act for themselves, attributed either to inadequate mental faculties (knowledge, understanding, memory) or, if this argument is invalidated by the competence and efficiency of the lodger, to the inadequacy of the integrative functions of judgement, orientation and adjustment. It is then the inability of the brain to control these functions that is indicated by a mode of thought which obeys automatisms and drives which are inappropriate to the social and material conditions within which the lodgers' work is performed:

> They can't work like we do. Even if they know how, or have the skill or the enthusiasm or the goodwill, it still isn't in their power. They might want to. There are some who are very enthusiastic and really want to work. I know a lot. Far from not working, they work a lot. But it's not just a question of working. You have to know how to organize as well. There are some who work harder than we do . . . But they don't know how to act for themselves . . .

This inability leaves its mark on the whole present and future life of the lodger. It prevents him ever attaining true professional status: "They don't have a job", or even simply performing any job in a consistent and profitable way:

> There are some who would like their freedom, but they wouldn't be able to get by. If they left they wouldn't manage it. They wouldn't be able to work for their living. They wouldn't be able to get a secure job.

And even if they were able to show their ability, the lack of control would once again stop them overcoming their changeable moods and their temporary physical and moral deficiencies, preventing them from facing up to the constraints of reality:

> Leaving the Colony is all very well but . . . they don't have a job. If you want to understand life, you soon learn that you can't live off nothing. They would have to get enough work to be able to get somewhere where they can live . . . They don't have a job . . . Because even with us there are always . . . but we're able to control ourselves. Still, there are days when you're not . . . You don't always feel the same each day. But with them it can happen the moment something goes wrong. Me, I don't think they could . . . I can't imagine they could control themselves well enough to accept everything you have to accept in civilian life . . .

A condition of existence, work also means social participation. It implies that the worker is able to take his place, keep it and accept it. Unable to govern himself adequately, the patient is debarred by the law of his desires to submit to the law of system either because he would be required to tolerate the moral and financial inequalities his state implies:

> He isn't sufficiently in control of himself to accept, for example, that he earns 50 francs while somebody else earns 100, and that he can't lead the same life as his neighbour who has twice as much money as him. There's one who left. He used to be placed in Berry. Don't try to tell me that that lad is capable of driving a tractor or handling agricultural equipment. He's never done it, so he can't. His bosses are always going to think of him as second rate. He'll just have to accept it.

or because he would be unable to dispose of his income sensibly and constructively:

> They aren't able to control themselves and look after their money . . . You can't have any confidence in them . . . They don't know the value of money. There's no point saying: 'I'll give so much money per week' or 'You'll have that much every month' because they don't understand it . . . They'll go and drink five, six coffees without even realizing. And if they've got some left in the evening, well, they have no thought for tomorrow. They would never be able to do enough work to pay for everything they want.

Despite all the efforts of work and the desire to succeed in it, the lodger's inability to manage his own affairs constitutes a social weakness which is all the more insurmountable because of the moral weakness to which it testifies:

> There was a time when they released a lot of lads like that. And it was always the same. They're able to work but they aren't able to understand enough. They often let themselves be exploited. They get work on a farm and the people see that they're not really normal because they're easy to exploit. I think they're better off as they are, provided that the family takes care of them, because they're looked after, they're supervised. Away from here, it's different. It's not good for people like that to be left in complete freedom, because they aren't able to . . . They haven't enough strength of character to organize themselves. They don't realize the difficulties. If they're let out of here then they have only one aim, to do everything they want to do. But they don't understand that it's them who have to earn the money. They're helpless. Of course they are. They have to be completely normal.

A prey to his own desires, the patient easily becomes a victim of exploitation:

> We had one who asked to return to civilian society. He was a good lad who deserved to leave because he was able to defend himself, and that's rare enough. But he had one weakness. He was a boy who would certainly have

worked hard, would have done his best to give satisfaction, but he would have been ripped off, he would have been robbed left, right and centre. And he was fond of women. A couple of kisses is all it would have taken to get round him. He was a lad who would never have been really happy because he wasn't able to look after his own affairs.

Finally these impossibilities combine and culminate in the impossibility of acceding to the most unambiguous form of social integration, marriage: "They can't look after themselves well enough to start a home or make a life for themselves."

And if, therefore, escape is only conceivable in the form of a return to the family, this is because the unseen workings of the illness, present despite the most positive surface appearances, undermine the lodger's ability to master his judgements, his acts, his drives and his desires and add the necessity of moral guidance to the need for material support. The lack of responsibility implied by the status of confinement accorded to the patient confirms this evaluation of the lodgers' social and moral state:

> Let me tell you about one case. There was an old woman who came for two months every year. She used to get into a right state over him. She would take him off on the Sunday morning and bring him back to his foster parents on the Monday. She wanted to take him away once and for all. I told her: 'You know that it's a lot of work. Because while they're here they're frightened of the doctors, the supervisors. But once they're free it's a different matter.' You know, the boys we've got here, if they were with their families they would be free. They wouldn't be worried by the doctors or the supervisors. They would want to leave and the parents wouldn't be able to do anything about it. And then it would all start again. Me, I think it's impossible. They're incapable of looking after their needs. The family has got to take the responsibility for them.

After disposing of all the levels of organic and active life, it is the mark of non-control which closes the door on social life. And on freedom.

The Pig-Headed and the Wrong-Headed

The inability to act for themselves has repercussions for the social life of the patients, not just in their modes of participation as productive, responsible agents within the community, but also in the forms of socialization and, it might be said, sociability, that are mentality and morality. What mental illness produces is then called deviance.

The image of the lodgers' "social ability" is a multifaceted one, each aspect corresponding to different spheres of social life. The facet underlying the establishment of a "way to get by with" refers to the lodgers' behaviour in society, in their dealings with the civilians. At this level, priority is given to the observance of codes and conventions. We also find a homogeneous conception of the sociability of the patients which encompasses their social attitudes, the relationships they are able to establish between themselves, their interaction with their immediate surroundings etc. This conception addresses the life of the group in highly specific terms, distinguishing between an interpersonal level at which affinities are established between individuals and a collective level characterized by genuinely social traits as if the common condition of the lodgers were a source of collectively shared attitudes and behaviour.

In fact, the analysis of the relationships between lodgers living, for example, in the same placement is based on psychological criteria, with harmony and conflict being referred to the degree of compatibility between the character, way of life and pathological behaviour of the lodgers. These vicissitudes of cohabitation are held to be a matter of chance. In contrast, the approach to group relations outside the placements, whether these are informal or develop within the structures of work or the hospital institution, is based on constants of temperament and consistent relational phenomena which apply to the entire population of lodgers. This approach involves a theory of the determination of certain social processes (gregariousness, contagion, dispersal) by the illness. The state of the patient plays a mediating role in that it modifies the relationship between the lodger and his peers, and between the lodger and the values which ordinarily define social relations. Identical social tendencies correspond to disturbed mental functioning in all the patients. These tendencies give way to anomic relations in which a counter-society, or at the very least, the potential for a counter-society, takes shape. And while the lodgers are denied a positive, constructive social expression, their association with one another is perceived as a negative force concealing moral danger and social opposition.

This can be seen most clearly in the field of work where the same inability to act for oneself results in isolation at the level of production, and gullibility at the level of remuneration. In effect, the foster parents believe that when the lodgers are reduced to a routine automatism, they adapt to the necessities of collective work because of their greater submissiveness to hierarchical organization and authoritarian supervision, whilst for the very same reasons they are completely unable to take part in autonomous, responsible collective activity. This is, in fact, the inability to support and cooperate. It is true that some are, perhaps jokingly, reproached with "wanting to have the upper hand", "to be in charge of the others", "to play the boss", behaviour which leads to provocative comparisons with the system of cause and effect:

> The two we've got get on well together. But in the end it's all the same. L never says anything, thank heavens, because if he started to grumble . . .
> But he understands. The other one, he wants to be the boss even though

he's more of a fool than L. He wants the upper hand. It's amusing to see how they go about it. Sometimes at noon he says: 'Send them off for a walk.' But the other one, L, who's also the older of the two and the more intelligent, he doesn't say anything. He knows how to listen and let him talk, and then the number of times he says he wouldn't live with anyone else. And then the other one goes to sleep at my mother's house and it's just the same, he tries to play the boss down there as well: 'You have to buy some this, you have to buy me something else . . . ' He was twenty years old when he arrived here and since then he's being playing the boss. It doesn't matter. And they're at it all the time. It's amusing to see how the pair of them get on.

However, the foster parents are unanimous in emphasizing, both in work and elsewhere, the existence of a withdrawal, an asociability whose obvious egotism only ill conceals an inadequate self-mastery. And in the same way that the negligence with which the lodgers are reproached because it contravenes the values of order, economy and social management character-izes the moral dimension of insanity, so the absence of cooperation, which runs counter to a basic principle of the organization of agricultural work based on exchange and reciprocity of services, emerges as a hiatus between divergent mentalities. In radically transforming the lodger's state of mind, the failings of the illness are rapidly perceived as dwelling in the far reaches of otherness:

> I don't think they're capable of getting by in life. And there's something about them . . . Let me tell you something strange. I used to live in Cameroon. When it comes to work I can best compare them with the Blacks. Because one of them washes up the crockery, and the other the glasses, but they won't help one another. They've both got their work and it's their work. Well, the Blacks were like that as well. It's strange, isn't it? Their work is their work. There's one who brings in wood for the stove. None of the others offers to help. No, it's his work. If there's no wood, there's no fire, because it's A who goes to get the wood. I can't find a better comparison. The Blacks, first of all they're lethargic and then they have to do that and not that, and that's all there is to it. It's just the same here. They don't help one another. It must be because of the illness, because, after all, they are Europeans. They're people from these parts. With the Blacks it's different, you can't compare them. But here, it's because of the illness. And I'll tell you why. Because if they weren't ill they would do like we do. They're incapable of being like us, of acting for themselves, for example, or earning their living or organizing their lives. That's to say that if they were free, they wouldn't be able to have a house, a wife and children to feed, to organize their lives. It's not possible.

The bipolar schema of non-control is echoed in the analysis of the relationships the lodgers maintain with one another. Autism is counter-balanced by suggestibility, the malleability of judgement by the rigidity of action. In the field of work, the lodger's inability to evaluate the worth of his efforts often leads him to demand a remuneration which is incommensurate with what the foster parents regard as his deserts, or even, as we have seen, his needs. He then proceeds to listen to the excesses of other lodgers who are just as ill-informed as he is. Finally, his demands are interpreted as an error into which he is locked by collective pressure:

> They can be quite stubborn when they get together. They talk. They think they can do the work of someone who isn't ill and so they want to be paid the same wages. Some of them say to the others, 'You're wrong to work for that money' and they say this and that and get ideas into their heads and on it goes.

Generally speaking, the expression of solidarity, of a community of condition, is attributed to the pathogenic effect of the environment and is seen as a confirmation of the illness:

> The last one [A], when we had him we saw well enough that he wasn't ill. Well, he must be a little bit ill or else he wouldn't be here. But we soon saw that he's not as bad as the others. But although he's normal, at the same time he's not. There's something which I can't quite put my finger on. One day I was angry with R who had lost some of the Colony's things. The other one [A] was making fun of him and I thought to myself: 'But he's realized that he isn't normal.' At the time he [A] was joking. Afterwards he said to me: 'Madame, R told me he must have left them when he went to visit his mother on holiday.' I didn't answer him and the next day my husband said: 'Did you sleep well, A?' – 'No, I slept badly. R was kicking up a fuss all night. He was angry. He's a nervous type. Your wife was wrong to argue with him like that.' He's normal and, at the same time, he's not. He can get into quite a state if you're angry with the others. He makes a joke of it at the beginning, makes fun of them and then later he defends them. It's difficult to know what to make of him.

It is clear that this type of reasoning serves the interests of the foster parents. By attributing any legitimate basis in the claims of the lodgers to lies, denials and bad influences, the foster parents are able to define their position, their entitlements and their rights in the way which is most conducive to the requirements of the placement. Far from being inspired by self-interest, this reasoning derives from the representation of the effects of the illness. And the vigilance of the foster parents, which in the majority of cases is designed to minimize contact between the lodgers, is established as a defence against the risk of contamination of fragile minds and against the fear of a moral danger. This is because it is one and the same weakness which shelters these minds behind the beneficent control of order and exposes them to the harmful power of disorder. The company of normal people "recuperates" the lodgers whilst contact with their peers makes them worse:

When some of them are at the Colony, they're different to when they are out in the country with the locals. It's good for their minds to talk with the locals. It's the same everywhere. If they're in a house where they are well guided, they can't guide themselves of course, but if they're in a house where the people talk to them, explain things to them, where they get good advice, it's indispensable for them.

The company of their fellows always has a deleterious influence on the patients which operates in many ways. It aggravates the patients' pathology through the effects of identification, mirroring and mimesis:

> I'm almost certain that being with people can improve their condition. When I go up to the Colony, I see large numbers of them under the trees. They're all together with others like them. You have to observe them a bit. Some of them are frightening, some of them are shouting. If they're together in an atmosphere like that, how are they ever going to get better? Generally speaking, you take on the colour of the surroundings you're living in. I expect it's always been like that. Well, if you put a large number like that together in an asylum, what is it they're going to hear all day long? They're all the same, all the same together. They can't do anything but make one another worse.

Such company encourages and thus reinforces deviance. In the presence of his peers, the patient always finds connivance in or acceptance of his dubious activities:

> They sell everything to one another. They sell all their belongings. I know a little chap who paints very well. He sold a lovely box of paints to one of my lodgers. It was worth about 300 francs or more and he sold it for 30 francs. I made him take it back and he sold it back to him. He sells everything. He hasn't got anything left. His watch, all his best things, everything. There's a group of them. They're all much the same. It's all they think about. Well, what do you expect them to think about? They don't have a job or anything. There are some awkward ones, some wouldn't harm a fly and others who would just as happily drive a car and get drunk every day. And of course if they weren't under our control. If one of them drinks and nobody says anything, then the others . . . 'If nobody's going to say anything to him about it then I'm going to do the same.' Well, you can see that it's an impossible life!

By transforming the mentality of the patients, group life disturbs the functioning of the placements and represents a threat to public order. And in this way we find an explanation of the disgust and anxiety felt by the population in the face of groups of patients gathered together outside the precincts of the Colony. Might such groupings not develop an autonomous culture in which deviance becomes the norm?

Ch'tits, *Real* Ch'tits

However, this influence and the power attributed to the influence of the group can only be fully understood when the suggestibility of the patient is seen to be based on a negativity which derives from his "patient's nature":

> What it is, is that these are people who you shouldn't leave together with others. You shouldn't let them meet other patients. Because they get ideas into their heads, they do stupid things to each other. I don't let them go visiting. I know they're not doing any harm and I can see what they're up to. I've got one who was used to calling from door to door. He had got into the habit, and then there was another one, a young one, who didn't dare to until this one came along and taught him. They get one another to behave stupidly. They could just as easily go and steal from someone as . . . That one has got sticky fingers. I've seen that at home. If I'm working outside then I take him with me because otherwise he's sticking his nose in everywhere. He'll even go into the bedrooms. And whatever he sees, he puts it in his pocket. Some of the things he picks up are just trifles but, all the same, he's that way inclined. If he found money to buy himself sweets with he would take it quickly enough. Sweets, tobacco, that's when you see that he was born ill.

It is no longer simply a question of moral weakness but of a potential for harm which reveals itself with the illness and the failure of mental control. This potential is also observed in the violence and wickedness attributed to the domination of nerves: "They're tough cases, they get stubborn, they act stupidly. They are *ch'tits*, real *ch'tits*."

In this area of France the word *ch'tits* is used to cover the bad, the wicked, the ill, the sickly and the depressed. A mad dog is called *ch'tit*. To be a *ch'tit* to someone means to make his life a misery, to torment him (Gagnon, 1972, p. 120). It is a new face of wickedness hidden behind the façade of illness. Alongside the voluble anger of nerves, it is the cold anger of resentment known as "malice" (*ibid.*, p. 225). Alongside the violent wickedness of nerves which threatens with blows, it is the sullen wickedness which threatens with malign deeds:

> What I'm always afraid of, even though they say that they've been placed and they're not dangerous, is that they're taken by a fit of madness and do some harm or that they'll set the house on fire just at a time when you're not expecting anything. I've always been frightened of that. I'm scared of fire. As for doing us any harm, I don't think they would. You would have to make them very angry. They would have to be very angry before they hit us.

Aggressive drives and the desire to harm are always present, whether evident or latent. In some it is immediately obvious in the "look, the heavy face", "the sullen silence" or in the malign intentions behind the way an axe or a knife is handled:

> The first one, we didn't keep him, he was a bit . . . He had stolen an axe which he took up into his bedroom. We didn't want him . . . not with all that. We said, well, he took it into his room, you can imagine how frightened we were. Even at the beginning he didn't look very pleasant . . . He wasn't very gentle, that one . . .

More commonly, the foster parents point to the more benign face of this potential in the "stupidities", "tricks" and "turns" of the lodgers: "They can be bad with the children, they can play some kind of nasty trick."

They expect to see the emergence of a maleficent potential in precisely the best-known and most adapted lodgers who, as they grow bolder, start to commit thefts or make excessive demands. However, when it is not reinforced by social contact with other patients, the potential for harm is generally only thought to explode in its full virulence, in characteristic acts of malevolence, when the patient is suffering from an attack:

> I've got patients who I'm not afraid of at all. They can be attacked by a fit of madness, but so can we. That's a question of illness.

It is at this level that mentality and character are joined in illness. The traits of the illness become moral traits often designated by the term "it's his vice", "it's his weakness" and reciprocally: "Some of them are liars, some of them are false, it's the illness." These traits sometimes appear to be etched on the being of the individual like traits of character:

> A violent character, that's a patient. It's because of the illness. Us too, you know, sometimes we're violent as well . . .

This assimilation emphasizes the dual nature of malice. On the one hand, it is rooted in the nature of the patient: "Some of them are deceitful, their character isn't the same as the civilians'."

On the other hand, it is aimed at others, either gratuitously or as a reaction to some act:

> You don't want to get on the wrong side of that lad. That's a failing of his. It just takes someone to oppose him. And he's often played tricks on us. He's dangerous. If you get him angry, and there are times when he deserves it, you never have the last word. He gets his revenge. He punctures a tyre or one day you find that something of yours is broken. We tell him not to do it. He's played us a few tricks like that. He's done the same to my mother. Let me tell you what happened with my mother. He got it into his head that she had broken his electric razor. She had a new pair of shoes and he threw

them into the pond. There's nothing bad in it. Nothing happens to anyone who hasn't done anything to him. He just takes his revenge. You can't tell what he's going to do. He doesn't say anything . . . but . . .

In all its aspects and at all its levels, *the propensity to wickedness always corresponds to a defect of correlative thought and the failure of the brain:*

He pays us a lot of bad turns. That side of him has developed more than the intellectual side. He can hardly read or write. With counting it's just the same, he can just about get by. In some ways he isn't difficult, but in others . . . You can't study the one side of him. If he wants to do something bad to you, he'll do it. If he wants to do you a kindness, he'll do it as well. Often it's sweets for the child or flowers for me, and then at other times he'll do you a bad turn . . . There's no point remonstrating with him. The next moment he's forgotten it, he doesn't remember. He's got an empty head.

In this way a study of the moral face of the patient complements the study of the biological, pragmatic and social faces and produces an outline sketch of the insane man.

The Functional Nucleus of the Organism

The way this representation is constructed obeys an underlying structural model which is presented in Diagram 1 (p. 195). This model identifies an elementary functional nucleus at the heart of the organism which is influenced by the workings of mental illness. This influence has a twin effect, impinging, on the one hand, on the order which regulates the functioning of the three components of the nucleus – cerebral, biological and nervous – as well as on their interrelations, and, on the other hand, on the material order which affects the types of production associated with them. The first effect of the illness is revealed in a central, regulatory dysfunctioning which defines, in the specific nature of its otherness, a *state of the patient*, while the secondary effects of this dysfunctioning at the level of organic, active and mental life determine the *states of illness* which may differ in degree and quality.

Observable in all the judgements made on the capacities, behaviour and potential of the lodgers, this vision constitutes a general framework which makes it possible to apply a norm of pathological distortion to which the differing expectations, control methods and attitudes of the foster parents correspond. The state of the patient implies a variable extent of cerebral and nervous regulation of organic and psychological life which is modified, oriented, guided to differing degrees by the "control" of the brain, or exacerbated, automated, biased by the excitation of the nerves. The gravity of these effects may range from a major dysfunctioning of the functional nucleus of the organism (FNO) to a paranormal functioning, ranging through

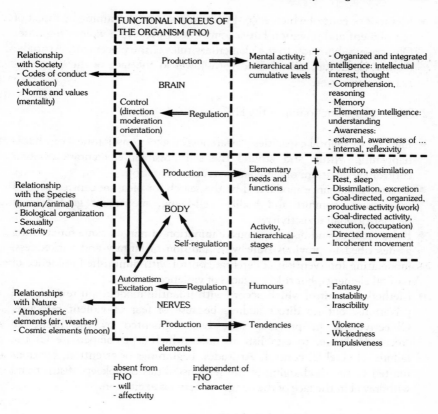

Diagram 1

Representation of the functional nucleus of the organism

a scale within which we can discern a number of constellations where the attributes corresponding to mental, bodily and nervous productions (summarized in Diagram 1) are interwoven with the behaviour and attitudes of the foster parents evoked in the last two chapters.

1 Major dysfunctioning of the FNO

- Maximum cerebral deficiency: mental activity and cerebral control almost non-existent.
- Maximum organic dominance, state close to bestiality with: lack of control of biological functions; excessive and blind satisfaction of needs; lack of coordination of movements, agitation, wandering or prostration; inaction.
- Autonomy and domination of nerves: instability, irascibility, violence (direct influence of natural elements).

- Methods of control which accord with animal model: training by threat of punishment and privation but accompanied by fear of a violent response. Objective: submission to the elementary rules of the placement. Attitude: disdain, revulsion, distrust and withdrawal in the face of the danger of nervous excitation.

2 Profound dysfunctioning of the FNO

- Elementary mental capacities: "awareness" makes consciousness of what is happening within and around the self possible; elementary cerebral control: moderation, organic and nervous orientation.
- Organic dominance modulated by the search for pleasure centred on oral satisfaction, comfort and bodily well-being, movement guided by a hedonistic goal; no activity.
- Independence and discontinuous domination of nerves: same functioning as described in previous state with addition of fantasy and wickedness; moderating intervention of cerebral control with diminished influence of natural elements, but risk of attacks of violence.
- Methods of control which accord with infantile model: oral rewards and privations, but no direct address because of fear of violent response. Objective: as in previous state but augmented by the desire to "recuperate", i.e. to establish an order which will compensate for the failures of cerebral control. Attitudes: beginnings of attention; relations limited to the discharging of the responsibilities of upkeep; distrust and withdrawal in the face of the danger of nervous excitation.

3 Reduced dysfunctioning of the FNO

- Reduced mental capacities: awareness is augmented by understanding and the beginnings of memory; increased cerebral control with the capacity for "direction". The possibility of social apprenticeship through imitation arises together with a limited social capacity but is accompanied by the risk of whimsical insubordination and the risk of "malice".
- Residual organic dominance: improved control of functions and needs, but focused on oral satisfaction and greed; coordinated movement; activity oriented towards a goal allowing for the more or less automatic supervised performance of minor tasks. But risk of instability due to influence of nerves.
- Relative independence and intermittent domination of the nerves: same picture as in previous state but with increased cerebral moderation; intermittent nervous excitation.
- Methods of control accord with infantile model, with recourse to admonishment. Objectives: education, adaptation, "to get to work". Attitude: beginnings of consideration, workplace relations, reduction of defence against risk of nervous excitation.

4 Minor dysfunctioning of the FNO

- Minor mental deficiency: good memory, beginnings of comprehension and reasoning; increased cerebral control (direction) over body, nerves and mental activity. This results in the possibility of education, integration into social norms, but with the risk of insubordination, malice and moral contamination due to contact with peers.
- Reduced organic dominance, emergence of differentiated activity: organic control, residual oral focusing which is counterbalanced by other pleasures or interests; attention paid to personal belongings (clothes, objects); more autonomous and responsibly organized, productive activity; search for leisure activities, gregariousness; persistent nervous instability.
- Reduced independence of nerves, intermittent domination: attenuation of preceding picture; the potential for nervous excitation is manifested in the form of temporary attacks or as the distortion of higher activities.
- Method of control: the model of infantile apprenticeship is augmented by flattery, the manipulation of needs and desires, advice. Objectives: as in the preceding state. Attitude: the same but with displays of familiarity and understanding of the individual.

5 Paranormal functioning of the FNO

- No mental deficiency: emergence of organized intelligence to complete comprehension and reasoning; high degree of cerebral control but persistence of inability to "manage one's life"; thought and intellectual interest with more or less anomic manifestations as a result of the integration of social norms and the perverse influence of the nerves; risk of weakness and moral contamination by environment.
- Residual organic dominance, development of activities: the traits distinguishing this from the preceding state are the acquisition of the capacity for professional work and a developed capacity for social autonomy. But a focusing on oral pleasures together with signs of instability can reveal insufficient cerebral control and the influence of the nerves.
- Diminution of nervous dominance: as in previous case.
- Methods of control: the methods mentioned earlier are augmented by the evaluation of performance and its reward, the acknowledgement of abilities in accordance with the model followed in interactions between adults. Objectives and attitudes remain as above, with an increase in esteem and integration into the family.

This typology is of course an artificial reconstruction whose characteristics are more rigid and systematized than the actual descriptions of individual lodgers on which it is based. Nevertheless, it does provide a faithful reflection of the way in which representations and behaviour are linked, illustrating in its structural and instrumental aspects the processes of objectification and anchoring identified in the theory of social representations. It brings to the fore the peculiarities of the hidden system which organizes the image of the mental patient.

This vision contains a certain number of striking characteristics: the dissociation of cerebral and nervous systems; the fact that the attributes and functions which are conferred on the nervous system give it the same importance as the brain with which it is contrasted; the hierarchy of aptitudes and levels of cerebral activity; the idea of a totally "cybernetic" control and interpretation of the development of human activity; the thresholds delimiting the passage between increasing levels of organization and ability etc. All these elements provide an overview of a naïve "theory" of man which is closely associated with the naïve "psychology" which it complements and justifies. And yet this vision still contains gaps, both surprising and revealing. Some dimensions and functions such as will, sexuality and communication are barely touched on. Nor is there the slightest mention of affectivity! Even if this is situated along with the other elements mentioned above in a zone not yet explored by the representation, it is still surely fundamental to the representation of human beings – unless it is radically lacking in the representation of the patient?

These questions, like those raised by the relationship between the brain and the nerves which mediate both a social order and a natural order, focus our attention on the investigation of the way the illness intervenes in the production of the effects and states we have observed so far, as well as on its nature and genesis.

Chapter Seven

Thinking about Mental Illness

> Listen, in their illness they all have a different
> way of being ill.
>
> The illness, that depends on how badly they've
> got it, whether it's by birth or whether it's by
> accident.
>
> Well, they're ill. They aren't people like us.
> They're people with something wrong inside.
>
> They have to get out a bit . . . otherwise it affects
> the brain.

The opposition of brain and nerves takes on a new and more precise significance when we turn to the description of the effects of mental illness on functions, aptitudes, behaviour and their explanation. The gradation of states of illness which ranges from the biological to the social is based on the regulatory dynamic of the brain and the nerves within the organism. Although this dynamic can be specifically referred to a dysfunctioning of the brain and the nerves, it is primarily viewed in its global aspect where it defines the nature of the mentally ill man as being radically different from the nature of the normal man. Equally, when there is a need to characterize specific individuals in terms of their illness and its origins, the target of the illness assumes prime importance: "with him it's the brain that doesn't work," "him, it's his nerves that have gone." The significance attributed to the organic substrate introduces a fundamental division into the population of patients. This is particularly clear when individual cases are under consideration: "It all depends on the type of illness he's got, whether he's a nervous case or whether he's subnormal," or when an appeal is made to historical comparisons:

> All the same, in the past I think the patients were genuine mental cases. It's
> different with the young ones today. When you see them you realize that
> they're bags of nerves.

In attempting to account for particular cases in the absence of any supporting knowledge, this distinction is complemented by a consideration of the conditions, both temporal and factual, under which the illness first appeared. This may be "by birth", "in childhood" or "by accident". These two points of reference, the zone and the circumstances of the attack, which are uniformly and universally applied, constitute the scheme through which the object, illness, is constructed. They combine to form an etiology. The period of confinement makes it possible to postulate the influence, whether simple or combined, of endogenous and exogenous factors in the morbid process in which defining different types of brain or nervous diseases vary depending on the degree of exposure of the brain or the nerves.

Whilst the regulatory function of the brain is always seen to be disturbed, the integrity of its intellectual aptitudes and functions may be preserved to a greater or lesser degree depending on the time when the illness took its hold. It is in this sphere of mental activity that the differentiation of cerebral attacks attains significance. This is illustrated by two typical cases. The first, the "innocent", is an extreme case in terms of the limitations of ability. The second, the "crackpot", is more ambiguous. Sometimes grouped together with the retarded, the crackpot is also related to the "nutter" or the "head case" in both of whom the nervous dimension predominates. In fact, it is in this way that the two apparently major mental afflictions are designated. These are *deficiency* and *breakdown* and they differ in their symptomatic and functional appearance as well as in their time of emergence.

Deficiency consists of the privation of certain intellectual aptitudes, the obliteration of certain zones of mental activity without any impairment of the functioning of residual activities. Breakdown is the disturbance of mental functions, the disordering of intellectual activity without impairment of abilities. Mental illness reveals itself in the two contrasted forms of inhibition in the first case and excitation in the second. We have already seen that excitation is imputed to the nerves and that distortions of thought can often be explained by nervous domination. This results in an affinity between mental breakdown and nervous imbalance which relates them in a number of clinical observations and blurs the line of demarcation between the crackpot and the nervous case, thus isolating deficiency in an order which is radically different from the other "mental illnesses".

This differentiation assumes its full significance when considered in the light of the notions which are associated with the designation of the time and conditions of emergence of the illness. To say that it comes *from* birth, *from* childhood or *by* accident is to mobilize biological, genetic and social representations which order the different types of affliction within a continuum which is bounded by the poles of innocence and nervous illness.

Innocence, Its Degrees, Reasons and Limits

Deficiency is thus embodied in innocence which, in local parlance, embraces all cases of retardation. Its appearance prevents the intellectual capacity from crossing a specific threshold known as "comprehension". On this side of the threshold, the various levels of deficiency reflect an image of the initial stages of cerebral evolution which determine mental age at critical periods of physical growth which are quite precisely related to real age. The elementary mental acquisitions attributed to the retarded individual are situated at between two and seven years. These are walking, the development of reflexes, and later "awareness" which makes a rudimentary education possible without yet allowing the development of true comprehension which consists in the immediate understanding of complex objects, the capacity to memorize and, most importantly, the acquisition of reading and writing:

> We've had L for twenty-five years. He's a child. He's not a lodger any more. He's like a very small child. When he came to us he was like a very small kid . . . He doesn't know anything. He's completely defenceless. You have to guide him like a small child. You can't let him out on the road because he doesn't understand the danger. He would wander around in the road, jump into it. He's like a very young child. He doesn't understand a thing, a two-year-old kid.

> I've got two at the moment. They were taken when they were four. You have to do everything for them. They can't read or write but you can teach them a few things. You can send them to do the shopping but at first they didn't know how to say good morning or thank you when they were in a shop. Now I always say to them: 'Say good morning, say goodbye, say thank you when you're given something.'

> There's one who has been in the asylum since the age of six. At first I thought that if he had been well looked after he could have learnt to read, but now I've realized that it isn't possible.

Seven years, school age, the age of reason, is the upper limit of the innocent. Beyond this age lie the social and academic apprenticeships which constitute the base on which the higher mental functions are built. Beyond this age, the patient leaves the framework of mental deficiency whose major attributes are inscribed in the three most current definitions of innocence: "they aren't aware," "they don't understand," "they can't read or write."

The explanation of these shortcomings is organic: deficiency is correlated with insufficient development, with an arresting of brain growth which keeps the patient in an infantile state. In "those who have it from birth", the "retarded by birth", it is the result of a congenital defect. In a "childhood case" the brain develops normally until something happens (accident, fall or illness). The patient then "remains" at the age at which the brain was "stopped":

> C. He's an innocent, isn't he? *He's a man who hasn't developed.* He had meningitis when he was small and that's where his brain has stayed. He's just the same as when he was very little.

Innocence is comparable to the atrophy of an organ and is held to be unchangeable. Of the brain which is "halted" or "withered", the foster parents say "it's empty in there" (in the cranium), whereas in the case of mental breakdown they say "the brain is empty", a reference to the affected organ. The state of the organ defines the level of aptitude and, consequently, the scope for education and improvement:

> He had an accident. He's got the mind, the conversation of a child. He's come to understand a bit more. He's improved. But I don't think he'll ever be able to understand more than that.

> A child who's born with a *withered brain*, you can do as much as you want for him. *There might be a very slight improvement* but he'll never be normal. It's the withered brain. Children who are born like that with their brain withered, *there's no hope that it will get any better.*

This makes it easier to understand the diagnostic value conferred on starting school. On the one hand, the efforts which this demands testify to the completion of the brain's growth and marks a decisive step in the development of the individual. Thus even those who show a level of understanding will still be classed as innocent if they were incapable of being normally educated. But to have experienced even the beginnings of school with a degree of success, that is to say, to know at least how to read and write, is enough to prevent the diagnosis of retardation. On the other hand, this qualitative leap out of infancy exposes the patient to outside influences and is thus also a leap out of innocence. Innocence implies a positive moral value which can only be explained by the conjunction of ways in which cerebral growth, the processes of socialization and the role of confinement are conceived of as the interdependence of organic development, mental development and the advent of maturity.

In fact, an illness originating in birth or childhood is not a sufficient definition of innocence as the same designation is applied to other patients who are judged to be intelligent but are also qualified as nervous:

> They are boys who have always been like that. You can't really tell whether the illness has changed them or not. Either they are really and truly innocent or they are there for some other reason. There's always a reason and there's nothing you can do about it.

> Little P. He grew up at Vaucluse. His mother threw him into the stairwell from the fifth floor. After that she abandoned him. He was found in a dustbin. He's not stupid or anything but he has trouble speaking because his whole face is deformed and he's nervous as well, very nervous. He suffers attacks of nerves.

In the case of those who are ill "by birth" or "from childhood", the age of confinement plays a decisive role in distinguishing between the innocent and the nervous. It serves as a reference point to gauge both the level of retardation and the state of innocence. Confinement is in itself a significant consideration. As we have seen, it is generally held that if a patient is confined then "something" (event, accident, incident, crime or crisis) must have happened during the course of which the illness "showed itself" or was "recognized". This schema is more complex in the case of retardation, as those who are considered to be truly innocent are often brought to the asylum in distress because of the failure of their vital and mental resources. The patient is generally thought to have been confined either after losing his family through abandonment or death, or, if the family still exists, because it does not possess the means (material, psychological or moral) to look after him, the decision to confine the patient in this case being made at the time the deficiency is recognized. Thus the age of entry into the asylum, excluding hospital stays which are known to have been dictated by other circumstances, is taken to be an indication of the mental age of the patient. Thus the foster parents speak of "the children of Vaucluse", "they are like children of four or five years". This age is also the guarantee of innocence because if the family defers confinement of the retarded child independently of any outside influences it can only be due to the actions of the patient himself:

> The old one we've had for thirty years, he came when he was sixteen. He's not like a man who fell ill as an adult. He's stayed like he was when he was very small, but he's always been a bit special. And what's more, his mother told me, he's still got his mother and sister, she told me it was because of that they put him inside.

From here we can return to the first case in point: "There must have been something" which is imputed to the illness and which is enough to prove that the entrant is no longer innocent, not retarded, but a different sort of patient:

> Twenty years ago, only one patient in fifty knew how to read. They were all illiterate, all backward. It's not the same now. They've got something. And obviously with the ones who have already lived normally it's a different kind of illness.

Confinement which occurs after school age points to a different illness from innocence and combines cerebral "breakdown" and not deficiency with nervous breakdown and often with "something" more:

> The patients who are put in the asylums at the age of seventeen or twenty, I wouldn't want them. They're nervous cases, whilst the ones I've got here, they were put there at the age of four. They are children who were placed in Vaucluse when they were four years old. Well, they're retarded children.

It is both curious and significant that a gap should exist in the representation of the age of confinement. There is no notion of hospitalization between the pre-school and post-adolescent ages. This gap introduces a discontinuity into the pathological process with the late confinement of the patient then becoming a source of anxiety:

> People who have it from birth, mental patients who have convulsions and things like that, people who were confined at five, you can readapt them. But the ones who enter the hospitals at seventeen or twenty, they are a lot more nervous. A lot of them are difficult to adapt to life here. And you can be sure they've done something bad, something like that.

Here we see the equivalence, retardation = childhood = innocence = harmlessness:

> Personally I prefer mental patients who are really retarded. The others, who have a degree of education, if you can put it that way, who understand a little without really understanding . . . but who get nervous anyway . . . who have illnesses which arrived later . . . well I think . . . you're not very sure where they come from or what they've done.

> Harmless people like that, the retarded ones, I'm not afraid of them. But the ones who are put in the asylums at twenty, you can't be as confident about them, they're nasty people. I had one. I was afraid of him. He was a boy who had definitely been put there because he had done something . . .

Moreover, an early entrance into a psychiatric institution becomes a guarantee of safety which opposes infancy to youth and thus, in combination with the time of the attack, deficiency to breakdown.

Isolated from society, the asylum allows those who enter it as children to retain their innocence. The "lack of awareness" or the "lack of understanding" which are determined by the patient's mental level are redoubled by his healthy ignorance of the things of the world or, at a less moral level, by the sheltering of a fragile mind from the example and temptations of the world. Thus confinement puts a premature end to any bad tendencies by depriving the patient of the stimulation of experience:

> The ones who went there as young children, who never knew civilian life, they don't know anything about reality.

> In general, the ones who enter the hospitals later are nasty people. They're there because of the bottle, I should think. Whereas a child who was put into the asylum at four, he doesn't really know what he's up to, does he?

Organ, Socialization and Breakdown

What does this mean if not that confinement interferes with a process of development which, as of a certain moment, demands for its completion a contribution which is derived from contact with external reality and social apprenticeship? This is because as well as hindering the actualization of certain tendencies, confinement leaves the patient's intelligence suspended in a void:

> He never left Vaucluse. He didn't know a thing. I tell you he was quite stultified when he arrived. He didn't know what a butterfly was, or a bird. Can you imagine it? And today he gets by in life. To be truthful, these people need to learn a lot.

> We had him when he was eighteen and he didn't know a thing. He came from an asylum and he didn't have a clue about anything. I had him and I taught him. And now you can see that he's quite a presentable lad.

What is being said is that deficiency is not imputed to confinement, rather that the emergence of qualitatively distinct afflictions which are marked by mental breakdown is associated with temporal and social dimensions.

In effect, when the development of the brain is completed – at approximately the tenth year, to judge by the type of scholastic knowledge such as reading and writing which is used as an indicator[1] – purely qualitative changes take place in mental functioning which bring the role of socialization to the foreground. This, favoured by the malleability of the brain, and mediated by the family environment, the immediate social environment or the structure of the institution, lies at the root of both normality and disorder. It also sanctions or strengthens the expression of a deviant nature and is, without doubt, the reason why a certain length of time is needed before such deviance, manifested in actions, provokes the confinement of the "youths" after their sixteenth year.

The family contributes to the formation of mentality through the education it provides and the models it offers. Any failure on the part of the family environment will have an immediate effect on mental functioning. This is particularly evident in the lack of firmness and discipline denigrated by the foster parents when they attack the liberality of middle-class education. In a changing world these tendencies and errors in the family environment contribute to the discrepancy in the mentalities observed in the youths and, as we have seen, correspond to a taste for an easy life, for money,

---

[1] This threshold of academic knowledge seems to correspond to the completion of middle school which previously formed the limit of compulsory education in France and which brought with it the certificate of primary education.

for waste and for immediate gratification. If educational discipline and rigour have such a high value, it is because their aim is the acquisition of consistency, effort and independence, and because in this way they contribute to the development of initiative and responsibility and have a direct effect on the personality.

First of all they "sort them out", teach them "a sense of what life's about":

> Living next to us, it stabilizes them, gets them used to life. We manage to teach them how to live. But there's no improvement at the mental level. Once you've got a lodger, if he doesn't know how to live in a certain way then he can't be cured. Looking at it another way, it teaches them a thing or two. It gives them a sense of what life's about. Because in the asylum they've got everything, they've got everything they need. They don't have to worry about anything, whereas here they have to think that it's tobacco day, that they mustn't miss the shower day. They manage to make their bed. They manage to think that if their shoes aren't well kept, they'll have to go without tobacco. They still have more to do than in the asylum.

Second, as the joint effect of an authoritarian hand and a model of firmness which the educator must show, they help to strengthen the patient's character, to "recuperate" him, giving him a mental framework without which there is neither rectitude of life nor adaptation to the constraints of the social environment:

> Maybe he didn't have a lot of natural strength of character, and his mother was a widow. She couldn't spend much time looking after him . . . I don't think he can have had a lot of will power when he was young, because he was there for a long time and he's said to have fallen in with bad company, and he certainly went on the bottle. And the mother was a widow with three boys so I think it's because of that they put him here.

> When the big one's mother came she was happy to see him but she didn't want him to wait for her before eating: 'Leave him, leave him.' She was frightened of changing his habits. 'Don't change his habits or he'll get confused.' That's how understanding she is.

The failure of education also eases the path of the illness by preventing the mind from constructing a defence against the harmful influence of the human environment. This, like society in the midst of the transformations which characterize the modern, urban world, is rarely conceived as exerting a beneficial influence. Because normality is defined in relationship to the rules of the environment to which the foster parents belong, modes of life which originate in another type of environment or society are thought of as favouring deviance and mental disorder. On the one hand, the bad example the youth finds in the company of his peers, who are increasingly left to their own devices as they grow older, threatens to push him sooner or later into misdeeds.

On the other hand, the temptations which an urban consumer society offers to the adolescent threaten him with the dislocation of an imbalanced way of life the effects of which will have repercussions for his mental functioning:

> There's no point saying he's innocent, because he's not. He's ill, but he's not innocent at all. I can promise you, he can argue and everything. What brought him here was a rather too tumultuous way of life, rather too fast-moving for his brain. I get the impression that it moved a bit faster than he did. What's more he's finished all his studies. His father was going to get him a job in Colmar, I don't know where. After that he wanted to go off with the beatniks and that's what he was like when he was taken in. And anyway he's always a bit like that. I don't know if I can explain myself well enough for you to understand, but I still think he had quite a well developed intelligence. He wasn't stupid. He knew very well. He was quite capable of writing a letter. He had a degree of intelligence. But there were times when everything was chaotic and he would tell mad stories or he would start singing and thumping the table. He was really . . . I don't know what you think about the beatniks but in my opinion they're innocent. At the time I used to compare him a bit with those people. As I see it, they are people with something which isn't quite right. I don't know if that's the way you ought to judge them but, really, I think they're off their rockers. But as far as teaching is concerned . . .

The same argumentation is applied to the question of academic instruction which is also foreign to the foster parents' world. An instrument in the formation of mentalities, it lies at the base of the differentiation between generations, making the young a little "stranger", inspiring a respect which is mixed with anxiety:

> The young ones today who have lived in the cities and have been to school, they're not country people, they don't have the same ways.

> The ones who are completely innocent, we're quite familiar with them. We involve them in the life of the family, it helps conversation. But the ones who have been taught, well, we leave them alone. They're more difficult because they understand more. At my mother's there was one who almost took his diploma. He's the sort you have to . . . you spoke with him like with someone of note, you had a certain respect. People like that, you're not familiar with them, you stay formal . . . I had one, an industrial designer. I was very formal with him as well. But he couldn't stay. He got bored, very bored. He wanted to work but it wasn't his job and you could tell he didn't know how. He was bored to death . . . That's difficult. When they're like everyone else it's more pleasant.

A Pathogenic Culture

The array of significations which is organized around the idea of academic education helps to explain the link between the organism and the cultural. Passage through "the schools" is seen as a potential aggravator of social factors in mental disequilibrium which may create an atmosphere within the organism which is favourable to the development of the illness. It can increase the risk of disorder through an exclusive involvement of cerebral life at the expense of manual and material activity, an agent of balance and an antidote to tedium. It is because of this that formal education is associated with specific functional problems which are characterized by breakdown (loss of memory, speech difficulties etc.), idleness (through practical inability or refusal to work), mental disorder (delirium, incoherence of ideas, morbid absorption in thought etc.) and – a trait with a fundamental significance for the characterization of juvenile mental pathology – nervous problems.

It appears that school education, which occurs during a critical phase of biological development, is itself able to cause cerebral disturbances. Culture is here seen to play a pathogenic role which can be translated into a scheme of symptoms which closely associates mental breakdown and nervous breakdown. Particularly evident in youths, this mental attack is radically differentiated from that of infancy or adulthood. This idea is found at its most powerful in the older foster parents who show no reticence in giving voice to beliefs relating to the part played by academic instruction in the etiology of mental illness. For them, "the ones we get now come because of the studying", "it's the learning that's brought them here", and this because of the following process. The accumulation of knowledge entails excessive cerebral activity which damages the brain and, as an indirect consequence, affects the nervous system:

> The one who does the shopping has lapses of memory. He used to have a job and now he's here . . . He was too educated. That affected his brain . . . The other one is just the same. He's always in his books. He studied for a long time. I don't know what. It doesn't matter what it was. It affected him. He was too knowledgeable. That's affected his nerves. I see him. He reads and reads. Either he's out or he's reading. If he's standing up he's got to be walking. He can't stay sitting down.

Sometimes the effect of intellectual work is aggravated by living conditions which are not commensurate with the required effort. In particular, insufficient food and sleep are considered to be a consequence of the decision to pursue intellectual activity:

> The young ones, they get tired when they study too much. And then some of them don't eat as well as they ought to if they're going to study like that . . .

And that's how it starts. They fall, they grow anaemic and it affects the brain.

There was one who's left now. When he was at school he was always first. He did his military service. He wanted to be an engineer and he had all the books. And his father thought that he ate in the evenings when he got back from the factory. Instead of eating he would be deep in his books. So of course he developed a nervous depression. While he was here if you told him to do something he would say, 'yes, I'll do it', but you couldn't tell him to do two things at a time. His head wouldn't hold it. It wouldn't stay there . . . There was nothing to be done . . .

More generally, everything which constitutes an over-intense stimulation of the brain becomes a cause of illness, for example the noise, speed and rhythm of urban life "which moves too fast for the brain":

They spend all their time running about, running here, running there, doing this, that and the other.

It's tiring. I haven't been in Paris much, but in Bourges it's bad enough. I told my daughter that I would never live there.

The ones who fall into a nervous depression, it's because they can't stand the noise.

With some of them it's because of the noise, because of the schools. Some of them can't manage, they just can't manage, their brains go off. They were perfectly all right and then their brains turned.

Images such as "fall" and "turns off" reveal a double representation which concerns both the organ, its process of deterioration, and mental illness. The deterioration of the brain is the cause of mental breakdown. The brain "turns off" like milk, "curdles" like butter. A naturalist vision, inspired by everyday experience, makes use of this analogy to attribute mental disturbance to a chemical and physical process. In the same way the foster parents say, "He had a plug in his brain which stopped him talking." It is the corollary of the representation which presents retardation as the halting and withering of the brain.

These linguistic traits have an even richer content in that they designate something of what mental illness is: "it", what is "it"? A still obscure agent of nature: an exogenous and polymorphous force which associates the phenomena of organic transformation with processes of a more or less material nature such as noise, speed, reading. It is a force against which one fights by eating and which can produce both anaemia and depression, affect the brain and the nerves, impede speech, bring lapses of memory or twitches or unrest. Is this not the unified, materialist vision of madness reemerging in order to unite the cultural and symbolic dimension to the organic dimension, to unite the nervous, a part of the natural universe, with the cerebral, a part of the social universe?

Today there are only a few people who express themselves in such clear terms and, more significantly, organize these terms in an explicit causal argument. But if we listen to the speech of those who record the representation in a more modern and more neutral language we find that it continues to operate implicitly. We find the repeated use of verbs like "to curdle", "to turn off", "to fall", the accentuation of the role of academic education and the associative contiguity which links this to the various forms of cerebral and nervous breakdown, the reassuring images of innocence and the disquieting images of nervousness, the multiform yet unified presence of mental illness manifesting equivalent symptoms of its diversity. All this indicates that the effort to understand mental illness draws on disparate elements including the type of attack, the mode of attack and, in particular, the period of confinement. These elements are assembled within a construction which borrows from the anxiety of the group in the face of alien values, those of youth, the city, the modern world, and from the immediate understanding it gains from the practical and natural everyday environment. This construction formulates a representation of mental illness which conforms to a latent model. Can we take this exploration further?

The significations attached to attacks which strike the grown adult confirm that the dichotomy between young and old, earlier lodgers and today's lodgers, corresponds to different conceptions of pathological processes. Disturbances of cerebral functioning which correspond to breakdown are similar in the youth and in the adult, but the organization of the clinical picture and the etiology are specific to each.

Where Does the Illness Come From?

When confinement, and thus the illness, appears in a grown adult, it is the circumstances of its emergence that come under scrutiny. The response of the foster parents is not a *why* but a *where from*. The movement from an illness of birth or of infancy to attacks which occur later in life is a movement from the *of* to the *from* or *by*, from the state which corresponds to a stage of development to the functioning which corresponds to the intervention of an external event or agent. This movement thus reformulates the question of history's determination of the organic.

In fact, mental illness in the adult is said to be "by accident": no conception of an endogenous process seems to exist in connection with this period of life. Nevertheless, the variety of cases encompassed by the term "accident", together with the stories told about many of the mental patients, shows that an internal pathological development cannot be excluded and can serve as an implicit criterion in the distinction of the various accidents.

Let us start with the distinction drawn between alcoholism and the other accidents. To say that "the illness comes from alcohol" masks a number of different conceptions: "With some of them, it comes from alcoholism, but nowadays it depends on the type of alcoholism as well." The first proposes a direct if restrictive causality. Drinking alcohol causes well-known problems, the most common of which is also the least specific and the most worrying, namely violence, the so-called "fighting drunk" which is seen to be related to nervous violence and wickedness:

> The other one was a drinker. He wasn't an easy type. You had to be careful not to say anything to him. I knew if he had been drinking and I kept my mouth shut. One day he threw his soup at the gate. Another day I was frightened that he was going to hit me. When he threw his soup at the gate I was shocked for a second. It's after that I started to be frightened. Now he doesn't drink any more. He comes in without saying hello or good evening. He doesn't speak. That's how he is. I don't insist too much. When he used to drink and behaved violently I never tried to change him.

This violence does not appear to be exclusively dependent on drunkenness, indeed this state awakens rather than creates it. In fact alcoholism appears to be a consequence of the illness in that it reveals a morbid maleficence. When the effects of drunkenness are less extreme, alcoholism is seen as a vice turned to by an individual who has been weakened by his living conditions, his education, external influences, or again as a refuge for someone who has been traumatized by unhappy events. It is an instance of addiction which can be imputed to a pathological personality structure:

> We had a very good one, a North African, who was truly gentle. He did a bit of handiwork. He liked to have something to interest him. He wanted to live his life again, if you like. But he started to drink. It was the illness. He told me a little bit about his problems. He lost all his family in Algeria. His wife had been murdered. He lost all his children. They died of starvation. And he came to work in France. He worked in a lot of places. And he must have started to drink, maybe because he was unhappy, maybe because he got used to the habit, the North Africans don't drink. He lost all his money. According to him he had a lot of money. And all that, well, it doesn't help you get better . . . If he had wanted to be really serious about it, he could have started to work again, he could have left . . . It's partly his fault.

Finally there is an alcoholism which is deemed to have a different "nature". This difference in nature comes from the fact that the illness derives from the alcoholism of the parents: "His father was probably an alcoholic, because a lot of them, most of them have inherited that."

The "heir to alcoholism" is not necessarily an alcoholic himself but he nevertheless carries another burden because his nervous system is irremediably damaged:

> If he's the child of an alcoholic you know that he won't be cured, that he's a nervous case, that he'll have to take medicine and that if he doesn't things will go wrong. And that's that.

In the first place, alcohol excites the nerves and clouds the mind. In the second place, it damages the functioning of the nerves. What we have here is more a view of the "organization" of the illness than of its heredity.

In its close association with the domain of the nerves, in its dual reference to a pathological domain – the one which engenders it and the one which it engenders – in the implied transition from a common vice or failing to an "incurable" and dangerous pathological state, alcoholism is profoundly different from other factors which lie at the root of mental disturbance in the adult. These other factors are characterized by a more selective action, relatively limited in time and defined by its effect. Furthermore, they do not entail total upheaval in the organization of the patient's personality, even if they profoundly disturb certain sectors of it. Nevertheless, these diverse pathogenic agents are all revealed by a breakdown which, despite the possibility of abatement, can regain its virulence at any moment. This encapsulates the entire problem of the adult patient:

> For the lodger maybe it's better if it's an illness of birth than if it comes by accident. He remains a child for the foster parent. You know that he's like that and that you can't change him . . . While with a man who has had an accident you're always saying to yourself: he might have, he might become . . . If he's looked after he might improve, but on the other hand he might break down again.

Whilst the cerebral problems which result from an organic or physical accident can leave certain faculties intact, they attack more specifically those which play an instrumental role in relationship to mental life (memory, attention or speech) and do not exclude the possibility of recuperation:

> I can't tell the future. Illness, whatever, might mean that it happens to us as well. My daughter was unlucky. She had her diploma and then at eighteen she got encephalitis. We had to teach her everything again, how to tell the time, to count and so on. So I said to myself that maybe the same thing happened to these people here.

It may even be that the accident leaves no mental traces or that only a physical handicap caused by the accident indicates that the patient has been confined:

> We had one who was released. He was a man who had had an accident in the underground. He was forty or so and came from a Paris hospital. When we saw him we said immediately: 'It's not possible. He can't be a lodger.' He was a good conversationalist, he wasn't retarded or anything. There was nothing about him, you couldn't tell him apart . . .

> And then there are disabled people who are there because they need to be looked after, because they're incapable of making a living but who, heaven knows, are hardly mentally ill any more, perhaps aren't mentally ill at all. I've had disabled patients who have done the shopping and you can't tell me that they are the only ones you don't notice. It doesn't seem like it. It looks as if it's just their disability which justifies them being brought here.

More specific than illness contracted during adulthood is the biographical accident in which the individual is forced to confront the unhappy or painful events of his past, with the consequent "shock" being the cause of mental breakdown:

> We didn't know her fate and we didn't know her life. At Dun there was a ruined countess. Her illness either came from her husband's life or her own.

In fact, a distinction is made between two types of "shock" which lead to noticeably different pathologies. On the one hand, there is the moral, affective shock which is associated with a private ordeal or difficult living conditions:

> It's an illness you can get from any kind of blow . . . The ones who have been attacked by . . . mental illness . . . There are a lot of things that can happen. It can be a misfortune, a death, family grief.

> There was one who stayed with my sister-in-law who you wouldn't have said was mentally ill in the slightest. He was a man who had done everything for himself. But he had all sorts of illnesses and had run out of resources. He hadn't been able to regain enough self-control to work and they put him in a home.

On the other hand, there is the nervous shock which is associated with a traumatic external situation a typical example of which is war.

The clinical picture which corresponds to the moral shock is relatively simple: minor mental disturbance; frequent signs of nervousness, generally limited to twitching; in contrast, frequent depressive states:

> Those people aren't really ill . . . a family grief, lapses of memory. But apart from that they're like anyone else. As far as work is concerned, the old one over there has got the willpower and the enthusiasm. You can talk with him well enough but the conversation isn't the same as with a normal person.

His weakness comes from the illness. There are gaps in his memory. He can't really keep up a conversation like a normal person. And if you remind him it can give him a shock. It can make him think, 'I'm not normal.'

They are people who've been traumatized by something or other, who have experienced some difficulty in remaining fully responsible for their lives. And that's why they are here. But apart from a few periods of depression, of I don't know what, they behave just like normal people.

Yet it is precisely these symptoms of depression which are charged with disquieting significance and reveal, despite the appearance of normality, the profound strangeness of the patient:

It's the toughest ones who become the most depressed, the ones who have been left by their wives. They're always thinking about it. Although they are well adapted and polite, it's always preying on their minds. That makes them more difficult. They have a tendency to spend their time in a daze. Sometimes they twitch.

What is disconcerting about the depressive is that the chain of thought itself might be affected, and unease is greatest when the mental faculties of the patient are most intact. This is because, as with the cases of youth, depression and academic instruction are often linked:

There are a lot of intellectuals. They are people who have been worn out, traumatized by family crises. There was one my salesman used to call M. He smelled like a goat and would come into the house with his boots covered in filth. And this gentleman had nearly won a *prix de Rome*, in architecture. An artist. He was responsible for the decorations at the *Société Théâtrale*, wonderful. And then there was a family crisis. His wife became the mistress of a lawyer. He was worn out, and the other one being a legal man he was able to see to it. Unless it was justified of course. In any case he was taken to a psychiatric clinic and then he landed up here . . . We're getting more and more of them. It's very depressing to see. We're getting more and more tired intellectuals.

Disturbances of thought are disorienting because they are difficult to discover and to understand. It is not for nothing that the bored patient is the one thought least able to work and that he is feared almost as much as the nervous case. The depressive appears to carry this sombre air "in himself" and his wickedness is expected because his disgust with life is intermingled with an urge to destroy:

He didn't want to eat. I went to find him and I said, 'You have to eat!'. To please me he said, 'I have eaten'. He had the knife on the table. He wanted to destroy himself. I felt a little sorry for him. Then I took the knife and closed the door. I made him a little bit frightened of me without being too aggressive towards him. I used to say 'You have to eat' without getting angry with him or anything like that, and I managed to get him to eat before I said anything . . . They are people, you understand, who you can't argue with. When they're angry you can't do anything with them. It's better to leave them alone or to treat them gently. I treated that one gently and everything went well. He was a nervous case, an extreme case. He was a man who had had a life before and who . . . when he arrived here there was no remedy for him. Later he started taking sedatives and that helped a bit.

This disruption of thought reveals the dominance of the nerves which is otherwise scarcely seen in the depressive. It is this which makes him an object of anxiety and groups him together with the young and the patients who have suffered a nervous shock:

Those people, their nerves are ill. They're nervous cases. Unfortunately there are a lot of them nowadays, especially amongst the young. A lot of civilians get nervous depressions. That's the fashionable illness nowadays.

The association of history and breakdown is further explained by the approach to nervous shock which, in the adult, is typified by the trauma of war. Such adults are thought to suffer a serious, primary attack on nervous functioning with, as a consequence, disturbances to both mental and active life. The importance attached to war extends to embrace all military situations. Military service, a biographical element which is every bit as crucial as academic instruction, figures amongst the proofs which show that the lodger "has known life outside". The adoption of a military career functions as a classificatory factor just as much as ethnic or national origin or the exercise of certain professions. The foster parents refer to "the legionnaire", "the paratrooper" in the same way they speak of "the North African", "the Pole" or "the teacher", and qualify them with negative characteristics: "hothead", "intolerable character", "bad tempered", "bold", "violent" and "complaining".

The roughness of military existence together with its more or less licentious peripheral aspects seems to create a different mentality which is particularly refractory to the regime of the Colony:

I didn't say anything to the paratrooper. He stayed together with the others and then suddenly he wanted to be with us all the time. Then one day I said to him, perhaps I shouldn't have, that he was a lodger like the others, that he wasn't any better than them. Perhaps I shouldn't have said that, things might have been different then, I don't know. I wasn't able to keep him. If he had soup he threw it away and said that he didn't get enough to eat. He said, 'In the summer I didn't get soup to eat in Paris.' I decided it couldn't go on like that, that there would always be something else. He had had a life with a woman. He couldn't get used to life in the Colony. He couldn't force himself to live like a monk. And you felt that there was something lacking in him.

At the same time, the apprenticeship and experience of violence constitute an incitement and a model around which relations with others are moulded:

> Some of them scare you, like the lodger who had been a paratrooper with his mania for taking machines to bits. He made a bad impression on me from the very start. I wasn't afraid for me because I knew that I could defend myself. But I was afraid for my husband, because he used to surprise you. My husband isn't really handicapped. He walked with a stoop when he was a child. Now he has arthritis and he wouldn't be able to defend himself because of his legs. I was frightened. I said to myself that if he ever got the idea of hitting him then my husband couldn't defend himself. And in his last placement the foster parent had been frightened as well, frightened that he would hit her, that he would attack her. He looked as if he would hit you. It's difficult to explain.

In the final analysis, whether violence is inflicted or suffered, it is an agent of aggression whose effects immediately influence the nerves:

> He was always going on about the same thing, that he had been in the war, that he couldn't work because the sun made him too hot or another time because he had been having too many drops, or because he wasn't paid enough. All the time there was something. At first he wasn't drugged enough and then after a while, you know, *the nerves get the upper hand. And then he started to shout. You couldn't get him to listen to reason any more. Impossible. He wasn't able to reason any more* . . .

And when military experience takes on an extreme nature, the memory of it continually recalls the accompanying upheavals:

> The other one is a legionnaire. If he didn't have his medicine then my legionnaire wouldn't be calm and gentle at all. He doesn't do anything, he wanders around and that's all. He amuses himself as he can.

> He became ill quite late, at the age of thirty-seven. *It was because he was scared. He was always frightened of bombardment. He was always afraid of the Germans. You can see it in his eyes, you know.* His mind easily goes back to when they attacked him and things like that. That's his illness. The last war. There are times when he's perfectly calm. And then, when he's eating or whatever, he thinks of it. He tells us what he saw in the Legion, what happened there. 'Oh Madame, that's what it was like.' I say yes. *What else should I say, because if I say no, he'll get into a state. If I contradict him! So I always have to agree with him. It's a fear of his but there's nothing wicked behind it. It's a fear which he's had and which is still here.*

When the event "makes an impression", its indelible trace is that of the emotion felt at the moment of the shock. It is not just a question of memory and reproduction, "the fear is here", it is the event and its repercussions which are etched in the being whose fundamental dimension it constitutes, a source of behaviour which is no longer adapted to the social environment, its codes and its norms. It expresses itself as violence and disorder because it is violence and disorder which mark the divide between the sufferer and the outside world. This is the reason why everything which is violent threatens to produce mental disorder and everything which is disorder threatens to provoke violence. War, as well as noise, speed, the city, any form of life which unsettles biological rhythms and natural balance, contravenes the established norms, menaces the individual and makes him menacing:

> We get more and more of that kind of illness with today's hectic life.

> The change in the patients, that's evolution. The evolution of everything as far as I can see. I have the feeling that life was more pleasant ten years ago. Today life is infernal.

> You don't feel as safe today. Nowadays we seem to get extreme nervous cases. I mean, it's because of modern life.

Moral disorder itself generates violence and the cause of certain nervous imbalances is thus seen to be the separation between the patient's parents.

Curdled Brains and Inner Force

Thus the nature of the accident which gave rise to the illness determines the type of affliction. In the naturalist representation, the emotional shock "goes to the brain" and causes a deterioration of the cerebral matter which is then revealed in irreversible functional disturbances:

> Him, it's that he could never get on with his father. *That soured him. But it can't be cured. If you've had your brain curdled like that it doesn't get better.*

It seems that, present within the being – "it's the illness that's here, it's here, there's nothing to be done" – the affliction in this case corresponds to an organic phenomenon of destruction or decomposition because, along with expressions such as "a plug in the brain" or the term "curdled", local vocabulary also makes use of words such as "off" in the sense of decomposed.[2]

The breakdown which follows the shock reveals itself in speech through

---

[2] In the French, *tranché* = decomposed, curdled, turned (when speaking of milk, wine, food), cut off (Gagnon, 1972, p. 323).

the patient's lapses of memory and, if the memory remains intact, through a disruption of thought – melancholy or delirium – whose aberrant path is subjected to the capricious and lunatic vacillations of the rhythm of the nerves, as we can see from this pathological sketch:

> Some of them became ill late, like the father . . . who's a good old man. During the first few years I had him, *it was still possible to keep up a conversation with him.* But now he's lost. You can't understand what he's saying, or anything at all. First of all it's a recurring illness, but that doesn't matter to us. He talks to himself. He sends messages, he telephones. We're not afraid of him, he's a good old man. You're frightened when you have nervous ones . . . *He's got a good memory and all that.* He's often told me what he used to be like. He hasn't told me that he was confined but he did tell me: 'they came to get me at work', he was a salesman at a chemist's shop. He said: 'My wife had a serious operation and then they came to get me, they took me and now I'm here . . . ' *He's ill of course. We know well enough that he's had something in his brain, maybe it was when his wife was ill that it turned,* maybe . . . I don't know.

The influence of the nerves makes itself felt at the level of the regulation of thought as a result of cerebral deficiency without necessarily expressing a fundamental breakdown of the nervous system. The chronic form of such a breakdown manifests itself as "agitation" and, in moments of paroxysm, as acts of violence (shouts, anger, aggressive actions) and "fits". The same is true of nervous shock which records the cause of trauma and the reactions which accompany it in the brain and in the body, in memory and in behaviour.

The sphere of the nerves is characterized by acting out. This is illustrated by the beliefs about the effect and the transmission of twitches which count amongst the clearest signs of an attack of nerves, so much so that it sometimes becomes the clearest indication of all mental illness. "Mental illness, we often think that it's if they twitch, they all do the same thing." Taken in its widest sense which embraces grimaces, jerky or uncoordinated movements as well as the more spectacular manifestations shown by the "nutter", twitching expresses nervous breakdown in the characteristic gesture of repetitious automatism. And in whatever degree it is manifested, it remains unpleasant and disquieting:

> First of all they are in their own room. We aren't in contact with them so we don't have to put up with them if they twitch, put up with seeing them the whole time.

This is because the spectacle given by the patient contains a danger. It is strange, it "shocks", it "makes an impression", it "frightens you". Confrontation with it entails the risk of suffering a nervous shock, of breaking down as well through a process of reproduction of what has been seen. No one is completely sheltered from it, but habit and an adult capacity for resistance, the knowledge of how to manage the relationship with the patient, constitute sound defences. The same is not true of the child, who is constitutionally less well protected and on whom the spectacle leaves a deep impression:

> Some of them have a twitch and that can have serious consequences for the children who can be affected by it. I know a little girl, four years old, who twitched dreadfully. I was intrigued at first and I found out that she had been in contact with a lodger who had a twitch and she had picked up this problem which had never occurred in her family.

In a malleable brain there is a direct transition from the witnessed gesture to the reproduced gesture, a contagion transmitted through an image, a mirror image of nervous breakdown. The behaviour which is dictated by the disturbance of the nerves serves as a model and produces the breakdown from which it originated. The disturbance becomes one with the manifestation in which it reveals itself. Transmission by sight, direct contagion, mimetic and organic reproduction: we find here a form of animism which confirms what is thought about epilepsy.

The representation which underlies this type of interpretation puts the autonomy and breakdown of the nerves on a par with cerebral inadequacy. Of the patient whose illness comes from nervous shock, the foster parents say that "there's something in there" but add that "there's something missing", that "the brain is empty", "is not in control of the body". Everything happens as if the disturbance of the body reverberates within the brain and unhinges it.

The fragility imputed to the children also shows that what is crucial is the capacity to resist the assaults of an external aggression which "goes to the head". The example of the control of fear, described under the heading of "custom", makes it possible to understand this process. Custom, too, appears to be a preventative technique, a mental prophylactic aimed at preventing nervous and cerebral breakdown. It is an effective technique because this kind of fear has no consequences for the robust, well-armed adult. It stops the affect and its bodily echo from ever etching itself on one's being in a definitive, repetitive manner. At the very most it can provoke the local malady known as the panic attack which may necessitate confinement to one's bed and is reminiscent of the "*sousto*" of the Amerindians.

The notion of strength of resistance appears as a key concept in the understanding of the genesis of accidental mental illness. The terms which recur in connection with illness contracted through emotional shock are "fatigue", "weakness", "strength" of willpower or the inadequacy of character to "regain the upper hand", in the same way that the alcoholic lacks the strength to resist the temptation to drink:

The industrial designer, he's got all his powers of reason. I ask myself why he's here. What's more he hasn't spent any time in an asylum, whereas the others come from Vaucluse, Villejuif, Sainte-Anne. Not him. He came straight here. I think he came after his mother died. That must have something to do with it. He was left helpless. He didn't have enough strength of character.

Some of the ones who are here, it's exactly what they're lacking. That's why some of them were drinkers. With a little strength of character they wouldn't have done it. That's what's lacking today, strength of character.

The patient isn't well enough armed to confront what is oppressing him, just as the young are ill-equipped to resist the aggression of the outside world. Everything suggests that this weakness, which is organic in the young, is "cultural" in the adult, as if what is needed, if cerebral integrity is to be preserved, is the exclusively "moral" barrier of mental frameworks which are provided by education and reinforced by the hard tests set by life. This relationship between moral force and organic balance reappears in the explanation of the healing of a doctor who had undergone an emotional shock:

I knew a doctor who fell ill. Of course, he was educated and he had a certain strength because he was in contact with the patients. His daughter was ill and when he realized that she wasn't going to recover it went to his head. There are some people who fall ill more easily than others. The doctor had *a certain strength behind him which helped him to rebuild his life. That's unarguable. He had a certain strength which prevented it going to his head. He was used to very ill people dying.*

The idea of inner strength goes back to the idea of propensity. The education received, the preparation for life can lead to a predisposition for the illness and explain the fact that the same traumatic effect can have a different effect depending on the past life of the person involved in it. Particularly relevant for cases of affective shock, this interpretation assumes that the patient is deprived of a positive strength of character. But this is not the only way in which the notions of strength and receptivity can be understood. In some cases the illness seems to depend on the existence of a negativity, either potential or effective, a predisposition to illness which corresponds to a genetically determined characteristic, and this is suggested by everything conveyed by the idea of "nervousness".

Nerves, Blood, Evil

For the fact is that those made ill by traumatic shock account for only a small proportion of the class of "nervous cases". They constitute the sub-group of "accidental cases" in whom the nature and intensity of the attack depend on an external cause. It is this that differentiates them so radically from the other "nervous cases" who are so often contrasted with those in whom the brain is ill because of the specifically endogenous nature of their illness. What dominates in these cases is a strongly negative conception of symptoms which may take on frightening proportions: breakdown gives way to excitation, agitation culminates in "fits" and violence in "evil":

> That's *what I don't want to have, extreme nervous cases.* I'm frightened of fits, *the extreme fits* they can have. It's not for me that I'm frightened, I could defend myself, but for the children. *I'm frightened of fits and great epidemics, basically of severe incurable illnesses.* I don't want that. With the rest it's always possible to get by somehow.

In the same way that the innocent offer a reassuring sight, nervous cases, who are their absolute opposite, impose a menacing vision. But apart from these unhappy fantasies, the foster parents remain vague about what constitutes an attack of nerves. It appears to correspond to an internal process which is closely associated with a constitutional propensity and whose destructive character evokes the idea of a negative force which meets with no opposition from any defensive resource in those whom it dominates.

Whilst in the case of nervous shock we find the representation of an "attack" of the illness – "the nerves have been attacked", they say, or "it's descended on the nerves" – the representation used for the "extreme nervous cases", those feared sufferers of "agitation", is rather that of a *state*, because of the predetermined and endogenous character of the affliction. This is how they have always been viewed: "born like that", they are "degenerate".[3] The illness, which is genetically inscribed in them, comes from predecessors who have transmitted a deficiency which either runs in the family or has been acquired at some stage.

The illness is transmitted through the blood and springs from its poor quality. Consisting of organic matter, like the brain, blood can turn[4] as a result of illness or the absorption of harmful materials (tobacco, alcohol).

> They're born from a bad blood or from alcoholics.

> With a lot of them, it's the parents who were alcoholics. There are young ones who get married, the father drinks, so does the mother, and then they smoke as well. All they think about is alcohol and they don't eat. Just think

---

[3] It is impossible not to be struck by the similarity between this conception and the theory of degeneracy which was adopted by a number of doctors at the Colony after its introduction at the end of the last century by Morel and Magnan (Castel, 1976).

[4] The images used in connection with the blood come from the naturalist vision described above. Thus, in popular medical vocabulary, pleurisy is known as "frozen blood", ecchymosis as "bruised blood" (Gagnon, 1972, p. 300). These expressions are uncommon today, and for this reason it is all the more remarkable that the vocabulary should have remained intact in connection with insanity.

of the number there are like that. And then when they have children what
are they going to be like?

This denaturation creates a sickly character which bears its traces and has a
low threshold of resistance:

> Him, *he was born with bad blood in his veins*. When his mother reached the
> critical age, *her blood cut off*. She didn't last long.

> You see families where the father's a drunkard and the kid squints, he's
> nervous, he's puny. It's not that the mother doesn't feed them but it's in the
> blood. It's the blood which is there and there's nothing you can do about it.

Some of the comparisons allow us to define the relationship between blood,
brain, nerves and body. In the case of mental breakdown the illness is
situated in the brain, in cases of nervous breakdown it is located in the blood,
thus confirming the heterogeneity of the blood and the autonomy of the
nervous system and its affinity with the body. In fact the nerves participate in
two sectors of the body's existence, motricity and blood. The denaturation of
the blood determines a functional degeneration which reveals itself, at the
level of the organs, as weakness, as rickets, as deformation and, at the level of
the nerves, as motor disorders. On the other hand, too hectic an existence
which has a direct influence on motricity has repercussions for the nerves and
aggravates the problems caused by "bad" blood:

> Some of them are nervous cases, children of alcoholics. There's nothing
> good about those cases. Most of those lads come from the city. It's too hectic
> for them, too much noise. If your head's weak . . . In the country you don't
> get any like that.

Whilst in the case of the brain the illness operates primarily through
inhibition (reduction of intellectual faculties and regulatory control), in the
case of the nerves it becomes excitatory (uncontrolled movement, moods,
inclinations). Any external excitatory factor is capable of arousing or
aggravating the illness in a subject who is already mentally weakened. In
everyday life every precaution is taken to prevent the excitation of the
patient by eliminating the causes of agitation, examples of which are games
with the children, arguments or the incitement to violence which may arise
when the foster parents fail to master their own reactions:

> They're nervous cases, but they aren't people who want to do any harm, not
> the ones I've got here. First of all you mustn't show any sign of being afraid.
> As we say here, you can spread butter further than vinegar. You mustn't
> always be on at them either.

In contrast, the illness is reduced by a peaceful atmosphere of fresh air:

These lads have got ill nerves. But the country calms them a lot. It calms them down after the city, because it's the noise there which gets them worked up.

I've seen one change. He was really . . . I don't know how I can explain it to you . . . He didn't have his feet on the ground at all. He was nervous. He would fly into a temper for no reason whatsoever. And it was no good shouting at him. You had to be gentle with him. If he got angry you couldn't shout louder than him. You should never do that with people like him. You have to know how to manage them. But he's got better and nowadays his fits are much less frequent . . .

They're less agitated in the country than they are in the asylum. It's because of the fresh air.

It's better for them to be here. At least they get some fresh air. It's better for them, it does them good. But cure them? No.

Between the sufferer from nerves and his environment, there is a fusion, an assimilation of influence, a direct communication of states. Once again we witness an animist vision of the illness, a belief which is corroborated by the representation of the nerves.

The representation of the nerves is very vague, evoking rather than the image of an organ, as in the case of the brain, a functioning, that is to say the exercise of a power. When this functioning is pathological, it is either brought into perspective within the organic system, with the foster parents claiming that "the nerves get the upper hand", or it is seen as an independent process, in which case they say that "the nerves tense up", "work themselves into a fit". What seems to be at work here is a kind of personification of the nerves which are seen to act autonomously, with their own particular demands, and which modify their state as a function of the environment in which they are situated and the activity in which they are engaged. Thus they demand to be nourished: "It's the nerves, they have to be fed," and lack of food becomes a key factor in nervous breakdown:

It's because of the lack of food, because of the lack of care. It's the way the children are fed. The parents work, the children go to school and half the time the parents aren't even at home. *They don't eat and that's it. They grow anaemic and it happens to them* . . . And then the girls want to slim and they don't eat. *It's bound to have an effect, isn't it?* . . . *It goes straight to the chest or wherever* . . . *then they fall into a nervous depression.*

At the same time, work may also exhaust the nerves: "If he works all day his nerves are worn out."

Atmospheric conditions can also function as an irritant: "When the weather changes the nerves grow tense."

In this way the double relationship of the nerves, a still vague entity, with blood and nature is confirmed. The fact that the food can have such an effect on their state shows that they are inseparable from the biological substrate, that which constitutes the living matter of the individual, the blood which "ripens with eating".

In fact, the nerves are conceived as a force, a potential for energy which animates the body and its movements. That it is their tension which lies at the root of vigour and motricity[5] is proved by the effects attributed to drugs:

> The ones who have drugs to calm their nerves, they immediately get tired. They don't have the strength to work.

The nerves seem to be the dark side of vital energy, a force which can break out in violence when left to its own devices, which can be transformed into wickedness when liberated from cerebral control:

> It's heavy, such an illness. When they're having a fit they don't hold back at all. He said it himself, 'I don't know what I might be capable of doing. Take care, I might be dangerous.'

The force which the nerves are or which they mediate also symbolizes the bestiality of man, his kinship with the living world which ensures his communication with other forces of nature, the atmospheric and cosmic forces from whose influence no living species, not even the vegetable, can escape. And it is without doubt this idea of natural power which has its place in the "savage" world that makes possible this emergence of violence and wickedness which are so specific to nervous cases.

The Dark Side of Mental Illness

But this vision, the depths of which can only be glimpsed through an examination of what is said about nervous cases and nerves in fleeting scraps

---

[5] In the interviews connected with the representation of the body and its functioning which were conducted under the supervision of S. Moscovici in 1961, elements were discovered which accord with this vision and which corroborate our interpretation. For older persons provided with a lower level of information, blood represents "the life and energy of the body" and the nerves are assimilated to the veins and the blood: "It represents strength, it's what holds us together. If we didn't have nerves we wouldn't be able to stand up. Nerves and muscles, that's all the same thing. There's fat, oil, muscles, it's the nerves . . . veins in fact. If we were only made of bones I don't know if we would hold together. The joints wouldn't hold maybe. I think it's the nerves which keep a hold on the muscles and all that, flesh and so on. Muscles are a bundle of nerves together, there's not a lot of meat in them. It's what lets us walk, stand upright, carry." As for food, "it's vitamins, it's energy, isn't it? What you've got in the blood, that's nerves."

Other investigations into popular medicine (Gagnon, 1949) confirm the relationship which is established between a nervous attack, the circulation of the blood and external excitation. Thus to counter an attack, it was the custom to cut one of the ear lobes to let out the blood, a process which was accelerated by the banging of cooking pots and saucepans.

of conversation, is far from being present as a conscious element of the representation today. Behind the overwhelming rejection of the nervous patient, the researcher runs up against a kind of conceptual void. Nothing more precise is said than that it is necessary to distrust nervous cases, because they are nervous, present a risk of fits and consequently of wickedness and violence. This is the menacing figure which haunts the hell of the foster parents, an imaginary hell as everyone vows to have nothing to do with this type of patient or to be soon rid of him.

Where then do the obsessive fear of fits and the notion of the fit itself come from? To discover this we have to turn to the history of collective experience and search for the only trauma known to it: epilepsy.

When asked to specify the type of mental illness they wish to have no contact with, epilepsy is the one which the foster parents turn to first, primarily because of the children:

> Epilepsy, I would be frightened of it because of the children. You can't catch it, it's a nervous illness, but all the same it's not a nice sight for the children. It makes an impression. I would be scared that it would frighten them, that it would affect them.

Epilepsy contains a number of frightening and menacing elements, the most important of which is the rapidity of its arrival and the fall which accompanies it. To see someone "fall down ill" is an unbearable sight to someone who knows nothing of mental illness:

> Epilepsy, it isn't the same type of illness. I've never had one and I've never wanted one because of the children. I'm afraid they would be frightened when they see them fall, that it would give a nervous shock to the children. It's things like that I'm scared of. It's the sort of thing you see as you grow up, it's not dangerous.

The fall brings to the fore the scandal and the disorder of an illness which is difficult, perhaps even impossible, to understand and which only experience can accommodate:

> I had one who used to have epileptic fits. I didn't want to keep him because of the little one. You know, he used to fall. It makes an impression on small children. For people like us, it's . . . My little boy was three years old and to see something like that, well it gave him a shock. And it was him who saw it first. He came to tell me that he had fallen. But I didn't explain that it was . . . He wouldn't have understood.

And the effect made by the fall is all the greater because of the secondary phenomena which accompany it and which themselves carry significations from which the fit also derives its danger. Amongst these phenomena, the most important are the gestures. These are interpreted in two ways. First, they are gestures of brutality, of attack:

> Nervous illnesses, they aren't at all pleasant. You're always frightened of seeing them fall down ill, do some harm, make gestures. The gestures, I'm frightened of people like that. I've seen them fall and it's left a mark on me.

and second, they are gestures of sexuality which are revealed in a paroxysm of violence:

> When they fall down ill they make all kinds of ugly gestures. I saw one fall in the mud and he made a gesture with his thing [his penis] as he fell. Well, that's a bad example for the children.

This circumlocution is necessary because of the great reticence in speaking of the anxiety aroused by the sexuality of the patients which, in nervous cases, appears to be hypertrophic and inseparable from an aggressive impulse:

> I don't like the nervous ones or however you call people like that, sexual people like that who are after the women. I live in horror of them. I had one who was very nervous. He was a violent man. He had this manner towards women. We only had him for two months. He would have hit us or even taken a knife and come at us!

Beyond this, might one not hazard the thought that, behind the brutality and the wickedness of which so many lodgers are accused, is hidden a sexual anxiety which the foster parents forbid themselves to express? A further aspect of the epileptic fit is particularly striking for the witness, namely the tendency to dribble. An old woman evoked her impressions in this way:

> In church, they put the lodgers' pews underneath the bells near to the children. One Palm Sunday one of them fell. He foamed at the mouth so much that I was seized with fear . . . After that we ate a stew and I felt sick. I only took some broth because I was expecting a child. To me it looked like the patient, the one who started to foam in church.

The fear comes from the unknown, but also from the violence of the fall and the violence of the rabid, both in its literal and figurative senses. We should not forget that a bad patient is a *ch'tit* and a *ch'tit* dog is a mad dog. Furthermore, this foam on top of the broth, which is made of meat, is that of the patient. It is the patient who is there, or his illness. In the ubiquity and transposition of the illness we see once again animism and the idea of infection which, despite all denials, remains present in the mind:

> I had one who was an epileptic. He used to fall. It wasn't very pleasant . . . he had . . . with his mouth wide open. Well, I didn't let the children in. I

telephoned and they came to get him straightaway. That was it. That isn't at all pleasant, especially when there are kids around. It scares the kids, even afterwards. They catch it, I think. I've heard tell that . . .

If foam, the slaver of an overheated, excited or rabid animal, recalls an instinctive and bestial element in human make-up which resides in uncontrolled strength, violence and sexuality, then the association of nerves and organic fluids, whose interaction marks phases of excitation, is also confirmed. Of the epileptic who succeeds in mastering his reactions, it is said that "he controls himself" but although there is no blood and no slaver, he still "goes white". And the nervous case will not fail to evoke the idea of the "fit" or of epilepsy as soon as blood turns his face red:

> We had one called X . . . He wasn't easy, he had his moments. I didn't notice that he had real fits but there were times when he turned violet and at times like that his eyes went funny and he really wasn't quite normal anyway. There was one day when he was having a set-to with Y . . . We heard them on the other side of the door, we weren't even up. My husband put on a shirt and he put him outside and Y . . . somewhere else. I don't know what he wanted to do. Another time, I've got a seventeen-year-old son who's quite sturdy, if he hadn't been there I don't know what would have happened. I had a pile of washing-up to do. I was surprised, he caught me by the arm and pulled me, he pulled me and stared at me and carried on pulling. I said to him, 'What on earth are you doing?'. He didn't say anything and he carried on staring at me. But my son wasn't far away and because I was speaking loudly he was soon there. 'What's happening?' he asked. 'I don't know,' I answered, 'he's grabbed hold of my arm, he won't let me go, he doesn't answer me.' So my son came up to him and said, 'Let go of my mother.' But he still wanted to take me with him and I still had my pile of washing-up. Well, there were no two ways about it, my son gave him a couple of slaps and he let go of me. When he turned red I thought that maybe it had been a kind of epileptic fit.

The unity of the nerves as an instinctive and organic force is expressed in the notion of the epileptic fit. The power of the blood and the power of evil are combined under the tangible and omnipresent shadow of the illness.

Nowadays the spectacle of an epileptic fit is very rare because "nowadays, there are less of them. They're looked after, they've got medicines. They don't fall down ill like they used to at one time." When we were able to obtain detailed eye-witness reports it was always from older foster parents. Today, the foster parents content themselves with saying that they are afraid of epilepsy because of the children, without drawing on any personal experience or providing any reasons for their fear. All that is left is the silence of fear, and medicines.

By suppressing the symptoms of epilepsy, medicines have been an agent of reassurance while, at the same time, their widespread use has made the risk of a fit so omnipresent that any patient who is treated with them is labelled as a "nervous case":

> Mainly it's the nerves. The medicines are all more or less for the nerves. It depends on age. All these people here take medicines and you've got to make sure they get them. It's very important to take medicines and you've got to make sure they get them. It's very important, very important. If they don't have their medicines regularly, they get worked up.

By concealing the fit, medicines have come to signify both it and its attendant menaces:

> They're not the same any more. They're more wicked nowadays. They're not the same any more. They receive a lot of treatment but they're more difficult. They used to be stubborn but that was all there was to it. They went to be treated once a week but it was nothing major. While today, what with the nozinan and largactyl and drops of I don't know what, they get too much treatment. It's for safety, that's all. For safety's sake, it's better that they have too many drugs. If they didn't, people would be shocked. The medicines act like a kind of guarantee. In earlier times they used to put them in the ward to punish them, not to treat them. It was to punish them. Big L swore at us. You should have heard the way he swore at us, and as for the gestures he made! We told the Colony and they kept him naked in the cell they use for people in straitjackets. He was like that for three days. When he came out, he didn't start again.

Whilst accentuating the physiological nature of the illness, chemotherapy also becomes the sign of nervous degeneracy in which *violence and disorder* are genetic characteristics:

> They've always had drugs. There are some patients who can't do without them. In my group there's only one who doesn't take them. He's mentally ill as well but he can behave himself all the same . . . He isn't bad. He's very nervous but he isn't bad. Whereas if the others weren't treated, well, you don't know what might happen.

In this way an exhaustive process of symbolic elaboration replaces the therapeutic value of medical treatment with a practical value and thus augments its capacity to provoke anxiety. The more they are thought to be reserved exclusively for incurable "extreme nervous cases", the more likely drugs are to be considered to have a merely sedative effect and help to define true mental illness, which is incurable. Consequently, not to take medicines means not to be ill:

> Mine are never ill. They don't take any medicines. There are some who take medicines, but mine, never. If anything, mine are just retarded.

To take medicines means to be incurable, or in other words, never to be free of the danger of one's illness and thus constantly to confront others with the menace of one's wickedness:

> You don't know what they might do . . . I don't think that they're dangerous . . . In general, as long as they take their medicines . . . The one I've got here has medicines to calm him . . . the medicines they use for people who are a little bit wicked. Perhaps he was wicked when they brought him here. If he had a fit maybe he would be wicked.

The circle closes by suppressing their outward manifestations, chemical treatment comes to signify all the pathologies which are associated with nervous disorder and, as a consequence, with what has traditionally always been thought of as the essence of that type of insanity which is not innocence – wickedness:

> Some people believe that if they're mentally ill it's the same as saying that they're wicked. That makes you notice straightaway that they aren't as bad as all that. You know, when they talk about the mental patients, they say that they're just as likely to take a hammer to you as kick you, that they're wicked . . . They say that the mental patients are madmen, madmen who you can't live with.

From innocence to wickedness, a long path in which we have followed step by step the construction of illness as an object, has also enabled us to discover all the forms which mental illness may assume by way of the factors which delineate it, express it, favour it or determine it. It is a relatively clear construction in which symptoms, periods and areas of attack fully exhaust the sphere of the known.

On the one hand, the brain, its development and the influence of society. On the other hand, the nerves, biological identity and savage nature. On the one hand, innocence and the slow progression of the illness which derives from the damage inflicted by society. On the other, wickedness and its obscure roots. On the one hand, the social frameworks of balance and the imitation of educational models; on the other, the forces of disorder and the notion of contagion which is found in animism. Between these poles we discover an entire theory of man and society, a rational construction which distinguishes between the various types of illness in accordance with the categories which experience and contact place at the disposal of the milieu which must live with the patients.

This construction exhibits all the characteristics of premedical knowledge (Foucault, 1971; Barthes, 1988; Augé, 1980): identification of the symptom and the affliction, absence of nosography and denomination of illnesses, morally or socially dominated etiology. It also exhibits considerable similarities with the psychiatric conceptions of the nineteenth century (contrasting of retardation and degeneracy, value of moral treatment amongst others) which were shared by the founders of the Colony. Alongside its dependence on old models, it brings to light the role of the axiological in its prescientific causal explanations and its recourse to the field of the biological when discussing the fears provoked by mental illness.

Here we are able to observe the close association between the processes of social representation: objectification and anchoring. When it comes to conceiving an etiology of mental illness, the functional nucleus of "brain – nerve – people of flesh and bones" which takes account of bio-psychological functioning and of pathological states appeals to a threefold support in the cultural heritage of the group, its "tacit knowledge". This is first of all the support provided by the moral opposition of "innocence" and "wickedness" which has clear roots in the Judaeo-Christian tradition. Next it is the transformation of this opposition into the terms of nineteenth-century psychiatry, "retardation" and "degeneracy". Finally it is the support of group values in the *a contrario* conception of the exogenous causes of mental illness: everything which contravenes the existential values pertaining to a way of life and a moral code becomes a source of disturbance. But within this construction a new phenomenon, the medicalization of insanity through the introduction of psychotropic medicines, produces the resurgence of old beliefs which have lain buried in the collective memory and thus turns the spotlight on the tragic, disquieting mask of insanity.

Chapter Eight

Acting Out a Conception of Madness

> My grandmother kept her cutlery and crockery
> marked her whole life long. The old people, they
> used to think of it more as an incurable illness,
> something you could catch.

> When I do the washing I keep the patients'
> separate from the rest. The washing-up as well,
> because having children here we started like that
> right at the beginning. Even if they're very, very
> clean because, after all, deep down they are
> human beings like us, but all the same . . .

> There's nothing to be frightened of in the illness,
> it's not contagious. But, still, a lot of the lodgers
> would quite happily kiss a child and I don't like to
> see that.

Successive approaches to grasping from where and how illness arises come up against the incessant affirmation that it "is there", "in" the patient. Behind the apparent rationality of a model whose progress from cause to the organ in which it is manifested suggests that the illness is apprehended differently in different individuals, we discover that everything conspires to see it operating identically in all. The construction developed around the twin poles of brain and nerves shrinks, when we turn our attention from the patients to their illness, to the unified vision of a mental or nervous "breakdown" produced by exogenous or endogenous causes. It narrows to the unvarying identity of the pathological process at the organic level, the illness which "curdles". The unity and identity which lie hidden behind this construction concern the nature of the illness. But does a clear representation of this essence of insanity exist? The recurrence of certain phrases and the implications of certain types of avoidance behaviour at work in situations of contact with the illness provide an outline of such a representation. But this does not mean that this conception of insanity is spoken out loud.

The forms of language employed to express the unity of operation of the illness which "curdles" the organic material are complemented by a substantial, transitive vision. The illness comes "from" or "by", "takes hold of" and becomes "part" of the patient, is specified "in" a multiplicity of signs, always ready to emerge even if there is no risk of "catching" it. Doubtlessly these turns of phrase reflect a process of "naturalization" which can be discerned in every social representation, a natural tendency of thought to objectify ideas, turning the pathological into a concrete entity, materially present in the body and the symptoms the body displays. As we have noted in previous chapters, it is also possible to see here the application of borrowings from traditional knowledge or from the shared experiences of the farming community. The schemes provided by such borrowings supply a conception of the processes at work within living material and it is these schemes which, in the absence of any other appropriate mental tool, are then transferred and applied to the pathological process. But the absence of alternative explanations within the community is not in itself sufficient to explain this process of borrowing and application. It seems to us that language also contains elements of a vision of insanity whose echo reverberates in certain modes of behaviour.

Showing through this behaviour is the idea of possible contamination by insanity, despite the assurances of the hospital in which the population claims to have complete faith. As we have seen, nervous contagion is avoided by banishing twitches and fits from sight. A resurgence of the illness is prevented by avoiding any reference to it when speaking with those who live in its shadow. This absolute refusal to speak of it wards off the alarming possibility of its appearance. These practices raise two issues. They indicate that explanations of a materialist type or explanations which imply the material circulation of mental illness cannot be fully accounted for by a process of objectification which is a characteristic of representations. The distress to which they testify corresponds to something more than a cognitive phenomenon. At the same time, the avoidance of the visual and verbal contact on which they are based reveals elements of a belief which is magical in nature (omnipotence of imitation, the look, the word in the transmission and creation of a thing), is difficult to reconcile with the frameworks of rational thought and, what is more, represents a source of anxiety.

One hypothesis seems to account for this state of affairs. Within the conception of the nature of insanity there would appear to enter elements of belief which, because of their archaism and ability to arouse anxiety, can only have a possible and authorized translation in the acts which they inspire. Such a hypothesis supposes a vision of insanity which, observable only as a trace element in certain turns of phrase, reveals itself not in what is thought but in a mode of action which is all the more difficult to formulate in explicit terms because it has its origin in an irrational universe which is dominated by fear. In other words, certain dimensions of the representation of insanity should be observable in the concrete relationship with the bearer of the illness in everyday gestures and practices, without there necessarily being a verbal, or indeed in some cases, a mental correspondence. This hypothesis then suggests a mode of action based on a conception of insanity whose significance can only be extracted through confrontation and which throws light on a considerable number of displacements and contradictions of speech. The problem posed by a logic which strives to construct illness as an object in rational terms but stumbles, as we have seen in the preceding chapter, on encountering the theoretically reassuring scientific fact of chemotherapy and consequently charges this fact with anxiety, invites us to lend credence to this hypothesis.[1]

We have already seen how medication, historically associated with the disappearance of fits, has come to define the nervous patient and to impute the greatest threat to those who are treated by chemical means, whilst retaining the old categories which teach a bipolar organization of the insane. But would it be possible for such an explanation to function with such rigour and arouse such distress if it were based solely on historical continuity and a number of case studies in the absence of any information concerning the purpose of the treatment? Can we not discover a source of anxiety in the significance of medicaments as an ingested material which has a specific effect on mental illness? The resistance to administering medicines shown by the foster parents suggests that this is the case.

---

[1] It is necessary to underline a methodological point in connection with the subject discussed in this chapter, a subject which is presented here in a very different sequence from the order in which it revealed itself to us. Our attention was drawn *at the very start* of the enquiry to the problems associated with medicines and the care of the patients' possessions. This indicates their crucial position in the organization of the field of representations concerning mental illness.

On the one hand, sources from the hospital environment freely spoke of the resistance to medicines and the allergic effects. At the same time they refused to suggest any explanation or to indicate on the census of placements those where they had noted cases of allergy or a refusal to administer medicines. This alerted us to the importance of the problem, striking and hidden at the same time.

On the other hand, the ethnological type of approach used during the interviews was decisive in determining the order of discovery of the most secret conceptions concerning the illness. By concentrating a part of each interview on the living habits adopted with the patients we were able to obtain crucial information without which an essential part of the representation of insanity would have been lacking. From the very first, our interviews revealed the hard fact of the revulsion in which liquids touched by the lodgers were held and further revealed that this revulsion was associated with separation of their belongings. Throughout the entire period of the enquiry it was necessary to return to questions concerning these practices and to try to discover their significance – generally in vain – in order to obtain some associated comments which would provide us with an indirect means of discovering the background of beliefs which they express. Using the associations articulated in connection with these methods of care, we shall here reconstruct the development and the classifications of this conception. This approach will bring us face to face with two sets of problems, both of a theoretical nature, concerning the relationship between representation, practice and symbolism, and the relationship between systems of practice and belief and social organization. As in the preceding chapters, the attempt to provide a precise description of the material revealed by the enquiry in order to discover the models which structure the field of representation (an attempt which is even more important here, where individual facts and details only become meaningful in connection with an incessant movement of *rapprochement* and confrontation) concludes by deferring their examination to a later stage. This examination is the object of the Epilogue.

Patients to Care For

Although distributing medicines and making sure that they are taken is one of the essential tasks of the foster parents, a task whose non-observance can lead to action by the authorities (temporary withdrawal of the patient or even closure of the placement), cases of failure to administer drugs are too numerous to be explained by the desire not to impair the lodger's ability to work or indeed his overall well-being, an argument advanced by many foster parents:

> Drugs don't always make them better. Personally I think they drug them up too much. I think the medicines they give them are too strong. I've got a patient who takes them. If you gave him his full dose . . . I've reduced the number of drops. It used to knock him right out. What's more it made him forgetful and destroyed his desire to work. It completely overwhelmed him.

The vet and the visiting nurse discuss some tasty pieces of gossip. The first has been treating ducks and other poultry intoxicated by the absorption of pills thrown away near the ponds or manure heaps. The second has discovered boxes containing several hundred dummy pills.

Today only a few refuse to touch or administer medicines, but in the past the refusal was universal:

> It was Dr . . . who told us to give them these medicines. We never used to have to do that. It was a big thing, getting us to do all that. It hasn't always been accepted by the foster parents. They formed a union and threatened to send the patients back.

Why this refusal? It is, of course, an extra and sometimes time-consuming burden, especially when patience and ingenuity have to be shown in getting round the more unwilling patients. But is this the only reason?

As we have seen, the introduction of medicines has transformed the way in which the patients are perceived, but this was only possible as the result of a modification in the way that illness itself is perceived. The testimony of a former member of the Colony allows us a view of the mechanisms underlying this movement:

> When I started there we didn't have medicines like there are now. There were four types of tablet. We used to make them ourselves. Some were made with methylene blue, some with rhubarb . . . it was all to get us to take the medicines. *It was harmless.* There were patients who came from Valigny to collect their medicines. They wanted to be treated. The doctor would say, 'Give him a dozen, fifteen, thirty,' or 'Don't take more than one a day and come back when you need some more.' *It was harmless* and it worked well. It's belief which makes you better. I knew a nurse at Ville-Evrard. There was a patient who used to play up until two or three in the morning. The nurse

wanted to know what he could do to get him to sleep. He rolled up some breadcrumbs, put the little balls into a box and covered them with liquorice powder. He made little pills out of them and gave one each evening to the patient, who slept quite soundly. Then the doctor called the patient and told him he was going to treat him. After a while the patient said, 'What you gave me isn't as good as what the nurse gives me!' The doctor got on his high horse and had a few words to say to the nurse. But afterwards he couldn't help laughing because he had done exactly the same thing! When they want to be treated you have to go along with them. There was one who wanted watercress syrup, asparagus syrup so I gave him some water with a bit of syrup mixed in with it just to keep him happy. They're like children who want to be indulged.

The imposition of medicines by the Colony and the medical authorities upset the cognitive balance which had been achieved by the milieu by favouring a "mental", that is to say purely cerebral or moral, interpretation of insanity. Up to that point it had been reassuringly easy to view the patients as "innocents", as "nutters" or, if absolutely necessary, as alcoholics. The principal attack was cerebral and the nervous breakdown which it sometimes entailed did not possess the same significance as that engendered by primary nervous attack.

The fact that the Colony was unable to defend itself against unrest except by recalling patients to the ward gave substance to the theory of moral wickedness which was deserving of punishment and which could be corrected by banishment to the cell. The absence of drug-based treatments prevented the illness appearing as organic. Dummy medicines were reassuring because they possessed no curative properties, their effectiveness being explained by reference to the illusions engendered by mental aberration. The advent of chemotherapy suddenly made the illness into something organic. The patient, the illness and the medicines themselves suddenly took on a new significance. As the therapy attenuates symptoms, the accent shifts to the direct attack of the nerves. In short, we see the return and the exacerbation of the threatening character of insanity which the population had sought to bury in the concepts of innocence, vagueness and moral weakness by reference to which mental otherness was explained.[2]

---

[2] A text by Renan (1883/1967, pp. 25–26) illustrates particularly clearly this reassuring vision of mental disease which allowed rural communities to live at peace with the insane: "Now, in those days the mad were not treated in the cruel fashion which has been more recently invented by administration and custom. Far from interning them, the locals allowed them to roam around the whole day through. *Tréguier generally has a large number of madmen like all those races of dreamers who spend their days in the pursuit of the ideal.* The Breton folk of this area, *when they are not kept on the move by an energetic willpower, are far too ready to abandon themselves to a state half-way between intoxication and madness which is often no more than the errings of a dissatisfied heart.* These harmless madmen, who covered the whole gamut of mental otherness, were a sort of institution, a municipal possession. People spoke of 'our fools' as in Venice they spoke of *nostre carampane.* They could be met almost everywhere. They greeted you, welcomed you with some disgusting joke which nevertheless made you smile. They were loved and they made themselves useful . . . "

Moreover, the medicines themselves lose their innocuous, their "harmless", character. The power they exercise over the body and the nerves gives them a disturbing force which demonstrates properties related to those of the illness they are treating. The power they express makes handling them dangerous, to judge by the allergic reactions which developed after their introduction: "Some of the foster parents were allergic to the medicines, you understand?"

Such cases, which can still be found today, are said to result from the handling of certain substances, notably largactyl, whose use is claimed to have caused numerous allergies amongst nurses working in psychiatric hospitals. However, we still have to ask ourselves about the significance of this response to chemotherapy – not omitting the professional response – whilst bearing in mind that largactyl was the first medicine used in the psychiatric hospitals and at the Colony.

Equally revealing is the way in which the foster parents interpreted their allergies. At first it seems that they considered them to be a "shameful" illness for which they consulted a doctor from outside their own town and that they refused to mention these ailments to the doctors of the Colony. Once the diagnosis had been made known and confirmed, information concerning the origin and the risk of allergy circulated freely from mouth to mouth. The result was an increase in the number of cases and avoidance behaviour on the part of the foster parents who no longer consulted doctors but instead went straight to the Colony to secure the withdrawal of the patient they were treating or, at the very least, a change of treatment:

> It's still common today. They tell us: 'Give us something else.' It's a strange business because there are people who have been administering largactyl for four or five years without any problems. And then suddenly there's something wrong with the eyelids, the hands. A lot of them don't say anything and go off to see a dermatologist or something like that. Some of them go to see a local doctor they know. It was a doctor at Lurcy Levis who was one of the first to discover it. They hadn't made the connection. But see how it's grown now. They're always talking to one another about it. As soon as there's something a little bit wrong with their hands: 'It's the largactyl.'

The foster parents have furthermore elaborated a "theory" according to which the noxious nature of the drug derives from its function of treating the nerves and its presence in the form of a liquid:

> It calms them. I've got a nervous case. He makes gestures. He grimaces. He strikes his hands and all that. Well, I've got drugs to give him. I've just told M [the nurse] . . . He gave me some and I ended up covered with spots. I told him, 'It must be the medicine.' And when he gave it to me in tablet form instead of liquid it was all right.

Following the incrimination of first largactyl and then of theralene, rejection was extended to all drugs. In fact the nature of the substance is less important than its liquid state.

It is on the basis of information passed on from mouth to mouth that these products must be identified because the Colony distributes its medicine in neutral packaging without specifying its name. At the same time, those foster parents who spoke to us of their allergies described the onset of attacks in such a way that they seemed to depend on the physical properties of the liquid, which is conceived as volatile and able to penetrate into the body:

> The drops, *I didn't touch them, I just breathed them* . . . It was largactyl, that's what gave me the allergy.

The effects of contact and inhalation are similar:

> I've changed two so far because I had to give them largactyl. It gave me eczema. *I spilled some drops. It felt cold and then it swelled. That developed into eczema.* I went to the doctor where I met a neighbour who said, 'Aren't you giving largactyl? You don't need to ask anyone else.' They changed the lodger. With another one it was theralene. That brought it on again. I saw the doctor and he said, 'There's no doubt about it.' They didn't want to believe me at the Colony. *Being touched by largactyl, theralene, has done something to me.*

Psychotropic therapies appear to be endowed with some kind of magic "property" which can diffuse into the organism without being absorbed. It is a property of differing value, capable of "calming the nerves" of the ill, but also of producing harmful effects in the healthy.

The allergic reaction reveals a double anxiety at the somatic level. First, the anxiety which is prompted by the reemergence of mental illness revealed in chemotherapy. Second, the anxiety provoked by the strange effectiveness of a remedy whose inhibitory action on the nerves is accompanied by secondary effects which suggest to the foster parents both a cerebral deterioration – the loss of memory, weakening of willpower and energy – and a physical deterioration – tiredness and inability to work. The representation which articulates this double anxiety seems to be borrowed in its entirety from an animistic type of vision which confers on medication a transmissible and transmutable negative power which is more precisely expressed by the liquid excipient and its exhalations. This vision is corroborated in every point by the rules of hygiene observed in connection with the patients and the practices relating to their care.

The Parting of the Waters

The references to the allergy and the medicines are unmistakably associated with the idea of a pollution caused by the patients and the hygienic prescriptions designed to avoid it. This "pollution–hygiene" pairing is related to the "liquid–odour" pairing. In fact what is feared is the direct contact of the patient with the water reserved for the use of the foster parents. In the days when water still had to be fetched, the worst trick the lodgers could play was to spit into the water they were carrying or to dip their capes into it.[3] And absolute horror grips some of the foster parents at the idea that a patient might touch the water which they use to do the household chores or soak their personal belongings:

> There are some lodgers who frighten us. When they gesture, when they get angry. One of them frightened me so much that I sent him back. And I think it's because I sent him back that they gave me this lame one who doesn't do a thing. Because you have to have a reason to send them back. He used to frighten me. *When I was alone and he was feeling agitated he would come and scratch near my water or put dirty washing in my basin.*

Testimonies such as this state in the baldest terms the relationship between the attack of nerves and the danger of contact mediated by water. At the same time they demonstrate the extent to which this fear is considered to be unjustifiable when considered in rational terms, despite its power and the panic it induces. In fact it is at this level that the simultaneous fear of contagion and the denial of it are constantly seen to emerge. And those who dare to admit it openly do not attempt to disguise its irrational basis:

> You feel as if there's something which might be transmitted, microbes or something.

> It's only a fear. That's all it is, because I don't believe that there are any microbes. The patients aren't contagious. It's just a fear. *The perspiration, the smell. It's all linked to the illness.*

The contradiction is of little importance. All that matters is avoiding the elements of the illness – or the medicines – which can be transported by the bodily fluids and whose incontestable signs, found in the odour of the lodgers, are the cause of the foster parents' preventive hygiene:

> They have a special smell, what with the drugs they give them. They smell bad. It annoys me because of the children. You have to be very hygienic.

---

[3] It is not insignificant that the introduction of drugs in the 1950s coincided with the end of the need to fetch water. The local authority started to install running water throughout the region in 1952.

> You might tell me that there are people who don't take as much care over it
> as I do, but personally I don't think that's very healthy.

The equivalent roles played by the illness and medicines in producing
perspiration and odour again confirms the role of chemical therapies in the
reawakening or the perpetuation of older beliefs.

One might question whether this really constitutes a return to, or survival
of, earlier beliefs. The concern with hygiene is justified given the dirtiness of
some lodgers. Moreover, even though the specific smell of the patients is
recognized by everyone, it is not always explained by reference to
perspiration, and therefore to the illness. For many it is the result of excessive
smoking or a lack of cleanliness. Finally, the repugnance felt in the face of
the medicines and the emergence of allergies is not universal. Might this not
simply be a case of a few phobic foster parents rationalizing their fear as best
they can, precisely stripping away the primary significations from hygienic
measures, the remarks made about the smell of the patients or the importance
attached to the cleanliness of the lodgers? To support this interpretation one
might point to the foundations on which the predominance of the criterion
of cleanliness-dirtiness in the explicit norm of the "good lodger" is based.

But have we not already shown that the emphasis placed on this criterion
derives from practical reasons, whether this is a question of the work required
of the foster parent or the material discomforts which dirtiness represents for
the placement? Have we not already demonstrated that the disgust in which
the bodily dirtiness of certain lodgers is held is by no means incompatible
with dealings with them? Nowhere in all this do we find the notion of
pollution or contagion. On the contrary, we discover a perfectly rational
evaluation of the burdens and inconveniences involved and, as a result, the
implementation of certain guarantees or defences.

However, the objection can be reformulated: What if this were simply a
question of collective rationalizations, with the few alleged "phobics" openly
expressing the fears and beliefs of all? What if dirtiness and pollution are not
located in the same register, or rather if alongside the "harmlessness" of
dirtiness there were the danger of "pollution"? And what if the preoccupation
with hygiene, crystallized around what the illness evokes or expresses, were
not aimed at dirtiness but at pollution? And what if, for precisely this reason,
the population were seeking to hide or disguise its meaning?

If we adopt this point of view a curious fact emerges: when the foster
parents speak of their work or even of life in the placement they never
spontaneously address the question of hygiene. If this topic is to form part of
the conversation, a context which evokes the illness or its treatment is
needed. Similarly, when describing their activity, they emphasize the
question of meals and housework without, themselves, ever volunteering
information concerning the care of the patients' personal belongings. Direct
questioning is required before such information can be gained, and even then

the foster parents are little inclined to speak at length on this subject. Now, the enquiry revealed that even if not all the foster parents are allergic, even if they do not all reject the use of medicines, even if they are not all equally intolerant of dirtiness, they nevertheless all adopt protective measures when it comes to the belongings of the patients or the objects which they have to touch in order to live. These measures, which go under the name of hygienic measures, prove to be significant social practices whose meaning reveals fundamental dimensions of the collective representation of madness and demolishes the hypothesis which suggests the existence of procedures and explanations which are specific to a few "phobic" foster parents.

First in this list of practices are the cleaning techniques used. These involve a whole ritual designed to separate the water used for the maintenance of family belongings and that used for the lodgers, more specifically the water used for washing clothes and the water used for the dishes. Although it possesses a stable basis and structure, this ritual, which is performed with almost obsessive rigour, can be observed in a number of different modes. As a result, the separation of water assumes apparently different forms from one foster parent to the next and creates the illusion of idiosyncratic habits which have no other basis than the preferences or household customs of the individuals concerned. One foster parent systematically separates all the washing belonging to the lodgers while another only washes the clothes separately but not the dishes or *vice versa*. Some take the principle of separation so far that they forbid the patients to enter the areas reserved for cleaning activities. Others even make the lodger wash his own belongings whilst there are some who believe that such a solution actually increases the risk of pollution. In a matter such as this where the thresholds of disgust and fear differ from one individual to the next, personal habits seem to escape any kind of communal system. In fact, observation soon reveals that in their own ways all the foster parents conform to a consensual order which establishes an absolute separation where protection is maximized, and a separation which is more symbolic than effective where protection is at its least stringent. But even in places where there appears to be little differentiation in the care of belongings, a degree of protection always remains.

Thus as far as the washing of clothes is concerned, those who claim not to separate their washing from that of the lodgers still under no circumstances "soak them together", and find a guarantee in the systematic and sometimes extreme use of "washing products". What is more, they make subtle distinctions between whites and coloureds, working clothes, men's clothes etc. Some "do the whites together" because then everything is bleached. Some wash the coloured clothes together because this does not include the underwear. Some will only mix their husband's working clothes with the lodger's clothes because "there's nothing to be afraid of in that", because they are worn over other clothes etc. The same is true of dishwashing. Even if the foster parent claims to wash the dishes together, she specifies that she washes the lodgers' dishes after the ones used by the family, or she avoids doing the glasses with the rest of the washing-up, or she takes special precautions – very hot water, frequent rinsing under running water, the use of detergents, bleach etc.

The only cases in which these rituals are not observed are in placements in which the lodger who inspires no anxiety is fully integrated into the life of the family. But apart from being exceedingly rare, these cases possess no real stability, being always conditional, subordinate to the feeling of safety on which the foster parent's sense of distaste depends, or to the "knowledge" of the person she is dealing with:

> They've got their own crockery which I wash after I've washed my own. Earlier, when we were on the estate, we used to eat with them and I did their washing-up together with mine. *You can't catch the illness. It isn't like tuberculosis. If they work, you're less afraid of them. There's nothing repulsive about a patient who's ill. It's in the brain. It's a depression. There's nothing repulsive about it.* Do you believe that there are no depressives amongst the civilians? Well, we don't find those people repulsive. Nowadays though, I wouldn't eat with the patients we get today. They aren't the same . . .

> We do their washing-up just like ours. There are some houses where they wouldn't have that. *We do the washing-up together. It's not as if we didn't know the patients, is it?* But some people, it's as if they had servants living with them.

These reservations clearly express what it is that the separation of the care of personal belongings is aimed against: *the danger in the illness, the unknown in the patient*. But the way in which these two dimensions which characterize the illness/patient pairing are represented remains unclear. So great was the ignorance and the mystery which enshrouded this point that we had to apply a systematic mode of questioning throughout the entire enquiry in order to deepen our analysis of it.

From the Silence of Prohibition to the Secret of the Liquid

With the separation of the water used for washing purposes, we are, in effect, in the presence of a social practice which is quite specific to the individuals who employ it. Although it is related both in its principle and its form to the rule of distance whose institutional and normative character has already been demonstrated, the practice of separation does not appear to proceed from the same origin or operate at the same level. Despite appearing to function as a rule, it lacks the normative character which, for example, characterizes the rule of distance. This is seen in the fact that those who adhere to it do not pronounce upon it in the imperative mode and those who do not observe it do not run the risk of being treated as deviants, neither do they attempt to justify their behaviour on "moral" grounds but in terms of material and psychological guarantees.

At the same time, the great differences which exist between particular modes of implementation make it clear that the social character of the practice is less a function of the relationship which it establishes than the representations which inspire it. The rule of distance institutionalizes the relationship with the lodger in order to maintain a social differentiation. This is not true of the separation of water. Although it does involve a social relationship (the prohibition of certain places and tasks, for example) this is as a consequence of measures of hygiene which are immediately dependent on the representation which is constructed of the illness. It follows that if the rigour with which these measures are applied varies with the level of personal fear aroused by this representation, then their structural similarity demonstrates the social character of the representation. Social in its inspiration, that is to say based on a particular, socially shared vision of the illness, the separation of water is only secondarily social in its objective, which is to regulate contact with the illness through the relationship with the patient.

Thus, while behaviour regulated by a social rule such as the rule of distance has a significance which can be derived directly from the relationships which it institutes, and which is easily comprehended by its agents who transpose it or rationalize it as an objective or a principle of action, the behaviour observed with regard to hygiene remains opaque and demands our attention.

This opacity is seen primarily in the obstacles which prevent the free circulation of information. Everything happens as if hygiene-related behaviour springs from a mysterious, inaccessible domain whose very existence is a secret. The secret character of such behaviour is not solely a result of it never being mentioned spontaneously during the course of the enquiry, a fact we have already mentioned, but also from the difficulty the foster parents experienced in accounting for it. Mostly the foster parents simply stated their customs without trying to provide any explanation of them, employing an attitude and a mode of speech which recall the refusal to speak about mental illness or to admit any knowledge of it. The opacity of the fact is rendered even more impenetrable by the opacity of the motives. For whenever anyone tried to satisfy our insistence on this point, we came up against the evidence of a deeply-rooted but unexplained custom:

> I take them their meals and it's me who collects their dishes. I do my washing-up and everything. I don't like anyone touching. That's something I insist on . . . I don't let them touch things which belong to the house. No, no, no. I do my washing-up first and then I do theirs . . . I don't know why . . . It's a habit of mine . . . They're healthy people, really . . . They see the doctor regularly and they are very well looked after at Ainay-le-Château . . . It's just a habit of mine. I wouldn't let them do the washing-up, no . . .

In the end it is an opacity which enshrouds the basis of action. The arguments explaining the customs of hygiene are never stated without reservation or contradiction, whether the potential explanation is contagion, dirtiness or the association of the smell and the illness:

> All the clothes are washed together. I don't make any distinctions. The dishes I do separately. I don't do theirs with ours. I wash their dishes once a day. I do their coloureds with my husband's washing. If they had any serious illness they wouldn't be here. They have a special smell because they smoke so much. That smells bad. But they are clean. I don't do a separate load for them.

However, this opacity reveals a keen awareness of the revelatory value of the separation of belongings, of the close association of this practice and matters of crucial significance for the group which, however, are not authorized to those outside the group:

> The washing gets done in the washing machine. There's no need to touch it. They are decent, gentle. As for the dishes, my wife does ours first and then she does theirs separately. *But that's something you don't have to mention in your report.*

More obscure, less constraining at the collective level and at the same time more demanding on the individual level, and perhaps more worrying psychologically than the institutionalized order they recall, surely the rules of hygiene present the same face as that shown in other societies by the relationship between equivalent rules and the sacred or the magical. As is the case with most phenomena and customs which are of decisive importance for the community (Lévi-Strauss, 1976), the meaning of the behaviour remains unstated. The representation which guides it is hidden somewhere in the concern for hygiene and the contradictory evocation of a denied contagion. It is a mute thought whose attendant actions designate its true belief: the transmissibility of insanity.

This unstated thought and the belief it conceals reveal their true nature with the gradual disclosure of the elements which are symbolically and materially associated with hygiene and the separation of water. To this end it is necessary to identify their specific significance, which is hidden by the details of their implementation in the fields of both dishwashing and laundry. At first sight the two appear to be equivalent. Justified by the odour and the dirtiness of the lodgers, they obey the same principle of hygiene, namely to protect the family's belongings from possible pollution by avoiding contact with water in which dirt can collect. But, here, the way in which hygiene is associated with the notions of pollution, smell and fluid reveals profound differences which can help us explain the real objective of the measures which surround them.

Smell, Liquid and the Prohibition of Contact

The concern with hygiene is presented differently in the case of clothes and in the case of dishes. As far as clothes are concerned, separation is explained by the smell, an immediately identifiable trace left by tobacco, dirtiness or perspiration. The same is not true of dishes, which carry no smell but rather imply a trace left by that which the illness has affected. Nothing is ever said of this trace, but one of its causes is constantly evoked – medicines, which point directly to the illness:

> I always wash the dishes separately and I always put some disinfectant in. First of all because they all take medicines. And for me the medicines alone . . . ugh . . .

In the case of clothes, the link between the odour and the medicine or the illness is provided by perspiration. The link is established by the indelible character of the mark which is left. The foster parents, who never doubt the quality of their cleaning, believe that despite their thoroughness the smell remains in the lodger's belongings. They then attribute this special smell to something specific to the lodger – a special type of perspiration which derives from the illness and its treatment:

> The medicines give them a very strong-smelling sweat. It's dreadful. Their clothes smell when you're ironing them, most of all when you're ironing them. I bleach their whites because they give me so much dirty washing that I have to disinfect it. And even after it's been disinfected and rinsed, you wouldn't believe it, the smell is still there. It's attached to their clothes. It's unbelievable. You can smell it. I'll take you up to their room and you can smell it as well. There's no point airing the place or using air fresheners. Nothing does any good. That's what they smell like. Personally, I think it comes from the drugs they're given. It's when they perspire, it gives them a special smell. And then there's the tobacco as well, because they smoke a lot, all of them. But basically I think *it's the medicines which give them that smell. After all, they're the only ones who have it. Because after all it isn't what we smell like if we've been sweating. It's a special smell.*

Surely what we find underlying this interpretation is a "materialized" representation of the illness. Everything suggests that a substance emanating from the illness mixes with the bodily secretions and is emitted along with them. It is as if the idea that this "perspiration, this smell which seems to come from the illness" implied that they express something which participates in the nature of mental illness and which can be found in the indelible mark which they leave even in washed clothes. This is doubtless the reason why the foster parents speak more frequently of the smell than of the dirtiness of the lodgers when dealing with the question of hygiene. Cleaning can overcome dirtiness but it cannot eradicate the pollution which is associated with the illness. More than simply incapable of being or making himself clean, the patient appears as a source of pollution because bodily contact with him risks the contamination of the object he touches, the transmission of his impurity and his illness, most particularly in a liquid environment in which his perspiration is free to mix. One horrified foster parent summed up the distinction between pollution and dirtiness for us:

> Let a patient do the washing? Have the water polluted? Have things drying in filth?
> No thank you! That means something, that does!

Contact with water does not remove the patient's dirtiness, instead it adds to it the pollution of his secretions.

Moreover, this belief is clearly indicated by the change of habit and attitude which accompanied the mechanization of household chores. The introduction of washing machines to wash the clothes seems to have authorized greater freedom in the washing technique. The foster parents who claim not to separate the clothes all use washing machines, whilst it has at least permitted the others to use the same cleaning materials. Formerly, the concern to avoid pollution meant that the washing utensils were separated just as much as the clothes to be washed:

> I had separate things for them. Now I've got a washing machine to do the washing whereas, before, I had a boiler for them, a basin for them, and a washing-up bowl for them. We had all the things for them because it doesn't do to mix, you know. It's a question of hygiene. Because, you know, they have a strange smell. They keep just as clean as we do and, yet, there's something about them. It's easy to tell their washing when it's dry . . . Compare one of your shirts with one of theirs and you can easily see the difference . . . Even if it's washed and dry there's a difference. I don't know, I suppose it's their perspiration and the drugs they get . . . When you get a lot of them together it's disgusting.

And the same foster parent carried on to tell us that the materials used in the construction of washing machines doesn't retain the smell which has also been eradicated by the detergents used in this type of apparatus:

> In the washing machine I do their sheets first and then their coloureds. *But the smell doesn't stay on the washing machine . . . I was frightened it would spread.* I didn't fancy that much but you don't smell anything with this washing powder.

The smell itself possesses a material substrate which can inscribe itself, "attach itself" to clothes or diffuse, "spread" through the air and attack other materials, just as the medicines do. It now becomes possible to understand how contact with the same washing water, the same recipient, if it is not completely tin-plated, the same area of infiltration, carries a material risk of transmission of a substance which resists traditional methods of washing and which can cling to any porous, gaseous or liquid support. It is a volatile, chemical substance against which modern materials are protected by their impermeability and their destructive action.

This argument, which is valid for clothes, does not apply to dishes. There is no question of washing the patients' dishes in the family dishwasher:

> I wash their dishes separately. Next year I'm going to buy a dishwasher and from then on I'll get them to do their own washing-up. At the moment I wash their things when my own are finished and I add some disinfectant as well.

The exclusion of this solution points to a difference in the way clothes and dishes are perceived as vectors of pollution. In both cases the separation of washing water is a defence against related but nevertheless distinct risks, differentiated at least in their level of gravity. On the one hand, the hygiene argument provided by smell and perspiration in the case of clothes is inadmissible where dishes are concerned because the type of contact these have with the patient's body is quite different. On the other hand, the traces left on dishes seem to be more resistant and more dangerous.

But what is this something which, associated with smell and perspiration, is related to the illness? To what phenomena, what specific process does the pollution mediated by dishes correspond? Silence, on this point, is absolute. During all our interviews, not a single foster parent told us what was at risk. What is the reason for this? Have the measures applied with regard to dishes become established through a process of generalization? Or do they testify to a representation which is as hidden as it is important?

In formal terms, it would be possible to opt for the hypothesis of generalization. Because "there is something" which is associated with the illness and which is transmitted to that which approaches the patient, everything he touches must be subjected to the measures of separation. But then the precautions taken with regard to dishes ought to be less rigorous than those observed in the case of clothes. Yet we find the opposite:

> I wash the clothes together. But the dishes, it's best to keep them separate. You feel as if there's something which might be transmitted, microbes or something. It's only a fear. That's all it is, because I don't believe that there are any microbes. It's just a fear. Even if they're very, very clean because, after all, deep down they are human beings like us, but all the same.

At the same time certain elements in the speech used to explain the measures of hygiene indicate that the dishes are seen to occupy a higher position in the order of protection, and therefore of pollution. In fact, hygiene is sometimes invoked in the name of the safety of the children but only in the context of dishwashing:

> When I do the washing I keep the patients' separate from the rest. The washing-up as well, because having children here we started like that right at the beginning.
>
> I do it all at once. No, I tell a lie. First of all I do ours and then I do theirs. You know, despite what they say, it's because of the children.

Reference to the children always indicates the highest level of anxiety, and to link the separation of the dishes to the well-being of the children shows that contact poses a danger of major proportions.

And in fact it is on this point that avoidance of contact becomes so systematic that it borders on a prohibition. It is not just a question of separating the water used for washing the dishes but also the dishes themselves. In the majority of placements today, and invariably in the past, it was an inviolable rule that the patients had their own eating utensils which were reserved exclusively for their use. Equally, the lodgers are or were absolutely forbidden to touch the utensils used by the family.

> They eat what we eat but that's all. My soup is their soup. It comes out of the same pot. We eat after they do. I do all the washing-up. They wouldn't do it as well and I don't like them doing it. If I couldn't do it my husband would. In placements where the lodgers do the washing-up the dishes can't be clean. They have their dishes up there, but they are dishes just like ours.

It is necessary to dwell on the relationship between contact and dirtiness. Again, as was the case with the washing of clothes, we encounter the idea that the lodger would not be able to do the washing-up properly. But there are two further aspects to be investigated here. First of all, when the dirtiness of the lodgers is evoked, as it often is in connection with the dishes, it is always understood in a specific way. What is meant is less bodily dirtiness than dirtiness at table, the dirtiness which prevents the foster parents eating with the patients. The reason given for the separate taking of meals is not the inability to correct the lodgers' table manners but the dirtiness they display while eating, the fact that the lodger dribbles, drops his food while chewing it or simply "eats with his head in his plate". The disgust felt in the presence of this unedifying spectacle is exacerbated by the revulsion inspired by the mixing of oral secretions with food and the receptacle in which it is served. Avoidance of contact is established as a protection against this dirtiness and is extended from the sphere of washing-up to apply to the utensils themselves. And this is the second remarkable element in the separation of dishes: the patient is forbidden to make use of the utensils belonging to the family. What is the significance of this if not that he will pollute them to such an extent that washing will not remove all trace of it, just as washing powder fails to remove the odour which is embedded in the lodger's clothes? That he will leave something there which risks being transmitted to those who subsequently use the implement? Transmission here operates via the mouth.

But whilst in the case of laundry the foster parents speak of perspiration, *when they are speaking of the dishes there is never any mention of the source of pollution. There is never any pollutant.* To discover and specify the nature of this pollutant a closer examination of behaviour is necessary. Even if every placement does not respect the old customs with the same rigour of this foster parent:

> They have their own dishes and cutlery. There are some who don't do it like this, but me, I bought myself dishes just for my use. But I still use disinfectant for their things, only for theirs. Perhaps I've got a bit of a bee in my bonnet about it . . .

There is, nevertheless, one custom which is universally observed, that of using special glasses for the patients:

> You know, they can be quite selfish as far as that's concerned. They all have their own glass and they all know which is theirs. It's a precaution, especially if you don't know them.

> It's the drugs. I've always done it like this, their dishes separately. When they come for a drink in the afternoon when they're working, it's normal to give them something to drink if it's hot, they have their own glasses. I don't let them drink out of the same glasses as us.

What is the significance of forbidding the lodgers to touch the glasses? To an even greater extent than the plate and the cutlery, the glass is a receptacle which comes into direct contact with the mouth, on which the lodgers' lips rest for a while during which time they are able to leave their deposit. The glass is equated with the liquid in the glass, the liquid which is swallowed. But it is also the receptacle at the bottom of which a residue will always be present. And it is this residue which has been in contact with the liquid which has passed through the mouth, liquid which has been in continuous contact with the mouth and which, in return, might have received a liquid secreted by it. The glass is the feared vehicle of the material which resembles perspiration and which is also secreted by the patient: *saliva*.

Saliva was never mentioned during the interviews and yet the idea of it was constantly present. During one interview a young lodger of the placement entered the kitchen. The foster parent greeted him whole-heartedly and entrusted him with her eighteen-month-old daughter. The young man's clothes and face were not as clean as one might have hoped and I was, I must admit, surprised to see him take the little girl on his knees. The conversation continued calmly whilst the child played with the lodger under the indulgent eye of the mother. Then the lodger put the little girl on the ground to pick up a small object which she had dropped and which he held between his lips for the time needed to sit down again and put the child back on his knees. When the child tried to recover the object her mother ran to her, seized the object and, pale, hurled it with a rare display of strength far out into the field. Not a word had been exchanged but the mother's reaction had been immediate. She had prevented the child from touching what the patient had held in his mouth. Another foster parent explained the difficulty of having lodgers while the children are still young:

> It's strange, isn't it? The children like to be with them. They go with them and you can't stop them. They like to play with the lodgers. But you have to watch them. Some of the lodgers can do them harm without even noticing. *There was one who gave my little girl something to drink. I couldn't stop him giving her a drink. He was drinking and then he took his glass and he was going to give her something to drink. There she was and he wanted to give her a drink.* I had to get angry to stop him giving her drinks. Oh yes, there are a lot of problems!

It is again saliva, and the illness, which is found in another much-feared contact with the lips, the kiss:

> There's nothing to be frightened of in the illness, it's not contagious. But, still, a lot of the lodgers would quite happily kiss a child and I don't like to see that. But you can't stop it happening just as soon as you can't see what they're doing.

And again it is saliva that we find in the most violent expression of the illness, in the foam which coats the lips of the epileptic.

Living Secretions and Contamination

The parallel between laundry and dishwashing is reestablished: in the first, perspiration; in the second, saliva. Two liquids of bodily origin, both of which can pollute water, with one, saliva, being accorded greater pollutant power. Where does this power come from and why does it act in so special a manner on this type of vehicle? For even if it is now clear that the hygienic measures are aimed less at dirtiness than at pollution by the illness, one question still remains to be answered. How can we understand the many foster parents who accept bodily dirtiness which they say is repugnant to them, tolerate living with enuretics and encopretics whom they clean and touch without batting an eyelid while they show such fear and such repulsion at contact with objects which they believe to be impregnated with liquids secreted by the body? Urine and faeces, a type of filth which can be cleared away by cleaning, inspire disgust but they do not entail the same "phobic" rejection as perspiration and saliva. The foster parents touch sheets wet during the night to dry them just as they touch defecation to dispose of it, yet these are also bodily excretions. How does this difference operate and what does it signify? More precisely, why are the first considered as dirtiness and the second as pollution, that is to say carriers of the illness?

An initial answer can be looked for in the representations which concern the body. As in every case where our investigation touched on domains where academic or scientific knowledge has not yet completely effaced all traces of traditional knowledge, it was the older foster parents with the greatest feeling for tradition who gave us access to the contents of the practice of hygiene. Such traditional knowledge is always closely related to the beliefs which serve as a base for popular medicine. A study of the customs and beliefs yielded by a folklore which lives on in the medical field where, alongside plants, organic substances have an important role to play, can give us a useful perspective on the representation on which separation is based.

And, in fact, the list of medical prescriptions (Gagnon, 1949) shows that animal substances have a certain but variable effect on the body depending on their origin. From this point of view it is permissible to classify them as *living secretions*, which include all the substances produced by a process of transformation and organic development and which are secreted at the skin or the mucous membranes (exudation, saliva, nasal mucous etc.), and *dead excretions* including peeled skin, the residue left by substances absorbed by the body and rejected after the assimilation of their active components. If this classification is taken as a basis for the examination of medical prescriptions, it appears that dead excretions always have a curative power – for example cow dung cures suppurations and human urine heals cuts. Living secretions, however, have an ambiguous effect, sometimes positively formulated – sores are healed by letting a dog lick them – and sometimes negatively – spitting into a frog's throat eases a cough. Lice are said to come from the transformation of crabs under the influence of sweat. Surely the positive value of dead excretions, which appears to reside in the substances themselves independent of the agent which produces them, should tend to neutralize certain human excrements, making those of the patients appear harmless? At the same time, would not the ambiguity of organic secretions whose value, positive or negative, appears to depend on the agent which produces them contribute to investing the saliva and perspiration of the patients with a pollutant power? Such a hypothesis seems to take account of the difference noted between peelings, bodily dirtiness and pollutant secretions. At the same time it strips nothing from the obscurity surrounding the nature of the power attributed to these and what it is in the productive agent that explains it. There are two reasons for this. On the one hand, the prescriptions and customs on which the distinction between living secretions and dead excretions is based themselves imply a vision of their efficacy whose nature still has to be explained. On the other hand, if it is true that the negative, disturbing nature of the substances emitted by the lodger results from the specific quality of the patient, it is again necessary to specify what it is in him that is the source of this danger and what it is, in others, that is at risk.

At the level of observable manifestations, the danger corresponds to the fear underlying the practices of hygiene, the fear of contagion. Now, this has been systematically eliminated. But as we have pointed out on numerous occasions, the affirmation of the mental patient's non-contagious nature brings proof of the contrary belief. It is essential for us to discover the nature of this contradiction. Of course, it reveals the discrepancy between a formal acceptance of the reassurances provided by the Colony and the precautions which grow from a conception judged to be erroneous or old-fashioned. Nevertheless, the vigour with which this contradiction is expressed invites us to investigate it further.

Is the explanation of this contradiction not to be found in the fact that we are here dealing with two sorts of contagion which can coexist without discord, despite deriving from different conceptual universes? The contagion which is denied is medical in nature, that which is still feared is a magical contagion. At one and the same time we can say that the lodger is not a carrier of germs or microbes, that his illness is not infectious or contagious in the sense that, for example, tuberculosis is, that the visits from the medical staff eliminate any risk of morbid disease, and yet continue to assert that contact with the patient entails a risk of contamination. But this contamination is provoked by phenomena which do not fall within the medical sphere. We have already seen how simple visual contact with the signs of nervous breakdown threatens the young child with contamination. Linked to a representation of organic development, we see the emergence of a notion inspired by a process similar to that underlying the idea of imitative magic according to which imitating something leads to its creation. In the same way, to consider that physical contact with the emanations of another organism – animal or human – can have a beneficial or harmful effect on the body is to appeal to a power with which certain objects or certain beings are endowed, and at the same time to appeal to a magical conception of contagion which is based on the principle that two things which are united and then separated remain in contact, the power of one remaining within the other (Cazeneuve, 1961). And as Mauss says about one of the laws of magic, the law of contiguity, magical contagion "is concrete, material and in all points resembles physical contagion" (1950, p. 59). This appeal to a magical mode of thought may appear excessive, transferring a type of reasoning and belief observed in other times and other societies to a population which belongs to our culture and our times. However, such an interpretation needs to be viewed in the light of the implications of the practices of hygiene.

First of all there is the model of illness implied by the idea of contagion. While admitting "a feeling that there are things which are transmitted", the population rejects the hypothesis of microbial contagion:

> I've always lived around here and I've never heard of any illnesses being caught from the patients. I don't know whether that's right or not. One winter there was an outbreak of flu but that didn't come from the patients. I've never heard of anything like that.

It is impossible to see here, as one might otherwise be tempted to do, a disguise for contagion in the medical sense. Today, as before, the population's worries seem to be firmly directed towards something other than "an illness like everybody gets". This is because what in the lodger is associated with the idea of contamination, the practices of hygiene and the avoidance of contact, is the fact that he is suffering from an incurable illness, one which "can't be treated", "can't be healed" and which, for this reason, is situated outside the medical domain. Of general application in earlier times, this conception is still current today. The recollection of one foster parent: "My grandmother kept her cutlery and crockery marked her whole life long. The old people, they used to think of it more as an incurable illness" finds an echo in the outburst of another: "I'm frightened of fits and great epidemics, basically of severe incurable illnesses."

Mental illness becomes consubstantial with the patient, inherent to his nature, and leaves its imprint on everything he is and everything he produces. In consequence those things which are most closely associated with him will harbour something of what he is, a "something" which is as fearful and effective as it is imprecise (like magic power), a "something" which carries the illness of which it is a part.

It is difficult to discover what the effects of contact with this something might be, precisely because the measures of separation are intended to avoid this very possibility. But the cases of allergy suggest that, at the very least, contact may result in physical disturbance. And even though during our enquiry we constantly met with the idea that "you can catch it", even though imitative reproduction of mental illness was specifically mentioned, there was only a single case in which the process of contamination through contact with a living secretion could be identified. A foster parent who was explaining how her washing machine helped her avoid contact with the lodger's belongings went on to explain how she had herself been a victim of the pollution of mental illness:

> Well, believe me, I cut the tip of my finger and it suppurated. I'd only cut the skin. And then M was making his handkerchiefs. *He used to collect handkerchiefs and roll them up.* He used to roll them up into big balls like that. Well, of course, *they got dirty. The material of the handkerchiefs collects the dirt*

and you can't wash it out. I said to myself: I don't know how I'm going to wash those. I took his handkerchiefs and put them into water to soak. Then I changed the water. I had soaped them well. But I still had that cut and *it must have got in, I don't know what it is, and it went bad and it suppurated*. And it's from his handkerchiefs that I got that. Because it stung, it started to sting immediately, and how it stung! Some of them are dirty, it varies. But M wasn't dirty. All the same this operation of rolling up his handkerchiefs. It got into the material and it wouldn't come out again . . . Nowadays it's better with the washing machine. Especially if you've got people like that. You don't have to handle it.

Everything is present. The illness and its sign: the operation of rolling up handkerchiefs, that is to say a behaviour dictated by the illness (in this case nerves, as the foster parent indicated to us at another point in her discussion of the lodger M). The pollution of the linen by a dirtiness, which is not a lack of cleanliness (this is explicitly stated) but a nasal secretion, irremediably penetrates the material under the effect of the "operation". This symbolic expression of the illness, which does not exclude a (magic?) material power – that of impregnating the dirtiness in the material so that it cannot be removed – then combines with the living secretion to pass from the handkerchief to the foster parent's skin, enter her body, sting her and *go bad*, resulting in suppuration. In the same way that its counterpart, the affective shock, goes to the brain and turns it bad. In the same way that nervous breakdown can change a patient's gait, "attack one side, leave one leg bad". In the same way that illness mediated by bodily fluids is transmitted to the body of the normal individual and turns bad as a purulent, destructive affliction.

It is necessary to identify precisely the elements used in this testimony if we are to interpret magical contamination. On the one hand we again find the representation of a biological phenomenon directly inspired by current experience. This story is reminiscent of a process familiar to vets who work with horses, in which a nasal infection known as glanders can acquire a cutaneous form through a process of contagion. On the other hand, it is possible to identify a representation inspired in two ways by magical belief. First there is the representation of the harmful power of the patient's nasal secretions which finds a direct correspondence in the beliefs of popular medicine with its theory of humours, which implies an extension of the illness to all the elements of the body which it then invests with a negative and harmful potential. Second there is the representation of mental illness as a force whose direct transmission can immediately affect all spheres of life in their mental, active or organic dimensions. In this representation we again find the magical belief in a spiritual power endowed with a material effect.

The global representation of the process of contamination is in some way invested with multiple significations, themselves determined at another level by elements which belong to different domains of thought and experience.

For the rest, in its most secret aspects, the illness appears here just as the analysis of its products and forms had suggested, as a unique, polymorphous force, both material and transitive. Moreover, it appears as a magic, harmful power capable of turning the organism bad, seizing and dominating the nerves, in close contact with the forces of the natural world. It forces activity, removes liberty, arouses malignancy. A foster parent who was emphasizing that dealings with the lodgers had modified his knowledge of mental illness rejected any idea of contagion. Asked to describe his discovery, he explained it in these words:

> It's given me an objective view of mental illness. Now I know what mental illness is. My God, *it's an infection of certain parts of the brain which affects* other elements . . . which affects the emotions, mobility . . . *It isn't a physical illness.*

Apart from the "hereditary defect", the only other cause of mental illness which he acknowledged was emotional shock. This revealed itself in "tiredness", "the inability to take responsibility" in those who "don't have enough strength in them to resist what's going to their brains". Previously he had been "content" simply to see the difference between the "mad" and the "sane" as "wickedness". These reasonings cannot fail to recall an animistic mode of thought. Through them the illness evokes a non-material force which reveals itself at the physical level and constitutes the magic power of beings and things (Greek *dynamis*, *mana*, *orenda* etc.). It is the force or fluid which gives plants their virtue and the magician his power. United with the material, this force or fluid, which is also seen as a spiritual power, is found once more in everything that comes from the body. In this way the sufferer, who is the bearer of this force, is seen to spread its negative power to others. Is it not this that the foster parents believe and fear when they use their authority to suppress the boldness of the patients and forbid them to open the door and watch when they are washing their children or giving their husbands an injection?

The Traveller, the Stranger and the Impurity of Difference

It is through this very process that insanity becomes a quality, a state, a force of the patient. It is to the patient that we return in order to explain a negative virtue which is never uttered but which is expressed through the behaviour of avoidance. We have to turn to the attributes which characterize the insane man to find a reason for the avoidance of contact with him. Alongside the danger of contamination, a property of the illness, we find the danger of contact, a property of the patient. Now, we have learned that those who do not apply measures of hygiene indicate that what is to be feared in the patient is the unknown. We have already seen the importance of knowledge of the patient in the process of adaptation and acceptance. This knowledge, which serves to identify the lodger's pathology and character in order to determine the behaviour best adopted towards him, is not sufficient to suppress the avoidance of contact at the maintenance level. We are therefore dealing with another type of unknown, one which points to the mystery of insanity, to its essential difference, the source of its negativity. The most striking connotations of this unknown appear in the associations which are brought out by questions directed towards the practices used to secure separation. For in these practices, the unknown borrows from the same background of culture to define both the madman and his illness.

In fact, the separation of belongings was not invented specifically for dealings with the lodgers. Rather, it was taken over from older customs reserved for certain characters on the social scene whom the community associates with the patients. This crucial piece of information was provided by an interviewee practically without him knowing it. In an attempt to justify the separation of belongings he turned to a tradition which was itself related to the separation of items of crockery. This slippage showed the deep-seated identity to be found between the separation of water and the avoidance of contact. Let us listen to him:

> You know, it reminds me of the old days when the 'travellers' used to move from farm to farm. They were the hippies of their day.
>
> Q. Were they gypsies?
>
> No, the gypsy had his caravan. The travellers, they were men who were out on the road with their bags, 'tramps' we called them. And of course they were put up in the farms. They were given some soup to eat and allowed to sleep in the hay. But they had their own glass. There was always a separate plate for the traveller. It wasn't right, you understand. It's the same with this lot now. They're no dirtier than the others. They shower more often than their colleagues out in the country, but . . .

Patient, traveller, tramp, three marginal characters whose evocation and contact are charged with meaning. In the patient, a disinherited being, dispossessed of his rights, cut off from his past, rootless, turned into a "drifter" by his illness, there is something of the tramp, a vagabond without hearth or home, living from alms or theft, passing from region to region, unlike the gypsy not even possessing the territory of his caravan. The stranger who has come from elsewhere is granted the hospitality of the region but, out of distrust and fear, is forbidden to share the table utensils.

The traveller, although he shares the wanderings of the tramp, has, according to students of folklore (Gagnon, 1972), both a trade and a power.

Contrary to the claims of our interviewee, the traveller is not a vagabond but a pedlar, roaming the country to sell the few bits and pieces he carries in his bag. Furthermore, his right to board and lodging derives not from charity but from magic. The traveller is thought of as a kind of sorcerer who can bring bad luck to anyone who refuses him a welcome. So malicious is he that he must give his matches to his host before entering the barn where he will sleep to ensure that he does not set fire to it. Viewed with suspicion because he left his home to embark on a career of wandering, he is invested with a harmful power as distinct from simple dishonesty as the pollution brought by the patient is from dirtiness.

In the rootlessness, both real and symbolic, to which his illness condemns him, the patient combines the dishonesty of the tramp, a thief like him, a source of damage, with the malice of the traveller, a sorcerer whom the patient resembles in his deceitful look and his propensity for evil and bad turns. The dimension in this evocation of the untouchable unknown which causes him to be invested with a negative power is his displacement, the incongruity of being away from his home, not where he belongs. It is the difference of the foreign. We should not forget that the patient's gaze is all the more feared if he comes from another country, and especially so if this country is far away. So much so that eventually "the look of the Pole" or "the look of the Russian" become synonymous with an evil look. Where does this difference of the foreign acquire its force?

The stranger is feared because of his origin. Because of it, he is not subject to the prevalent code of conduct and is thought to be capable of all kinds of aggression:

> They had given me another one. He was a Russian and very stubborn. I didn't like to be alone with him. I wasn't frightened because I know they have to be very certain of them before they let them loose. On the other hand, he used to drink. One day when he was very drunk he said to my husband, 'What would you do if you were attacked?' And he had got into a nasty habit. As soon as my husband left in the morning, he came knocking on my door. This Russian, I wasn't really afraid of him, but it was the way he was, he didn't go about things the same way as a Frenchman. They don't have the same ideas about things.

Foreign origin also implies a difference in blood which can readily give rise to every shade of wickedness, from the multifaceted cunning of the Slav to the routine brutality of the North African:

> We used to have an Algerian, a pig-headed man. And he wasn't small either. I was frightened by him because he was brutal. He used to push us as he went past. In the middle of August he would still be wearing his pullover and coat . . . He was brutal, but not towards my husband. You had to make sure you didn't annoy him. You had to get out of his way, not annoy him. It

was impossible to get him to change his clothes . . . For example, if I took
him his food and put his plate in the middle of the table when he didn't
want it in the middle he would snatch it from out of my hands. I would just
be putting it down in one place and he would put it somewhere else entirely.
That was a type of brutality. He never came after us. He never actually tried
to hit us, but it was his way of behaving . . .

Furthermore, blood lies closer to the root of evil if it is mixed. The purity of
its origin represents in some way a guarantee of human qualities while
admixture, revealed in the colour of the skin, signifies its deterioration.

At the moment there are a lot of Blacks here. Not real Blacks, but a lot of
North Africans. The black Blacks are easier to get on with than these
yellow-skins, the half blacks. They're a bad bunch. They aren't really
yellow, a bit darker than that. They aren't black but they aren't white
either, and they're worse. I spent the whole of the war with Blacks and they
were all right. But there were some yellow ones as well and they were
difficult to get on with.

Different countries, different customs, different blood. Like the stranger, the
patient offers an image of displacement and impurity. Because insanity,
wandering, aberrance is also in the blood. The untouchable unknown is a
threat because of the strange powers of the foreign, that is to say of mixture
and bad blood. It is impossible to avoid the comparison with the
representation of nervous attack, so similar are the two schemata. The
agitation which drives the nervous case to his chaotic wanderings, to a
physical and spiritual "drifting", has its origin in the degeneration of the
blood which results from the decomposition and absorption of foreign
substances – alcohol, tobacco, bad food – or to an unregulated life,
contaminated by the pollution of the cities. A stranger himself, the patient
degenerates through a process of denaturation and impurity. To compare the
patient with the traveller is to bring together insanity, sorcery and otherness.
To extend the rules applied to the traveller to the separation of water is to
remember the magic force of the illness and to fear in the water the impurity
which comes from the patient's blood. Water remains a symbol of purity and
fertility in a region where the beneficent influence of sacred fountains once
spread in profusion; or where during the long years of wandering, Saint
Menoux, the healer of madmen, enjoyed not only the power of curing mental
illness but also that of washing clothes cleaner and removing spots (another
obscure way of indicating the relationship between insanity and fluid,
pollution and secretion).[4]

---

[4] It is not without significance that the legends connected with Saint Menoux himself are
somewhat disturbing. Able to chase the wolves from the forest (he is generally seen as a magician
who could make wolves obey him), he punished farmers who refused him alms when he appeared

To say that the substances which emanate from the patient pollute the water is to establish their impurity and their harmfulness which, in an organic view, is related to the deterioration and otherness of the blood, a source of pollution which is mediated by living secretions. When the blood is pure its power is beneficial. Renan, writing once more about the madmen of Tréguier, evokes the insanity of a young girl who, falling from high rank into poverty, had sunk into melancholy. He describes her father, who had become a flax grinder, in these terms:

> He was a patriarch . . . they thought that, as the leader, he was the repository of the gifts of his race and that his saliva and his touch had the ability to cure the ill. They were convinced that such healing powers could only come from a richly noble heritage which he alone possessed. There were days when his house was surrounded by people who had come twenty leagues to see him. If a child was slow to start walking, if his legs were weak, he was brought. He would wet his fingers with his saliva, anoint the child's kidneys with the liquid and the child would grow stronger. (Renan, 1967, p. 30)

It is impossible to state more clearly the relationship between the power of saliva and the quality of the blood. Entrenchment within the group (race) guarantees the purity of the blood. Superiority (nobility) ensures that the group qualities and powers which are transferred with the saliva are retained. The reasoning used in this case sheds light on the reasoning applied to the patient. Uprooted, external to the group, his blood possesses neither its virtues nor its qualities. If he has a force, and he does – that of the illness: "They're strong these illnesses, they're powerful" – contact with it can only degrade the force of the group.

There are two ways in which living secretions pose the threat of impurity. By spreading the properties of a blood which has degenerated under the influence of an incurable illness, they can also degrade the blood of those who approach them, causing weakness or infection:

> I do their washing after mine. The first one we had was a syphilitic. They didn't say anything about it. We didn't catch anything . . . but . . . there was one who caught a bit of a cold. I don't know if it had anything to do with his illness. As far as washing is concerned, I do their clothes in the washing machine. I do the whites together with mine because I put bleach in. But I don't let it all soak together. If we were to catch something now

---

in the guise of a beggar (like a tramp) by turning their bread the colour of blood (an act of sorcery) and setting fire to their hemp crop (as the traveller threatens to do). A punctilious guardian of morals, he causes the death within a year of young people whom he accuses of dancing too much or of making fun of him – as one makes fun of the insane. The only saint in the region who cures insanity, he is also the only one to be associated with so dark a legend, so laden with maleficence. In all its aspects, the universe of insanity always casts the same shadows.

after two years!. . . I'm not afraid of them, but the syphilitic, he's syphilitic after all. It's an illness which can't be treated and can't be cured.

What emerges here, as in the illness of the nerves, is the link between sexuality and deterioration. The chaos of that excitation which unleashes organic needs and aggravates sexuality corresponds to a disturbance of the blood by sexuality. This lies at the origin of the revulsion felt for the female lodgers whose manner of nervous excitation has already been seen to point more clearly to disturbance of and by sexuality than is the case with the men. This disturbance, which is present in their personal secretions and menstrual blood, makes contact even more frightening:

> I prefer men, for reasons of hygiene mostly. A man, good, if he's washed more or less, he'll do, whilst a woman, I don't know what you might catch. I certainly wouldn't like it. This hygiene question worries me enormously. Some neighbours of my mother-in-law had three of them. She told me that there were times when it was dreadful. With a man it's different. There's less special hygiene needed than with a woman. That must be very troublesome, very unpleasant.

What emerges here, alongside rootlessness and denaturation, is one of the fundamental dimensions of the patient's impurity. This combination means that the contact with living secretions threatens in another way: by making him who touches them impure, denaturing him, impairing his integrity and, through the individual, the integrity of the group.

Representations of the biological and the social are interwoven with animist beliefs in a cultural symbolism. Pollution and impurity testify simultaneously to the extraordinary character of insanity and the otherness of the patient. Against a background of an organic representation of the illness and a magical vision of its transmission, the practices of separation point to the unknown, strange and therefore malefic, and the untouchable, impure and therefore dangerous, in the patient. The danger of contamination by contact is aggravated by the danger of degradation through intermixture. The untouchable unknown is the impure stranger, strange to those around him, threatening their integrity with his otherness:

> I do the washing-up at the same time. I've nothing to fear. It's not like other illnesses, illnesses brought by microbes, things like that! . . . And I've got the right products as well and I use very hot water, not boiling, but I heat a basin of water as much as I can and still be able to touch it and I rinse the things twice under water. Well, like that . . . I know, there are people who think . . . When I had tuberculosis, it was during the war, they sent me butter and I would say 'Go on, have this butter, I haven't touched it,' – it was me who was afraid of infecting the others – 'Have it. I haven't touched it.' But the nurses, they had had tuberculosis as well. What can you do

about it? Tuberculosis, it happens, cancer, they're diseases and yet they still eat off the same plates. But these other diseases, mental illness, it's not the same thing . . . We wouldn't eat . . . because they're strangers . . . If at least they were part of the family, then we'd know them.

Knowing the other is to know that he is like you, as is illustrated by this conversation which took place during the course of an interview with a woman who was visiting a placement. She explains why she has no desire to take a lodger:

> I'm not very patient. I don't put up with much . . . They aren't children but . . . I see little X . . . in front of the church. That's just about the most I could put up with. The poor man is a bit loopy. He gets a pension. He comes from the region. We grew up together.

> The foster parent – I can tell you I was surprised to see him at your house the day you were handing round a drop[5] . . . I didn't even know.

> The guest – There's one of them, that's all.

> I ask – Do people treat him differently from the lodgers?

> The guest – Oh yes. He's a child of the region. He's like a four-year-old. Everybody knows him. He's called John-the-Pipe because he likes his pipe. That's all there is to it. We were at school together. People make a lot of fun of him, even with the lodgers around. He's more stupid than the lodgers. But, after all, we do know him.

Similarity, either through the fellowship of condition or of group, guarantees against the impurity of contact. If the child of the region bears that mark of otherness which is insanity, then knowledge of his origin and his roots makes it possible to establish his natural identity as a group member. The fellowship of blood guarantees its purity and eliminates the threats posed by the illness. Similarity and identity authorize the union symbolized by the contact of salivas. Contact is possible because mixture is not to be feared. Otherness establishes the impurity of contact. Contact indicates identity. Thus, if the avoidance of contact is a way of guarding against impurity, it is also a means of indicating difference, maintaining a lack of identity. When the foster parent turns the stranger into an untouchable, she saves her own integrity from the risks of otherness by confining the latter within the notion of

---

[5] The drop (French *goutte*) is a small glass of local brandy. To offer "a drop" is a sign of acceptance. At the start of the enquiry a visiting nurse told me, "When you go to see the foster parents, if one of them offers you a drop at the end of your visit you can consider yourself accepted." I was offered it only once, by a woman who was preparing to open a placement.

difference. Even those who do not fear contact are well acquainted with the stakes:

> I take them their food and they bring me their dirty plates. I do all the washing-up in one go. No, Madame, there's no difference between them. I wash their glasses with mine. First I wash theirs and then I wash mine. I do what everybody else does. If I had a patient I knew had some disease, but my patients are perfectly well. I've no reason to treat my patients any differently from my children.

The avoidance of contact is the establishment of an order which protects the group. The separation of water and table utensils, explained as measures of hygiene, manifests similar effects to the rule of distance. However, the significances attached to it go much further and it is charged with images which at all times have been associated with evil, wandering, the impure, the defence of the group and its territorial identity. The "drifting" of the madman, the incrimination of the nervous case always considered as "evil", suggested to us a comparison with the penal usage of the notion of stain whose original form has been analysed in Greek society and traces of which can still be found in certain local traditions in which Talion's principle is still operative (Glotz, 1904; Jodelet, 1926). A crime was a stain on the group to which the victim belonged and purification was only effected with the exile of the criminal, his social elimination. He was not allowed to share anything with the group, not even to walk on the same soil for fear of polluting it. Do we not find here a relationship with the ignominy attached to vagrancy? If the criminal was killed, his corpse was taken to a crossroads to be stoned, the throwing of stones having a magical character of purification. Is there not here a relationship with the custom of throwing stones at madmen? And how can we fail to think of the sorcerer whose powers emerge at the crossroads, a crossing of paths which belongs to no territory? Finally, it has been shown that the concept of stain in the legal sphere emerged at a time when social solidarity was crumbling and no central legal power had yet established its authority. The idea of stain became a means of repression. Is the same not true of the community we are studying, a community which is insecure in its own defence? But what is the repression we are dealing with?

In this network of multiple signifiers which is provided by the acting out of a conception of madness, contact and illness are associated with magic power and pollution on the one hand, and with the otherness and impurity which give rise to social differentiation on the other. This association is only possible given a shift of emphasis away from the illness and towards that which it attacks, from direct contact to social contact, that is to say from the human body to the social body, passing in this process from representation to symbol. The pollutant power of the illness, a magic force transmitted by contact with living secretions, becomes in the patient a sign of otherness proper to his nature as bearer of an insanity whose impurity threatens the integrity of others. The avoidance of this contact, a measure of hygiene adopted to protect the human body from contamination, becomes a social division established to protect the social body from mixture. This process is illustrated in Diagram 2 (below).

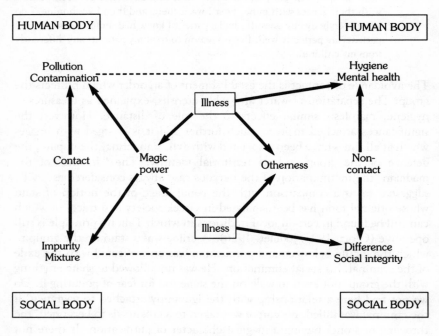

Diagram 2

But in integrating the rule of distance by means of this displacement, these practices of separation invest differentiation with a new weight of meaning. Between the *institutory practice* which defines the normative frameworks of the relationship with the patient and the *signifying practice* which, based on the representation of the object, patient/illness, reveals the dangers of this relationship, something has slipped which is related to private experience: direct, close confrontation with mental illness and its bearer. Not the public or semi-public confrontation of everyday coexistence and activity but the intimate confrontation of physical proximity. This something, together with all the symbolism which has grown up around it, has to do with physical contact. How then, despite the heavy veil of silence, can we not search in the rejected image of the contact of saliva, in the imprecision of the limits between the self and the other which characterizes animism, in the defence of identity in the face of the stranger, in the evocation of blood and sexuality, impurity and intermixture – all those things which are reaffirmed by the ritual repetition of phobic behaviour – how can we not search here for the phantasm of the fusion of bodies?

The practices of separation, at once protective, purifying and discriminatory, protect the individual and the group from sexual intermixture (and the temptation of it). This was rarely said and when it was it took the form of a confusing associative logic:

> They do their dishes themselves. As for their washing, I do it in the washing machine, of course, but I don't wash it with mine. Because they have a smell which you don't. It isn't that I'm afraid of infection, not at all, because their illness isn't contagious. If there's something wrong with the lungs, tuberculosis or something like that, it's very soon found out because they go for radiography once a year. It's not that I'm frightened of it. But no . . . it wouldn't be proper to leave the children with the lodgers. Especially, I don't know if you follow me, especially with the little girls. There are some who have been caught unawares.

In its polysemy, hygiene designates that which is the real threat to the group and against which the only defence is an individual one, sexual pollution:

> The female patients, they're the worst. You'd have to see it to believe it. And the rules. Everything has to be washed, you know . . . And then the stories there have been, that they don't just take up with the male patients but want the men of the region as well.

To get this far it was necessary to delve into the most secret retreats of the thoughts which invest insanity with magical and malign powers and the insane with their otherness. Our path has passed through the signifying practice which permits the expression of the real or imaginary experience of that on which the institutory practice bears. It is a path at the end of which, when the illness has revealed all its secrets, the patient takes on another face, that of the rejected object.

Epilogue

Face to Face with the Loonies

Refused object, sexual prohibition? Might we not be pushing our interpretation too far? And is it possible to assert at one and the same time the social symbolism and the personal symbolism borne by the signifying practices we have just examined? The general employment of these practices has enabled us to rule out the hypothesis of individual behaviour of a phobic nature. But in returning to the idea of sexual prohibition are we not running the risk of reducing the collective significance of these practices and of ignoring the social nature of the representations which they motivate? However, the representations associated with these domestic rituals, like certain data yielded by the enquiry, oblige us to consider this aspect of matters, to confront the problem of a multiple symbolism, of the polysemy of interdiction, of the overdetermination of the behaviour which derives from it. In short, of the psychosocial production of meaning and of the role played by the representations and the dynamic of the group which produces it.

We should not forget: what has been described here derives from an institution whose direction and maintenance is the task of the women. The institutory practices which record the distance at which the patients are kept belong to an order established and perpetuated by the women and justified by the protection of their children and the family home. And, as we have already had occasion to note, although their strength is sometimes a valuable asset in confrontations with the patients, the menfolk's fraternity of work and gender with the latter means that they exercise less authority over and maintain less distance from them. The signifying practices, on the other hand, are related to the techniques used to rule the domestic universe which Bourdieu has shown to be the place of a "practical truth" and of "private, shameful and everyday secret use" of a feminine symbolism which is different from the "official, public, solemn, extraordinary" masculine symbolism (1980, p. 394). And, in fact, as the meanings associated with these practices were revealed, it was only the men who spoke of the stranger and the "traveller" with reference to their former social utility and their implications for the community, whereas the women emphasized the risks of contamination through proximity and the importance of a knowledge of the other which roots him in the community. If, therefore, as protectors of the group it is the women who have possession of its practical truth, we must search for the ways in which they affect the production of the symbolism of their acts in the light of their pivotal position between the civilian group and the group of *bredins*. Here we encounter the perspectives opened by Douglas (1978) in her analysis of religious and secular pollution.

The customs concerning the patients' belongings and their maintenance belong to what Durkheim called "negative acts" with "the function of preventing mixture and unwanted contact" (1976). But what is their precise status? They obey an ambiguous ritual which is related in its form to the obsessive ritual, and to the magic or even religious ritual in its contents – the representations associated with it – and in the conditions under which it is implemented. Acts of tradition, domestic in their function, they occupy a position within this "confused mass of deeds whose specific character is not immediately apparent" which, according to Mauss, "extends" between the poles of magic and religion (1950). They possess the three properties of magic: the instrumental value of protection against the dangers posed by certain properties of the patients; the secret, intimate way in which the patients are kept; and, in the individual variability of the rule-keeping established in different individuals, a character of necessity without moral obligation. From religion, they have the character of prohibition aimed at ensuring respect for and thus preservation of the family circle which is considered "sacred".[1] We find ourselves in the presence of practices which are charged with history and yet etched on our own times and, as a consequence, difficult to unravel. Durkheim himself wrote of the subtlety of distinctions in this regard: "Folklore contains prohibitions of which it cannot easily be said whether they come from religion or magic" (*ibid.*). If, as Douglas thinks, our ideas concerning pollution and our ideas about religion – we would add magic – are only distinguished from one another by a "conceptual specialization" which is proper to our societies; if the rituals of purity and impurity remain today, despite their veil of hygiene and pathogenesis, "essentially religious acts" by means of which it is possible to "elaborate the symbolic structures, bring them into the full light of day" (1978); then examining how the practices which we have brought to light have come to signify what they do can help to explain the symbolic and mental functioning of the community which we are studying.

Let us concentrate first on the form which these practices take. A comparison with the obsessional rituals of isolation suggests itself for more than one reason. There is the compulsive character of the behaviour, its instability and the displacement of its application which simultaneously indicates and masks the fear of contact. This function of obscuring and protecting which is fulfilled by social and obsessional rituals in the face of the fears aroused by situations which are avoided has been amply demonstrated

---

[1] The characteristics listed here come from Mauss (1950) and Durkheim (1976).

by psychoanalysis (Fenichel, 1953, p. 327). The way in which the behaviour is described and justified reveals feelings of fear whose nature remains most often unformulated, if not unconscious. Two points make this comparison worthy of our attention. On the one hand, it is important because it brings to light, alongside fear, an emotional dimension of behaviour over which an interpretation in terms of social symbolism can stumble, as has happened to an author such as Douglas, and we shall insist on this point later. It is important, on the other hand, because it allows us to attach to this behaviour sexual connotations which are not without a concrete basis for the population.

The Risks of Sex

In fact a number of striking thematic slippages during the course of our interviews were sufficient to convince us that fears of a sexual nature were present in these domestic rituals, not to speak of the symbolism with which the bodily fluids were invested and the association made, via epilepsy, between saliva and sexuality. We find here the mechanism underlying the fear of infection which derives in part from animism. Various psychoanalytical texts surveyed by Fenichel (*ibid.*, pp. 197, 259) have shown the link between the fear of infection and unconscious sexual fears or desires (castration, impregnation, incorporation, destruction etc.), as well as the correspondence between ideas of contamination and the development of a defence against sexuality. In a general way, the idea of infection seems to serve to rationalize feelings linked with the "archaic taboo of touching" which, for Freud, could be associated with any drive irrespective of its instinctual nature (aggressive, tender or sexual) in that one of its aims is always to touch the object.

Even when this correspondence has been posited, however, it is still not possible to apply the schema of an unconscious link between the prohibition of contact and sexual prohibition without taking certain nuances into account. The unconscious character of the sexual significance attached to behaviour is not absolute and there is a clear awareness of the sexual risks brought by a masculine population of mental patients despite the supervision and selection guaranteed by the hospital. It is still necessary to ask whether this behaviour might, at the very least, conceal an unconscious fear and if so, where the danger stems from, and where the desire.

Can we content ourselves with thinking that sexuality returns to the private sphere because it is veiled in the public sphere? The enquiry showed that it is difficult to approach this question openly and spontaneously and that it is simultaneously emphasized and denied in social discourse. Let us remember that sexuality – like affectivity – is not present as an explicit element in the clinical picture of the patients and that we needed to follow a detour through the etiological description of the zones and periods of attack before discovering it to be associated with the most frightening element of the illness: nerves, blood, evil. Similarly, the attention paid by the officials of the Colony to the selection of patients testifies to an unabating concern with overcoming any sexual dangers. These are the very dangers to which the outside observer is referring when he attacks the negligence of the public authorities and reproaches the population with "lessening themselves" through sinking into close personal contact with the patients.

And it is precisely here that the discrepancy arises. The silence or the ambiguity of the declarations alerts us to an unease which cannot be explained by the behaviour of the lodgers alone. Of course, the constant vigilance of the population testifies to the insecurity to which they feel a prey, with their fear of aggression and seduction, particularly in the case of the young:

> I don't like to see the lodgers hovering round the school, in the middle of all the young girls. The children don't distrust them enough.

> After five years he began to get the urge to chase girls. He was at that sort of age . . . He used to visit the cafés. He certainly set the alarm bells ringing. We told him he shouldn't do it. And then he got more and more angry because he said we were stopping him seeing the girls. I was annoyed with him for chasing after the women.

> Those people, the loonies, they haven't got a clue. But you can teach them. It takes a year, maybe two, but after that they know. People say 'they're just idiots' but they're not as idiotic as all that. They watch the house but they don't live in the house. I don't like it. They don't come in here because with girls here, you can never tell. There have never been any problems but I'm always afraid they might get the idea into their heads. I'm always afraid.

And yet, it is stated quite clearly, there are ways, one of which is separation, to protect oneself against the danger posed by the lodgers. What remains is the problem of the attraction the women themselves might feel for certain of the patients. Is this not the real risk against which the population is defending itself? The internal peril, that of intermixture and its consequences?

> The presence of the lodgers has brought problems, and it still does. At the start there were women who had relationships with the lodgers and it's the same today. The children of the lodgers are more obvious now than they used to be.

> In my class there were five children of lodgers out of sixty. One was a delinquent and will always be a delinquent. He's a homosexual, he steals. The intelligence of the others is reduced.

The community was able to mobilize its defences in the face of this evident threat. In his anxiety to disprove the gossips of neighbouring regions and demonstrate to me the mental health of the population, one of our interviewees told me that for many years the community had benefited from the services of an "abortion specialist who knew when it was necessary to prevent a birth: that's why there aren't any idiots in the region." Another interviewee told us that a custom of "strongly encouraging miscarriages" had once existed in the area:

> They used to manipulate the mother's stomach. There was even a doctor who used to kill the subnormal and the mongols at birth.

This rule of custom went some way to sanctioning the transgressions which the women had a number of reasons to commit. As proof let us quote this spontaneous testimony which argues for the exclusion of the lodgers from the category of civilians:

> They aren't men. They've had their civil rights taken away which means they aren't men. Look, there are young people here who are the children of the idiots. Monsieur X is the grandson of one of the madmen. Perhaps he doesn't even know it himself. Me, I know it because I used to live in . . . and his grandmother had her son from an idiot. That man was quite all right. And his son as well, there's nothing wrong with him, and X, too, he's perfectly all right. But there's something wrong with his son. The child's as big as that. It isn't normal.

> Me – Are there a lot of children of lodgers?

> Well, there have been others. There was a little girl. The patient left and then she got married. And then there was Mademoiselle . . . who had one staying with her who was her lover for twenty years. She's left now, lives with him somewhere near Vichy. She's married. And then there was a little girl . . . the girl got married to a very healthy lodger. These things don't happen so much nowadays. I don't know the reason why. The young people have got other things to do than think about that. Life is freer – not freer exactly but . . . It's the same with the women, they can find something other than the lodgers. It was different before. The women didn't go out much. They stayed at home and they had more contact with the lodgers . . .

> Me – Were the lodgers better then?

> Generally speaking, the ones who did things like that, apart from the little one who went off with . . . he was really ill. The older ones weren't too bad at all. Some of them were better than the men from around here. The Parisians, they're better than the men from the country . . . There wasn't much to say to them. It was none of our business. There was another one who set up at the crossroads . . . as a seller of . . . that was a good twenty

years ago. We talked about it. It was a part of life like everything else. Nowadays you don't hear that sort of thing being talked about. Nowadays if a patient does something a bit more enterprising in one way or another, he's probably up to no good.

Me – Aren't the new patients liked, then?

Well no. It isn't the same any more. They aren't men. They aren't good. After all, in the past there were men who, although they were ill, were distinguished men, good men. At that time we had all sorts. There was the innocent one, and then there was the distinguished type who was . . . you couldn't really call him ill. Well you know, that type of person could give pleasure, of course. They were certainly better than the husbands. So it was bound to be like that. Whereas now, the ones who come are young lads, little head cases. There was one quite recently who was taken back. If it doesn't work out, they take them back and that's that.

Me – Are you frightened for the girls?

We're more afraid for the very young ones, for the little girls. We're more afraid for them. Generally it's the parents' fault. They let them get away with too much. The children who are like that are a bit neglected. Little boys, little girls. I wouldn't say they don't do things like that. That's the fault of the parents. The children are left to hang around. There are only a very few of them, always the same, always the same category, even as they get older, even as the generations change, it's always the same ones.

For this old foster parent who was prepared to confide in us, difference in class once justified and excused the inclinations of the women. This is no longer true today when the youth of the new arrivals seems to have made its impact, much to the displeasure of the mothers whose anxiety is reinforced by a nervous pathology:

Having a daughter is a worry for me. I'm afraid of it. It happens so quickly. The old ones are safe enough. But I'm always thinking of the little girl, wondering where she is.

Nowadays they've all inherited something. They're all much bolder. But you can get them to respect you all the same. They have to be a bit afraid of you, the men. The old ones are better than the young ones. All the ones who arrive now are young ones. They aren't the same at all. They aren't the same sort of lodgers we got ten, twelve years ago. You have to be wary because of the little girls. It's not the same sort of illness.

This is the reason behind a highly organized defence mechanism in which the vigilance of the population is complemented by the supervision exercised by the Colony. I had the opportunity to observe the plans and strategies employed during the course of a dance which took place regularly in the back room of a café. The dance is open to all, giving the lodgers the right of entry. The lodgers have their place to the right of the orchestra. Grouped together there, they face the dance floor which they dare not cross in order to sit in the square with its tables and chairs, reserved for the people of the region.

Two young men join the group of lodgers. They are well dressed, elegant and easy, with close-fitting trousers and brightly coloured shirts. Are they strangers to the region who, unaware of this spontaneous division of groups, have been mixed up with the patients, or are they lodgers who have joined the rest of their clan? It is impossible to resolve the doubt. One of them hurries to invite a girl to dance. The first time he is turned down by a young woman who is chatting with her friends, but then, spotting a woman who has been left alone after her friends have moved onto the dance floor, he bows in front of her. Alone, unprotected, the woman hesitates and then accepts. As soon as the dance is over she hurries back to her table. From that moment onwards she is constantly asked to dance by the men at her table or those at others and is thus unavailable for the young man who has now been identified as a lodger. This goes on for the entire evening and indeed none of the other women is left on her own. Without consultation, without a word, but without an error, the group has come to the defence of its women. The lodger continues to lie in wait and when a mother, of ordinary looks, enters with her daughters, he springs on them. One of the young girls accepts his invitation. He holds her tight and she appears to be happy with this state of affairs. The mother is plunged into disarray. She takes advantage of a lull in the music to call her daughter and drags her off with her sister. There is something tragic and pitiable in this humble, isolated woman pushing her children towards the exit without daring, as others would, to repel the advances of the lodger with a curt, superior refusal: "No, no, Monsieur, go back there, leave us, leave us." The crowd, which has suddenly fallen silent, parts to let them through. No one moves as the man follows them into the road. But the Colony has already been alerted and tomorrow the preparations will be made to return the cause of this disorder to Paris.

The Taboo of Marriage, The Taboo of Emotion

But this is not the sole social regulation of dealings with the lodgers. A further danger exists, and here the group is prepared to make no compromises: the overt, legal setting up of a life together. When a woman transgresses this law, she is excluded. For example, we met a woman who was ignored in her village for living together with a lodger. Her presence was still tolerated because she had not actually married him. But if the pair marries they have to leave the region. Since the founding of the Colony (Vié, 1941), none of those who have married a patient have remained in the area. The fault can be overlooked, its consequences hidden or prevented. The inadmissible thing about marriage is that it makes the lodger a fully fledged member of the community. The unthinkable hybrid is not so much the child of the patient but the loony who has become a civilian.

The fact that sexual *mélange* is tolerated provided that it is not given official sanction shows that the point of the prohibition of marriage is the maintenance of a social hierarchy. The main risk is not the deterioration of the population through the transmission of insanity to its children, but invasion by the insane themselves. It is the risk of an effective, legalized *lack of differentiation* whose consequences would be catastrophic for the image and the identity of the group. After all, the child of the lodger keeps his local roots, is only known to his family and his neighbours and can be hidden. The lodger who has become a civilian is the impure stranger raised to the rank of citizen who can, at any time, express his double social identity, remind the population that it is possible to be both civilian and insane. This is the fear which feeds the anxiety of the group. The feeling of collective integrity can only be maintained by securing the overt exclusion of the patient from any legitimate niche in the social structure, other than that authorized by his privative status. Here we rediscover the process at work in the home, where the integrity of the family can only be preserved by establishing distance and the approximation of the "as if".

We are now in a better position to understand the private and social meaning of the negative rituals to which the women submit themselves and which form the counterweight to their obsession with maintaining distance and limiting boldness, as well as to the equivalence they suppose between distance, respect and authority. In passing, we could underline the link between the prohibition of contact and position within a hierarchy. The nurses in a psychiatric hospital justified their refusal to eat at the same table as the patients with the risk of losing their authority (Lévy, 1969). This linkage was established by Dumont (1981) who used it as a tool to investigate social differentiation. It also plays an active role in protecting against the fusion which Canetti (1981), in his analysis of mass phenomena, identified as a tendency in social life, and which Park (1950), the inventor of the concept of social distance, saw as the historical consequence of the cohabitation between different ethnic and national groups. And in our enquiry we are dealing precisely with a question of fusion. As the representatives and protectors of a family and a social order of which they are the weak link, the women can only perpetuate this order by erecting hierarchical barriers and symbolic prohibitions which preserve them from contact with that by which the order is threatened.

At the level of signifying practices and their overdetermination, we observe the genesis of the symbolism of pollution in its concrete fundamentals – the temptations and the risks of transgressing the sexual prohibition and the social fears it arouses. Even if the probability of temptation is low, given the type of patient found in the placements, many of whom are far from appetizing, it nevertheless remains a potential for social sin which may arise in a placement where an attractive man is housed. We have already seen how many customs are rigidly perpetuated within the placements, sometimes without justification, in order to find a way of coming to terms with all types of lodger, especially the most troublesome or worrying ones, as well as with the possibility of a change of behaviour. When this state of affairs is generalized, all contact becomes dangerous, always synonymous with lack of protection against non-differentiation.

And when the individual fails to establish a separation, it is the community which reestablishes the partition by rejecting him. Alongside the territorial exclusion of women who join themselves to a patient in marriage and the contempt shown towards women who have been seduced, there are more subtle, veiled, even unconscious processes operating within the group itself, divisions which depend on the type of contact entered into with the patient. The ostracism practised with regard to the employees of the Colony is one example, but it is sufficient for the individual to be placed in circumstances which favour more intimate contact with the patients for this process of division to intervene. Thus, the fact of belonging to a family which kept a placement results in a differentiation which can be immediately observed at the level of the marriages contracted within the community.

The distribution of marriages revealed by our enquiry indicates, in contrast to Girard's study (1964) of the "choice of spouse",[2] peculiarities which are significant when viewed in the light of the social and psychological consequences of the presence of mental patients. It is possible to observe both how the placement zone forms a closed circle and how, within it, a local instability arises which differs from tendencies observed at a national level. Whilst the proportion of marriages between people born in the same district is clearly lower than the average, geographical homogamy is greatly overestimated within the placement boundary, even showing a considerable tendency towards homochtony (marriages between districts up to 30 km apart). By contrast, the number of households set up by couples coming from the same *département* or the same region is lower, with the number of those coming from further afield seeing an increase. The placement boundary therefore seems to create an endogamous cultural zone which is relatively unattractive to individuals coming from the region but which is open to outsiders.

These characteristics are largely explained by the way the choice of partner is affected by whether he or she comes from a family of foster parents. People who were brought up with lodgers show a considerable tendency towards

---

[2] Given the age of the population of foster parents, the data yielded by Girard's study was perfectly relevant as a comparative survey of the marriages contracted by and between the foster parents.

endogamy: they marry one another just as those who were not brought up in such families remain together.[3] What is more, the matrimonial fate of individuals born into a family of foster parents follows a distinct path. The "field of the eligible", to use a term coined by Maisonneuve (1968), is very narrow. If a man has spent his childhood with a lodger, he will not find a woman to marry in his district who has not also grown up with a patient.[4] If he is to marry in his district of origin or within the boundary of the placement zone, he has to find a woman who was brought up under the same conditions as he was, and to find a woman who does not come from a family of foster parents he will have to look further afield.[5] Although less rigorous at the district level, this tendency which governs marriage with persons external to the group of foster parents also applies to women.[6] The movements of the population within the perimeter of the placement zone are explained by a mode of selection which is a function of the proximity to the patients and which tends to reinforce and isolate the lineage of the foster parents.

The preference of the children of foster parents for each other may correspond to a similarity of social condition which is generally low, especially in the case of the farmers. However, it remains the case that this tendency testifies to an evident social branding which confirms the aura of stigma which the population associates with contact with the patients. And the fact that this branding is more clearly observed in the case of the men alerts us to the extension of the meaning of the prohibition of contact and its generalization. We have seen that the men are considered to be more familiar in their dealings with the patients as a result of being of the same sex, the reduced supervision exercised by the parents and, later, by the camaraderie which develops with the sharing of agricultural work. The men's difficulty in finding a woman, a common phenomenon in country areas, is exacerbated by an additional rejection of those who have lived in the proximity of patients on the part of women who do not come from a family of foster parents.

Such a phenomenon, which shows the unconscious effect of the everyday proximity of the insane, requires some comment. It confirms the representations of a pathogenic sensitivity in the young. It denotes a tendency towards the development of a "foster parents' culture" which social exclusion has caused to close in on itself and in which the development of defensive reactions, already visible in certain signs such as the strengthening of the habits of partition, is to be expected. Finally it indicates that approaching the patients in itself involves a risk of contamination and that the significance of the prohibitions of contact go beyond the simple sphere of sexuality.

This fact provides a proof which points us towards the moral dimension of the prohibition of contact. Anyone capable of entering into a close,

---

[3] x^2 significant at $P < 0.001$.
[4] x^2 significant at $P < 0.01$.
[5] x^2 significant at $P < 0.001$.
[6] x^2 significant at $P < 0.001$.

interpersonal relationship with a mental patient is simultaneously rejected, hidden by the group and accused of insanity. This I had to learn to my cost as, in the course of the enquiry, I approached homes in which the lodgers were integrated, thus uncovering the secret of a local deviance which informants at the hospital had attempted to hide. The latter showed their disapproval in verbal aggression and manifestations of "boldness" which made my relations with them so difficult that I had to suspend my contact with the hospital. But let me recount a final anecdote. Towards the end of the enquiry a motoring accident caused something of a commotion in the region. Two Swiss tourists had taken a picturesque country road joining two trunk roads. As they left a turning, the silhouettes of two men walking at the side of the road became visible. As the car drew level with them, one of the men raised his arm, tottered and then, all of a sudden, fell into the middle of the road. The rapidity of the movement made it impossible to brake in time. The man, a lodger, was hit by the car as he fell and died instantly.

I was to hear the news of this accident on the evening of the day it occurred during the course of one of my habitual stops at a café. There was quite a commotion and one of the customers recognized me and called across:

Have you heard what happened today?

No.

There were two Swiss women who were out of luck. They ran over a patient. It was because of the tobacco. He must have been feeling unwell. There are some who say it's like a suicide. I think he was unwell. Just before he'd said to the other bloke, 'I don't feel well.' The doctor came. At the Colony they come straightaway in cases like that. *Once the report has been made, there's nothing else to do. They went on their way, the poor women.*

A funeral oration for a phantom. The file is closed on a barely legally acknowledged existence, lacking any interiority which might excite compassion. Even in death, the victim is a burden to others, not because of the responsibility he involves them in, but because of the shock he produces. In this case violent death is not the drama which strikes at the individual, the grief which descends on a home or a community. It is the accident which puts an end to a crippled fate, the instrument of ill fortune for the civilians. The speaker knew all about it. It was he who drove the vehicle which served, depending on necessity, either as an ambulance or a hearse. He knew the significance of these deaths which caused him neither grief nor sorrow. His reaction is the image of that of a group to which grief is unseemly.

And yet, during the course of our interviews, there were a few individuals who had a tear in their eye as they evoked the memory of a dead lodger. What psychological mechanism, what pressures can explain this hardening of manners? Granted, the patients are not part of the community. Even their place in the cemetery recalls this. They are buried in a square, set aside, with crosses at uniform intervals such as are found in military cemeteries. Moreover, they are scarcely persons. They are more like pawns, interchangeable figures in the placements who are so often seen to disappear for reasons other than death. For example they are transferred to other psychiatric sectors or other hospitals. For the foster parents this has no other effect than to empty a bed which needs to be filled again. Abandoned by their own people, why should the lodgers expect those who house them to supply them with the family they lack? But are these the only reasons for this show of indifference? The accident in which the Swiss tourists were involved was to provide an opportunity to understand something of its collective background.

The placement in which the dead lodger had lived formed part of the sample to be interviewed. I tried to get in touch with the foster parent. I heard from a variety of sources that this person was very distressed by the death for which she felt partly responsible because she had not, as was her custom, accompanied the patient in her car. The hypothesis of suicide only added to her unease. When I announced my intention, some employees of the Colony started to laugh: "So you want to see . . . *she puts on the best show in the region.*" At the same time, they asked me to postpone my visit for reasons of discretion: "She's very upset", "She's most distressed." In fact, it seemed to the informants very incongruous that I could hear of an emotion being expressed with reference to a patient, even if this emotion was presented as a sham. Nevertheless, I was able to meet the husband of the foster parent while I was interviewing his sister. Did he come on purpose? Perhaps. In any case, he was clearly anxious to speak:

The sister – Well, how are things going? [*turning to me*]. One of their lodgers was run over.

The brother – They brought me one this evening. He hadn't heard from his family for two months. He used to talk about that every day. He had been to the Colony. In fact, he didn't quite get to the Colony. He came back. We don't know what happened . . . He fell under a car . . . He must have, according to the other lodger, he stretched out his arm when he saw the car and said, 'I can't walk all the way back to Ainay. I'm tired.' And then when he stretched out his arm . . . but it didn't touch his legs. He fell and it killed him, but it didn't touch his legs. He had a hole in his shoulder. But he didn't do it on purpose. He wanted to stop the car, but it was going too fast, 160, 150 or even 100. Madame, he was a patient, he smiled at them, he stretched out his arm, he smiled at them, to stop them maybe, but . . .

Me – It's painful for you?

The sister – Well, you know, they were used to him. The patient used to be lodged with his daughter.

The brother – He was clean. It was him who took in the tray for the others. And then he knew the different vegetables and the rooms and everything. He used to come into the house. There were days when he used to say: 'I can't go on, I'm tired, I'm tired, I'm no good for anything any more.' – 'Don't worry, Roger. Go and rest, go and lie down.' And then the next second he would be back again. 'Good, go and fetch some bread, Roger.' There were times when he said no. And other times, 'Yes, from Bessais if need be.' Clean, absolutely clean. He used to clean the rooms for all the others, everyone in the house, everyone at my daughter's.

The sister – [She] must have gone away because of Roger, X . . . it shook her up badly. My sister-in-law, he lived together with her all the time. You find a way to live together with them. You grow attached to them. It shook her up badly, that did! And then he was useful around the house. He cleaned the rooms. He took the others their food and all that. And when he felt in the mood, he used to cut back the privet hedges. It wasn't a long job. And like that things ran well. He was the sort of man . . . you have to know how to get on with him, that's the most important thing.

The brother – And that fool X . . . Yesterday I was at the door and the postman said to me, 'I didn't know he was one of your lodgers.' He knows all the lodgers. And that other idiot said: 'If only they were all shut up in a park. We don't need that on the roads.' Well, I said to him, 'You, maybe you'll be there tomorrow, lodger.'

Later, at the Colony, I was to hear the following comment:

They made a great song and dance about the whole thing. And it's been said that he was acting like a psychiatric case himself. *You can't talk of contagion, but they're worried about the illness.*

To enter into close contact with the insane is to be near to becoming it oneself. However, the affection shown towards the unfortunate victim was most certainly conditional. Is it therefore necessary, before one can show one's affection, to disguise it as utilitarianism? In order to be able to feel compassion for the insane, is it necessary to be familiar with the inner workings of the condition? In any case, that is how one is viewed. The "presumption of similarity" which Maisonneuve (1968) counts amongst the processes of projection which underlie interpersonal affinity is the basis of the social judgement passed on those who show any sympathy for a lodger. It is true that there is a saying which runs "birds of a feather flock together", but here we have moved beyond simple popular wisdom. Perhaps we are in the presence of one of those "sentimental aphorisms" in which Mauss (1950, p. 119) sees the originating – and magical – forms of the induction which reveals a social need, a "state of collective sensitivity". The similarity between the insane man and those who are fond of him would then derive from the social and socially affirmed contagion of abnormality. Infringing the common rule of distance debars the transgressor from membership of the group and removes him to the field of abnormality. The deviant then suffers the same fate as the impure stranger. He is relegated to the margins of the acknowledged social sphere. This ability to displace the partition within the heart of the group preserves its order. In other words, the language of the prohibition of emotion, the interdiction of contact, completes the implementation of the defence of the collective identity.

Sexual taboo, marriage taboo, emotional taboo, organic contagion and physical contagion join forces to multiply the protective partitions. The partition between the civilian and the loony at the collective level, duplicated at the level of the placement by the partition between family and lodger; the partition between the children of families of foster parents and the others; finally, the partition at the community level between those who uphold the local norm and the deviants. The sexual taboo serves to avert "the peril of pollution through the blood" (Morin, 1969), the marriage taboo defends against the integration of the insane into the social framework, the emotional taboo prevents the breakdown of the collective psychological defences. But if social opprobrium and discredit can master the transgression of the last of these taboos just as expulsion can master infringement of the marriage taboo, the same is not true of sexual transgression, which can remain secret and entails no other punishment than contempt if it becomes known. This penalty is incommensurate with the risk in which transgression involves the community.

It now becomes possible to understand the full significance of the negative domestic rituals. In observing them, the women are, in two senses, acting and thinking as members of the group. They are not just bearing in mind the collective damage which could result from a private failing. Douglas observes that the belief in sexual pollution emerges, amongst other things, when no concrete punishment exists for transgression, when societies are based on a paradox and a profound contradiction. In the face of the contradictions implied by the institution of the Colony, the compulsive concern with hygiene shown by the foster parents takes on a symbolic value as a reminder. It reminds the women of the importance of preserving the social body, incarnated in the sacred body of the family. In the face of the lodgers' desire for equality, their demands for integration in which the threat of fusion lurks, the recourse to the idea of organic pollution makes it possible to legitimize the arbitrary nature of segregation. The appeal to the biological gives discrimination a natural basis. By cordoning off the supreme good, the home and the children, the practices of separation serve to maintain and express the value of the group identity. If one equates, like Dumont (1981), the process of making sacred with the assumption of value, these practices are not denuded of religious symbolism.

However, one question remains to be answered. These rituals, which do not consist solely of the sexual, also do not consist – so it seems to us – solely of the symbolic. The fear which motivates them in the minds of people is based on a very concrete danger: the transmission of the illness through bodily secretions. Can this belief be thought of as the symbolic apparatus whose conditions of implementation have been established by a number of different authors? We know that the imputation of magic powers and properties arises in the presence of signs or attributes such as abnormality, ambiguity of biological or social status, marginality, an abnormal or unwarranted social position. Mauss even speaks of a topographical or territorial definition of magic powers and draws a picture of the potential magician which closely resembles that drawn of the nervous type by the population. Seeing in the impure and in dirtiness something which is misplaced and which must be excluded if the order is to be perpetuated, Douglas (1978) gives pollution the "austere function" of reinforcing existing social structures. All these elements are related to the situation we are studying. But to accept a purely symbolic interpretation of the practices and beliefs we have discovered would be to ignore, on the one hand, the context of the representations which form the everyday knowledge which guides action towards the patients, and, on the other hand, the social energy which underlies the emergence and functioning of these representations.

This type of symbolic interpretation is exemplified by Douglas who, in equating ritual pollution and secular pollution, supposes that "our ideas of dirtiness are themselves the expression of symbolic systems and that behaviour *vis-à-vis* pollution only varies, from one end of the planet to other, in its details" (*ibid.*). Her theory is that "certain pollutions serve as an analogy for the expression of a general idea of social order", and function "as the symbolic expression of the relations between different elements in society, like the reflection of a hierarchical or symmetrical organization which is valid for the whole of the social system". The biological content of these symbolic reduplications is thought to come from the fact that "the human body furnishes a basic scheme for all symbolisms". In her explanation of pollution, each social group would draw from the symbolism of the body those symbols which are best able to express the dangers which oppress it. To whatever part of the body it refers, the power of pollution would then become "inherent in the structure of ideas, a power which allows the structure to protect itself".

Representations and Practices

This intellectualist conception which postulates a direct passage from the social structure to the structure of ideas does not take account of the psychological and social dynamic which is set in motion in modern societies by beliefs and rituals relating to pollution. Thus it does away with the social function of the ritual which is to provide support for the values of the group and to help social agents in the accomplishment of their role (Radcliffe-Brown, 1939). Eliminated, too, are the social sentiments which, lying at the base of "practical ideas" and the logic of magic, testify, for Mauss, to a "social state of unease and sensitivity", as well as to a "magical solidarity" of groups, signs of which are still alive in our societies (1950, pp. 130–131) as Favret-Saada (1977) has illustrated with regard to sorcery in the Bocage.

It is true that to pay attention to the emotional sources of social or mental life is not always considered to be scientifically legitimate. Thus Lévi-Strauss, in his introduction to the work of Mauss, sees the latter's recourse to affectivity as a historical weakness which threatens to seduce the researcher, or at least the ethnographer, with an "idle refuge", reducing "social reality to the conception that man – savage man, even – has of it" and resulting in a "verbose phenomenology" (1987). Yet Lévi-Strauss himself does not eliminate the role of "psychosocial tensions" in the institution of a cultural order, as we have seen. And for social psychology, armed with the results of the study of cognitive phenomena, the consideration of affectivity and its roots in social dynamics is essential if we are to understand the functions involved when the members of a community arrive at a construction of their reality. It is also essential if we are to come to an authentic theory of social knowledge. This approach should also help us to relate the study of rituals to a "social theory of knowledge", as Durkheim predicted, by viewing these rituals within the overall system of representations and practices in which they are inscribed. This is not achieved by the model which explains the beliefs associated with pollution by means of the formal and linear effect of the symbolic duplication of the structural aspects of society.

Our observations have brought to light: the high level of social and psychological investment in the practices of separation; their crucial value to the group; the role they are given in the affirmation and maintenance of a discriminatory hierarchy, in individual homes as in the social fabric; their association with representations of insanity and the insane, whose face, hidden but repeatedly evoked in speech, they reveal. It follows that, in our particular case, we must concentrate on the relationship which exists between the representations of mental illness, the symbolic practices and the psychosocial dynamic within which both the former and the latter are realized.

This is all the more important because a crucial problem concerning the relationship which exists between practice and representation is raised by the tacit knowledge which we have discovered below the surface of the behaviour which expresses the taboo of contact. This taboo has been primarily associated with modes of thought both by Durkheim and by Freud, although with differing implications. For the first it is the exclusion of ideas, the "psychic incompatibility" which results in a dissociation of acts: "For ideas not to coexist, it is necessary that things are not in contact, that no manner of relationship exists" (1976). For the second (1936), it is because touching is prohibited that ideas are separate. The intellectual mechanism of isolation, which can take on a normal form in logical reasoning or classification, or a pathological form in the case of obsessive thought, has its origin in the prohibition of contact which in turn has its roots in human drives. We have here a difference of perspective which reiterates what we have just said about the symbolic interpretation of negative rituals. On the one hand, the hypostasis of society in the sacred, with the respect and mental inhibition it entails, lies at the source of the practice. Acts are at the service of ideas whose origin is to be found in a society conceived of as a unique, homogeneous whole. On the other hand, the regulation of the drives is transformed into acts which reecho in the mind. The drives imply energy and a link with something which is not the self. This perspective seems to be more appropriate to the approach to the conflicts and interdictions which are associated with a relationship between groups than the perspective employed within the Durkheimian tradition which treats the social group as closed on itself, even in cases where it needs to manage functional failures by symbolic means.

When we turn to the relationship between thought and social practices, whether these are apprehended at the individual or the collective level, we cannot avoid answering the question posed by the energies which are released in the relationship to the other. This requirement is of special concern in the case of the relationship with insanity which, as we have seen, aims at the avoidance of fusion with the other and mobilizes phenomena of a highly emotive nature which are associated with the safeguarding of identity. This dynamic of relations governs both practices and representations. The question then becomes one of understanding how the practices come to function as a symbolic apparatus. It is necessary for us to examine whether the representations contain elements in which the symbolic value of the domestic rituals is founded. Further, we must explain why these should be more expressive than speech relating to the vision of insanity, when we take account of the context within which both the one and the other have developed. To understand the social logic at work in this symbolic elaboration, we have to link it not only to the strategies overtly employed by the community, but also to the representations of mental illness which guide these strategies. It is in these representations that the community expresses the specific nature of its real-life experience of its situation.

Called on to welcome into its homes those whom society normally hides behind the walls of an asylum, the population of Ainay-le-Château and its environs have invented a social institution which permits it to integrate an exogenous group without incorporating it. This it does in its own best interests and its own defence. The interests of the population give the institution its strength in the face of the system of the Colony to which it dictates its own law. This defence was to have other consequences for the population's psychological development and fuse it into a community closed in on itself.

A *Community on the Defensive*

The explanation of a social protection as careful and well-armed as the one we have discovered can only lead to a collectively shared defensive psychological structure. The psychological profiles tend towards a uniformity manifested by socially regulated modes of behaviour. All the alloplastic measures which have an educational aim – designed to contain the lodgers within their own ranks and reduce the potential for aberrance, the "you never can tells" of sex, violence or malice – are matched by autoplastic measures of self-control and obedience to everyday codes of conduct or morality. Each individual learns from the group a way of acting, of behaving, of feeling. This, of course, has an effect on the individual psyche. Everyone thinks and acts as a representative and protector of the group, a state which also modifies their image of themselves and their internal dynamic. The members of the social body start to function in unison, in a sort of living consensus.

In general, in the study of the processes which grow from the contact of different social groups there is a tendency to subordinate the individual to the group by showing how their social membership, or their desire to demonstrate this, influences their behaviour and their cognitive mechanisms. It seems to us that our results place the emphasis elsewhere. Certainly the members of the community act, think and feel as a group and fall under its influence, but this they do primarily for the group and in its name. Everyone is in the same boat, shares the same fate, works together to ensure common survival and a minimum of collective harmony. This collective militancy, this active identification, is also mobilized by the desire to preserve the environment in which their own identity is rooted.

If this is indeed the case, as we believe we have demonstrated, we no longer need to proceed from the idea of a collective consciousness or the apparatus of a group psyche to understand how a community develops psychological mechanisms – defensive or other. In contrast, it is essential for us to take account of social communication and the representations it mediates.

But let us concentrate on the hypothesis of defensive functioning. Signs of it abound. The rigour of customs and behaviour reserved for the lodgers, invested with the authority of tradition, applied systematically without taking account of individual particularities except in so far as these may indicate the best methods of manipulation. A cloak of secrecy covering the everyday truth of life with the patients and, above all, everything which degrades the respectability of the group image; sensitivity to the disapproval and judgement of an external observer with whom one identifies in the denigration of deviants. Emotional taboo and a temporal displacement in the expression of emotions (anger, fear . . .). And the other obvious trait: the defence against guilt.

We have already seen how, in the invocation of the force of custom, the need to find a justification shines through when the foster parents are speaking of the way they treat their patients. It is not with impunity that individuals are treated as "flesh and bones", "not completely as if they were animals"; it is not with impunity that they can be subjected to the exploitative and the arbitrary. The support of the group is a defence against guilt. But it is not enough. It is here no doubt that we can find the basis for what is said about the lodgers and about the necessity of behaving as one does. And it is from this fact that certain characteristics of the representations, to which we shall return, arise. Guilt also shows through in the accusations of bad treatment inflicted on the lodgers. The foster parents experience a regular need to speak of it. Even if the occurrence belongs to other times or other places, it is an abomination which continues to haunt them. Finally, how can we avoid seeing in the insistent emphasis of the material advantages of the Colony system, alongside the overcompensation for the unease caused by close contact with insanity, the emergence of a type of reaction which sometimes resembles cynicism? The anomic feelings which accompany the population's display of its standing and economic pride give us proof of this. This movement from bad conscience to false conscience does not fail to leave its mark on the representations.

Going further, we have observed the presence of a defensive conflict underlying a mentality which is related to the "obsidian mentality" depicted by Delumeau (1978) in connection with the fears of the West. This conflict is a constant which pervades every aspect of community life at whatever level one cares to look in the course of a detailed inspection of all its past and present moments, all its public and private places. It is the contradiction between self-interest and fear. Both dictate conduct, both impose rules and demands on the function of the Colony system. They do this by establishing their domination over social agents in the course of a long process of invention in which the community has mobilized all its knowledge and all its expertise in its fight to survive.

To survive, that is what is at stake. To survive economically; to survive within the unity of a group threatened from within and reproached from without. To survive as if nothing special had happened: to show the placid and respectable face of normality whilst bearing the signs and marks of aberrance; not to see insanity and to fear it at the same time. Enslaved by its economic needs, the community has to live with its fear in order to survive. But whereas objective evidence of the need and its consequences are easy to find, the fear, polymorphous and secret, is less accessible in all its dimensions. The fear of feeling that the group identity is under threat is easy to discern, but the other fear, that of the illness, that which insinuates itself from all corners, in certain looks, in certain gestures, in the erection of barriers, the fear which surrounds the children, the fear which even creates a local pathology, "the panic attack", the fear which causes the allergies, this fear could only be understood through the intermediate study of the representations. And the representations remain to spell out the significance of all the practical measures of defence, just as their construction serves to bring about the coexistence of self-interest and fear, to surmount the conflict of accepting, in order to survive, what one would like to remove.

What do these representations tell us? To provide a satisfactory answer to this question it is necessary to find out where they come from and how and why they appear and are organized as we have found them.

The Manufacture of a Representation

In distancing itself from scientific knowledge and confronting it with a purely practical, effective mode of knowledge, the community we are studying places us in a position to observe how representations are produced and function within a delimited mental and social space. This established and acknowledged self-separation from all scientific knowledge is conducive to the construction of an original mode of thought aimed at mastering the data provided by objective experience and by intimate first-hand experience of real-life situations. At the same time, it is in some way separate from and contradictory to present-day knowledge. This accounts for the fact that certain aspects of the representations are explicitly mediated by speech and others are hidden in practice.

The situation of our community, fused together in its isolation, presents us with a first particularity: the importance assumed by social communication for the management of life with the patients as well as for the equilibrium of the members of the collective group. At various points in this study we have seen how necessary contact between foster parents is in helping them to overcome fears and difficulties, to find solutions to the problem of adaptation, to instigate rules and norms. Equally, we have seen the extent to which the social interchange which grows up around the lodgers is felt to be a sign of their integration into the communal universe, the extent to which opportunities to meet are valued as a vital group activity. All this combines to create a rare case of circulation in, and cohesion of, social discourse. So much so that during the course of our enquiry we often had the feeling that we were listening to a single person speaking through the various mouths of our interviewees, each picking up and continuing a single dialogue in which the questions raised by a remark made in one place found an answer in a statement made in another. It was as if the investigation were progressing within a discursive, homogeneous material with a unifying effect on the representations which was to surprise us.

In our interviews of individuals who differed in the way they integrated their lodgers into or excluded them from the life of the family, we had expected to encounter different representations. But everywhere we found the same model of insanity, organized around the opposition between the brain and the nerves. This model was always developed in the same way to describe the state of the mental patient and specify his organic, mental and social status, to explain the form assumed by the disturbances and the processes associated with their endogenous or exogenous origin. Is this to say that representations are independent of conduct? And yet, the methods of control used to "educate", "adapt" the lodgers are closely bound to the image formed of the insane man, the representations in this case serving as a direct guide for action. And yet, the reluctance shown by the Colony to let us approach the placements in which the lodgers live on an equal footing with the foster parents suggests that a radical difference exists between those who deviate from the norm of distance and the others. We have witnessed this difference in the capacity for attachment to the lodger. No relationship therefore between representation and affect? And yet, even those who refused to implement a partition lent their support, if only timidly, to the idea of a divergence of conception and ethic. No relationship between representation and value?

The answer is simple and is fully present within one of the representations, that which distinguishes between an attack of the brain and an attack of the nerves. What changes with proximity is the choice of partner. Privilege is a reserved status. The patient with whom one shares one's home and one's table belongs to a single category, the "brain" patient, not the patient who has been put there "because of the nerves". The innocent patient who is treated as if he were a child of the family, the worker whose activity demonstrates a minimum of cerebral control, the patient whose mental functioning has been disoriented by life's misfortunes, these are the only types of figure with whom the foster parents permit themselves a proximity of contact. This proximity can correspond to a psychological need or a moral attitude in the foster parents; it can derive simply from the desire to rationalize life in the placement or come from the chance discovery of a sympathetic case. However, it is always selective, excluding the patients who are dominated by a nervous affliction with its many attendant defects: degeneracy, agitation, indocility, lack of control, wickedness. Close ties are only established with the harmless.

The model which structures all the fields of representation concerning insanity thus introduces a radical division into the domain of the real. This explains how behaviour as different as partition and proximity can coexist even when the same representations are shared. The popular theory defines classes of patient about whom all are agreed. Those who for personal reasons are inclined to enter into closer contact choose the "good" lodger from one, and only one, of the classes without in any way abandoning commonly held conceptions. Their precautions and defences are less generalized than those of the other foster parents, that is all. And in a certain sense they provide an even more striking confirmation of the principle of division which guides the perception of the lodgers. This perception implies a judgement of the patients which always obeys the same laws, is always based on the same premises and always applies the same type of knowledge.

Here we touch on another particularity of the production of representations which derives from communication, the mode of elaborating knowledge developed by the milieu of the foster parents. In its instrumental character, aimed at evaluating the patient, finding out whether one is "well served", whether he is "serviceable", discovering ways of influencing him, this knowledge is based on and oriented towards practice, a practice whose rules and formulae are transmitted from one foster parent to another, from one generation to the next. It is thus a knowledge constructed of diverse elements and related to the "bits and pieces" (*bricolage*) to which Lévi-Strauss refers in connection with the thinking of the savage. Deprived of the support of a codified system of interpretation and confronted by the unknown in the form of the patients and their afflictions, the community seeks an answer in the informational resources, in the categories and criteria of judgement which are provided by collectively established modes of action, by modes of speech spread by communication, by modes of thought drawn from the cultural heritage. The contents of the representation which are forged in this way to provide an idea of what the mentally ill man is in his various degrees of gravity, what his illness is in its diversity of symptoms and origins, form kaleidoscopic tableaux consisting of a variety of constituents. It is necessary to identify these elements and the relations between them as they appear in speech, and to isolate the fields of representation which appear as *concretions* of their components.

The Constituents of the Representation

There is a first group of constituents which has a direct relationship with practice. This is the first-hand information which provides direct experience of contact with the patients. These constituents are inferred from everyday observation and are related to the symptomatic traits of a pathology. They appear in the enumerations whose partial, precise and variable character has already been emphasized. These traits are not organized as homogeneous case descriptions, do not lend themselves to real generalization but to a purely inductive type of knowledge. In contrast, certain recurrences in the designation of traits testify to a process of selection which implies that there are criteria for the observation of the pathological which come from other spheres of collective experience and from implicit schemes which are passed on by communication.

Thus, underlying the designation of the signs of the illness, we find a second set of constituents which refer to the values of the group and its lifestyle. Already the position of the pathological, alongside character, in the natural order, standing in contrast to the cultural order expressed by mentality and education, shows the intervention of the normative in the evaluation of morbid disease. A confirmation of this is provided by the use of codes of practical morality to evaluate, for example, the patient's sociability or his ability to organize his work. Or again, in connection with the genesis of the illness, by the questioning of bourgeois, urban ways of life, of modern liberal education, of the dissolution of families, of training etc. The group uses and projects its values in the construction of a representation of the illness as deviance or the product of deviance. At the same time as it expresses itself in this representation, it defines one of the major criteria in the differentiation between the we and the not-we: moral identity, the sharing of the same codes of life and the observance of these codes. So much so that if no other sign of insanity is present, it is seen in deviation from local norms or, by generalization, in deviation from the norms of the group to which the patient belongs.

Another type of constituent with its roots in local culture is drawn from the background of traditional knowledge. We have met such constituents in a variety of forms. In the residual significance of certain words of folklore which point to a biological knowledge either directly (cut-off blood) or metaphorically (*ch'tit*). In the reference to certain organic processes noted during the course of everyday work (glanders, substances which go off like milk). In certain psychological conceptions such as the formulation of feelings of affection in terms of flattery, the conception of reciprocity in interpersonal relations. In the games of arousal entered into with animals or the village idiot who are teased to the limit of their endurance and in the danger of their response. In the customs reserved for the "traveller" and the "tramp". . . . All these elements of folklore constitute a reservoir to which the population can turn to satisfy its need for explanations or interpretations when these are not imposed as *a priori* categories of classification, denomination or action.

The typical and mythical figures of the social world around whom anxieties and prejudices have crystallized belong to this same cultural background. There is the sorcerer who is never named but whose frightening look of cunning and malice is evoked. There is the man from the East, the Russian or Pole who is the embodiment of fearful, far-away lands. There is the military man and his warlike aggressions . . . Has it been noticed that the Jew is not mentioned here? This theatre of the imagination is peopled only by emblematic figures of violence and evil, an echo of the deep dichotomy between innocence and wickedness, the original classification of the world of insanity.

The Christian origin of this classification shows the influence of religious discourse, and we should not exclude the hypothesis that beliefs of a magical type are supported by the modes of thought which this discourse perpetuates. In the same way, the papal encyclical *Mysterium Fidei* reaffirmed the realism of the "transubstantiation" (the conversion of bread into Christ's body and wine into Christ's blood) as a mystery of faith and communal fidelity to a language which assures that it remains so despite the passage of time (Marlé, 1965). The same process is suggested by the foster parent who identified the dribbling of an epileptic whom she saw having a fit in church with the bubbles of grease on the top of a stew: "To me it looked like the patient, the one who started to foam in church." The legend of the local saint, Saint Menoux, who transformed bread into blood, points in the same direction.

The power attributed to blood does not fail to evoke the belief maintained by the royalty of the healing power conferred on the "thaumaturgic kings" whose history and dynamic has been reconstructed by Marc Bloch (1983). From the Capetians onwards, the fact that the kings were anointed with holy oil at the moment of their coronation conferred upon them the power of transmitting, through the contact of their hands, an invisible power to the bodies of the sick and miraculous properties to the water which they touched. At the start of the 19th-century Charles X continued to promote this institution which Bloch emphasizes was "borne along by the deeper currents of the collective consciousness". "[T]he expression of social forces of an obscure and profound nature", it became an instrument by which royalty assured its strength, establishing the link between the power of a group and the quality of its blood. Bloch has also shown that the official ritual of touching scrofula became "a medical commonplace", "the vitality and even the expansion of these primitive practices". We have found an echo of this in Renan, and what is said about the blood of the mental patients is one of its applications. This hierarchical classification of the power of the blood is underlined by a schema which has in all ages structured the language of racism, the explanation of the smell of the stranger by the impurity of his blood. Since early times this has been a particularly explicit operation in the case of the Jews (the *faetor judaïcus*) and, since the Middle Ages, in the case of the Hypocrites who were accused of sorcery (Delacampagne, 1983). This schema can no doubt be identified in the inferences which base the measures of protective hygiene on the smell of the patients, even if these inferences might have been encouraged by certain medical conceptions.

And how can we fail to count amongst the cultural constituents of representations the traces left in the collective memory by conversations with the medical staff of the Colony? In fact, striking similarities exist between the statements made by our interviewees and those which surface in the reports of the directors, themselves reflections of conceptions belonging to their own or earlier times. Information circulates despite the prohibitions. By way of proof let us cite some examples taken from reports on the Colony: the allusion to the belief that insanity can be transmitted through water; the idea that the "centres of affliction" determine the breakdown of organic functioning or the violence of the nerves; the evocation of the drifting which is observed in the insane; the opposition of the violence of degeneracy and the harmless character of weak brains which have to be protected from shocks and strain; the pathogenic role attributed to urban life, its stress and its sophistication; the regenerative value of rural life for the mental faculties and moral qualities etc. More recently this similarity has been seen in the change in the way the patients are "considered", a change attributed to the influence of certain medicines. And there are also the few foster parents who speak of the education which has allowed them to understand the reason for their lodgers' behaviour. Such examples are not frequent of course, but they do testify to the effective circulation of ideas between the medical environment and that of the foster parents. It is true that the development of "counter-knowledge" as a response to the "errors" of judgement of the doctors (for example, believing the words of patients judged to be liars) indicates that the milieu of the foster parents only retains that which accords with its expectations and preconceptions. However, this fact does not prevent medical knowledge from contributing material or categories to the representations and thus strengthening those which have persisted in time or those which form part of the culture of our society.

In this respect, although we have not found any formal trace of it in the speech of the population or the writings of the hospital doctors, we must also take into account certain of the medical conceptions which were widespread at the time the Colony was founded. An example of this is the osphresiology which links the odours of the body to the elimination of secretions exhaled through the emunctories and which associates the strength of the smell with the composition of the secretions, themselves coming from the seminal fluid and the animality of the individual (Corbin, 1982). The same would apply to the explanation of syphilis which the "syphilographers" of the beginning of the century said could be transmitted through the bodily fluids with the consequence that objects placed in water represented a danger of contamination for the "innocent" (Corbin, 1977). Even if we suppose that the spread of medical knowledge has given a "scientific" basis to the fears of the population and may thus have reinforced these fears, this still does not suffice to explain their orchestration within a magical symbolism or their resurgence on the introduction of chemical therapies. To explain this we must penetrate the internal logic of the construction of the system of representations.

With the exception of data provided by direct observation of the patient, these different constituents imply either second-hand knowledge or knowledge transferred from other areas of activity, borrowed from the ethos of the group, from popular wisdom or from the surrounding culture. Knowledge gained from contact with the patients, descriptive and partial, needs to be structured within external frameworks if it is to acquire meaning. It is constituents of the second type which serve to construct these frameworks by providing observational analogies, criteria of classification or categories of designation, codes of interpretation and explanatory schemes. Circulating in the words, the linguistic expressions, the contents of social discourse, embodied in gestures, these constituents exist as the storehouses of the collective memory which is nothing other than the memory of the transmitted words and the moulded body, an influence which pervades everything. These constituents form a sort of reservoir of referents used to pass a verdict on the patients and their state and to establish a position which can be adopted towards them. Everyone invokes them in accordance with the dictates of the situations which have to be confronted, including that of the interview which makes it necessary to formulate things which have been so frequently excluded from thought.

This depository in which the constituents of the fields of representation of patient as an object and illness as an object are anchored does not present itself in what is often considered to be the latent form of representations, that is to say as a structure. Rather, it seemed to us to take on the form of a fluid, fuzzy, and not intangible, reservoir whose actualizations vary with context and use. One and the same referent can be used for different thought operations: for example, the norms and values of the group make it possible to decide on the value of a behavioural trait as a symptom (respect of the division of tasks between two working lodgers is interpreted as a pathological sign with regard to the local norm of cooperation and reciprocity), to form a moral judgement of an individual (as the notion of boldness testifies) or to locate the origin of the illness (way of life, urban, bourgeois . . .). One and the same thought operation can also mobilize different referents, for example forecasting the lodger's adaptability involves a whole range of observations, both moral and psychological (with the notions of character, mentality, education), organic (with the evaluation of cerebral control), etiological (with the attribution of the pathological signs to a historical or organic source), imaginary (with the evocation of typical figures in the human landscape) etc.

There is nothing surprising in the syncretic character of this mode of thought when one thinks of the type of knowledge it serves to create. It is a purely practical knowledge which has the aim of "managing to live with" the patients and which is sometimes driven by the urgency of unforeseen events to find a possibility for mutual accommodation. This supposes a cognitive activity which, unable to apply a predefined interpretative model, arms itself with all the materials hidden in the collective heritage of knowledge, values and images which have the aim of managing the day-to-day relationship with the environment. All this cognitive activity does is to displace onto a new object the procedures generally employed in the maintenance of everyday knowledge, for which all the elements of the cultural stock are often equivalent and interchangeable.

This process finds support in the fact that the thought operations required to elaborate a knowledge of an ill individual, to imagine the population of lodgers or to imagine an abstract type of mental patient are restricted. They include the designation of a case, the description and interpretation of behaviour, the identification of a symptom and evaluation of its gravity, the detection and decoding of a pathological sign, the evaluation of the state of the patient, his future within the placement and in life in general. When addressed to specific cases situated within specific circumstances, local reasoning operates in accordance with the same logic: it *identifies* (by designation, observation) *a fact* (case, behaviour, symptom, sign, illness), *describes* it and *understands* it (interprets and diagnoses it), finally *explains* and *evaluates* it. These operations are interdependent and it is rare for the chain of reasoning which leads to knowledge not to be completely worked through. From which derives the necessary appeal to the totality of the available local resources whose individual elements are frequently interchangeable. This also explains the way in which representations elaborated in this way gain their character of concretion. This notion of concretion appears to us to be doubly relevant to a designation of all representational formation, irrespective of whether the representation applies to an isolated object or an entire field of real-life experience. This is not simply a question of borrowing a metaphor from the geographical or even the medical domain with the object of unifying elements within a single body with its own particular consistency. Psychology also provides us with a usage of the term which is dominated by the idea of a totality, produced by the fusion of the elements (images, sensations, ideas, habits) belonging to the present and the past of subjective experience or borrowed from a variety of historical origins. This usage corresponds to the particularities we have just described.

Moreover, these mental productions exhibit characteristics which frequently come to light in the construction of representations. Their anchoring in a shared practical and cultural background invests the representations with specific contents and shades of meaning which translate something of the cultural identity and the mentality of the group. Thus the organic processes which contribute to an analogy-based conception of the illness as a deterioration which makes the brain, the nerves, the muscles, the organs "turn bad" borrows from modes of activity to be found in the rural environment. In the same way the conceptions expressed with regard to the work and the laziness of the patients are, in the main, the expression of the interests and values of the group.

It is possible to observe other marks of the processes specific to representations. By way of example, let us cite a fact which illustrates a characteristic moment of objectification, namely selective construction: not all the elements which belong to the lay psychology of our population are to be found in the clinical picture of the patient. Affectivity, willpower, even sexuality are missing even though these find an application in other fields such as the etiology of the illness or the methods used to control the lodger, for example. The description of the social partner obscures, along with affectivity and sexuality, those traits whose acknowledgement in everyday interaction is forbidden by the prohibitions and fears of the group. In the case of the will, the image records the absence of a dimension, and the reason for this can be found in the implicit theory of insanity – another aspect of objectification: naturalization. The attribution of dangerous nervousness to degeneracy of the blood leads the population to consider Africans less dangerous than those from the Maghreb because the skin of the former is black and their blood thus purer than that of the second, whose skin colour gives rise to the idea of a mixing of blood. As far as our community is concerned, local beliefs and conceptions provide the representational processes with original material for the production of representations specific to the group whilst allowing a certain latitude for individual variability in the articulation of the cultural elements of practical experience.

A Ternary Operator

What is more, these amalgams and constructions are not the products of disorder. We can identify here constants and regularities which are not implied solely by the modes of reasoning used to respond to practical needs or to integrate signs provided by specific situations. In the different fields of representation we have identified schemes of thought which are uniformly applied in the management of both inductive and deductive reasonings. Thus a classification of the states of the illness is described by deducing the manifestations assigned to the spheres of organic, social and moral life from a tripartite scheme of biological functioning (brain – body – nerves). In this way the illness is explained by the use of an etiological model which sees the mode of attack (the brain or the nerves) and the circumstances of the attack (birth or accident) as important factors. A figurative core is again found to underlie these schemes, a representative node which can be identified in every field. It is on this node that the opposition between the brain and the nerves within the organism is focused in the attempt to account for the whole extent of the human reality which has to be understood.

The existence of this core is the third particularity which characterizes the thinking of our community. In fact its existence as such is not surprising and simply confirms the central moment of the process of objectification, a structuring schematization. The opposition of brain and nerves appears as a significant, organizational structure. But this says little about the particularity demonstrated by the constitution and functioning of this structure when we concentrate on the nature of its terms, its ternary construction, on the fact that it operates in every field of representation and that it can be directly observed in the production of speech.

It is a general tendency in the field of the study of representations for the works which reveal a schema of this type and describe its structuring role to refer to a specific field of the representation of an object or a situation. In the same way, recourse to the repetition of a binary structure in each of the diverse sectors of reality covered by the representation is really the implementation of an equivalence between the different terms existing in each sector. Moreover, some critics consider that such modules are reconstructions produced *a posteriori* by researchers which risk unduly immobilizing the flow of ideas and speech. Finally, structural elements are often abstract notions or qualities which are held to be concrete entities.

Now, what we have found in our enquiry differs in all counts from what is described above. In the first place, the terms of the "brain", "nerves" node are concrete terms, images of organs. In this they are homogeneous with the figurative productions which characterize representative thought, intermediaries between percept and concept, linking figure with sense. However, one nuance exists. We are not dealing with reified abstractions but with concrete objects which develop into conceptual operators and help to fill in gaps in knowledge. In fact, the polyvalence of their descriptive, topological and explanatory uses confers on them a complex cognitive status. They function simultaneously as percepts, concepts, schemes and even as personified entities. We have heard descriptions of their appearance as phenomena: "The nerves which have gone bad", "the empty brain", "plugged up", "withered", "halted"; of their properties: the brain is "in command", the nerves "gain the upper hand": they are localized, like the disturbance they cause, in different parts of the body; both cause and effect, they are the zone of operation of processes from which they suffer or which they engender; they subsume behaviour, gestures, expressive forms into a general category: "twitching, it's the nerves", "lapses of memory, that's the brain". When we turn to the process of personification we see that this is most marked in the case of the nerves: "it has to be fed", "it needs to wear itself out". What is more, they possess the implex character which Burloud attributes to certain concepts formed by the relationship between highly diversified but specific images. In effect what they produce, what they manifest, also comes from the domain of the concrete and the practical: the body, its expressions, its realizations.

This takes us to the second specific characteristic of the structure, namely its ternary nature. Brain and nerves cannot be dissociated from "people of flesh and bones". Their opposition only acquires effectiveness, meaning and value within the totality given by the unity of body and mind. It is this totality which allows two terms to be repeated, applied with no variation of image or name irrespective of the field of representation concerned. The ternary node of "brain – nerves – people of flesh and bones" functions as an elementary structure of the image of man and his avatars. And this structure is made operative by the qualitative aspect of its terms, their relative position within the system which confers on them properties, qualities and connotations of lasting value, a semantic charge which varies with the universe which man, whether sane or ill, is conceived to inhabit according to the perspective from which he is considered.

There is nothing of an *a posteriori* reconstitution in this core. Its terms have nothing of the generic designation of elements which analysis might identify as equivalent in speech. Neither is it an abstract module postulated as the residue left in thought by experience, as cognitive structures are sometimes conceived. It is found at work at the source of descriptions, judgements, explanations, evaluations, always using identically designated terms. This structure is not latent but generative. It is found within every instance of speech, whether it is a question of cataloguing the loonies, of describing the man as mental patient in terms of the gravity of his state; whether it is a question of defining forms of behaviour which make it possible to guide the relationship with the lodger, of elaborating the "knowing how to deal with" which allows the foster parent to adapt to the lodger while obtaining what they want in terms of everyday life and work; whether it is a question of reading the symptoms of the illness, decoding their signs, passing judgement on their nature and genesis; whether it is a question of constructing defences or establishing prohibitions. This ability to transfer between the fields of a representation in which the patient and the illness themselves form a whole, in which speech and practice are equally expressive, comes from the ternary structure and the concrete quality of its elements. The first assures the unity of the mental medium – man in his nature, his acts, his environment – at the heart of which the oppositions and their antagonisms, the differences and their hierarchy, are conceived. The second makes it possible to modify significances which vary with the context in which the terms are used and the attributes and images with which they are associated.

It is necessary to state that with the terms of brain and nerves we are not dealing with neutral, "innocent" notions. They are echoes of a biological vision which across the centuries has made them into the universal supports of soul and matter.[7] They have always embodied the polarity of the finite creature and they continue to do so in our community where they are spatialized depositories for all the evocations which have crystallized around a generic human duality, in its cultural past and in the history of its experience with the insane. Everywhere in speech the brain and the nerves function simultaneously as real objects and symbolic objects: biological entities, vectors of good and evil, of inhibition and excitation, of the social and of nature.

The operations of social communication have transformed them into idea-images (Moscovici, 1981), into memory-images able at any moment or in any situation to restore the accumulated meanings laid down as the sediment of history. This is indeed what is revealed by the employment of words whose implications unfurl or reactualize in different ways depending on the context of speech in which they are used. Everything suggests that layers of sense are captured in these images and indicates a phenomenon of *semantic desiccation*. This phenomenon of reduction, of compression linked to social transmission,

---

[7] As early as Homer, we find Anticleia teaching his son Ulysses, who had descended to the realm of the dead: "All mortals meet this judgement when they die. No flesh and bone are here, none bound by sinew, since the bright-hearted pyre consumed them down – dreamlike the soul flies, insubstantial."

is evident elsewhere: when we see young foster parents using the same words, gestures, even the same utensils as their mothers without feeling any need to search for a meaning or a reason.[8] Words, gestures, habits preserve the memory of the group, conceal a tacit knowledge which no longer needs to be continually expressed. The same is true of the organic images whose common social use makes it possible to preserve the full semantic wealth of the images without the conceptions and the significances corresponding to them having to be continuously or openly employed. They form the *representational primitives* from which everyone can derive implications and generate representational meanings and contents.

The Ideological, the Axiological and the Symbolic

The question which now presents itself concerns the mobilization of these memory-images, the conceptual application of these idea-images in accordance with the circumstances and contexts in which they are articulated. Everything depends on the conjunction of two phenomena. First there is the ability of these images to refer to objects, both real and symbolic, thus to speak of them in biological terms or to exploit their contents or their expressive potential. Second, there is the intellectual position adopted when dealing with the dual object of patient/illness. This is the principle behind the organization and the specific functioning of the fields of representation.

Thus the field of representation which concerns the states provoked by mental pathology proceeds from a dual *description*, that of the effect of the illness on the individual; that of the mental patient as a person and a social partner. The first description refers to the dominance of the biological dimension of the organic images, seen from the point of view of production, regulation and functional effects. The symbolic dimension intervenes secondarily in the moral evaluations and connotations of the aspects of organic, active and social life. The second description entails a specific use of the terms of the node and *an ideological type of representational functioning*. The individual and the patient who is described is not just anyone. He is a lodger, that is to say a social partner whom the community invests with a particular status (resident, worker) but whose integration on a footing of equality is forbidden. What is it we find here? An advancement of the regulatory functions of the brain and the nerves which is not explicitly formulated anywhere else. This regulatory aspect is reminiscent of the control imposed by social organization. Its implications can be developed in two directions.

On the one hand, it points to the stigma attached to the traits which

---

[8] Remember the case of the woman who, surrounded by a profusion of modern equipment, continued to use earthenware plates and wooden cutlery for her lodger, just as her mother had done (see pp. 112–13).

directly affect the interests of the foster parents (for example, the lodger's inability to control his appetite, his inability to maintain self-control at work) and which justify differential treatment and exploitation. It is interesting to note in this regard that work, which acquires such value in the eyes of the social whole as a reassurance against the fear of the ill, possesses no such significance here. It is invoked as a sign of good mental regulation or deprecated in the name of poor cerebral control. The symbolic and practical evaluations do not serve the same interest or obey the same logic. The contradiction is easily surmounted by the division established between the "arguable" and the "unarguable".

On the other hand, it demonstrates the impossibility of the patient taking a normal place in society and thus becoming part of the group bearing "civilian" status, because the lack of cerebral control prevents him from correctly managing his professional or his private life. This argumentation is strengthened and legitimated by the biological character of social incapacity. Moreover, it is a mode of reasoning which always makes it possible to find a sign of incapacitation, even in those who have given proof of their normality.

Turning to the *explanation* of the pathology, we find the invocation of another aspect of the biological dimension of organic images, namely the material aspect. The material substrate comes onto the scene to account for an etiology which combines endogenous and exogenous factors. In effect, the explanatory model of mental illness uses two approaches: first, the zone of attack (brain, nerves) and second, the circumstances of the attack (by birth, during childhood, by accident). This explains why the different pathologies find their definition at the point at which organic material and social influence meet. The age of confinement serves here as an indicator which localizes the damage, defines its constitutional or conjectural nature, and passes judgement on the role of socialization and its limits. The cerebral matter and its physical growth and the nervous matter with its relationship to the blood designate the two endogenous origins of mental illness. Innocence and wickedness, generic forms of insanity, derive from the differential nature of the *organic matter which in this way gives it its value. In the same way it is the values of the group which are left to define the exogenous factors of mental illness.*

What do we observe here? The institutional and the social intervene simultaneously to determine the diagnosis of the types of affliction and account for those which are not congenital. Two institutional criteria make it possible to distinguish between the "good" illness of birth (cerebral) and the "bad" illness (nervous), namely psychiatric confinement and schooling. In signifying that cerebral development has been completed, the latter changes the meaning of confinement. If entry into an institution happens before the child has started school, it is equated with a mode of assistance made necessary by the failures of the family. Later confinement is seen as imprisonment and identifies the criminal nature of the young person, his passage from innocence to wickedness. Twin resources of the social order and socialization, the asylum and the school are reference points which make it possible to judge the domain of the organic.

As for the disturbances which arise "by accident" and concern only the adult (with the exception of certain "childhood" accidents which are associated with somatic episodes), these are always social in origin. This social causality is explained with reference to the values and meanings with which the community invests its way of life. Conditions of existence which contrast with the virtues of rural life are considered to be pathogenic: the city, noise, the speed of city life, the comfort of modernity and money; so too is anything which contravenes the ideal of the family (infidelity, adultery, divorce, abandonment of the children or simply the diminished attention provided by a working mother). Another cause of morbid illness can be found in activities and forms of existence which are foreign to the culture of the group: military existence and war; "studying" and the intellectual professions which combine an unnatural way of life (undernourishment, lack of work) with a continual excess of effort; bourgeois mores whose permissiveness makes the individual a prey to private disorder and trauma and whose lack of rigour coupled with an excess of protection sap the victim's inner force. And as we have seen, it is in this inner force, which is purely moral, that the healthy adult finds the best defences against the pathological risks of existence.

When it is not related to the organic domain with its positive and negative potentialities, the idea of cause also implies the notion of responsibility. The responsibility of the individual is implicitly questioned by certain ways of life which suppose a personal choice. In other instances, responsibility relates to the patient's human environment or that of society and the living conditions it imposes. Now, one thing is remarkable here: whether individual or collective, responsibility is defined by the deviance from local norms. For a community which feels the proximity of insanity and the presence of mental patients as a threat to its equilibrium and its integrity, the assumption of its own values is a means of reaffirming its identity and projecting the risk of the development of insanity away from itself and onto the counter-values of a world which is foreign to it. In an etiology of mental illness in which a correlation is maintained between the endogenous and the exogenous, the division within the organic substrate is an initial means of separating the good, represented by the harmlessness of a deficiency which permits socialization, from the bad, implied by the degeneracy of the blood, the negative force of an otherness of nature. The axiological introduces a further division within the social or the cultural by distinguishing between the group and the rest of a pathogenic society. By barricading itself behind the purity of its identity, the community defends itself against the emergence of insanity in its midst and thus affirms insanity's social otherness.

It is precisely the conjunction of biological otherness and social otherness which is brought about by the third application of the cognitive node, which is involved in providing a conception of *the nature, the essence* of insanity. Here we are dealing with a tacit knowledge, mediated in discursive practices by all the nominalized forms which are used when speaking of mental illness and in the factual practices which have the aim of guiding the relationship with the mental patient and through which a material, transitive vision of insanity is constructed.

It is at this point that the *third term of the node, the body*, becomes operative. In fact this knowledge, whose roots draw their nourishment from deep in the terrain of popular medical tradition and cultural background, specifically points to intra-organic functioning and its substrate of blood and humours. It indicates the environment in which cerebral regulation and nervous regulation display their antagonism and their influence, the vehicle and the sphere of their action, the site where culture and nature meet. The representation takes us inside the body with the idea of a substance or a force which circulates within the biological environment, via the bodily fluids, and can "attack" and "sour" the organs as it "falls" on them. But this inner power is also communicated between bodies, back towards the outside social world from which it may have come. The world of biological knowledge provides a notional tool which allows the community to think of another type of contact between illness and society via the contact of bodies. The representation thus creates a mental space which can be occupied by social symbolism. The order of the natural gives us access to the *order of the symbolic*. The relationship established between bodies creates a means of expression for the relationship between the community and the group of patients. We can now see that biological knowledge needs the support of magical belief: the sympathetic chain established between bodies must remain unbroken for the logic of symbolism to function.

Thus the core of the representation of mental illness is the mediator through which social symbolism takes its place in the continuum which also embraces the ideological and axiological systems which govern the relationship with the insane. Let us look more closely at how this is to be understood. With the node[9] "brain – nerves – people of flesh and bones" we have brought to light a cognitive structure which constitutes the model of the popular theory of mental illness. Their ability to condense semantic elements laid down by time gives the terms of this structure the status of primitives which are used in the actualization of specific meanings in accordance with the conditions of their intellectual and social usage.

The description of the mental patient and the explanation of mental illness are based on the application of a normative position. In the first case this position is expressed in the evaluative mode: the representation of the state of the patient cannot be separated from an evaluation which is based in

---

[9] Borrowing the term "node" from acoustics enables us to account for the dynamic and generative aspect of the cognitive structure. It is a knot and a source of multiple semantic "vibrations".

the interests of the community and its members. The evaluation legitimates and justifies a social relationship of exploitation and exclusion. In the second case this position is expressed in the axiological mode: in the absence of expert knowledge, the explanation of the illness is entirely constructed from the conjunction of the group's system of values which serve to define, *a contrario*, its exogenous causes, and an endogenous "theory" which embodies an evaluative vision of the good and bad insane man in the idea of the organic. In both cases the biological furnishes self-interest or fear with the argument of the representative construction. Norms and values express the community in the identity of its needs and its conception of man.

When the illness is understood as the cause of a functional state, it points to social relationships and is embedded in *ideological speech*. When it is understood as an effect, it points to a theory of man and is embedded in *expressive speech*. The actualized meanings which surround each term pass from the universe of rules to the universe of values. In both cases we witness the invocation of a social order which the community wishes to establish and preserve. And here we are already in the realm of the symbolic in so far as it implies the implementation of an ordered relationship between the civilians and the *bredins*. But the meaning of this relationship still has to be revealed. This meaning will appear when we enter the realm of the ontological, when illness is thought of as entity. It then points to the idea of totality, whether organic or social, and to the negative or positive force which circulates between its elements. Embedded in *symbolic speech*, it sets out the structure and the principle of its life, or its survival, which simultaneously unites and separates. The appeal to the biological plays a specific role here. It is not used, or at least not solely, to legitimate a social order. It is the condition which makes it possible to think, with no contradiction, of exclusion within inclusion and is thus the instrument which allows the community to perpetuate its ambivalent relationship with the insane.

The Metaphor of the Four Ls

Let us pause for a while at this notion of symbolism which is so frequently employed in connection with social representations which are designated as symbolic processes. It seems to us that it is necessary to release the meanings of this notion if we are to examine the way in which representation and symbolism are linked and draw from this explanation the implications which are relevant to the phenomena we are investigating. To do this we shall use a metaphor, the metaphor of the four Ls. Why four Ls? Because these four terms, all starting with L, seem to us to cover the primary and generic, but often dissociated, senses in which the notion of symbolism is employed. L like *lieu*, L like *lien*, L like *law* and L like *leavening*. These terms refer to a status and to a function.

L like lieu: the symbol is in lieu of, takes the place of. What is intended here is the vicarious status of the symbol and the representation; the semiological relationship which they, as signifiers, maintain with the signified; their function of evocation, of expression. It is also the sense in which symbolism is most commonly referred to and which involves the least difficulty or need for explanation.

L like lien: here we must turn to the etymology of the term: the item divided in two which both parties keep in order to recognize one another. Recognition, unity, participation, social bond. This is also the significance conferred on the symbolic, via communication, by theories as different as those of Durkheim and Mead. This notion of lien can also be found in the idea of relation which is fundamental to the structuralist conception of the systems of expression which constitute culture.

L like law: this designates the ordering function of the symbol as it has been formulated by authors such as Lévi-Strauss and Lacan. It is a logical, structuring function which extends from the establishment of social order to the organization of language. This function can also be seen in the flow of symbolic interactionism with the idea of a "negotiated" social order which emerges from the interaction between social agents.

L like leavening: an image which restores the creative character acknowledged in symbols. That is to say, their capacity to reveal or invest with meaning, notably in the case of language and myth, and their effective character within rituals and institutions.

These four aspects are present in the field of representations which touches the essence of insanity and confers on it its symbolic power at the individual and the social level. The images and the beliefs which are embedded in language or in domestic rituals express a tacit knowledge whose forms are perpetuated by everyone and whose contents are recreated by all in the name of the identity of the community to which they belong, a community whose weak link they risk becoming if they relax their protective vigilance. These images and these beliefs fuse the group into a whole by separating it from its intruders.

Isolated in a social environment which condemns it (in both senses of the word) because of its life with the insane, the community constructs through its internal workings a symbolism of defence and restoration. These "magic" representations which crystallize in the verbs and prepositions of language acquire an expressive, ordering power when they pass into everyday gestures. Thus the group speaks of what it is and what it must not become, as is shown by two specific characteristics of the rituals of the avoidance of contact.

If, in connection with these, we have used the term "signifying practices", it has been with a concern to take account of both their difference from the "institutory practices" which govern life with the lodgers, and their status as carriers of hidden, otherwise inaccessible representations.

The two types of practice establish a dual order. But their procedures, their orientation and their meaning are not the same. Seen from this perspective, only the domestic rituals are, properly speaking, derived from the order of the symbolic. In fact, the ways of handling, treating and educating the lodgers (instituory practices) set up impassable barriers through the explicit formulation of rules and prohibitions and in the creation of situation signs. These practices establish, clearly and knowingly, an order which is imposed by authority on the social partners. It is a question of making social partition effective and ensuring that the other is aware of it. Nothing of the kind can be found in the "signifying practices" which are most often observed in secret and scarcely have any influence on the manipulation of the other. They serve as reminders and warnings. They recall the necessity for the radical separation of bodies which is psychologically vital for the community. They make it possible for every man and woman to define for themselves both the otherness against which they must defend themselves and the dangers which it brings. As ritual acts they comprise within a single signification – the affirmation of a transmissible and maleficent bodily force – the two faces, private and social, of a single threat: otherness. At the same time they assure the passage from the universe of biological representations which base the danger of intrusion on the danger of contamination, to the universe of representations of the social which makes the integration of the rootless stranger (whose prototype is the pedlar-sorcerer) into an act of aggression towards the social body. Here and there it is a question of purity, the integrity of the private body being the condition for that of the social body.

It now becomes possible to understand the persistence and form of this dual appeal, biological and social, to ancestral, indeed archaic, representations of insanity with their magic contents borrowed from the realms of animism and sorcery. This population prides itself on its modernity, a few hours from regional capitals and from Paris, and soaks up television. It receives all the possible reassurances from the hospital. For what reason does it continue to live with beliefs which are so hard to bear and so full of anguish? Why do these beliefs retain a power which is attested to by their violent reemergence in the face of the introduction of progress in medical treatment, chemotherapy?

The embedding of these beliefs in the language codes which are transmitted by communication and the everyday acts which are transmitted by tradition, both conditions of collective memory, suffice to explain their permanence, not their intensity of character or the veil of secrecy with which they are covered. Certainly there are times when the population measures the divergence of these beliefs from that which it is fitting to think in the society which surrounds them, but if it hides these beliefs it does not turn them into an inert residue. The memories borne by secular or religious culture, the leftovers of outdated medical knowledge can, as we have seen, fuel conviction and render it acceptable or plausible. But this does not fully explain the reasons for and the form of adherence to it.

As far as its form is concerned, this immemorial background of beliefs concerning insanity acts as a catalyst of fear. This is probably the reason behind its incarnation in the body. The domestic rituals, gestures, acts of silence keep the representations alive without the need to utter them: the materialization of thought remains operative even though it is suppressed. Operative or simply present. It only takes the intervention of an external event, a change in the population in the placements, the introduction of drugs, for it to be actualized once more. But why should knowledge of this type remain dormant only to be reawakened at times of "social excitation"? Everything points to the existence of a system of interpretation which is not allowed to die out, which is kept alive by social memory and held in reserve in case the emergence of new situations should make it useful. It is a kind of guarantee against the future unknown. This is how Halbwachs concluded his work on the social frameworks of memory:

> From which it results, not only is social thought essentially a memory, and that its contents are entirely composed of collective rememberings, but also only those specific and individual memories survive which societies, working within the conditions prevalent in any given age, are able to reconstruct.

When we attempt to understand the reemergence of these memories, we must turn to the social situation which thought needs to master. The prohibition of contact, pollution, the establishment of hierarchies are the elements of a symbolism so widespread that it is possible to see them as universals. Without having recourse to a collective, timeless imagination or unconscious, we can see here categories which emerge whenever a social situation exists where measures against an internal threat have to be elaborated by a social group. This phenomenon arose in Greece when the subject matter of pollution passed from the domain of religion to the domain of legislation. It was observed with regard to the Hypocrites and the fears of medieval Europe. It was with the danger of sexual liberation which came to the surface during the 19th-century that the nightmare belief in the transmission of syphilis through the bodily liquids took hold of even the most informed of medical establishments. The fear of AIDS and its transmission by saliva or sweat are also a part of this phenomenon. And how can we fail to think of the exploitation of social memory by the extreme right which unites in one and the same anathema the stranger and the AIDS sufferer, prescribing the creation of reserved spaces for the protection of society against contamination?

The community we have been studying places us in a position to understand the dynamic which leads to adherence to these delirious productions. The psychiatric system assures no protection against the intrusion of this threatening element which is the insane man. Indeed it favours it. In order to defend itself from what it considers to be a danger, the population invents an order which it defends by material and symbolic means. Uncertain as to its rights, it clings to archaic beliefs which can coexist with modernity, despite the psychological cost entailed by their symbolic function. In this community, which is obsessed by the idea of being socially demarcated and feels threatened from within, collective adherence to this body of representation is a means of affirming its unity, defending its identity. Recalling a vital prohibition, it makes each individual into a defender of the group, someone who will institute its internal divisions. When the change worked amongst the patients by the introduction of new therapies or the development of new methods of recruitment makes the risk of their assimilation more immediate, does the resurgence of older visions not become a prerequisite for survival?

When a society opens itself to otherness and the nightmare of fusion draws closer, the appeal to biological fear gives birth to a negative solidarity. But for this to happen, is it not necessary for "untamed images" to continue floating in our heads and in the atmosphere of our time? And have we really left behind us that "immense magical conclave" of which Mauss spoke?

Bibliography

Abric, J.C., *Coopération, compétition et représentations sociales*, Cousset: Delval, 1988.

Adorno, T.W., Frenkel-Brunswik, E., Levinson, D.I.C. and Sanford, R.N., *The Authoritarian Personality*, New York: Harper & Row, 1950.

Allport, G.W., *The Nature of Prejudice*, Cambridge, Mass: Addison-Wesley, 1954.

Arensberg, C.M., "The community-study method", *American Journal of Sociology*, 60:2, 1954.

Aron, R., *The Opium of the Intellectuals*, translated by Terence Kilmartin, London: Secker & Warburg; New York: Doubleday, 1957.

Augé, M., *Symbole, fonction, histoire: Les interrogations de l'anthropologie*, Paris: Hachette, 1979.

Augé, M., "Anthropologie de la maladie", in *Encyclopedia Universalis*, **18**: 168–70, 1980.

Balandier, G., *Sens et puissance*, Paris: Presses Universitaires de France, 1971.

Banton, M., *White and Coloured*, London: Jonathan Cape, 1959.

Barthes, R., "Sémiologie et médecine", in R. Barthes, *The Semiotic Challenge*, Oxford: Basil Blackwell, 1988.

Bastide, R., *Sociologie des maladies mentales*, Paris: Flammarion, 1965.

Becker, H.S., Geer, B., Hugues, E.C. and Strauss, A.L., *Boys in White: Student Culture in Medical School*, Chicago: Chicago University Press, 1961.

Belisle, C. and Schiele, B. (eds), *Les savoirs dans les pratiques quotidiennes*, Lyon: CNRS, 1984.

Bellelli, G. (ed.), *La représentation sociale de la maladie mentale*, Naples: Liguori, 1987.

Berger, P.L. and Luckmann, T., *The Social Construction of Reality*, New York: Doubleday; Harmondsworth: Penguin, 1966.

Bertolini, C., de Cutrone, F. and Pavan, L., "L'attitude de l'opinion publique envers le malade mental par rapport aux changements politiques et à la reforme psychiatrique en Italie", Symposium du IXe Congrès de Psychiatrie sociale, *Psychologie Médicale*, **15**:2387–90, 1983.

Biadi, A., Faraut, F. and Paoli, J.F., *L'internement psychiatrique: Médecins, familles, hôpitaux et la loi de 1838*, Paris: IDRASS Prins, 1979.

Bloch, M., *The Royal Touch: Sacred monarchy and scrofula in England and France*, translated by J.E. Anderson, London: Routledge & Kegan Paul, 1983.

Bonvalet, M., Bonvalet, P. and Gominet, P., "Impressions au cours d'une visite de centres de placement hétéro-familial de malades mentaux en Belgique et en Suède", *Informations Psychiatriques*, **38**:3, 262–7, 1962.

Bonvalet, P., Bonvalet, M., Robert, P. and Robert, L., "Organisation et réflexions à propos du placement familial des malades mentaux à la Colonie familiale d'Ainay-le-Château", *Informations Psychiatriques*, **40**:7, 446–68, 1960.

Bonvalet, P., Bonvalet, M., Robert, P. and Robert, L., "Perspectives d'avenir du placement familial: Reconversion de la Colonie familiale d'Ainay-le-Château en un mode d'assistance adapté à l'évolution actuelle de la psychiatrie", *Informations Psychiatriques*, **42**:3, 227–34, 1966.

Bourdieu, P., *Le sens pratique*, Paris: Ed. de Minuit, 1980.

Bourdieu, P., *Ce que parler veut dire: L'économie des échanges linguistiques*, Paris: Fayard, 1982.

Bramel, D., Bell, J. and Margulis, S., "Attributing Danger as a Means of Explaining One's Fear", *Journal of Experimental Social Psychology*, **1**:267–81, 1965.

Brockman, J. and d'Arcy, C., "Correlates of Attitude and Social Distance towards the Mentally Ill: A review and resurvey", *Social Psychiatry*, **13**:69–77, 1978.

Bruner, J.S., Olver, R.R. and Greenfield, P.M., *Studies in Cognitive Growth*, New York: Wiley, 1966.

Canetti, E., *Crowds and Power*, translated by C. Stewart, London: Penguin, 1981.

Castel, R., *L'orde psychiatrique: L'âge d'or de l'aliénisme*, Paris: Ed. de Minuit, 1976.

Cazeneuve, J., *La mentalité archaïque*, Paris: Colin, 1961.

Changeux, J.P., *Neuronal Man: The biology of mind*, translated by L. Garey, New York: Oxford University Press, 1987.

Charuty, G., *Le couvent des fous*, Paris: Flammarion, 1985.

Chombart de Lauwe, M.J., "Changes in the Representation of the Child in the Course of Social Transmission", in R. Farr and S. Moscovici (eds), *Social Representations*, Cambridge: Cambridge University Press, 1984.

Cicourel, A.V., *Cognitive Sociology*, Harmondsworth: Penguin, 1973.

Clark, H.H. and Haviland, S.E., "Psychological Processes as Linguistic Explanation", in D. Cohen (ed.), *Explaining Linguistic Phenomena*, Washington D.C.: Hemisphere, 1974.

Codol, J.P., "On the System of Representations in an Artificial Social Situation", in R. Farr and S. Moscovici (eds), *Social Representations*, Cambridge: Cambridge University Press, 1984.

Corbin, A., "Le péril vénérien au début du siècle: Prophylaxie sanitaire et prophylaxie morale", *Recherches*, **27**:245–83, 1977.

Corbin, A., *Le miasme et la jonquille*, Paris: Aubier-Montaigne, 1982.

Cox, G., Costanzo, P.R. and Coie, J.D., "A Survey Instrument for the Assessment of Popular Conception of Mental Illness", *Journal of Consulting Psychology*, **44**:6, 901–9, 1976.

Cumming, E. and Cumming, J., *Close Ranks: An experiment in mental health education*, Cambridge, Mass: Harvard University Press, 1959.

D'Arcy, C. and Brockman, J., "Changing Public Recognition of Psychiatric Symptoms? Blackfoot revisited", *Journal of Health and Social Behaviour*, **17**:3, 302–10, 1976.

Daumézon, G. and Bonnafé, L., "Le malade mental dans la société", in *Documents de l'information psychiatrique*, Paris: Desclée de Brouwer, 1946.

Delacampagne, C., *L'Invention du racisme*, Paris: Fayard, 1983.

Delumeau, J., *La peur en Occident*, Paris: Fayard, 1978.

Denis, M., "La notion de représentation imagée: Sa place dans les théories récentes de la représentation", *Bulletin de Psychologie*, numéro spécial: "La mémoire sémantique", 1976.

De Rosa, A.M., "The Social Representations of Mental Illness in Children and Adults", in W. Doise and S. Moscovici (eds), *Current Issues in European Social Psychology*, 2, Cambridge: Cambridge University Press, 1987.

Doise, W. and Palmonari, A. (eds), *L'étude des représentations sociales*, Neuchâtel: Delachaux & Niestlé, 1986.

Dollard, J. and Miller, N.E., *Personality and Psychotherapy*, New York: McGraw-Hill, 1950.

Douglas, M., *Purity and Danger: An analysis of the concepts of pollution and taboo*, London: Routledge & Kegan Paul, 1978.

Douglas, M., *Natural Symbols*, Harmondsworth: Penguin, 1973.

Douglas, M., *How Institutions Think*, Syracuse, NY: Syracuse University Press, 1986.

Driver, E.D., *The Sociology and Anthropology of Mental Illness: A reference guide*, Amherst, Mass: University of Massachusetts Press, 1972.

Duby, G., *Les trois ordres ou l'imaginaire du féodalisme*, Paris: Gallimard, 1978.

Dufrancatel, C., "La sociologue des maladies mentales", *La Sociologie Contemporaine*, 16:2, 1968.

Dulac, G., *La recherche sur les attitudes en santé mentale, questions, instruments, résultats*, Rapport OMS, Douglas Hospital Research Center, Québec, 1986.

Dumont, L., *Homo Hierarchicus: Caste system and its implications*, translated by M. Sainsbury, Chicago: University of Chicago Press, 1981.

Durkheim, E., *The Rules of Sociological Method*, New York: Free Press, 1958.

Durkheim, E., "Représentations individuelles et représentations collectives", *Revue de Métaphysique et de Morale*, 6, 1898; republished in E. Durkheim, *Sociologie et philosophie*, Paris: Presses Universitaires de France, 1951.

Durkheim, E., *Elementary Forms of Religious Life*, translated by J.W. Swain, London: Allen & Unwin, 1976.

Evans-Pritchard, E.E., *The Nuer: A description of the modes of life and political institutions of a nilotic people*, Oxford: Clarendon Press, 1940.

Eysenck, H.J. and Wilson, G.D. (eds), *The Psychological Basis of Ideology*, Lancaster: MTP Press, 1978.

Farr, R.,"Les représentations sociales", in S. Moscovici (ed.), *Psychologie sociale*, Paris: Presses Universitaires de France, 1984.

Farr, R. (ed.), "Social Representations", special issue, *Journal for the Theory of Social Behaviour*, 17:4, 1987.

Farr, R. and Moscovici, S., *Social Representations*, Cambridge: Cambridge University Press, 1984.

Favret-Saada, J., *Les mots, la mort, les sorts*, Paris: Gallimard, 1977.

Faye, J.P., *La critique du langage et son économie*, Paris: Galilée, 1973.

Fenichel, O., *La théorie psychanalytique des névroses*, Paris: Presses Universitaires de France, 1953.

Festinger, L., "A Theory of Social Comparison Processes", *Human Relations*, 7:2, 127–40, 1954.

Flahaut, F., *La parole intermédiaire*, Paris: Seuil, 1978.

Flament, C., "Structural Balance and the Representation of the Group", in R. Farr and S. Moscovici (eds), *Social Representations*, Cambridge: Cambridge University Press, 1984.

Flament, C., "Pratiques et représentations sociales", in J.L. Beauvois, R. Joule and J.M. Monteil (eds), *Perspectives cognitives et conduites sociales*, Cousset: Delval, 1987.

Fodor, J.A., *Representations*, Brighton: Harvester Press, 1981.

Foucault, M., *Madness and Civilization: A history of madness in the age of reason*, translated by R. Howard, London: Tavistock, 1971.

Foucault, M., *The Order of Things: Archaeology of the human sciences*, London: Tavistock, 1974.

Foucault, M., *Discipline and Punish*, London: Allen Lane, 1977.

Freeman, H.E. and Simmons, O.G., *The Mental Patient Comes Home*, New York: Wiley, 1963.

Freud, S., *The Problems of Anxiety*, New York: Norton, 1936.

Freud, S., *The Origins of Psychoanalysis*, translated by Eric Mosbacher and James Strachey, New York: Basic Books; London: Imago Publishing Co., 1954.

Freud, S., "Inhibitions, Symptoms and Anxiety", in *Standard Edition*, **20**: 77–172, 1926.

Gagnon, C., *Le folklore bourbonnais, I: La vie matérielle*, Moulins: Crépin-Leblond, 1947.

Gagnon, C., *Le folklore bourbonnais, II: Les croyances et les coutumes*, Moulins: Crépin-Leblond, 1949.

Gagnon, C., *Le folklore bourbonnais, IV: Les parlers*, Moulins: A. Pottier, 1972.

Garfinkel, H., "Studies on the Routine Grounds of Every Day Activities" *Social Problems*, **11**:3, 225–50, 1964.

Garfinkel, H., *Studies in Ethnomethodology*, Englewood Cliffs, NJ: Prentice Hall, 1967.

Giami, A., Humbert-Viveret, C. and Laval, D., *L'ange et la bête*, Paris: Presses Universitaires de France, CTNERHI, 1983.

Gilly, M., *Maître-élève: Rôles institutionnels et représentations*, Paris: Presses Universitaires de France, 1980.

Girard, A., *Le choix du conjoint*, Paris: Presses Universitaires de France, 1964.

Glotz, G., *La solidarité de la famille dans le droit criminel en Grèce*, Paris: Fontemoing, 1904.

Godelier, M., *Rationalité et irrationalité en économie*, Paris: Maspero, 1966.

Godelier, M., *L'idéel et le matériel: Pensée, économies, sociétés*, Paris: Fayard, 1984.

Goffman, E., *Asylums*, New York: Doubleday, 1961.

Goffman, E., *Stigma: Notes on the management of spoiled identity*, Englewood Cliffs, NJ: Prentice Hall, 1963.

Goldberg, D. and Huxley, P., *Mental Illness in the Community: The pathway to psychiatric care*, London: Tavistock, 1980.

Green, A., "Le corps et ses images", *Evolution psychiatrique*, **2**:181–216, 1964.

Green, A., "L'homme machinal", *Le Temps de la réflexion*, **5**:345–69, 1984.

Grice, H.P., "Logic and Conversation", in P. Cole and J. Morgan (eds), *Syntax and Semantics*, New York: Academic Press, 1975.

Griffin, J.H., *Black Like Me*, Boston, Mass: Houghton-Mifflin, 1961.

Halbwachs, M., *The Collective Memory*, New York: Harper & Row, 1980.

Héritier, F., "Symbolique de l'inceste et de sa prohibition" in M. Izard and P. Smith (eds), *La fonction symbolique*, Paris: Gallimard, 1979.

Herzlich, C., *Health and Illness: A social psychological analysis*, London: Academic Press, 1973.

Herzlich, C., "La représentation sociale", in S. Moscovici (ed.), *Introduction à la psychologie sociale*, Paris: Larousse, 1972.

Hood, R.W., "Dogmatism and Opinions about Mental Illness", *Psychological Reports*, **32**:1283–90, 1973.

Jalali, B., Jalali, M. and Turner, F., "Attitudes Towards Mental Illness", *Journal of Nervous Mental Disorders*, 166:692–700, 1978.

Jankélévitch, W., *Traité des vertus, 2: Les vertus et l'amour*, Paris, Bordas, 1970.

Jodelet, D., "Réflexions sur la notion de représentation sociale en psychologie sociale", in B. Schiele and C. Belisle (eds), *Les Représentations: Communication, information*, 6:2, 3, 15–41, 1984.

Jodelet, D., "Représentations sociales: Phénomènes, concept et théorie", in S. Moscovici (ed.), *Psychologie sociale*, Paris: Presses Universitaires de France, 1984.

Jodelet, D., *Civils et bredins: Rapport à la folie et représentations sociales de la maladie mentale*, thèse pour le doctorat d'Etat, Paris: EHESS, 1985.

Jodelet, D., "Malades du cerveau, malades des nerfs", in G. Bellelli (ed.), *La représentation sociale de la maladie mentale*, Naples: Liguori, 1987.

Jodelet, D. (ed.), *Les représentations sociales*, Paris: Presses Universitaires de France, 1989.

Jodelet, F., *Naître au langage*, Paris: Klincksieck, 1979.

Jodelet, M., *La conception de la peine chez Platon*, Rouen: Darnétal-lès-Rouen, 1926.

Johnson-Laird, P.N. and Wason, P.C. (eds), *Thinking: Readings in cognitive science*, Cambridge: Cambridge University Press, 1977.

Jones, E.E., *Ingratiation: A social psychological analysis*, New York: Meredith Publishing Company, 1964.

Kaès, R., *Images de la culture chez les ouvriers français*, Paris: Ed. Cujas, 1968.

Kaès, R., *L'appareil psychique groupal: Construction du groupe*, Paris: Dunod, 1976.

Kaès, R., "Eléments pour une psychanalyse des mentalités", *Bulletin de Psychologie*, 34:451–63, 1980–1.

Katsching, H. and Berner, P., "Comment estimer les préjugés du public à l'égard de la maladie mentale", *Psychologie Médicale*, 15:2329–31, 1983.

Kird, S.A., "The Impact of Labeling on Rejection of the Mentally Ill: An experimental study", *Journal of Health and Social Behavior*, 15:2, 108–17, 1974.

Lapière, R.T., "Attitudes versus actions", *Social Forces*, 18:230–7, 1937.

Le Cerf, J.F. and Sébille, G., "Dimensions sociales de la psychopathologie et de la psychiatrie", *Revue Française de Sociologie*, 16:3, 380–417, 1975.

Lévi-Strauss, C., *Introduction to the Work of Marcel Mauss*, translated by Felicity Baker, London: Routledge & Kegan Paul, 1987.

Lévi-Strauss, C., *Structural Anthropology*, Harmondsworth: Penguin, 1976.

Lévi-Strauss, C., *The Elementary Structures of Kinship*, translated by J.H. Bell and J.R. von Sturmer, London: Eyre & Spottiswoode, 1969.

Lévy, A., *Les paradoxes de la liberté dans un hôpital psychiatrique*, Paris: Ed. Epi, 1969.

Lévy-Leboyer, C., *Psychology and Environment*, translated by D. Canter and I. Griffiths, Beverly Hills, CA: Sage, 1982.

Linsky, A.S., "Who Shall Be Excluded: The influence of personal attributes in community reaction to the mentally ill", *Social Psychiatry*, 5:166–71, 1970.

Lorenz, K., *On Aggression*, London: Methuen, 1966.

Lyketsos, G.C., "L'attitude du public face aux maladies mentales", *Psychologie Médicale*, 15:2403–4, 1983.

Maget, M., *Guide d'étude directe des comportements culturels*, Paris: CNRS, 1962.

Maisonneuve, J., *Psychosociologie des affinités*, Paris: Presses Universitaires de France, 1968.

Mandler, G.M., "Representation", in J.H. Flavell and E.M. Markman (eds), *Cognitive Development*, New York: Wiley, 1983.

Marlé, R., "L'encyclique *Mysterium Fidei*", *Etudes*, 544–58, 1965.

Mauss, M., *Sociologie et anthropologie*, Paris: Presses Universitaires de France, 1950.

Michelat, G. and Simon, M., *Classes, religion et comportements politiques*, Paris: Editions Sociales, 1977.

Miles, A., *The Mentally Ill in Contemporary Society*, Oxford: Martin Robertson, 1981.

Miller, G.A., "Practical and Lexical Knowledge", in E. Rosch and B.B. Lloyd (eds), *Cognition and Categorization*, Hillsdale, NJ: Lawrence Erlbaum, 1978.

Minsky, M., "Frame-system Theory", in P.N. Johnson-Laird and P.C. Wason (eds), *Thinking: Readings in cognitive science*, Cambridge: Cambridge University Press, 1977.

Morin, E., *La rumeur d'Orléans*, Paris: Seuil, 1969.

Morvan, S., *Représentations des situations de handicap et d'inadaptation chez les éducateurs spécialisés, les assistants de service social et les enseignants spécialisés en formation*, Paris: Presses Universitaires de France, 1988.

Moscovici, S., *La psychanalyse, son image et son public*, Paris: Presses Universitaires de France, 1961, rev. edn 1976.

Moscovici, S., "Préface", in D. Jodelet, J. Viet and P. Besnard, *La psychologie sociale: Une discipline en mouvement*, Paris-La Haye: Mouton, 1970.

Moscovici, S., *Age of the Crowd*, translated by C.J. Whitehouse, Cambridge: Cambridge University Press, 1985.

Moscovici, S., "On Social Representations", in J.P. Forgas (ed.), *Social Cognition*, London: Academic Press, 1981.

Moscovici, S., "The Coming Era of Representations", in J.P. Codol, *Cognitive Approaches to Social Behavior*, The Hague: Nijhoff, 1982.

Moscovici, S., "Le domaine de la psychologie sociale", in S. Moscovici (ed.), *La psychologie sociale*, Paris: Presses Universitaires de France, 1984.

Moscovici, S., "The Phenomenon of Social Representations", in R. Farr and S. Moscovici (eds), *Social Representations*, Cambridge: Cambridge University Press, 1984.

Nadel, S., *La théorie de la structure sociale*, Paris: Ed. de Minuit, 1970.

Nunnally, J.C., *Popular Conceptions of Mental Health*, New York: Holt, Rinehart & Winston, 1961.

Park, R.E., *Race and Culture*, Glencoe: The Free Press, 1950.

Pélicier, Y., "Aperçus généraux de la psychologie des transplantés", *Concours médical*, **86**, 1964.

Phillips, D.L., "Rejection: A possible consequence of seeking help for mental disorders", in S.P. Spitzer and N.N. Denzin, *The Mental Patient*, New York: McGraw-Hill, 1968.

Piaget, J., *Principles of Genetic Epistemology*, translated by W. Mays, London: Routledge & Kegan Paul, 1972.

Piaget, J., "Le rôle de l'imitation dans la formation de la représentation", *Evolution Psychiatrique*, **27**:141–50, 1962.

Piaget, J., "Pensée égocentrique et pensée sociocentrique", *Cahiers Vilfredo Pareto*, **14**:148–60, 1976.

Poirier, J., "Problèmes d'ethnologie économique", in J. Poirier, *Ethnologie générale*, Paris: Gallimard, 1968.

Polanyi, M., *The Tacit Dimension*, Garden City, NY: Doubleday, 1966.

Rabbie, J.M. and Horwitz, M., "Arousal of In Group–Out Group Bias by a Chance Win or Loss", *Journal of Personality and Social Psychology*, 269–77, 1969.

Rabkin, J.G., "Public Attitudes Towards Mental Illness: A review of the literature", *Psychological Bulletin*, **77**:153–71, 1972.

Rabkin, J.G., "Who Is Called Mentally Ill: Public and professional views", *Journal of Community Psychology*, **7**:253–8, 1979.

Radcliffe-Brown, R., *Taboo*, Cambridge: Cambridge University Press, 1939.

Ramognigno, N., "Questions sur l'usage de la notion de représentation en sociologie", in C. Belisle and B. Schiele (eds), *Les savoirs dans les pratiques quotidiennes*, Lyon: CNRS, 1984.

Rapport de la Commission sur l'attitude de la société à l'égard des maladies mentales, Quatrièmes Journées de la Santé mentale, *Hygiène mentale*, **1**:39–40, 1959.

Redfield, *The Little Community*, Chicago: University of Chicago Press, 1955.

Renan, E., *Souvenirs d'enfance et de jeunesse*, Paris: Calmann-Lévy, 1967 (1883).

Robert, P. and Faugeron, C., *La justice et son public: Les représentations sociales du système pénal*, Paris: Masson, 1978.

Robert, P., Lambert, T. and Faugeron, C., *Image du viol collectif et reconstruction d'objet*, Paris: Masson, 1976.

Rokeach, M., *The Open and Closed Mind*, New York: Basic Books, 1960.

Roosens, E., *Des fous dans la ville? Gheel et sa thérapie séculaire*, Paris: Presses Universitaires de France, 1977.

Saint-Claire, L. and Turner, J.C., "The Role of Demand Characteristics in the Social Categorization Paradigm", *European Journal of Social Psychology*, **12**:307–14, 1982.

Sapir, E., *Anthropologie*, Paris: Editions de Minuit, 1967.

Schaff, A., *Introduction à la sémantique*, Paris: Anthropos, 1968.

Schank, R.C. and Abelson, R.P., "Scripts, Plans and Knowledge", in P.N. Johnson-Laird and P.C. Wason (eds), *Thinking: Readings in cognitive science*, Cambridge: Cambridge University Press, 1977.

Scheff, T.F., *Mental Illness and Social Processes*, New York: Evanston, 1967.

Schutz, A., "The Problem of Social Reality", in *Collected Papers*, I, M. Natanson (ed.), The Hague: Nijhoff, 1962.

Searle, J.R., *Intentionality: An essay in the philosophy of mind*, Cambridge: Cambridge University Press, 1983.

Sherif, M., *In common. Predicament: Social psychology of intergroup conflict and cooperation*, Boston, MA: Houghton-Mifflin, 1966.

Sperber, D., *On Anthropological Knowledge*, Cambridge: Cambridge University Press, 1985.

Srole, L., *Mental Health in the Metropolis: The midtown Manhattan study*, New York: McGraw-Hill, 1962.

Star, S.A., *The Public's Ideas about Mental Illness*, Chicago: National Opinion Research Center, 1955.

Strauss, A., Schatzman, L. et al., *Psychiatric Ideologies and Institutions*, New York: Free Press, 1964.

Szasz, T., *The Myth of Mental Illness*, New York: Harper & Row, 1977.

Tajfel, H., "La catégorisation sociale", in S. Moscovici, *Introduction à la psychologie sociale*, Paris: Larousse, 1972.

Tajfel, H., *Human Groups and Social Categories*, Cambridge: Cambridge University Press, 1981.

Turner, J.C., "Social Identification and Psychological Group Formation", in H. Tajfel (ed.), *The Social Dimension*, 2, Cambridge: Cambridge University Press, 1984.

Vié, J., "Le placement familial des aliénés et des psychopathes: Sa portée médicale et sociale", *Annales médico-psychologiques*, **II**:1, 1940; **I**:1, 2, 3, 4, 5, 1941.

Wallon, H., *De l'acte à la pensée*, Paris: Flammarion, 1942.

Wattie, B., "L'attitude envers le malade mental reflétée dans le réseau médico-hospitalier canadien", *Psychologie Médicale*, **15**:2397–2401, 1983.

Wittgenstein, L., *Philosophical Investigations*, Oxford: Basil Blackwell, 1953.

Wittgenstein, L., *Tractatus Logico-Philosophicus*, Paris: Gallimard, 1961.

Yarrow, M., Schwartz, C., Murphy, H. and Deasy, L., "The Psychological Meaning of Mental Illness in the Family", *Journal of Social Issues*, **11**:12–24, 1955.